Writing from within

The Next Generation

• • •

"Very deep…
very deep is the well of the past."

— Thomas Mann, *Joseph and His Brothers*

T0160600

DEDICATION

To Jeff, Will, and Gail
The kindest and most loving
children and former wife possible

Also by Bernard Selling

Writing from Within
Writing from Deeper Within
Writing from Within Workbook
The Art of Seeing
Character Consciousness
The Duke's Musician (novel)
Predators (novel)
The da Vinci Intrusion (novel)
Fortune's Smile (novel)
Henry, Boy of Barrio (film)
First Year, A.D. (film)
Three Miraculous Soldiers (film)
The Flying Machine (film)

Ordering
Trade bookstores in the U.S. and Canada please contact
Publishers Group West
1700 Fourth Street, Berkeley CA 94710
Phone: (800) 788-3123   Fax: (800) 351-5073

For bulk orders please contact
Special Sales
Hunter House Inc., PO Box 2914, Alameda CA 94501-0914
Phone: (510) 899-5041   Fax: (510) 865-4295
E-mail: sales@hunterhouse.com

Individuals can order our books by calling **(800) 266-5592**
or from our website at **www.hunterhouse.com**

Writing from within

The Next Generation

Bernard Selling

Hunter House PUBLISHERS

Hunter House Inc., Publishers
PO Box 2914
Alameda CA 94501-0914

Library of Congress Cataloging-in-Publication Data
Selling, Bernard.
Writing from within : the next generation / Bernard Selling. — [25th anniversary ed.].
p.   cm.
Includes bibliographical references.
ISBN 978-0-89793-617-0 (pbk.)   ISBN 978-0-89793-628-6 (ebook)
1. Autobiography — Authorship.   2. Report writing.   I. Title.
CT25.S45 2012
808.06'692 — dc23   2012030706

Project Credits
Cover Design: Brian Dittmar Design, Inc.
Book Production: John McKercher
Developmental Editors: Jude Berman and Jack Duffy
Copy Editor: Susan Lyn McCombs
Managing Editor: Alexandra Mummery
Editorial Intern: Tu-Anh Dang-Tran
Acquisitions Coordinator: Susan Lyn McCombs
Special Sales Manager: Judy Hardin
Publicity Coordinator: Martha Scarpati
Rights Coordinator: Candace Groskreutz
Customer Service Manager: Christina Sverdrup
Order Fulfillment: Washul Lakdhon
Administrator: Theresa Nelson
Computer Support: Peter Eichelberger
Publisher: Kiran S. Rana

Printed and bound by Sheridan Books, Ann Arbor, Michigan
Manufactured in the United States of America

9 8 7 6 5 4 3 2 1   First Edition   13 14 15 16 17

Contents

Part II: "Writing from Within": Advanced Work 167

Additional stories discussed in this book or that are good examples of the techniques taught in this book can be found at www.WritingFromWith in-Stories.com. The stories appearing there include:

    Rosalyn Cron — "Grass and Trees"

    Dale Crum — "My Sister's Shadow"

    Gail Field — "Appearances"

    Gail Field — "'Goodbye to All That' (Summer 1975)"

    Gail Field — "Information I Don't Want to Know"

    Sam Glenn — "The Board"

    Sam Glenn — "The Ring"

    Bernard Selling — "The Jewish Wife"

    Bernard Selling — "Mom's Trip North"

Writing
from
Within:
The Next
Generation

viii

Preface

Following the publication of the first edition of *Writing from Within*, in 1988, I received a great deal of valuable feedback about its effectiveness. A number of people responded strongly to the personal glimpses I had given my readers, so in this edition, *Writin from Within: The Next Generation*, I have tried to provide a few more where they make my teaching a little clearer.

This new edition incorporates a number of new techniques that have become central to my teaching, such as experiencing the stories as mirrors of ourselves and ways to expand and manage our creativity.

In order to write quality life stories, we have to search our lives for the events that have been most important to us, events that have helped to shape the way we think about and experience life.

Some thirty years ago, I began my own process of life review by thinking about the salient events of my early life, events that nudged me toward understanding the value of what I did not have: my father and mother's reflections and thoughts about the experiences of their lives. This process of life review formed the content of the Preface to the 3rd edition of *Writing from Within*, written in 1998, and appears in part below.

● ● ●

When I was sixteen years old, my father died—an unexpected and painful event for me. He was an enigma: a prominent psychiatrist, the possessor of seven college degrees, an angry and charming man, highly ethical, overbearing, and accomplished. A heart attack eight years before his death caused him to stumble toward the finish line of his life like an exhausted marathon runner whose sole purpose in life was to stay alive until his children finished high school. He almost made it.

For weeks after his death, I read copies of all the letters he wrote during his years of public life. Nowhere could I find anything personal about him: who he was, where he had come from, where he thought he was going.

Beyond a few facts and remembrances and a few funny stories, I knew very little about him. My mother died a few years after my father, and I reached young adulthood in the 1950s feeling like an existential antihero—free to make choices but not guided by an immediate past or a family history—truly alone.

In the intervening years, from Dad's death until the present, my father's sister, the one person who could reveal more of him, showed no interest in telling me more of his life, particularly his thoughts and feelings. "People of our generation do not dwell on such things," she would say. "I don't have time." So it appeared that my father's history, both family and personal, would remain shrouded in darkness, consigned to oblivion. And indeed it has come to pass. This has saddened me enormously.

Much later in life, I became interested in my mother's family. The results of this interest are discussed in Part I, Unit IV, "Writing Family Histories," starting on page 129.

When asked to teach the classes from which this book was drawn, I thought how much it would have meant to me to know my parents well: how they were raised, the things they did, and, most of all, what they thought and felt as they experienced their lives. This became my touchstone for teaching the class—actions and events accurately described, feelings about them honestly and vividly captured.

As the classes developed over several years, I began to realize the importance of what we were accomplishing.

First of all, the writing process was immensely therapeutic for each person. It was plain to see that once the participants had overcome a fear of writing, the process of getting their life stories out and on paper had a revitalizing effect on them.

Second, being congratulated for good work and encouraged by other class members to keep at the task was equally therapeutic.

Third, the warm acceptance of their work by family members revealed to each writer that he or she was filling a genuine need within the family.

Fourth, and most inspiring, was the awareness that, as each writer became more skilled, the quality of his or her legacy would itself become a guide for the family and inspire histories to be written by generations yet unborn. Occasionally, someone would comment after a particularly good story, "What would it be like for us if our parents and forebears had left memories as well written and revealing as the stories coming to the surface in our workshop?"

Ultimately, this is the great lure of life-story writing: to be able to affect the future of the families into which we are born; to give direction, amusement, and perspective to our children's children and their children; to write so well that a hundred years from now those who follow can clearly see the footprints we made and can begin to gauge their own paths by our direction.

• • •

In the years since 1998 my approach to writing and teaching writing has continued to evolve. Over the past decade and a half I have written a number of novels and screenplays as well as nonfiction books exploring the ways we can use life stories to help us know ourselves better (*Character Consciousness*); ways to look at the arts, especially films, with a critical and knowing eye (*The Art of Seeing: Appreciating Motion Pictures as an Art Form and as a Business*); and ways to go further within ourselves to write with a high level of creativity (*Writing from Deeper Within*). At present I teach fewer and fewer beginning writers and more and more professional screenwriters, novelists, and nonfiction writers.

Since 1998 my personal life has continued to evolve as well. My long friendship with my first wife, Gail, has resulted in a loving relationship with our two sons, with her son from her second marriage, and a close bond with our daughter-in-law, her family, and our young grandchildren. My experiences teaching life-story writing extend to our family as well: Gail has written her experiences of her relationship to her second husband for her son from that marriage; our son, Will, a Marine who served in Desert Storm and Operation Iraqi Freedom, has written stories of his life and experiences in the military; and our granddaughter has begun writing her own imagined stories.

How do all these experiences come together for me as a writer and teacher of writing? After thirty years teaching writing skills to life-story writers as well as fiction writers, I am aware that most of my efforts have been directed toward helping them (and myself) probe deeper into the human condition. The techniques and approaches to writing that I have developed, observed, or recommended are almost all presented to writers for the purpose of enabling them to take their observations of life to a deeper level of "knowing" and expressiveness.

For many of us, relating fully to another person in a love relationship is no easy matter. Many of my students tell me that, as members of our writing groups, they get to know each other far better than they know their significant others. I don't doubt they are right. Revealing ourselves to another person, face to face, is difficult—often very difficult. At least it is for me. Often the best way of saying what one wishes to say to another person is to write a story of the particular difficulty the two duelists may be having and then hand that story to each other. In this regard, please see the delightful stories written by Jeff Thompson and Mary Molinar on pages 120–122 about the impossibility of finding something they have had in common to write about after twenty years of marriage.

As writers we have to uncover, discover, recover, borrow, or bend a whole host of techniques and approaches that allow us to unearth deeper levels of inner awareness than we usually communicate to one another. In this regard, I encourage you to read the stories of Gail Field (see page 279 and www.Writing FromWithin-Stories.com), who writes about her marriage to and divorce from her second husband with insight, tenderness, and growing awareness of the difficulties of living with, loving, and finally letting go of illusions about one's significant other.

Exploring techniques that allow for greater expressivenss, however, is just one piece (tessera) of the mosaic that is story writing. Another important piece is giving sufficient *shape* to our expression of what we see in the experiences that we have lived and the stories we invent. I do everything possible to help my writing students create a picture of the world outside themselves as well as perceptions of the inner life of their characters. At the same time, I urge them to cast their picture in a shape that is distinctly artistic, meaning that their stories need to be written with a sense of the *principles of art* at work—repetition, balance, symmetry, variety, contrast, etc.—so that the writer's stories will be remembered. In this regard, I especially urge you to look at the Dale Crum's story "Smoke Rings" (see the complete story on page 275) and Karl Grey's "The Garage" (see the complete story on page 273)—"guy" stories that have an unusual sense of shape and form, making them "unforgettable," as the song goes.

This book constitutes the shape of my life teaching creative writing. The first task has been to assist people in sketching from life—writing stories of their lives. This meant observing and then practicing some thirteen steps that enable almost anyone to write a viable, interesting, perhaps even captivating story about one's life experience. The second task entails finding ways to go deeper into the human condition, uncovering techniques and approaches that allow for greater intimacy among the characters, the writer, and the reader. The third task has to do with employing the principles of art so that each story, whether fiction or nonfiction, has its own unique shape, a shape that will render the story memorable. After all, if we are going to take the time and expend the energy to write the best story we can, we want our readers to remember what they have read, for days, weeks, months…years…perhaps a lifetime.

Writing
from
Within:
The Next
Generation

xii

Acknowledgments

Writing from Within has been alive and well and thriving for almost thirty years, its existence due mainly to two men—Joseph Campbell, mythologist and editor of the texts of C.G. Jung, psychologist and philosopher; and Kiran Rana, publisher (Hunter House Publishers) of *Writing from Within* (1988, 1990, 1998).

• • •

A personal and professional crisis in the late 1970s led me into a period of self-examination, during which I began attending consciousness-raising workshops. A friend suggested "The Hero's Journey," a workshop by Paul Rebillot in San Francisco, based on Joseph Campbell's work, especially *The Hero with a Thousand Faces*. I began reading Campbell's many works, including his massive *The Masks of God*. I suspected my path to be similar to that of the hero; I had undergone a spiritual death and was ready to reemerge in a new skin. Soon, I attended Campbell's workshops at the Jung Institute in San Francisco and elsewhere and got to know him personally. We had many things in common, not the least of which was an interest in C.G. Jung and James Joyce and in playing the baritone sax.

Within a year, an accidental meeting with the principal of an adult school in Los Angeles brought me to a class of older adults whose students wanted to learn about writing life stories. Although I knew next to nothing about teaching creative writing, I soon realized that, in fact, I knew a lot, not because I had a graduate degree in English literature but because of the work I had done with actors as a film director.

I also found that as I saw certain threads of excellence in their stories, threads that I would later turn into *Writing from Within*, I began to overcome my own difficulties in writing creatively (which had led me to make documentary films for many years instead of writing).

• • •

In 1984 Kiran Rana attended a party where he chatted with a student of mine. Her glowing reviews of our life-story-writing class prompted him to get in touch with me. At the time, I had created a thirty-page pamphlet that I sent to him. A year later, a book emerged, a prepublication edition of *Writing from Within.* "We may not sell a lot of copies initially, Bernard," Kiran said in his soft voice, "as we are a small press, and it is not easy for us to get face time on book shelves, competing, as we do, with larger presses." I blanched. But he continued, "However, the book will still be alive twenty-five years from now." Indeed, he was right. Despite having sold no more than ten thousand copies between 1988 and 1998, Kiran authorized a third edition at that time, a much more complete and expanded look at "writing from within" and the concerns of life-story writers. His direct sales of this edition, coupled with those of Barnes & Noble, made it a semi-bestseller.

• • •

I also would like to express my appreciation to Bill Rempel for contributing material to Chapter 31 in this book, much of which relates to his book, *At the Devil's Table.* I had read his series of articles on Jorge Salcedo in the *Los Angeles Times* while teaching at a local community college and had let him know how valuable I thought the articles were. Rempel, in turn, volunteered to talk to my students, and I accepted. By the time he came to speak, the class had read every article he had ever written. He was stunned at how well prepared the students were and at the quality of the questions they posed. A high-quality discussion ensued, and we became friends.

• • •

I also wish to acknowledge the contributions of the following writers: Liz Kelly, Sam Glenn, Karl Grey, Roy Wilhelm, Dale Crum, Paula Diggs, Gail Field, and Dirk Tousley.

— Bernard Selling
Topanga, CA
December 2012

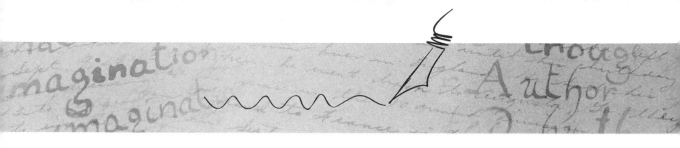

Introduction

Writing from Within: The Next Generation presented me with a unique opportunity to update the work I have done exploring and teaching personal writing. The previous editions of my book *Writing from Within* (1984, 1988, 1998) had done well in the marketplace, and Kiran Rana, publisher of Hunter House, asked me to consider revising the book again. A great deal of the "writing from within" process is as relevant today as when I described it in the 3rd (1998) edition. Some of the material from that book, however, was either dated or I had expanded upon it considerably in the years since.

As a result, Kiran and I decided it would be appropriate to publish three new books. The first, *Writing from Deeper Within,* is a volume devoted to the work I had done between 1998 and 2013, and is for those who have already purchased *Writing from Within*, 3rd edition, and want to know more. The book has a significant appeal to those who desire perspectives on screen, novel, and short story writing, especially writing in a deeper, more intimate way in these different mediums.

The second book, *Writing from Within Workbook,* describes the "writing from within" process in an even more thorough and compelling way. The intent of this workbook is to breakdown each step of the process into several writing and rewriting tasks, appropriate for fourth graders to senior populations.

The third book is the book you are holding in your hands. *Writing from Within: The Next Generation* (I love the Star Treky name!) is an update of *Writing from Within*, 3rd edition, with the addition of the work I have done over the past fifteen years. Yes, it is a melding of *Writing from Within* and *Writing from Deeper Within.* But it is also more.

Writing from Within: The Next Generation is a skeletal outline of my own journey as a writer. Unlike so many writers who know from an early age that they want to express themselves through writing, I did not know that writing would be part of my life's journey. Oh, I had always done well with academic writing in school, beginning with a research paper I had written on the United States Navy in the 10th grade, (an effort my father applauded in no uncertain terms. *Yay!*) However, my few fledgling efforts to write creatively, in my early twenties, went nowhere and my later efforts in creative writing, when I attended UCLA's film school, were a disaster. I immediately began to direct documentary films and later short fiction films, staying as far away from writing screenplays as I could.

This defect, lacuna, empty space in my resume eventually came back to bite me in the rump, big time. In learning to work with actors imaginatively, I had discovered a part of myself that seemed to be highly creative, a part that could connect to other imaginative people on a high level of creativity. But although I was able to direct cinematically, I was unable to write creatively, I couldn't come up with *the* screenplay that would enable me to launch a film career.

Depressed about life, work, self-worth, finances, and the future, I returned to academic teaching with my tail between my legs…hurting deeply. (*World, please, just give me a @#$%^ job!*) I still felt I had the potential to contribute a great deal to the world around me, but I didn't see a path to realizing that potential.

As life would have it, the answer appeared in front of me, as if it were an apparition. Despite my deep hurt and sense of purposelessness, I had done two things well: loved my sons and befriended my former wives. Gail (ex-wife #1) suggested I go to a consciousness-raising workshop—Life Spring. The workshop turned out to be less frightening than I thought it would be. *A door cracked open.* Then a friend suggested I explore the work of Joseph Campbell, the mythologist. *The door cracked open a little more.* Following that, the principal of an adult school where I worked suggested I teach a course for senior citizens in writing life stories.

This will be dull work, I thought. It wasn't. In fact, all of the work I had done learning about storytelling and working with the imagination of actors came pouring out of me as I worked with these older folks who desperately wanted to be able to pass along their life experiences to the generations to follow—the very thing I had wanted from my father who died when I was so young. *Bingo.* The door opened far enough for me to see where my energies and my desire to contribute to a better world could come together.

What I couldn't see at the time was that my own path to writing creatively, which I had sought for such a long time, was also opening up. During my first year of teaching life-story writing, I simply noted all the things that worked in the stories my students wrote. They liked the way I analyzed their work and compared their efforts to those of the major writers whom I had studied and whose works I had taught at various universities. When they had difficulties, such as hearing a critical voice within themselves that brought them to a halt, I had answers for them, *answers that actually illuminated my own difficulties with writing.*

Then I saw it. The root of my difficulties. My highly educated father (two PhDs and an MD) stood out in my fantasy life as a figure that said, "this isn't good enough." In an effort to "do better" I had always tried to make my writing more objective, more impersonal, more clinical—more like his writing. Exposed to the very interesting lives of my students, I began to see that the kind of writing toward which I gravitated was quite different: Simpler stories seemed to be the most powerful. The more childlike the stories of youthful experience, the better they seemed to me and to my students.

When I tried writing in this way, many of my problems in writing creatively disappeared. I freed myself of the need to be intellectual and "smart." I could create strong pictures with very simple language, and so could my students. I could grasp subtle nuances of relationship and get them on paper. I could articulate my long suppressed inner life and get these thoughts and feelings on paper. (Yay!)

I started to enjoy writing. And so I began to write a book about writing—a fifteen-year journey exploring how one learns to write creatively. *Writing from Within.* Perhaps, more importantly, I began exploring how I could learn to use my own personal writing as a means to looking at myself and, in viewing myself differently, I could change the way I related to myself and others: *Writing from Within* and *Character Consciousness.*

My lifelong dream—suppressed and inarticulate for a quarter of a century—became visible. *The door opened so fully that I began to see my path as much broader than I ever imagined.* I saw that I was, and always had been, a creative person. Yes, I could make films, if I chose. I could parent as I had, and teach, as I had. And make music, as I had. But more importantly, I could create, as a writer.

In this way, my long nurtured desire to write books about the Italian Renaissance crept into my consciousness. From the time I had studied art history in college, I had always been transported to the past by studying the history of art and artists. I loved history as much as my worldly father had—my father who took me to visit every Civil War battlefield from Charleston to Gettysburg. My father who drove the two of us thousands of miles to see old trains. My father, who took me to the Museum of Natural History in Washington and recited poems about old fossils: "said the little Eohippus, I'm going to be a horse and on my middle fingernail, I'll run my earthly course."

I took trips to Italy over some ten years and photographed castles, villas, and haunts in Northern Italy where my fictional and actual characters sailed and stumbled through life. Then I began to write. But the central character, the Duke of Milan in the late fifteenth century, just wouldn't come into focus. He remained too elusive.

In frustration, I asked myself, "Who would you be if you had lived back then?" The answer came immediately. I would be me. Well, at least the "me" I would have wanted to be: a musician. The son of a doctor. A man who loved women. Whose loves always got him in trouble. A man with such talents that every level of society welcomed him…and wanted something from him. So he became an acclaimed musician. And a beloved figure at the courts of Italy. And a spy.

Little by little, the novels became finished works. I wrote screenplays—and I was able to write them, develop them, and complete them in weeks, not months and years. "Yes," I was able to say to myself at last, "you are a writer."

And of course the shape of my own path as a writer became reflected in the shape of the paths that I opened up with and for my writing students. Many who had been with me for years had written elegant statements of life experience. And many of them wanted to experience more: to write novels and screenplays and short stories—fictional work, based on life stories already written. And they wanted to explore deeper levels of experience in their writing, whether fictional or nonfiction. So, together, we went to those places. That is the work to be found in *Writing from Deeper Within*.

However, *Writing from Within: The Next Generation* represents a larger step in my journey as a writer and as a creative person. It encompasses my journey from a certainty that I could never write creatively to realizing that I could turn out work that transported people to another time and place and provided them with insights and connections to things they had glimpsed but not thought about, a resonance that often existed within themselves, unseen and unknown.

The details of my particular journey are, of course, my own. But the general nature of my gradual understanding of the obstacles that lay before me, and my strong desire to move past them, are not unlike the journeys many who write and create must face. Thus, within the pages of *Writing from Within: The Next Generation*, you will find strong support for your own journey, from crawling out of the slime of ignorance to standing erect on a path of knowing and creating.

This path to creating and producing is not unlike the path outlined in Joseph Campell's *The Hero with a Thousand Faces*. The Parsival-like person who sets out with great ambitions, hopes, dreams (or perhaps with none of the above) encounters various teachers whose significance may remain unseen at the time, descends into a kind of catatonic state of depression and mindless self-flagellation, and finally emerges revived, reinvigorated, reinvented, and re-born—ready to create. This is the path of *Writing from Within: The Next Generation*.

— • • • —

The following paragraphs, which form the introduction to *Writing from Within*, 3rd edition (1998), refer to Part I of this book and are taken directly from the Introduction of *Writing from Within*, 3rd edition.

— • • • —

In the years after World War II, America saw an unprecedented rootlessness developing. Easterners moved west, Southerners moved north, corporate Americans moved everywhere. But in the years since Alex Haley's *Roots* (and more recently, the popular television show *Who Do You Think You Are?*) entered the consciousness of American society, we have seen a distinct shift toward respect for roots. And with it, we have witnessed an increasing respect for the wit and wisdom of those who have gotten us where we are—our parents and grandparents. For a writer and teacher who works with mature adults, this is a welcome change.

This volume, derived from the life-story writing classes and workshops I taught between 1982 and 1998 is written for those who wish to inform their children and grandchildren about the life path that they, the writers, have followed. It is also a self-help text for those who wish to use this writing as a means toward greater self-understanding.

Some of you may wish to read this book through from beginning to end before starting to write. In that case, you may wish to jot down notes as ideas, incidents, and people from the past come to mind.

I encourage you to work in a leisurely manner; there is no need to rush. It may take weeks or even months to move from one chapter to the next. That is to be expected. How many stories you write while developing the techniques presented in each chapter is very much up to you. You may well take six months to a year or longer to work through the book.

In the first few weeks and months, you will be spending a great deal of time rewriting, time that you might prefer to spend on the next recollection. To achieve the intimacy and depth of feeling and observation that are possible using the techniques described in the book, allow yourself the extra time and effort. Reread the book several times, and you will gradually make the techniques you have read and thought about a part of you. Using them will begin to feel comfortable—and you will be happy with the results.

At the end of several sections on composing, I include a short personal note. These notes are intended to guide you into the actual writing, for I do urge you to begin writing when I say *now*. Don't bother fussing, worrying, or protesting. Whatever comes out is a first draft, which can be revised later. If you wish to read through the whole book before beginning to write, that is fine. But do allow the book to help you get down to the task of writing, not thinking about writing.

I am often asked, "Should I write my stories chronologically, or should I write as my inner urge dictates?" By all means, write as that urge dictates. Your stories ought, generally, to be arranged in chronological order if you print or publish them, but you, as the writer, need feel no compulsion to write them in that order. The vivid memories are the ones most likely to pop out at you at any time of the day or night.

I do suggest that you write several early memories first, learning to write from the child's point of view before skipping around and writing about different phases of your life. Writing a number of early memories enables you to start with simpler memories and to discover the power of writing "authentically," that is, writing in a voice that is consistent with the age of the person you were. By getting back to that person, you will discover much of your past that you have forgotten or remembered inaccurately.

The style you will be developing will be forceful, immediate, and intimate. It will be full of dialogue and your inner thoughts and feelings. You will be developing your own authentic writer's voice, while you learn how to "write from within."

———•••———

The next paragraphs refer primarily to Part II of this volume, and also appear in *Writing from Deeper Within*.

Your Writing Process

A great many people who *want* to write have deep concerns about whether they actually *can* write. They wonder, "Will I be able to find an audience, get an agent, solicit a publisher, overcome writing blocks, and perhaps make a living at writing—all in the same lifetime?"

The answer: Who knows? But one thing is certain: Anyone intending to write seriously has to find a way of doing things that feels right and yields results. Everyone wonders whether they have talent. But the larger question is: Do you have what it takes to assume that you have talent and just go do the work? If you can get over that hurdle of doubt (which will return each time you experience a setback), then the next question is: Do you have the discipline and confidence to find your way through the maze of obstacles to create a body of work? Discipline and confidence are important, as is the belief that you have talent.

Five other clear and distinct concerns become visible in the labyrinth that is writing, each worth attending to:

1. Do you believe that a path exists that will get you through the maze of obstacles to completing a work?
2. Do you have a consistent, reliable plan for creating whatever you need to create?
3. Have you foreseen and dealt with the emotional obstacles to completing your work?
4. Are you willing to do the ruthless self-examination that writers must go through to complete their work?
5. Have you truly understood the messages that lie beneath the writing instruction that I will be outlining in subsequent chapters?

The Path

A small percentage of people know their talents at a very young age. The majority of us know what we would like to do but seldom know that the talent for doing so exists within. Discovering what your best qualities are (a process outlined in Chapter 22) is a big part of gaining belief in your talents and abilities to write. Writing well in school almost doesn't count, because academic writing is logical and analytical, and rarely creative. If you have an engaging way of presenting this information, that's fine, but it has little to do with becoming a writer.

The writer inside us sees the world in a fresh and perhaps different way. This side of a person finds itself fascinated by human relationships, not as described in texts by Sigmund Freud and Alfred Adler, but in the way relationships unfold, as they do in the works of Henrik Ibsen, August Strindberg, Billy Wilder, and Jean Giraudoux. Psychologists want to know *why* things happen concerning human nature. Writers want to know *how* things happen—how people act in certain circumstances.

To make the leap from being an observer of the human condition to becoming a writer about that condition, you must believe a path exists for you to follow, one that will yield a finished work. If you don't have that belief, then you must assume that you will find that path as you go along. And you will. But this path is your path, no one else's.

In his book *The Hero with a Thousand Faces,* Joseph Campbell describes the path of the transcendent hero, be he a person who crossed the face of this earth at some point in time or a philosopher's invention, a writer's creation, or a theologian's supposition. That path looks remarkably similar for all heroes: A naïve young person starts out on a quest, receives a talisman or charm, fails badly in some way, struggles to right himself, fails again, and falls into a pit of despair, loneliness, and confused direction. This pit becomes a spiritual death from which the hero emerges transformed and better armed to meet the challenges ahead. Usually this transformation includes a softening of the self and the ego that drives a young person and accompanies a new way of seeing things—often an ability to see into the hearts of those around him.

Campbell's path of the hero looks very much like that of many artists, musicians, and writers. To bring something into being, one must make mistakes and take false steps. In a labyrinth, a turn unexplored is a turn where light may exist just around an unseen corner. Exploring all of ones options takes time.

The Plan — Your Personal Mantra for Writing

The *plan* unfolds as a natural byproduct of, belief in, and willingness to follow the path. The plan is usually simple. The first part is adopting *a workable code or mantra to live by.* Your plan may be, "I will not take at face value anything that I am told." Such a code enabled George Orwell to endure bureaucratic oppression and poverty and see through Fascist, Communist, and Colonialist propaganda. Another code may be, "I will do more than my father." This code drives many people forward. My own code seems quite simple: "Play when others work; work when others play." Your mantra, in whatever form it takes, provides you with ample time and space to work on your craft while making as many mistakes as necessary.

The second part of the plan is *understanding your audience* fully, knowing what it needs and expects and trusting its responses without trusting its reasoning. This means that early in your creative life as a writer, you will need to be willing to make your work visible to the outside world. You do not have to do what your audience tells you to do. It only means that you understand what it needs and expects. It remains your choice whether or not to give it the expected.

It also means you will seek out mentors who can see where your work wants to go, as well as enlist the energies of others who want you to succeed in your artistic endeavors. One of the more effective creative people I have met in my lifetime, jazz great Buddy Colette, used to say, "We are all trying to get to the same place; let's go there together."

The third part of the plan is *articulating your beliefs about the fundamental nature of man and the universe* in your writing. Is man, at heart, good? If so, how do you explain the mistakes he makes, the dilemmas he creates for himself and others? Or is he ultimately bad? If this is the case, must he be trained and thus forced to conform to a moral order? But what happens if he rebels? Is there no hope for him? One aspect of your plan must be to investigate this question as you see it playing out in all the arenas of your experience. The characters you create (and observe) must all have their own take on this issue (and the universe that surrounds them), for this attitude will ultimately drive their quests, their goals, their obsessions, and how they decide to proceed.

Emotional Obstacles

Many obstacles stand in the way of anyone who wants to write (or create) in a serious way. Some are practical concerns—paying the rent, having significant relationships, fulfilling obligations. Often, however, you face less tangible concerns, ones that you hardly know exist—a backstory to your life that may include loss, abuse, neglect, and the like. These concerns may take a toll on your commitment to the craft and art of writing unless you pay attention. Like soldiers going into battle, you must train yourself for the battle ahead, while knowing your strengths and weaknesses and fine-tuning your mechanism for understanding the world around you.

Because obstacles do exist, you can best help yourself by learning early on what character qualities you have and what kinds of talents lie within you. If you function with a clear head, these obstacles, character qualities, and talents may even become a part of what you write about, in one way or the other. Having been a musician all my life, it came as no surprise to me that, in beginning my first novel, I focused on the life of a young musician. My father, a doctor, became the model for this character's father—a fifteenth-century physician.

Often you have to clear away or surmount emotional obstacles before you can write in an energetic way. When my film career stumbled, I spent years getting clear about what I wanted and what was stopping me. Finally, the path became clearer—I had defined myself in a narrow way that had held me back. Once I defined myself not merely as a filmmaker but as a creative person, many opportunities opened up, including my path to writing creatively.

Another obstacle facing many people is the question, "How do I incorporate others into my 'writer's life,' a life that can be quite lonely?" One answer is that at every turn of the road, you will need people to help you, and you will meet people you can help. A writer—in fact people in all walks of life—needs a strong support system which includes family (wife, ex-wife, parents, brothers, sisters, and children) and friends. Creative people function poorly if they try to exist/live/work in complete isolation. You also need to find people who are doing what you do (write) and find groups in which to exchange feedback about your work. Putting effort into finding people who give quality feedback (insightful but not hurtful) to your work is something you continuously need to do, and you will find it worth all the energy you put into it.

Self-Examination

Many creative people find the work of C.G. Jung, Joseph Campbell, and Abraham Maslow helpful in their personal quests for identity and support. Why? Unlike Freud and those who followed him, Jung investigated the human condition without a preconceived agenda. That is, he made no assumption about whether man's fundamental nature was evil or good. He saw people in the same way that his contemporaries Ibsen, Strindberg, and Anton Chekhov saw them—as fascinating creatures acting and reacting to the world around them, intent on surviving. Campbell, the editor of much of Jung's work, saw mankind operating in the same way, although his fascination lay in uncovering common threads in the footprints of stellar individuals through civilizations. Maslow saw nothing but enormous possibilities in human beings and believed that everyone needs to do what they can to live up to their potential.

As a creative person, the time you spend pondering the lives of individuals such as Jung, Campbell, and Maslow as well as their arcs (the beginning, middle, and ends of their concerns about the human condition) will give you strength and determination to see what others do not see, to uncover what others prefer to ignore, and to make visible what others find invisible.

• • •

The complete stories by many of the writers mentioned in this book may be found in Part III of this book or at www.WritingFromWithin-Stories.com.

If you would like to follow a step-by-step guide with exercises in order to complete the first fourteen steps of the "writing from within" process, I suggest you obtain the *Writing from Within Workbook* from Hunter House Publishers.

For those who wish to know more about setting up a helpful, noninvasive feedback group, please see the Appendix at the back of the book.

To observe the ways in which another group of creative people—filmmakers—answer many of the questions posed in this book, please look at my book, *The Art of Seeing: Motion Pictures as an Art Form and as a Business.*

"Writing from Within": The Basic Approach and Techniques

The first part of *Writing from Within: The Next Generation* contains five units. Part I, Unit I, "Acquiring the Basic Techniques of 'Writing from Within,'" looks at the basic techniques of life-story writing. Unit II, "Amplifying the Basic Steps in "Writing from Within": Narrative, Dialogue, and Inner Thoughts and Feelings," explores a few of these basic techniques more deeply. Unit III, "Using the Basic Techniques with Challenging Subject Matter," applies these techniques to unusual subject matter. Unit IV, "Writing Family Histories," examines different approaches to writing stories of a family's past history. Unit V, "Expanding and Managing Your Creativity," looks into some of the problems encountered when making the effort to be creative.

Part II, Unit I, "Advanced Perspectives in Writing Creatively," explores a host of techniques that allow for the creation of a more sophisticated, more complex, and more intimate story. Unit II, "Exploring Character Through Rewriting" suggests ways to reveal character and character qualities by sharing a character's innermost thoughts and feelings and describing character qualities through actions and details. Unit III, "Leaping into Longer Work" presents an opportunity to see how these techniques can move a story from sketch (short story or life story) to a full-length novel, screenplay, or play. Unit IV, "For the Future," imagines other uses for the techniques of life-story writing to understand ourselves and to provide a richer experience of writing in school systems across the country.

• • •

Acquiring the Basic Techniques
of "Writing from Within"

As I walk up the steps to the second floor of the Musicians Union in Los Angeles, I wonder what this class will be like. For years I have been teaching people to write their life stories in classes and workshops around California, and I have been a musician since I was twelve years old. Now I hope to combine these two passions by helping musicians—mostly older, both male and female, black, white, latin, and Asian—gather together to share their stories of life on the road and in the studios with bands big and small.

The first session, which we had last week, was fun. I had moved another class to this location in order to include these musicians, and the members of the old class welcomed the musicians with a lot of warmth. The new members did a short exercise in which each shared his or her earliest memory out loud. Then I showed them how to tell their memories again in a way that would bring the stories to life. In this session we will find out how their writing is coming along.

"Good morning, Herr Professor." Dave Schwartz, a highly respected, retired violist gives me a wry smile as I open the door.

"Hello, Dave, how are you?" I've come to see that Dave, who is pushing eighty and looks sixty, is not only one of the class wits, but a very sharp-minded man.

"Hey, Bernard," Eddie White greets me. "How's it going?" His shy smile lights up the room. A small, kindly man with snow white hair, Eddie has been with me several months now and has shown over and over again remarkable storytelling gifts.

"Hey there, Edward, you got a good one for us?" I ask.

"It better be good," laughs Buddy Collette, the great sax, clarinet, and flute player who, with Charlie Mingus, Britt Woodman, and Chico Hamilton, formed the first postbebop band after World War II. "He called me at three o'clock this morning to read it to me." We all laugh.

"Well, I sort of lost track of time," Eddie chuckles. The smile never leaves his face.

"Eddie's always had a problem with time." Jack Burger, a long-time drummer in the Hollywood studios, laughs.

"Yeah, sometimes I play three beats to a measure and you guys are playing four." Eddie enjoys poking fun at himself. "That's why I hardly ever play in public."

"You're lucky. You played music because you loved it." Jack leans back in his chair. "The rest of us were cursed with talent and had to earn a living at it."

Dave nods toward Jack, a little smile on his face. "Not all of us who earned a living at it were cursed with talent, Jack."

I laugh with them while other members of the class, the nonmusicians like Doris Argoud and Roz Goldstein from the earlier class, settle into their seats. Listening to musicians trade stories and gentle barbs is one of the highlights of my week, as it is for Roz and Doris.

"Buddy has a story," says Eddie. "I asked him to read it to me, but he wanted to wait for your comments, Bernard."

"Well, let's hear it," says Doris, a whimsical, supportive woman in her late forties. "I'm dying to know his earliest memory."

"This is just a first draft, you know," replies Buddy. Tall and distinguished, a true elder statesman of jazz, he takes several sheets of paper from his briefcase and puts on his glasses. As he reads, I reflect on what I know of him: A superb musician, Buddy is (and has been for a long time) a force in the creative community of Los Angeles, conducting workshops, concerts, and performances for kids in schools. In the early 1950s, he was instrumental in bringing the black and white musicians' unions together to form a single, integrated union. He later became the first black musician to break into the studios. Thanks to him, our class is now held at the union building.

I've known Buddy for several months, after a chance meeting brought him to the class in which Roz and Doris were students. Right away, he invited relatives and friends, including Eddie, to join the group. These new, creative storytellers have brought a wonderful energy to the class, and I'm impressed with Buddy's philosophy: "We're all moving forward, so let's move forward together." I find myself wondering, *What has enabled Buddy to become so positive and forward-looking, able to ease past obstacles that would stop another man?*

In this first story for our combined class, he writes about a time when, at two years old, he sees something on the other side of the street and runs across the street to get it. A Model T Ford runs him down, and Buddy disappears under the wheels. Buddy's mother hurries to the scene and sees only the scarf in the spokes of the wheel. "My baby…" she whispers. A few moments later Buddy is pulled from under the car, stunned but alive.

As I listen, I imagine Buddy's mother growing hysterical and angry, as I imagine most parents becoming…as I myself became when my younger son ran out in the street.

But no, Buddy's mother sweeps him up in her arms, saying, "Oh, my little darling, I'm so glad you're all right."

How intriguing, I think to myself, as I listen to Buddy describe the little tests his father devised to teach him independence and resourcefulness. His parents' attitude seems to be, "If you want to do it, it must be worth doing."

I begin to reflect on the nature of parenting. From noncritical, supportive parents comes a sense of wholeness to our lives, the kind of wholeness I also see in creativity such as Buddy's. But for most of us, I think to myself, loving, attentive, supportive elders are, like wholeness and creativity, something for which we yearn, but seldom get. I feel a little sad.

Unlike Buddy, I grew up with a sense of something missing in my life. *What is it?* I kept asking myself all through high school. *What's missing?* I wonder whether it had anything to do with my parents, though they were pretty normal. Dad was my hero, a successful, highly educated psychiatrist who survived a serious heart attack when I was eight and who coped with my mom's emotional illnesses.

Of course, Dad was not always my hero. Highly critical, with a mind as sharp as a razor, he absorbed book knowledge with ease. The unspoken rule of the house was "read books, do well in school, win Dad's approval." As I looked around our library at home, I was intrigued and overwhelmed. How could I ever hope to read all those books? I became quite critical of myself, and Dad's occasional dark rages that he directed at me added a whole lower octave to the voices of my inner thoughts: *You won't be able to do that. You don't deserve to get that. You won't finish that. You've reached a plateau, and that's where you'll stay.*

I reflect that my experience with my parents was probably not much different from that of most people: one parent highly critical, the other more supportive but often afraid to interfere. *Ah, that demonic inner critic, so ready to devour us. How sad,* I think to myself. *How sad.*

"What a wonderful story, Buddy," says Doris. "It gives us a lot of insight into you."

"My mother was a great lady," murmurs Buddy. "She gave a lot of thought to everything…like the music lessons we all got."

I glance around the room. Dave's face has a bit of a frown. "Dave, you have a question, I think?"

"I've always wanted to write about playing with Toscanini, Leopold Stowkowski, and Glenn Miller. But it just sounds like bragging. 'Big important me.' I get frustrated and stop writing."

"What voice is that?" I ask, expecting that those who have been with me a while will recognize it immediately.

"The voice of the critic," answers good-natured Roz. Dave still looks puzzled. "The voice that's telling you not to write or is finding fault with what you do...that's the voice of the critic."

Dave turns to me. "Is that right, Bernard?"

"Dave, when we were small, most of us were playful and we created endlessly...in the sandbox or at the beach, right?" The others nod their heads. "But too often our strongly critical mind—our 'critic'—simply overwhelms our 'creator' side. It makes it very difficult for us to see our deep-seated creativity and keep it going."

"So the perfectionist in me makes it impossible even to start writing," Dave muses. Roz and Doris nod their heads in agreement. "Very interesting...the conflict between my self-critic and my creativity is what's holding me back? Then how do I get unstuck?"

"In the course of writing our stories, we will often find these two sides of the mind fighting with each other. When this happens, we need to calm ourselves, to drain away emotions, particularly frustration—to allow our creative side to regain momentum." Dave stares at me intently. "I do a couple of things: I put a play-along jazz album on the turntable, pick up my clarinet, and accompany it. This calms me down, and I return more focused. Or I lie down and doze off. My mind calms itself down."

"You actually let yourself go to sleep?" asks Dave.

"He fell asleep during a story I wrote last year," laughs Roz.

"And he woke up and gave a great critique," adds Doris, racing to my defense.

"This balancing process has a very positive effect on the stories we write," I continue, "if we let it happen."

"It's had a positive effect on my life, too," adds Doris. Jack frowns at her. "Really, Jack. It's allowed a lot of my feelings to come out. Feelings that were buried for a long time."

"I was just thinking that nothing can help Dave put his life in balance," Jack chuckles. "He spends all his time carrying residuals to the bank."

"Don't I wish," laughs Dave. "But that does remind me of a story...anyway, go ahead Bernard."

Already I notice the men in the room becoming uncomfortable, joking and laughing as soon as we begin talking about feelings. This is not unusual. Buddy and Eddie are exceptions; Eddie's stories of growing up in the South are rich with feelings (see his story "Blind Lemon Jefferson Sings the Blues" on page 282).

"You know, when I was just starting to write," Doris offers, "I would sometimes get really emotional. A part of me would say, *Don't write this. It's too personal.* It took me a while to get up the courage just to go on and see where the story wanted to take me, what it would show me that I had forgotten."

"Writing isn't like playing the viola where I can just practice harder, is it?" Dave muses.

"Or listening to a record and stealing from the great artists," Jack smirks.

"Oh, Dave would never steal someone else's interpretation," adds Eddie with a sly grin. "He would make it his own."

"Don't bet on it," Dave laughs.

"Go ahead, Bernard," Buddy urges. "You were talking about feelings and writing?"

"Let me put it this way," I say. "When we are young, many things come along that hurt, embarrass, or frustrate us, yes?"

"You bet," Doris pipes in.

"Well, we soon learn to use language to keep that hurt at a distance…so we won't feel it as we write. As a result, we write in the past tense and use complicated words, anything to avoid reliving the pain of early childhood."

"So we actually use language to keep people from getting close to us when we write?" Buddy ponders this.

"Exactly," I answer. "Most of the time, we think we want to bring our readers into our stories; but in fact, we are filled with such fear of their discovering a lot about us that we actually keep them far away from the experience we are writing about."

"And the critic enters the picture, saying, 'You're bragging, don't do that,' and we silence ourselves even more," Dave adds.

"That's it," I answer. Dave is beginning to understand what has been holding him back. I turn to Buddy. "This is why we enjoyed your story about the Model T—because you let us inside the experience." I look around. They want more. "For example, many of us were taught in the early grades that it is self-centered to use the word 'I' in a sentence."

"I've never had a problem talking about myself," chuckles Eddie. "But go on. I like to listen to you talk, Bernard. Yes, sir, you sure can talk. Uhuhhhhh."

I suppress a laugh and continue. "Very often my students, in writing about themselves and their brothers and sisters, will say something like, 'We went to the creek and we were feeling good,' which is different from saying, 'My brothers and I went to the creek. I was feeling good.' There's a difference, yes?"

"A writer cannot make statements about the thoughts and feelings of 'we' and be believed, but he can speak about 'I' and be believed," answers Roz, who has been with me for several years.

"So it's a matter of belief, not exactness, that matters?" asks Dave. I enjoy the sharpness of his questions. "We have to make the audience *believe* what we are talking about?"

"Little differences in language, such as these, enable us to bring the audience closer to our inner experience or to push our audience out of our experience." I glance from face to face as each person digests these words. "We have so many ways of hiding our feelings and our thoughts from ourselves and from others."

"It's so true," says Doris, who writes vividly of growing up with an alcoholic mother. I hear the sadness in her voice.

"What we need is to find a way to express ourselves that keeps us in close touch with ourselves and our audience. In the next few weeks and months, as we go through the steps of 'writing from within,' we will learn how to express our experience of events and of ourselves in a way that draws our readers into our universe and keeps them in our orbit for the duration of the story—that allows them to believe what they are reading. A compelling story gets told and, at the same time, we have every opportunity to be at the center of our universe for a brief moment—and to make our universe interesting to others. 'I am here' rather than 'We were there.'"

"I'm with you Bernard," says Dave. "Open the door."

"Uhh uhh uhhh," murmurs Eddie. "Bernard, you sure can talk. You shoulda stayed in the air force. You'd have made a great general, or a politician." Everyone in the class laughs, including me.

"Just remember, some tears may flow," adds Roz. "And that's just fine." She smiles. "When I recalled the deaths of my mother and sister, tears were pouring out of my eyes the whole time. But I just kept on writing. I discovered a great deal about myself and my family as I wrote through the tears. I began to recover something I had lost a long time ago. It was wonderful."

"Let me just talk a bit more about how we can achieve this kind of wholeness and balance," I continue. "While discovering our creative side, a side many of us have never known, we may begin to recover something much greater, a part of our soul, the part that Roz is talking about."

"Writing from Within": The Language of Intimacy

"Writing from within" is the act of exploring vivid moments in our lives from the point of view of the age at which we experienced them, and then writing those moments with an intimacy of emotional detail that balances the outer world of actions, relationships, and events with the inner world of thoughts and feelings.

Little by little, we will find "writing from within" to be a process that will take us into the center of our own universe, propelling us through time and space toward an experience of ourselves that brings the past into the present, allowing us to see ourselves in a multitude of ways, as if we were many selves, moons circling our larger self. Exploring these old parts will help us uncover and deepen our sense of importance and worth. It will enable us to find our own authentic writing voice, to step out onto the center stage of our own lives, and to take our journey of self-discovery in an unusual direction.

Using the "writing from within" approach, we will (1) learn a process of storytelling that yields a mode for getting at the truth of our experiences, which is different from what we could accomplish using other methods; (2) learn a process for creating a story that has quality as a work of art; and (3) create a product that can be shared, savored, reviewed, and rewritten in company with others. By using the feedback methods taught in this book, our writing will yield a clear and unexpected view of important experiences too often hidden in a cloud of numbness and self-deception.

We will also learn to look at our stories in a way that allows us to gain further insight and clarification from them.

Clarifying Who We Were and What Happened

One part of the self-discovery process is seeing ourselves and our reactions to life experiences as clearly as possible. For example, if we have had a loss of some kind in our lives, such as a death in the family, it is important to see that loss clearly, to understand what that loss looks and feels like, and then, perhaps, to see the patterns of behavior we use to cope with that loss.

This part of the process is not easy. Most inventories, as they are called in alcohol and drug rehabilitation programs and self-help books, look like unending links of sausage, narrative burdened with excessive judgments of the shoulds and shouldn'ts of life, without beginning, middle, or end. They often do not get very close to the actual events and the quality of the insights may not be revealing or stimulating.

In "writing from within," we choose specific moments to write about. Each story has a beginning, a climax, and an ending, so we do not have to assess more than we can handle in the course of the fifteen minutes to two hours most stories take to write. Yet in this short period of time, we are transported to another time and place, making it possible to see ourselves as we were decades ago.

The numbness I mentioned earlier is only one way that we cope with emotional and psychic pain. When we have a physical wound, the tissue around it becomes raw, even infected, as red and white blood cells rage to fight off the invasion.

When we are wounded emotionally, there is a great deal of pain. We may try to anesthetize it, but unlike bodily injuries that tend to heal themselves, psychic wounds often grow if unattended. We look for ways to drain off the whirlpools of emotion long enough to enable us to go looking for the source. By seeing as clearly and fully as possible the experiences that haunt us, we are able to release ourselves from their weight and move on to handle other aspects of our lives.

For the past twenty years or so, the journal writing process has become a helpful outlet for people to release their emotions on paper without any form of criticism being leveled at them. Automatic writing, writing with the non-dominant hand, and the like are other effective ways of draining off emotion while beginning the process of self-examination.

Sharing Our Experiences and Achieving Peace of Mind and Body

While the prospect of starting to write may scare us at first, we can learn to overcome the fear. As our stories begin taking shape, we see powerful feelings elicited in our readers. How immense is our satisfaction when we realize we have the power to touch others' minds and hearts? Likewise, sharing these stories unlocks for us, as writers, a greater unfolding of the experience (feelings, perceptions, more of the story), which would not take place were the story not told and shared with others. The more powerful and honest the story, the more penetrating the insights that come to us.

Deep within all of us there is a protector that exists to keep from us recollections it believes would be too painful for the conscious mind to bear. It acts as a kind of emotional circuit breaker in our unconscious, causing us to grow numb, to forget. Our protector keeps these events and experiences well hidden in our unconscious until it is convinced we are ready to handle them. "Writing from within," however, slips past the protective layers of forgetting and selective memory.

In the thirty years I have been doing this work, I have been fascinated by this process—bringing something hidden to the surface, facing it, and taking a giant step toward regaining a lost part of ourselves, a part of our soul that has been missing. When we do this as part of a group, it encourages us to see that what we experienced is much like what others have experienced: We are not alone.

However, when we get together in writing groups, we do not spend our time discussing the psychology of what has taken place in our lives—the motivations, causes, and the like. For the writer's protection, we, the listeners, only discuss our "feeling" responses to the writing. Guidelines for giving feedback are established about what is OK and what is not OK. In this way, we, as writers, are protected from intrusive scrutiny and from criticism of our work or the way we handled our experience. The sharing process, as outlined in the book, is positive and supportive as we continue to dig in the sands of life experience for the truth of what happened to us in the past.

When we write a story and dig for its truth, the characters come alive. Our thoughts and feelings are out there on paper as the listeners hang on the edges of their chairs to learn what happens to these people they have come to know intimately. There is a great satisfaction in this. Our greatest pain becomes a substantial asset.

Using "Writing from Within" As a Metaphor for Moving Toward Wholeness

As a graduate student at the University of Michigan more than thirty-five years ago, I was introduced to a wonderful concept the fifth-century Greeks had for creating and maintaining a balance among the various parts of the self as well as the universe surrounding the self. This concept, *kalokagathia*, has stayed with me. I raised my two sons with it in the back of my mind—creating and maintaining a harmony among mind, body, and soul.

We might say that the *kalokagathia* of a good story is the harmonizing of three fundamental elements: narrative, dialogue, and inner thoughts and feelings. *Narrative* is the unfolding of events in the world through time; *dialogue* is the path by which we find and explore relationships among people (including ourselves) within that world; and *inner thoughts and feelings* are our deepest selves, made visible to others through our writing, giving us a sense that we are completely present in this universe of relationships and unfolding time. As we allow narrative, relationships, and inward-searching energies of our own thoughts and feelings to unfold and find a balance within each story, we also bring into balance our own life energies. In this act of writing and balancing, we reinvent ourselves. We discover our *kalokagathia*, our balance of mind, body, and soul.

This balancing is not as easy as we might wish. After all, the world may be a stage upon which we are the players, as Shakespeare said four hundred years ago, but for a great many of us, taking center stage is quite frightening. Our minds will distort recollections so that our fears are softened, our pain is pushed away, our anxieties are lessened. All of this is reflected in the way we write our stories, at least in the beginning. Some of us will relate a story and leave out all sense of relationship of the people involved and without including ourselves, as writers, in the picture. Others of us will write vivid dialogue but without a sense of a story unfolding. Still others of us will dwell so deeply inside our world of inner thoughts and feelings that we will appear to have little sense of relationship to the outer world or to the people in it.

These unbalanced ways of writing create distance between ourselves and the event and our audience, protecting us from the emotion of reliving the experience and the possible criticisms of our audience. They relieve us from taking center stage in our lives, from reclaiming our feelings, and from gaining the spotlight that we deserve, but of which we are so afraid.

Each step of the "writing from within" process will soften our fears and help us see and overcome the ways we create distance between ourselves and life around us, both as we live our lives and as we re-create it in our stories. Each step assists us in writing a more vivid story, but also helps us move past anger and rage, hurt and numbness, confusion and forgetting, past the need to keep life at arm's length. As we use these steps over and over from one story to the next or from one draft of a story to the next, our memories yield different versions of each event. We persuade our unconscious that we are serious about learning what really happened way back when, and rewriting becomes our primary tool for searching out more and more of the truth.

Using "writing from within" to create a more vivid story and to rewrite our stories to uncover more and more of the truth lures our energies away from our self-critic and toward our creator. We thus have an opportunity to discover a great deal about ourselves as we hold up the mirror of the ever-deepening story, asking, "Who am I in the mirror of this story?"

As we learn how to use the process of rewriting our stories to nudge to the surface more and more truths about events in our pasts, we set the stage for us to see life events with ever-more-innocent and inward-looking understanding and to value more deeply the profound dimensions of our own creativity.

chapter 1

Overcoming Fear

To tell one's life stories, to explore the sad/happy, exciting/boring, fascinating/fearful experiences of one's long life, seems like a wonderful idea. But how many wonderful ideas have we had in our lives that never became anything more than ideas? Quite a few? What stopped them from becoming reality? It was probably lack of motivation, or fear, or both.

If the idea of writing your life story strikes a chord within you, sets off a bell, causes you to salivate—or fills you with unspeakable dread—then you are ready to write your story. What is holding you back is not lack of motivation, but fear. Stark, naked fear.

Fear of what? Fear of being unable to write well and being criticized by friends and relatives? Fear of being unable to finish, of getting off the track? Fear that you might say too much and embarrass someone? Fear that you may dig up old, painful "stuff" that you can't handle? Fear that you just don't have what it takes to write well?

Research into the way the brain operates has revealed that there are two sides to the brain, right and left. Much of our fear of writing comes from the way these two sides do or don't work together.

We might term the right side of the brain "the creator," for apparently it allows us to do creative things—make connections, manifest ideas, imagine situations, see pictures of events. The left side analyzes, categorizes, recalls words, and performs its learning functions in a step-by-step manner.

For our purposes, what is important to know about the analytic left brain is that it has a little attic on top that houses "the critic." The critic is the person in us who says, "Watch out! You can't do that! You'll fail, so don't even try. You know you're no good at that!"

Perhaps you would be right if you said the critic sounds a lot like dear old

Mom or Dad: "If I've told you once, I've told you a thousand times, you may not do (something you really want to do) until you carry out the garbage"—or clean your room, wash the dishes, get good grades, and so on. Sound familiar? Believe me, I know. I, too, am a parent…and remember being a child.

Parents are great, but they do tend to be critical. They are our guides in the world, but too often they do more than guide us. They tell us not to do certain things, and then we become afraid to do them.

Our critic becomes a problem for us when we want to create something out of nothing—say a story or a painting—because the right brain, in which our creator stirs every now and then, is very tender, very sensitive to criticism. So if our left-side, tough-minded, parent-critic brain says, "Forget it! You can't do it," our right-side, tender-minded creator says, "Fine! I'm going back to sleep. Talk to me in a few weeks."

And so our deep desire to create—in this case, to write our life stories—gets buried once again.

How do we counteract the critic? We calm him. We stroke him. When he emerges, we become aware of his presence, but we do not fight him. We can enjoy his antics, be amused by his swordplay as he cuts away at our confidence, but we must keep out of range of that slashing saber. And we must avoid a confrontational stance. "What do you mean, I can't do it! I can so!" To the critic, that is merely a call to arms. On the other hand, a flexible stance—something like "You'll be surprised what I can do" or "I've been doing pretty well, so I think I'll keep on creating, even if it seems hard"—will deflect the critic's thrusts and keep our creative juices flowing. So enjoy the critic, be amused by him, but don't try to duel with him. He will actually be valuable at a later stage when he is calmer and able to look at your work objectively, suggesting ways and means of changing and expanding it.

We human beings have an almost infinite variety of ways to censor ourselves. Fear not only keeps us from writing, it inhibits us from letting the world see our work when it is done. We tend to be very hard on ourselves as writers. In fact, some very good work may be lost because of our pessimism.

The following is a fine story that the writer had tossed in the garbage. The writer revealed what he had done, and the class responded by insisting that he resurrect the story and bring it in, which he did, complete with stains from coffee grounds and fried eggs.

My Friend Jake   *by David Yavitts*

From a small town in eastern Russia, our family arrived in the Midwest of the United States, in St. Paul, Minnesota, a short distance from the banks of the Mississippi River.

Our house was on two and a half acres, partly in a hollow. The front of the house; that is, the parlor, living room, and dining room, were on street level. The kitchen and bedroom were on the hollow portion, held up by posts.

It was there that life for me began in this country. In the next couple of years, we had acquired a cow, horse, chickens and ducks. My responsibility was the ducks, keeping their quarters clean and feeding them.

I became very fond of them, gave them names and learned to recognize them by color and size. My favorite duck I called Jake, because we got that particular duck from our neighbor Jake's farm.

As I spoke the English language poorly, I did not have any friends, and I adopted Jake as my friend and confidant. He listened to me and would cock his head and did not move until I was through speaking. He would always wait for a while.

Jake grew faster than the other ducks, and his feathers, especially around his neck, were a ring of black. The rest was white.

That winter the ducks became full grown and plump. In the spring, I was assisting my mother in cleaning the stovepipes. They were full of soot and as I removed the soot much of the black powder made my face and hands black.

It was time to feed the ducks and I couldn't find Jake, my duck. I looked everywhere and called him. There wasn't any response. I finally went into the house; my mother was at the stove baking what she said was a chicken. I explained to her that Jake, my duck, was lost and that I couldn't find him. My mother told me, if the duck was lost she would get me another one—not to worry!

At this point, my older sister came in the kitchen and said, "Is the duck done yet?"

The sky fell down and I shouted, "That's Jake!" They could not pacify me. I cried and told them they were mean and bad to kill Jake and I ran out of the house, saying I didn't want to live there any more. I said I was going to my uncle's house across the bridge, over the river.

They didn't believe it, but I started my journey.

I knew where the bridge was; I could see it from my home and headed in that direction. Here was a dirty-faced kid about three and a half who cried as he walked toward the bridge. In my mind, I knew my soft-hearted uncle would solve my problems.

Well, I didn't get very far on the bridge when I was stopped by a policeman who asked, "Where are you going, young man?"

He repeated that question many times. I did not understand too well. I spoke Yiddish, and that soft-hearted Irish policeman spoke English with a brogue. He took me to the police station. There, an officer who understood me got my story, figured out where I lived, left me at the station, and eventually called my mother. She got my older sister out of the classroom at school and sent her to the station. My sister thought she would have to bail me out. There I was, my sister said, sitting on a table with an ice cream cone in my hand and crying. The tears ran down my face, washing the black soot off in white streaks. The ice cream washed my lips. I was a sight! My mother said, "Come home, dinner is waiting."

I said, "Mother, I don't eat duck!"

— • • • —

Having read the story, we can see that it is complete and effective. The details and observations are sharp; the dialogue is appropriate. It has a beginning, a middle, and an end; it is personal and deeply felt. Yet, despite its obvious excellence, the writer had dumped it in the trash. Imagine what would have happened, not only to the story but also to the man's future as a writer, had the class not insisted that he retrieve it.

Once we understand how our left-brain critic operates, we can begin to work on our memoirs, knowing that we can defuse our fears by identifying the pressure of the critic when he appears.

You may say, "I don't really have any fear and I don't think I have much of a critic." That's wonderful. But let's give ourselves a little test in order to find out. Let's suppose we've been given a writing task and have about a paragraph written. Myself, I am inclined to stop at this point and review what I've written. What about you? Do you go on? Or do you keep working on your first paragraph until you feel it is "correct"? In the next chapter, we will see what the answer to this question tells us about ourselves and our critic. We will also begin to work on our first life story.

chapter 2

Finding Your
Earliest Memories

"So, Bernard, let me ask you a question." Dave Schwartz has a thoughtful look on his face as we walk into the conference room at the Musicians Union.

"Sure, Dave, what is it?" I reply as we settle into our chairs.

"As you know, I want to write the stories of my experiences playing viola with Toscanini and the NBC Orchestra as well as the Glenn Miller Army Orchestra and the Paganini String Quartet."

"Yes?"

"Well, you mentioned that it is important to start with early memories of our lives," Dave continues. "But I want to write about things that happened to me from the time I left the Curtis Institute when I was twenty."

"First of all, writing early memories is important in the same way that every musician has to learn *Twinkle, Twinkle, Little Star* before he can tackle Bach, Beethoven, or Brahms."

"I see. Well, that makes sense," Dave replies with some uncertainty in his voice.

"But," I add, "there are other, equally important reasons, one of which is that in writing early memories we have a chance to see what the world was like from the point of view of a child, which is the place where we begin the search for our own artistic voice."

The other members of the class are listening, so I continue. "Your earliest memory is a good place to begin writing because it is something you see in your mind's eye, but it is not too complex to describe. It will probably be a fragment of something, a piece of a picture. That is just fine. It doesn't have to be a story. Even a few lines will do.

"You may be surprised how interesting, revealing, and important that little fragment really is. One of my students had been told all her life that she had hit her baby sister over the head with her bottle. What a traumatic memory to live with! But when she went way back to the incident, she recalled hitting the bottle on the side of the crib, and the bottle breaking and then hitting her sister. Suddenly, she was relieved of a guilt that had haunted her all her life, and the relief was wonderful!

"Earliest memories are often dramatic—a birth or death in the family, leaving or arriving at someplace special, a medical emergency. Sometimes, though, they can be as simple as remembering a shiny thing that hung over your crib. No matter how simple, write down what you see in your mind. Just that. Nothing more."

Getting Ready to Write

First, find a journal or notebook that you feel comfortable writing in. I suggest using a standard-size notebook (8½ by 11 inches) so that you don't feel cramped. Even if you plan to do most of your writing on a computer or typewriter, you may find that at times you will feel more relaxed writing the old-fashioned way, so having a journal on hand is still a good idea. Then, before you actually set pen to paper, take time to consider the following things.

Relax Yourself

Even if your mind is racing with solve-me-now problems, your childhood memories are not very happy ones, and your youthful writing experiences were unpleasant, you can relax into writing. Here are a few tips:

Create a backward-looking ceremony. Put on a favorite shirt or dress from twenty or forty years ago; reread a beloved novel from childhood; cook a meal from childhood (French toast for me); revisit a beloved place from long ago (Maine, in my case); talk to friends and relatives from years past; or gather pictures that bring back the happy memories of earlier times (railroads, particularly narrow-gauge ones, do it for me).

Choose a comfortable place and time in which to work. Find a quiet, comfortable place in which you can work undisturbed (although some writers seem to prefer coffeeshops or outdoor cafés, where the noise may be comforting); something relaxing in which to sit—a bed or a chair; and a place where the light is adequate and not distracting. It is equally important to find the right time to write. Our brains often whirl with problems to be solved; we need to find a time when we can put problems aside. For many people, sometime between eight in the evening and noon the next day is the best time to do this. Our right-brain creativity is most at work during these hours, whereas during the afternoon our left-brain, analytical, problem-solving energies are at their peak. So, if you don't feel like writing in the afternoon, don't force it.

Get out of town. If you are willing to invest the time, energy, and money to get a good start on this project, reserve a room for yourself at a quiet bed and breakfast in a peaceful town well away from the care and concerns of everyday life, or go visit a childhood haunt. (As I write this, I'm sitting at a table in my cabin beside a pond in southern Maine looking out over the water.)

Embrace your imperfection. Remind yourself that your writing does not have to be perfect. It is a part of a process to be learned. Fears are natural, and overcoming them is possible. (I used to believe that improvising a jazz solo, like writing, was something God-given and useless to try to learn. Twenty years of studying music and putting words and pictures on paper have taught me otherwise.)

Pump yourself up. Create an image of yourself as a knight in shining armor poised to seek adventure, like Lancelot and Percival or Joan of Arc going out into the world to do battle with their fears.

Drift off. The next time the urge to sleep strikes you when you start to write, give in to it. If you find yourself growing sleepy, you do not need to resist the urge, battling it for ten or fifteen minutes until finally you fall asleep only to awaken some time later feeling depressed because you have let yourself down. But you really have not. It's OK to drift off. It is your brain's way of switching from the everyday, problem-solving, left-brain mode to the creative, right-brain mode.

Calm your mind. Close your eyes, take a deep breath, exhale, do it again...and again. Listen to your breathing. This technique is used by professional athletes—tennis players waiting to receive serves, batters standing at the plate waiting for the pitch—to relax and focus at the same time.

Return to the Past

Use your daydreams or reveries to channel your thoughts back toward the deep past. Now that you are comfortable and relaxed, and perhaps semi-sleepy, allow your mind to float back in time, way back to your first memory. It really doesn't matter if that memory is from when you were three months old or three years old. It doesn't matter if it is not a story. It may be just a fragment of a picture. That is fine, as long as you see something.

Composing

Composing is the first phase of writing your life stories, and it involves the following elements.

Start Writing and Keep on Writing

Once you have begun your story, keep writing. Resist the urge to go back and make that first paragraph perfect. That urge is your critic speaking. Just plunge in, and don't stop.

Write from a Child's Point of View

Write down what you have just seen in your mind's eye from the point of view of the baby or child you once were. If you were in a crib, the reader would expect to see a bit of the crib and perhaps Momma and Poppa staring down at you. Create a strong and vivid picture of what you see: the place where the event is occurring, the sounds and smells around you, and the atmosphere of the scene. It is important to record all these details. Seeing the world through the eyes of a child, when the world was new and fresh, makes fascinating reading.

Here are some topics that may trigger your earliest memories:

- my earliest happy experience
- my earliest sad or shocking experience
- my first experience with a birth in the family
- my first experience with a death in the family
- my first day in school or the first day I remember in school
- my first experience of being all alone without Mommy or Daddy
- my first experience in the hospital—tonsils out, or illness
- my first experience eating, or playing, or riding on a train or a bus, and so on

At this point, we are ready to write. To make this easier, I will give you a little prompt to follow so that your self-critic—the urge not to write—will recede into the background. If, however, you would prefer to take a more step-by-step approach to this writing moment, please turn to the "Exercise" section at the end of this chapter. After you have completed that, you may wish to return to study the material in between. The following is your first writing prompt:

I know what to do, so it is time to do it. I am ready to begin. I am in a favorite, comfortable place. There are no distractions. It is quiet outside and in. There are *important objects around me and I may even be a bit sleepy. My mind begins to drift back, way back. I am very relaxed. I am beginning to see the first thing that I remember. I am going to write it…**now**.*

Form a Group

Working with a group of friends or acquaintances who are also interested in writing their own life stories is very desirable for several reasons. Reading your memoirs aloud to a group will tell you whether or not your stories are coming across well. It is also fun to share remembrances with friends, and often someone else's story will remind you about similar experiences of your own. Another benefit is that sharing stories with friends who are also interested in writing is less intimidating—everyone knows that his or her writing will be rewarded.

Reviewing

Having found your earliest memory and written a first draft of it, you have completed the initial writing phase. The next phase is to review what you have done to see how your work comes across to a listener or reader. Like composing, the reviewing phase has several steps.

Resist the Urge to Make Changes

The urge to make big changes and to be critical is always strong at this point. ("It can't be any good—I better change it.") Resist that temptation. Read over the story and make only a few corrections, such as cleaning up grammar and spelling. What you need most at this point is some feedback about the quality and effectiveness of what you have written.

Get Feedback

Writing is 50 percent self-expression and 50 percent finding out what the audience needs to know. At this point, you need some responses from friends about what you have written. It's rather scary to ask for reactions, but it will turn out OK. My own preference is to have a group of like-minded people review it. Friends and relatives may be either too critical or too patronizing, and neither of these attitudes is helpful for a beginning writer. So find a friend and read it aloud to him or her. (See the Appendix, "Creating a Supportive, Noncritical, yet Insightful Writing Group," for assistance on how to do this.)

Write Visually and for Impact

Ask those who listen to your stories two things: Are the stories visual (can they *see* them clearly in their minds)? Do they have an emotional impact (what do the listeners *feel* as they listen to them)? If a story has impact, listeners will often tell you it reminded them of a similar time in their own lives. This is a very good sign.

Rewriting

We are now at the final phase of putting together your first memoir: rewriting. The first phase, composing, frees you up to get your story on paper without stopping, that is, without letting the critic grab hold of you and drag you back to redo that first paragraph, as so often happens. The second phase, reviewing, helps you to get some objective feedback about your work by having a friend or group listen and respond to it. In the final phase, rewriting, you will learn how to make your story more vivid and substantially clearer to the reader, while deepening its impact.

Later we will explore rewriting more thoroughly, but this first memoir needs only a bit of tinkering to make it work. It is, after all, just a moment from your childhood, probably not even a complete story. Like a pianist learning to play the scales, a note at a time, your present task is only to make this moment dramatic and believable.

Below are guidelines to keep in mind when rewriting your first memoir.

Write in the Present Tense

In the rewriting phase of our work, we can explore using the present tense (using "is," not "was"), which gives the reader a wonderful sense of being present at or in the event. When we read a story written in the present tense, the events seem to be happening now; they seem to be happening around us rather than far away as if recollected through a tunnel. Small details suddenly become clearer and more vivid in our memories when we write in the present tense.

A child knows only what is directly in front of his or her eyes. Therefore, we believe a story written from a child's point of view more easily if it is written in the present tense. We may lose some information, but we gain a great deal in dramatic impact and believability.

Writing in the present tense is not easy for some of us. We have been accustomed to writing in the past tense for so long, we can hardly conceive of another way. It also forces us to use our imagination. An additional advantage is that writing in the present tense somehow puts our critic to rest for a while. We get out of our reflective, all-knowing, critical adult self and into a seeing, feeling, more-innocent self.

If you can use the present tense, do. If you are not comfortable with it at first, keep writing your stories in the past tense. Then, from time to time,

*Finding
Your Earliest
Memories*

experiment with the present tense. Just change all the past tense verbs to present tense: "I walked" becomes "I walk" or "I am walking."

Write in the First Person

Some of us find writing in the first person ("I was/am" rather than "he was/is" or "we were/are") troublesome. Many of us were taught in school that it is self-centered to say "I." This makes it a bit difficult to write one's life story.

In one of my classes, a tall, burly ex-Marine named Joe Page begins reading: "Joe P. got on his wagon and went down the hill really fast and then Joe P. nearly bumped a lady crossing the street. Joe rolled the wagon on its side. Joe really hurt himself."

"Joe," I say, after he has finished, "how long have you been out of the Marine Corps?"

He gazes at me for several seconds with his sad, tired eyes. " 'Bout thirty-five years," he answers in a soft voice.

I glance around the room. The fifteen other members of the class, all women, are very quiet. "Well, Joe," I say, "It's OK to say 'I.'"

"You ever been in the service?" he asks, eyeing me closely. I nod. "Then you know." He pauses for a long moment. "When 'a first went in, 'bout 1926, my first sergeant, he says to me, 'You boys ain't people no more, you're part of the Corps. It's 'we' and 'us' and 'the Corps,' hear? I catch any you sayin' 'I' this or 'I' that, I'll bust your a___. So don't let me hear that d____ word from any ya!!'"

"It's another time and another place, Joe," I say. "It's OK to say 'I.' Try it."

He nods, looking down at the page in front of him. "Mmm...mmm..." he stammers, wiping his face with a large red handkerchief. "Mmm got in the wagon and went down the hill." He glances up at me for an instant, then goes back to reading. "I got in my wagon and went down the hill," he mutters. His eyes meet mine for a moment, a hint of a grin on his face. "I nearly hit a lady and I turned my wagon over on its side...and I fell out."

Joe looks at me, then at the others in the class. The silence turns into relaxed, amiable chatter. "I know just how you feel, Joe," says one lady, touching his sleeve. "I was raised the same way." Many of the others nod in agreement.

More about Writing
from a Child's Point of View

Writing from a child's point of view—stripping your story of adult language—is perhaps the most important consideration for this early story. Be sure your memoir sounds as if it were experienced by a child.

You are probably asking, "How in the world can I write as a child would when I'm not a child? Shouldn't I just write as an adult looking back?"

The answer is no. You may not be able to write exactly as a child would, but you can *avoid certain writing patterns that mark the passages as those of an adult.* You are, after all, trying to recapture the world as seen through a child's eyes. *Avoid using vocabulary, diction, and phrasing that a child could not possibly use.* Consider the following passage:

> There were times, I suppose, when it seemed as if one would never be permitted to mature at a pace that was reasonable for my age. No, I was forced, albeit in a kindly fashion, to repeat *ad nauseam* the chores and duties attendant upon childhood: taking out the garbage, playing sports, minding my manners, and obeying the strictures of my parents.

No one reading this passage would suppose for a moment that a child had written it. Why? Because children don't talk or write that way. Let us look at specific parts of this passage to see what is unchildlike about it.

Vocabulary and phrasing: "permitted to mature," "reasonable for my age," "ad nauseam," and "attendant upon" are all phrases no child, other than one attending college at a remarkably early age, would ever use.

Qualifications: Statements that are qualified or modified are virtually never used by children. "I suppose" is a qualification, as is "albeit in a kindly fashion."

The objective voice: "One" is the objective voice and is almost never used by children.

Lists: Cataloging chores and the like in an orderly manner is an adult way of organizing. Children may do it, but they are less orderly and logical.

Now, let us look at the passage after rewriting it in a way that may not be childlike but at least is not obviously adult.

> From the time I was six or seven until I was eleven, my dad insisted that I take out the garbage every Thursday. What a chore that was! It seemed as if he'd never give me any real responsibility, just chores. But I remember one time when he…

Here you have a voice that could be adult or child. The passage is simple, straightforward, and visual. The narrator's voice and point of view do not intrude on the action or the progress of the story.

Let's take another look at the garbage incident, now written in the present tense:

I am twelve years old. Dad makes me take out the garbage every day. Yuk. Every day for six years. *When do I get a chance to do something important? I wonder.*

Suddenly, the story is more intimate, more vivid, more personal. This is a direction for us to explore.

In the first and second drafts of the story below, you can see the differences between a childhood story and a rewrite told exclusively from a child's point of view.

Willem   *by Jade* (FIRST DRAFT)

I have no recollection of the first years of my life. Looking way back into my early childhood, I come up with this little picture, a picture that has surfaced every once in a while whenever I am thinking of the old days.

I must have been three or four. There was a big sprawling backyard. A tall hedge concealed the main house, some distance away. The house was quiet; my mother must be resting. It was siesta time, the time after lunch when the shimmering tropical heat made people drowsy. It was also Sunday, the drone of my father's machines was not there. My father must also be resting. My father had a house-industry at that time. He bought up spices such as pepper, nutmeg, cloves, cinnamon, etc., from the farmers overseas on the other island, then he ground and bottled them in a special building on the grounds. To assist him he asked Willem to come over from his hometown on a far island to work as his foreman. Willem also lived with us in an outhouse.

I liked Willem, because he always spent time with us, whenever there was a chance. That afternoon was no exception. He showed my brother and me some magic tricks and then he said, "Kids, I am going to show you how strong I am!" He asked Joni, another workman, to go fetch the bicycle. Then he lay down on the grass and Joni was told to drive over his chest. I was greatly impressed when Willem stood up unhurt. Then he said, "And now the van will drive over me." Again he lay down on the thick grass and supposedly the car drove over him. I was in awe that nothing happened to Willem. This was where I got befuddled. I am sure I had not told my mother then and there, because she would have taken some action regarding Willem's way of entertaining us and she would have remembered the incident. As it was, when years later I talked about it, my mother said, "Nonsense, he must have tricked you." But I still wonder, did it really happen or was it just my imagination?

Jade *Jade (a pseudonym) grew up on a Borneo rubber plantation in the years before World War II. She came to the United States in the 1960s. She is married and a mother, and she came to life-story writing to "review her life and leave something for the grandchildren."*

—•••—

After hearing the story, members of the class suggested that the writer simplify the vocabulary and tell the story exclusively from the child's point of view, letting go of the inclination to set the stage, which takes the reader out of the child's experience. We also suggested she write the story in the present tense. Here is the result.

Willem *by Jade* (REWRITE)

I am sitting in the grass. The grass is cool and green and very thick and soft; I sink in it. I like to sit there. The sun is very bright, but the hedge behind me makes a shade.

My brother is here, too. He is bigger than I. Papa and Mama are not there. I know they are in the house a little far away behind the hedge. But Willem is there. He is very big, almost as big as Papa. I like him. He always has something nice for me and my brother.

What will he do today? He is lying in the grass. There is also Joni. I do not know him too well, but he does not matter. Willem is there!

Willem is saying, "*Anak mau lihat Willem digiling sepeda?*" ("Kids, want to see the bike run over me?") Joni already goes to fetch the bicycle.

Here he comes straight at Willem lying in the grass. Then the bicycle is already on the other side of Willem and Willem is standing up and laughing. He laughs at us kids. And then, with a laugh in his eye, he tells us that Papa's big truck will now run over his chest. Again he lies down in the thick grass, the car comes and it is over him; only his head sticks out, and he is laughing at us. I hide my head. I am afraid, and I grab my brother's hand. But I still look. Willem is already up again. Willem can do anything!

Years later when I talked about it, Mother said, "Nonsense, he must have tricked you." But I still wonder, did it really happen?

This rewrite of "Willem" is a much simpler story than the first version, isn't it? This version gives us the feeling of being in the event rather than of watching it from a distance. In fact, we feel as if the event is happening to us, as if we are the child watching the truck go over Willem, wondering how such an awesome thing can happen.

An approach that works well if you have a group around you is to tell your earliest memory aloud, then tell it again, consistently using the present tense. Notice how you suddenly remember more of the incident. Then write the incident down on paper.

If you find yourself avoiding "I," perhaps by saying instead, "We did such and such," remember: The days of your being unimportant are over. You are at the center of your autobiography. You may report what others are doing, but you are the person through whose eyes and ears we, the readers, experience the event. You are important. It is another time and place. It is OK to say "I."

If, at the end of your memory or subsequent early memories, you would like to add some background information or some of your present adult feelings about what happened back then, do so. But keep the adult reflection on the event distinct from the child's point of view. Jade's last line, "Years later when I talked about it, my mother said...but I still wonder," is a good example of including an adult reflection while keeping it distinct from the child's experience.

In successive stories we will continue to write from the child's point of view, although as we begin to write our more recent stories, we naturally know more of past and present and can set the stage more fully.

Please see Eddie White's story "Blind Lemon Jefferson Sings the Blues," (see page 282) which is an example of a powerful memory seen from a child's point of view. Also, Sam Glenn's story, "Epiphany" (see page 284).

 EXERCISE

PART 1: MY EARLIEST MEMORY   (FIRST DRAFT)

Step 1: Think of the first thing you remember when you were really young. Do you have a picture of it in your mind, perhaps just a very vague picture? Picture it even if it is just a fragment.

If you are having trouble remembering an early, early memory, turn back to the topics list on page 29 to jog your memory.

Now, if you are working in a group, tell your story out loud to the others.

Step 2: Write it down. Start with "I was _____ years old." Tell your story in the *past* tense.

PART 2: MY EARLIEST MEMORY   (REWRITE)

Step 1: Once again, tell about the first thing you remember. Tell it out loud to your group or to a friend or a family member, and this time in the *present* tense ("I am," not "I was"; "I remember," not "I remembered"; "I do," not "I did").

Step 2: Think about what differences you feel when you tell your memory in the present tense rather than in the past tense.

Step 3: Now *write down* what you remember of your earliest memory. Write the story in the *present tense,* beginning with "I am…" (giving your age when the moment happened to you).

Here is an example:

> I am four years old and I am learning to tie my shoe. I keep trying. I have finally done it. Now, I can go tell my mom I've learned to tie my shoe.

You can see from this example that your first memory does not have to be lengthy. It can be very short and still be a good place to begin.

Now that you have finished writing your earliest memory, you have done what every writer does: composed, reviewed, and rewritten. These are the same three steps you will follow with every story you write. As you write your earliest memories, you will find that even earlier incidents and experiences will come to mind. The process of putting pen to paper seems to call up memories. Write these as soon as they become vivid and significant. Many life experiences block feelings. Writing unblocks these feelings and allows you to move ahead, free and unencumbered.

Uncovering Your Most Vivid Childhood Memories

"You know, Bernard," chuckles Eddie White as the Musicians Union class draws to a close one afternoon. "I just have no idea what story to write next. After all, a lot has happened in my seventy-five years."

"Oh, you'll learn," smiles Roz.

"What would you tell him, Roz?" I ask.

"Search out a memory between the time you were born and when you were about twelve years old." She turns to Eddie with a grin. "A memory that's really vivid. Find the climax to it, then begin the story just before the climax."

"Very good, Roz," I reply, tongue in cheek. "You remembered."

"This is my seventh year," she chuckles.

I turn to the other members of the class. "Remember, almost everything we write is a story of relationship—you to your parents, you to your loved ones. Pick out the relationships that remain vivid in your mind, whether they were happy and loving or not."

Composing

When we pick up the pen or stare at the blank screen on the computer to begin writing our first stories, we may be haunted by fears and uncertainties. Calm yourself and follow the steps outlined in this chapter.

Warm Up by Writing

As you begin composing, direct your mind back toward your earliest *vivid* memory, one that truly stands out in your mind.

This new vivid memory should not be confused with your earliest memory, which may simply be a tiny fragment of a recollection, like some archaeological relic from a prehistoric time. Now we are looking for an early memory that has power, a memory that is very strong.

Up to now, I have suggested you begin the story with, "I am ___ years old and I am…" Many of you will tire of this beginning before long, and well you should. "Where *should* I begin?" you ask. A good method is to establish what the climax of the story is, and then begin just a little before the climax.

"What about background information and setting the stage?" you ask. "Isn't that important?"

Setting the stage is less important than you may think, and background information, or *backstory,* can be provided in the second paragraph of a story. What is important now is that you begin the story and then build momentum.

The details are coming back to you. You are *warming up.* That is, you are doing what every artist must do: Musicians play scales, actors do voice and facial exercises, writers write. You work your way into the story, establish where the events are taking place, who is there, and who you are in the story. We are not worried about crafting the beginning of the story, only about building momentum. After all, the best way of handling your self critic who is saying *you can't do this, you shouldn't do this*—is to pick up the pen, or sit down at the computer, and begin. Later, we will find out how to establish the beginning of the story from the material that you have created as a warm-up.

Here are a number of "firsts" that may bring to mind some of the vivid moments of your life between, say, two and twelve years old:

- my most vivid memory of Mom or Dad
- my most embarrassing moment in school
- my first adventure
- my first time being really afraid
- my first success in school
- my most vivid recollection of grandpa or grandma
- my first kiss
- my first time getting into trouble
- my happiest time in school
- my best friend in school

If you wish to take a step-by-step approach to writing and rewriting, turn to the "Exercise" section at the end of this chapter.

— • • • —

*I am ready to return now to my storehouse of childhood memories. I am sitting in the right chair…the music may be playing…perhaps there is a fire in the fireplace…I am ready to return to the time tunnel. Back I go…to a distant moment in time, keeping details in view, searching out lost ones…stripping away the wrapping around my memories until I can see the moment clearly. I am ready to write…**now.***

• • •

Write down everything you saw and experienced, all at once. Don't stop, even if the pieces are disconnected. Don't stop, even if the memory makes you want to cry. If you begin crying, cry. But keep writing.

Now, how does the story read? Is it one story or fragments? Are the details sharper than in your first memoir? Are the feelings stronger? If you have written a series of fragments, would you like to fill in the gaps? If not, OK; go ahead and take this memoir to your group or chosen friend. Read it aloud and listen carefully to each response.

Reviewing

During this second phase, we will learn more about what to look for when evaluating our own writing. I will also talk about how to listen and offer helpful critiques when other people read their stories to us.

Let us begin with a checklist of the first steps in reviewing:

- Resist the urge to change, to be too critical.
- Get feedback: Go to a friend or group to get responses.
- Ask if the work is visual and emotion-producing.
- Listen to your own comments to see if something was left out.
- Express your stories as experiences seen from a child's point of view.

Let's go into some of these concerns a bit more thoroughly. It is very important for a story to have an emotional impact on the reader. So the first thing to do is to add your feelings to each story. From there, you can enhance the visual clarity of the story by focusing on actions, by bringing the story closer to the reader with appropriate dialogue, by focusing on one incident at a time, and by listening carefully to feedback from the group and from yourself.

Add Your Feelings

One of the first things you can do to make your stories more vivid is to incorporate your feelings. "I am nervous," "I am sad," and "I am excited" are the kinds of feelings that will make a story more interesting. They glue the reader to the page: Through feelings, the reader connects to the writer's experience.

What you need to remember is that feelings—our feelings (that is, the feelings of the narrator) and those of the characters—have to be added *to each moment* of the story. It's not enough to mention a feeling at the beginning of the story and another at the end. That's not really adding feelings to the story—it's more like showcasing a feeling just to make your teacher happy. So, come on, add feelings each moment of the way.

> I am walking down the road to my house. I know Papa will be angry when he sees my report card. I'm a little nervous (*narrator's feelings*). As I get closer, I see him on the porch of our farmhouse. He has his arms crossed over his chest. Oh, oh. He's mad (*other character's feelings*).

In the course of teaching life-story writing for more than thirty years, I've noticed what great difficulty men have in writing down their feelings. It's not that we men don't have feelings. More likely, it's a matter of us not being aware of our feelings even as we are possessed by them. After all, we are human and we do have feelings.

If you are a man, you may have to work on becoming aware of your feelings and making sure they are in each story. You can start by simply adding feelings in a mechanical way.

> He has his arms crossed over his chest. Oh, oh—he's mad. Now I'm really scared.

If you add feelings mechanically, you will reach a point where you will be able to unearth your real feelings, even the more painful emotions, without a lot of difficulty.

In Chapter 5, we will explore this question in more depth: How do we get our feelings into the story as fully as possible?

Create Vivid Details

The first objective in writing good narratives is to make the events visible. The easiest way to do this is to bring the events into sharp focus by including little details that make the picture unique. Look at the following passage from "Uncle Eli" by Rose Rothenberg, the complete version of which appeared in the second edition of *Writing from Within*.

> Uncle Eli is a dapper man and extremely meticulous about his person. His shirts are always pure white, at least until they yellow a bit with age.

His dark serge suit is always well-pressed and clean. It does not yellow with the passage of time but takes on a shine that competes with the gloss he maintains on his high-button shoes. In the summer months he sports spotless white buckskin oxfords—the same pair year after year. His straw hat is worn at a rakish angle and, rain or shine, he is never without an umbrella.

The details in this passage—the shirts "always pure white until they yellow with age," the suit that "takes on a shine," and the umbrella that is carried "rain or shine"—suggests a great deal about the man's character: his stubbornness, inflexibility, and pride in the face of changing circumstances.

Now let us look at another passage rich with revealing details. This is taken from a longer story, the complete version of which appeared in the first edition of *Writing from Within*.

Life on the Railroad *by Eugene Mallory* (EXCERPT)

The year was 1904. Not a good year for the overbuilt, midwestern railroads or the ever-distressed farmer either.

The Missouri Pacific Red Ball freight was two hours out on a night run west. The nearly new Baldwin 4-8-2, burning clean Colorado coal, was really showing what it could do.

Conductor William Sidel was riding the high seat in the cupola of the darkened caboose and pondering what he should do with his upside-down life in general. First as a boomer brakeman, so called because he and many other bold young men had followed the railroad expansion of the late 1800s wherever the new rails led. Always moving on to new runs, new towns.

Then a bit of luck, and a bit of the old blarney, and he had his own train on the Hampton, Algona and Western, riding the varnish, not a crummy caboose. Even if the varnish was only an old combination coach; half seats, half mail and baggage, and his little conductor cubbyhole. The coach had to be there to satisfy the franchise, and he had trundled it up and down the 90 miles of lightweight rail that was all the Hampton, Algona, and Western ever amounted to. No matter that many grand names had been painted over or that the old coach was hung on the end of an untidy string of freight cars and seldom exceeded 20 miles per hour, it was varnish.

A perfect old man's job, while he was still young, had perhaps made him old in too few years. God forbid!

But why was he uneasy on this perfect prairie night? True, when he had totaled his manifests, the weight of this train had shocked him, and now his certified reliable watch said they had covered 40 miles of track in the last hour. Things had changed while he had vegetated on the "branch."

Eugene Mallory   *Gene was born in Iowa on a farm near a town hard-hit during the Depression. He has always loved writing, and traces his forebears back to Sir Thomas Mallory. Eventually, Gene moved to Los Angeles, where he worked for North American Rockwell.*

• • •

The phrase "riding the high seat in the cupola of the darkened caboose and pondering what he should do with his upside-down life" gives us a vivid picture of a man perched up high, looking out on the moving train and inward on his life in the darkness. Another phrase, "no matter that many grand names had been painted over," gives us an equally vivid picture of time passing.

These phrases are good examples of the power of using well-chosen details to convey information and feeling. What you will want to avoid is giving lots of details about objects when you are describing, say, a room or a place. Select details carefully, or they can become repetitive and boring. The most interesting and useful details seem to be those that give a glimpse into the characters in your stories.

Seek Out Your Authentic Writer's Voice

For many years, I was a college English teacher (as you can tell by the way I write sometimes). Student after student wrote lengthy sentences, inflated with high-sounding phrases. "Why do they write this way?" my colleagues and I asked ourselves. Years later, when asked to teach senior citizens to write their life stories, I was struck by the fact that many of them wrote the same way, using complex sentences that reflected their thoughts, not their feelings or what had happened.

Little by little, it began to dawn on me: Most of them didn't *want* to relive the past and bring it to life. They wanted to keep the past, and their feelings about the past, at arm's length. In fact, a great many of us do the same thing—adding a lot of "head stuff" to our writing to keep our vulnerability, uncertainty, and hurt well away from ourselves. To cope with trauma of any kind, we explain, analyze, psychologize, and bury the event under a barrage of jargon. Sometimes we romanticize it with wonderful literary-sounding phrases that give it "quality." It's a neat way to put as much distance between ourselves and the experience as possible.

"I would have loved to write purple prose of the kind popular in my day," George Orwell once wrote, "but the age [of the struggle between Fascism and Communism] did not permit it. The age demanded a clear look at things, expressed in language that did not prettify."

If we intend to view an event clearly without editing or injecting our adult point of view, we need to eliminate anything in the story that sounds adult or literary. This is particularly important as we go back into our childhoods seeking out our experiences of an early age.

It is also true of our stories from a later time in life. The innocent, uncluttered, direct point of view that we will develop through writing our early stories is essential in our later stories as well.

Why is this voice so much more reliable as an indicator of the truth? Because the child in us knows how to feel. The adult in us is always cautioning us to be careful. "Hold it back," it says; "that may not be acceptable to others, and to ourselves." The voice that echoes the darkest and deepest criticisms we've felt (often the voice of our parents) may be the voice that does not want us to see that we can be ourselves, not mere echoes of someone else.

The act of stripping away the adult language in a story is not something to worry about as we first begin writing. It is part of the rewriting phase of the process.

For an example of a story made more vivid and believable by stripping away anything that sounds adult, read both versions of the excerpts from "My Mother's Death" by Stephanie Bernardi found on page 89 (the complete story can be found on page 285). Here, the truth of the event becomes clearer in the rewrite as the adult voice is stripped away and the honest, more-childlike voice is heard.

Some of my students ask, "Why am I writing in this childlike way in later years, when I'm not a child?" The answer is that the pure, direct, emotional language we find in ourselves as children is our voice as an artist. I am not asking us to write as children when we are adults; I am asking us to eliminate anything that *sounds adult,* which is synonymous with *distant, intellectual, analytical.* Simple, direct, emotional, visual language that creates pictures and feelings will aid us in finding the hidden moments from our past.

This step of the process helps us tell a story more effectively and gives us a path to the secrets we hold inside ourselves. We get our cake and we get to eat it too. But we will need courage when we write a bit differently than we normally do and to face the truths that lie inside.

Go ahead and reread your story now. You may find the event coming back to you a bit differently, perhaps more fully.

Get and Give Supportive Feedback

Most of us think that artists, particularly writers, create in isolation, that they are intent on expressing themselves at all costs and to heck with what the world thinks of their work.

Some writers do create that way. But an equal number rely on trusted friends to give them feedback that will inspire their next steps. I, for example, could not have written this book without the feedback of a group of valued friends.

For most people who are not writers, their self-critic is so strong that they must actually reeducate it. The inner critic might say, "This work is no good, forget trying to do this story" or "You are revealing too much, it's too personal" or "You have nothing to say, so don't expose yourself to criticism."

However, a group of friends trained in giving feedback from within would probably take a different approach. "Good, not good. What does that mean?" I can hear one of my students, Judy Klein, saying to a member of the class. "It's all about the impact the story has on us, the readers. If you write about just one moment in your life and tell it in the present tense, with feelings, add some dialogue, and get rid of all that adult stuff, we will feel something."

I suggest that those giving feedback pay attention to three things:

1. Does the story create a picture you, the listener or reader, can believe?

2. Are the feelings of the characters and the narrator in the story?

3. How are you experiencing the story?

The third aspect is far and away the most important: To help the writer in a positive way, we do not give feedback about the story. *We give feedback about our experience of the story.*

In other words, when we listen, we must give our attention to the story and how we are reacting to it—where we are touched, where we are pushed out of the experience, where we are fully with it, where we find our minds wandering.

We need to avoid such judgmental statements as, "I was bored in the beginning, but then it got better." A fairer comment would be, "I found my mind wandering in the beginning, but later I got scared and worried about would happen to you, the central character." This kind of feedback helps us take risks in our own writing, for the gentle but accurate way we give feedback to others is the gentle, accurate way we will begin to give feedback to ourselves.

Writing in the present tense and eliminating anything that sounds adult launches us into the child's world of experience, well away from our own. It helps us get around our fears. It also creates an artistic distance between our listeners/readers and the child's world. The present tense helps us leap into this world of the child. The challenge for the writer is to keep us there. Getting rid of anything that sounds adult helps that happen.

T.S. Eliot, quoting Wordsworth, once said, "The artist's task is to create a willing suspension of disbelief," and that is exactly what we are after. The present tense and the use of simple language propel us from adult skepticism and disbelief into another world where everything is new and rich and never experienced before, a world where it is safe to feel again, where no one will criticize us, only support our expression of all the powerful things we feel inside but have been afraid, as a person and as a writer, to express.

Sometimes, when we fall into the old habits of using adult language, we cause the reader to come out of this rich world we have created. The belief is broken, perhaps just for a moment.

The other steps we will be exploring—writing dialogue, expressing inner thoughts and feelings, finding a vivid beginning and climax—also help create belief.

Dialogue, in particular, is a powerful way of transcending the gap between the listener's world and the writer's experience. Characters come to life through dialogue, which in film terms is a way of creating close-ups.

When we have accomplished writing from the child's point of view, we want to continue to express ourselves in this simple, vivid, emotional, unsophisticated language and style. This is the language of the artist that burns within us, the artist in us who sees things in a fresh, real way. It is the language of the artist in all of us who refuses to be bound by psychological jargon and other ways we have of keeping distance between ourselves and our experiences. It is the language of the artist who wants to risk seeing the self as it truly was at *vivid* and *critical* moments in our lives, a language that can touch our subconscious and provoke it into giving up its protections, so we may at long last pull the scrim of fear from our eyes and see ourselves clearly.

Gather together a group of friends and practice giving feedback from within about your stories. Can you see the picture? Can you feel the feelings? These are the two important questions to ask. Be sure each member of the group is giving feedback about his or her own *feeling experience* of the story, not what he or she *thinks* about the story. Did the story take you, the reader, somewhere, and keep you there? Did it cause you to feel something along the way?

The highest compliment you can pay a writer is, "I was there with you every moment of the way. Nothing caused me to come out of the moment. I saw every picture and felt each feeling." (For more information on giving feedback, see the Appendix, "Creating a Supportive, Noncritical, yet Insightful Writing Group."

Recover Voices and Faces
from the Past Through Dialogue

Another important step in getting to know our past is to grasp, as fully as possible, the relationships in our circle of experience as they swirled around us when we were children.

One of the most effective ways of seeing this is to begin adding *dialogue* to our stories. Dialogue is what people say to each other. It usually comes out of vivid emotional moments in the narrative. Most of us begin to write dialogue quite naturally at the high point in the narrative, which is also the point where we most want the characters to speak for themselves.

We may say, "I don't remember what was said," but in fact we have within us worlds of hidden experience that we may uncover. To illustrate, I like to tell of the time I was taking classes in directing from Lee Strasberg of the Actor's Studio. One evening he was giving demonstrations of how an actor can get hung up in the process of merging himself with the character he is playing. A young actor was reading a part, and it wasn't going well. Strasberg stopped him.

"Where is the problem, young man?" he asked. Strasberg was a wizened, intense little guy. The actor was terrified. His fear of displeasing the master was written all over his face.

"What part of your body?" Strasberg asked. The young man pointed to his shoulder. "And what is the memory?" continued Strasberg.

The young man then told a story having to do with his father, the same sort of experience the character in the play was facing. Rather than being able to identify with the character's problem, the actor was paralyzed by his similar experience. After he finished telling the story, the actor returned to the scene and did it beautifully.

In this way I learned how we carry around our memories in various parts of our body. So let's improvise some dialogue. Suppose I write the following: *Momma yelled at me to get up the stairs in a hurry.*

The line cries out to come from Momma's mouth, as: *Momma yells, "Get up the stairs! Now!!"*

This is a big improvement. It becomes even more effective if we put the "he says" or "she says" at the end of the first phrase of dialogue, or at the end of the sentence if the sentence is short: *"Get up the stairs! Now!!" Momma says. "And no back talk!"*

Before long, we will find our dialogue sounding like what Mom and Dad actually said. On the other hand, if we try to re-create dialogue and it just doesn't sound like what took place, we need to drop it and move to another place in our story.

Anytime we wish to get closer to an event, we can try improvising and adding dialogue. One caution: If in reality we could not have heard what was said, we need to avoid trying to re-create it. The reader must believe what he or she is reading. There is no point in trying to fool them. The reader's belief in our narrator's honest telling of a story is our greatest asset.

We will also find that adding dialogue will make the story far more interesting than telling it all in narrative. The following excerpt is an example of good dialogue, well remembered.

Jefferson Barracks, Missouri *by John Strong*   (EXCERPT)

We stepped outside for some fresh air. As luck would have it, the pigeon air corps was practicing dive bombing with Ford's new green sweater as target.

"Why did those damn pigeons pick on me?" lamented Ford, as he tried to wipe the droppings from his sweater with his handkerchief.

"Because they knew we were headed for the air corps and wanted to show us some expert bombing!" I joked.

"This isn't funny, John," protested Ford.

"Maybe they hate Irishmen and you're Irish and wearing green," I laughed.

"But you're Irish and a bigger target. Why didn't they pick on you?" asked Ford.

"Oh, can it, Ford," I yelled. "I'll give you the money to get it cleaned. This is trivial compared to the army life we've gotten into."

"Maybe Jefferson Barracks will be better," offered optimist Bill. But when we pulled into St. Louis next morning, Ford was still talking about the big stain on his sweater, the size of a pancake.

I went to a phone in the station, collecting my thoughts for my official call to Jefferson Barracks as the officer at Harrisburg had instructed.

"Sir, this is recruit John Strong, with recruits Bill Bee and Ford Smith. We are coming from Harrisburg, Pennsylvania. I have all the necessary papers," I recited in a good strong voice, trying to make a favorable impression.

On the other end of the line, I heard a childlike voice squealing, "What son-of-a-bitch stole my comic book? It was a Dick Tracy one, too. Come on, cough it up." Then he grumbled to me, "Say that again," which I did.

His next words really startled me. "What the hell do you expect me to do about it?" I thought I had a captain's young son on the phone, so I remained silent for a moment. "You got a tongue, ain't you? Now tell me what you want me to do," the brat ranted. "I have no papers on you at all."

"Maybe you can suggest how we can get to Jefferson Barracks," I offered, with a slight sneer in my voice.

"No one told me you were coming. The only way you can get here is in the mail truck. It's due at the station in about fifteen minutes, so get your asses to the entrance or you will have to walk the fifteen miles to get here. If you don't get here by midnight, you will be AWOL." With that, the jerk slammed the phone down.

John Strong   *John is a strapping man, six feet three inches and two hundred and forty pounds, from a patriotic family of Pennsylvania coal miners. Many of his ancestors fought for the Union during the Civil War, and John was brought up on stories of war and heroism. He writes vividly of his boyhood years growing up in Pennsylvania, of his young manhood as a coal miner during the Depression, of his disappointment at not gaining an appointment to West Point, and of his days as a soldier during World War II.*

——— • • • ———

Notice that new characters are introduced quickly through dialogue: "I heard a childlike voice squealing, 'What son of a bitch stole my comic book?'" Soon we learn that this is his new commanding officer—a quick, unexpected glimpse of a new character. This is good dialogue at work.

Focus on a Single Event

A vivid memory may in fact be a *series* of vivid memories, so you must develop a sense of where an episode begins and ends, and write only one episode at a time. This is called *focus.* Classically, in an Ibsen play for example, the story begins after some important event has taken place—a death, a crime, or the like. In your work you may start with a similar event, or just before the event. What is important is to express the reactions of the major characters throughout the episode and to know when the incident or event ends.

Focus is also related to finding the "spine," which we will discuss in greater detail in Chapter 6 under "Form and Structure (1): Find the Spine of the Story" (see page 76). For a good example of a well-focused story, see Dale Crum's story "Smoke Rings" in the "Stories" section at the back this book (see page 275). Focusing on what the episode is about—where it begins and ends—and writing visually by using details makes up what we call *narrative,* or storytelling. Ultimately, you will be seeking a balance among narration, dialogue, and your inner thoughts and feelings.

Rewriting

You are now ready to begin rewriting your second story. You have a greater fund of techniques at your disposal and a more thorough grasp of what those techniques can do. You have the responses of your friends or classmates to help you. Likewise, you have a better grasp of how to look at your own work after writing that first draft.

We tend to think of rewriting as very taxing, perhaps boring, maybe even painful. But the results are almost always worth the effort. To have one's work go straight to the mind and heart of the reader feels wonderful, as you are no doubt finding out. At this point, let's review the steps we discussed in rewriting your first memoir—

- Use the present tense.
- Write in the first person ("I").
- Include your feelings to create emotional impact.
- Write from a child's point of view (eliminate adult-sounding vocabulary and phrasing).
- Add the concerns we have just mentioned in our review phase: details, dialogue, and focus. Do not try to rewrite on a step-by-step basis, however. Once you have given thought to these various areas of improvement, read your story over and make gut-level changes where it feels right to do so.

Having done your rewriting, take your story back to your friends, relatives, and classmates. I think you will be pleasantly surprised. And if you want to write several more "vivid memories" before going on to the next chapter, please do so.

 EXERCISE

PART 1: MY EARLIEST VIVID MEMORY   (FIRST DRAFT)

What memory of your life between birth and twelve years of age do you have that is more vivid in your mind than any other, one that you remember better than any other? Tell it in the *present* tense.

Here is an example:

I am twelve years old. I'm walking into my brand new school. As I walk into my homeroom, I feel as though everyone is staring at me. I think to myself, "What if my friends get lost and don't meet me at the lockers—then who am I going to hang around with?"

I hope I don't arrive late to any of my classes cuz I'm afraid that the teacher might tell me something in front of the whole class.

The day goes by pretty fast and I have no problems. I finally go home.

The writer wrote about a very common vivid early memory—the first day in a new school. Other common vivid memories may be a birth in the family, a death in the family, a separation or divorce, or a special family event, such as a birthday or a religious celebration.

If you are having trouble remembering something vivid, try remembering the first time something happened, such as the first time you went with your father or mother on an adventure, or the first time your schoolteacher told you to behave.

Now, *write* your earliest vivid memory. Start with these words: "I am ___ years old and I am…"

PART 2: MY EARLIEST VIVID MEMORY   (FIRST REWRITE)

Now you will write your vivid memory over again. First, be sure it is in the present tense, then add the steps below.

Step 1. Ask yourself, "Are my *feelings* in the story?" If not, *add your feelings* ("I feel sad," "I feel happy"). As before, begin with the words "I am" and tell us your age when the event happened.

Below is the revision of the story about the first day at school, incorporating the narrator's feelings.

> I am twelve years old. I'm walking into my brand new school. *It seems so big and scary. I can feel the butterflies in my stomach* as I walk into my home-room. I feel as though everyone is staring at me. I think to myself, "What if my friends get lost and don't meet me at the lockers—then who am I going to hang around with?"
>
> I hope I don't arrive late to any of my classes cuz I'm afraid that the teacher might tell me something in front of the whole class. *How embarrassing.*
>
> The day goes by pretty fast and I have no problems. *I feel relieved* to finally go home.

Do you see how much more interesting the story is when it includes feelings? It grabs you and pulls you into it. Try to do more than put your feelings in at the beginning and the end of your story. Every time an action takes place, bring your feelings into the picture.

Remember, you may know how others feel from their actions or the expressions on their faces, but you know *your* feelings from the inside. Tell the audience what those feelings are. After a while, you will begin to include your feelings as you write your first draft, but for now adding them into the rewrite is fine.

Step 2. Take out any words or sentence constructions that sound adult and would not be very believable coming from a child.

Step 3. Get some feedback on your rewrite from your classmates or friends.

PART 3: MY EARLIEST VIVID MEMORY   (SECOND REWRITE)

Now we will add another step to the writing process: We are going to add *dialogue*.

We can often make dialogue out of narrative. For example, *Mom told me to go to the store* can easily be turned into *"Go to the store," Mom told me.*

Now, let's learn how to separate speakers. Try to rewrite the following passage so that it is clear who is saying what.

> How do you know if I am speaking or you are speaking when writing looks like this I ask my students. It sure is confusing one girl answers. So Mr. Selling tell us, huh? Huh? another student says.

"When a person is speaking, use quotation marks so readers will know that he or she is speaking," I tell my students.

"How do I know if you are speaking or I am speaking?" one of my students asks.

"Each new speaker gets a new paragraph," I tell her. "And put quotation marks around the actual words a person says."

So every time a new person speaks, he or she gets a new paragraph, and quotation marks are placed around the words that tell us someone is speaking. Following that guideline, the above passage would be correctly written like this:

> "How do you know if I am speaking or you are speaking when writing looks like this," I ask my students.
>
> "It sure is confusing," one girl answers.
>
> "So Mr. Selling tell us, huh? Huh?" another student says.

Try adding some dialogue to the rewrite of your story. You may not remember exactly what was said, but that's OK. You can invent what was said, as long as it feels like the truth. When you have finished writing, ask yourself whether or not your story is improved by your use of dialogue.

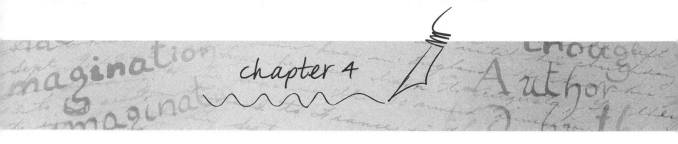

Uncovering Your Most Vivid Teenage Memories

I walk into homeroom the first day of school in the eighth grade and look at my schedule for the year. I am stunned. Fourth Period—Senior Band. *Senior band?? Me? Why me?* I wonder. *I'm not a very good clarinet player.* But it's true; the bandmaster has promoted me along with a half dozen other eighth graders into the senior high school band. I feel so proud—and grateful—that I practice hard. By the end of the year, I am close to the top of the clarinet section. Also, during the year I go from mooning over the ethereal Sue to liking the curvaceous Gail. I discover basketball and swing dancing. More often than not, my father and I come into conflict with one another. I want to do things my way; he wants things done his way.

Hormones have struck, as they do all of us between the ages of twelve and twenty. Those are exciting, often difficult years, filled with change. To grasp the excitement of those years and to embrace the depth of what we felt at the time, we will need to expand our range of story-telling techniques. Therefore, in this chapter we will explore more fully (1) how to start writing a story and (2) how to define the characteristics that make the people in a story interesting.

Composing

When we write, we need to establish a point of view from which the action is being viewed. In life stories, the point of view is that of the person who is both writing the story and narrating the story. The story itself may not even be about the writer who may be content to be an observer of other people's actions.

Establish Yourself as Character and Narrator

One thing you can do to help yourself as a writer while you are warming up and looking for the point at which to enter the story is to be aware that *you, as a character, must be in the story at all times.* Why is this so? Well, if you are not in the story, the audience will have great difficulty knowing through whose eyes they are seeing the action and they will not believe what they are reading. Consider the following story:

It's a hot summer day here in Macon, Georgia. A light breeze is blowing and my aunt is sitting on the porch fanning herself.

Suppose somewhere in the early part of this story we add the line: *I am sitting on the porch playing with my toy trains.* This awareness helps the readers in many ways. They will know where you are and from what point of view they will see the action, that is, close to the ground because you are small.

Now let's suppose you look for some details to fill out the picture. Oh, yes. There is a newspaper with a large headline. Let's see if we can make it out. Ah, there it is. "Wall Street Crashes." So let's add that. *A newspaper lies at her feet. The headline reads, "Wall Street Crashes."* So now we have:

It's a hot summer day here in Macon, Georgia. I am sitting on the porch playing with my toy trains. A light breeze is blowing and my aunt is sitting near me fanning herself. She has a funny look on her face. At her feet is a newspaper with the headline "Wall Street Crashes." I wonder what a walled street is.

Here we have a wonderful paradox: The writer as character is innocent and wide-eyed; the writer as narrator is giving powerful details to which the character responds in this believable, whimsical way. (Later we will find out that we can go one more step and place the line *I am sitting on the porch* at the beginning of the story—but that's yet to come.)

How do we create a sense of belief in the audience? First, we begin by making sure that the narrator's voice always sounds appropriate for the age at which the events are happening to the narrator. Thus if you were seven years

Create Belief

When we begin a story, we as artists have one purpose: to carry the reader on a voyage from where they are to where we wish them to be—in another time and place.

At that point our objective is to create belief, which is about the only way we have of keeping the reader in that altered time and place. In our day and age, readers tend to believe only a particular person's point of view, not a general perspective. This is why the great nineteenth-century writers like Herman Melville fell into such disfavor with readers in the twentieth century. The educated readership of the early years of the twentieth century did not believe the world to be orchestrated by an all-powerful, Godlike power, and therefore refused to believe anything written from an omniscient narrator's point of view. Thus, the most powerful charm we take with us on our story-telling voyages is our amulet: belief.

old when the event happened, the audience wants to believe that the event is being experienced by a seven-year-old.

When you as the narrator are a little older, say nineteen or twenty, the audience will believe your experience if you keep them in touch with your feelings at every point in the story, while continuing to keep the language simple—emotional, not intellectual. If you were, in fact, an intellectual nineteen-year-old, let that be reflected in the dialogue.

These three things—level of language, presence of feelings, dialogue that is appropriate to the characters—will create a strong sense of belief in your reader.

Establish a Point of View

Take a look at the paintings on the next two pages. In each painting, notice the perspective from which the viewer sees the action and how the perspective helps the viewer comprehend and believe the painter's meaning and message.

The first is Leonardo da Vinci's *The Last Supper*. We are placed directly in front of Christ, able to see the effects, on either side of him, of his statement, "One of you shall betray me." We are neither below nor above the action, neither awed by nor superior to it. It is happening directly in front of us, in a clearly defined space in which a fifteenth-century Tuscan valley unfolds behind the head of Christ. We know where we are and from what position we are seeing the action. It is "real" to us.

In the second painting, Pieter Bruegel's *The Fall of Icarus*, we are high on a hill overlooking a distant harbor in a place that resembles northern Europe. It is early in the sixteenth century.

Leonardo da Vinci's *The Last Supper*

Pieter Bruegel's *The Fall of Icarus*

We are placed near a peasant whose chores will take him down and to the left in the painting. Our eye is led to distant vistas: to the new round world beyond. Because of our position near the peasant, we would most likely ignore anything in the lower right portion of the painting, such as the leg of Icarus, who has just fallen out of the sky. (You may recall that Icarus and Daedalus escaped from the labyrinth of King Minos by making wings of wax. Though advised by his father not to fly too close to the sun, Icarus disobeyed and plunged into the sea when his wings melted.)

What is the meaning of this painting? Perhaps something like, "We are all so preoccupied with our daily tasks, we hardly see the truly important events in life taking place. We are distracted by the boring necessities of life (the peasant's tasks) and the world's concerns (opening up the world and viewing it, not as flat, but as round)."

The settings of these paintings and the perspectives from which we view the action have a great deal of influence on their message and impact on us, and it is similar with stories.

The writing techniques I am suggesting are cinematic. Many modern films begin with a tight shot and then widen to include everything important, so your establishing shot might come after a line or two of dialogue or some action at the beginning of the story. I often advise my students to begin with action or dialogue to get the reader into the story quickly, and then "widen out" to bring more into view.

Another technique, which early filmmakers often used, is this sequence: first, the establishing shot, a wide-angle shot encompassing a whole city or village; next, a medium shot, bringing us closer to the dwellings or places we are going to inhabit; and finally, a closer shot of the characters important to the narrative. If you are writing stories of your life when you were younger than ten years old, that is, writing from a child's point of view, establishing shots might actually be unbelievable at the beginning of a story. The child's world is tiny and narrow, though fascinating. So an establishing shot—a more comprehensive, adult view—might come at the end of the scene or story. After the story ends, you may also wish to tell the reader how the event described has affected you over the ensuing years.

As a young child, I see the world through a very small window. I know little of what others are doing. I know nothing of past and future. It is a very particular stage setting. As I mature, the window through which I see the world widens. I know more of past and present, of life beyond myself; therefore, I can set the stage more fully.

As a writer, I ask my reader to suspend his or her normal disbelief and believe what I have written. From a child, the reader can believe the world only as seen through the tiny window of a small child's awareness, but from a more mature youngster or an adult, the reader can accept a much more fully set stage.

Reviewing

In reviewing our stories, we want to continue to add to our techniques and concerns, so we will now address an additional aspect of writing: creating interesting people.

Create Unforgettable Characters

Unlike the Lilliputians in *Gulliver's Travels,* into whose world a big person was suddenly cast, we are all born into a world of big people. Mothers and fathers, in particular, loom especially large in our lives and our imaginations. Sometimes they appear distorted. My father, for example, appeared to most people as a strong-minded, humorous, thin-skinned, and occasionally imperious man. As I was growing up, he appeared so powerful to me that, until well into my thirties, I had dreams in which he appeared as a pursuing monster and I was a frightened Lilliputian.

Family members, many of whom have great power over us, must be dealt with in our memories honestly, clear-sightedly, and fearlessly. Since our view of them changes as we grow older, it is both appropriate and necessary to see them as they were experienced by other members of the family and by ourselves at different times in our lives.

Let's consider what makes a character in a book, a play, or a movie interesting, and see how it applies to our parents and the rest of the family. We might begin with the following definition: An interesting person is someone who wants something badly (*what* she wants is usually very clear) and takes an interesting, unusual, or difficult route to reach that goal (*how* she is going to get it is also clear). To the degree that the goal is dangerous and the means employed involve risk, the person might move up the scale from interesting to heroic.

Uncover Character Qualities

How a person goes about getting what he or she wants reveals certain character qualities. Charm, determination, humor, honesty, self-assurance, dependability, opportunism, and perfectionism are all qualities that get us what we want; they may also, tragically, defeat us in other ways.

After you have had a chance to think about and discuss several kinds of interesting characters, take some time to write about one yourself. Follow these six steps:

1. Think of a character you consider interesting.
2. Recall an incident, event, or series of actions that were typical of this character.
3. Find a word for the memorable quality or qualities he or she possesses.
4. Ask yourself if the incident you recalled really brings out the quality you have identified. If it does, go ahead and write about it; if not, you may wish to select a different incident.
5. Remember that the most interesting characters have several strong qualities, sometimes contradictory ones.
6. Include yourself in the story, making certain that your character qualities—as the narrator—are also evident in the story.

Here are some interesting or important people in your life you might want to write about:

- my grandparents
- my parents
- my sisters or brothers
- my best friend from the time I was ___ years old
- my first teacher, mentor, or guide
- my first boss

- my "black-sheep" relative
- my companion through a difficult ordeal

If you wish to use a step-by-step approach to writing and rewriting a story from your teenage years, turn to the "Exercise" section at the end of this chapter.

———— • • • ————

I lean back in my chair. The images of the past rise up to meet me through the murky depths to the present. The place and person become clearer. I begin to write… ***now.***

Rewriting

Many of you may be feeling that rewriting is still beyond you, that it takes time and you are not sure what the benefits will be. Virtually all writers go through a rewriting process that involves considerable change. Many of us write first drafts that are undistinguished and uninteresting. What counts is what we do *after* we have made it through the first draft.

Develop Your Own Writing Process

So that you can see the process I myself go through, I am going to write about an interesting character using the techniques I have given you so far. What you are about to read is exactly what comes from my head and my keyboard. Will it be any good? Will it be interesting? I have no idea. I will follow the steps I outlined for you and see where they lead.

1. Think of a character you consider interesting.
   My father…

2. Recall an incident, event, or series of actions that were typical of this character.
   Hmm…I'm not ready for that…

3. Find a word for the memorable quality or qualities he possesses.
   His curiosity…his desire to know…but the way he died? Ah, there's the incident…his death…what kind of curiosity could kill him…uh, hmm… pickiness, his insatiable desire to pick at the surface of things. That's it!! His intellectual curiosity and the way he died, together.

Dad's Death *by Bernard Selling*   (FIRST DRAFT)

My father had an insatiable desire to pick away at the surface of things. Intellectually, it caused him to be unendingly curious, devouring books, thoughts, and concepts hungrily. He loved learning and absorbing and analyzing, acquiring two PhDs and an MD. As director of the Recorder's Court Psychopathic Clinic, he was an innovator in the field of traffic offenses, alcoholism, and emotional disorders. Yet this insatiable desire to pick away at the surface of things had another outcome.

In the winter of 1955 he found a wart on his foot, a wart that bothered him. He picked up a razor blade from his shaving kit and began to pick away at the wart. The razor was dirty and infected. By the end of the month he had blood poisoning and was hospitalized. Shortly after, under the threat of having his leg amputated, he got up in the middle of the night, slipped, broke his hip, had a heart attack, and died. My mother and sister and I could hardly believe what had happened.

●　●　●

Now I've finished this first draft and I look it over. I realize I'm not in the picture, nor are my feelings. I begin to look for me in the picture to see where I am and how I'm feeling. I go back to the time he was in the hospital and see how I feel. I begin to write:

> I am sixteen and bewildered. How can he have done this? I wonder.
> He is smart. He has two PhDs and an MD.

I think back to how I feel after his death. I am so angry at him for dying. I can almost burst. *Why?* I wonder. *He and I have been battling with each other,* I answer myself. *Only recently does he even begin to know who I am, sort of.* Am I only angry? "I miss him," I write. "The funeral is a blur."

I review the story again. Yes, I'm in the story and so are my feelings, but the whole thing sounds rather academic and feels kind of remote. *How can I put this in a book on writing?* my critic asks. *It's OK,* my creator answers. *I'm letting them see how I get past the first draft.*

If this were one of my students writing, what would I suggest he or she do at this point? "Find out where the story begins." So I look over the draft again. Ah, there it is: "In the winter of 1955, he finds a wart on his foot." *Maybe it's going to be a different sort of story,* I say to myself. *Go on, make changes, see what happens—and try it in the present tense.*

Dad's Death (REWRITE)

One day, Dad finds a wart on the bottom of his foot. It is winter, 1955. He is fifty-three years old and not too well. He coughs a lot during the winter. I know he had a heart attack eight years ago. I worry about him. We all do. With a razor blade from his shaving kit, he begins to pick away at his wart. Nobody tells him not to. Nobody can tell him anything. A month later he has blood poisoning and is hospitalized. Shortly after, he is told that he may have to have his leg amputated. I am sixteen and bewildered. *How can he have done this? I ask myself. He is smart. He has two PhDs and an MD. His brain cuts through stupidity, error, nonsense, and people's bullshit all the time. I'm afraid he'll cut through mine sometime.*

Mom and Lee, my fourteen-year-old sister, go to see him in the hospital. I don't. It's Saturday and I play tennis with the guys instead. Afterwards, Lee tells me that Mom and Dad were like young lovers.

"He was telling all his old dirty jokes," she says, "and Mom was laughing and giggling like a schoolgirl. It was so... erotic, you could cut it with a knife."

I nod, feeling numb, wondering what I have missed.

Sometime after New Year's, he is still in the hospital. The doctors want to operate. He's outraged, I'm told later by my mother. He gets up in the middle of the night, slips, breaks his hip, and...

No, that's not quite how it is. I look back to see where I have gone off... Ah, that last paragraph.

Sometime after New Year's Day, I am in my room. I am working on a model train. The phone rings upstairs somewhere. I hear Mom answer it. A few moments later she comes into my room.

"Lopo died this morning," she says quietly. "He got up in the middle of the night. He was angry at the doctors. He slipped, broke his hip, and had a heart attack."

I listen. I walk away—or does she? We say nothing to one another.

I go to school the next day. Everyone knows he is dead. His picture is on the front page of the Orlando paper. I can see they are shocked that I'm here in school.

Finally, Bill Bledsoe comes up to me. "I'm sorry to hear what happened," he says. "I liked your dad." I mumble something. Later in the day, Bill Nichols comes up and says the same thing. No one else says anything about my father. Friends say nothing. Teachers say nothing. Mom says nothing.

Dad is dead. No more arguments. No more fights. No more misunderstandings. No more laughter. Would he have forgiven me for my breaking his prized Spike Jones records in a fit of anger if he had lived? Could I have found out why he got so furious at me for holding hands with Jeri B. when I was thirteen and staying out in the canoe with Pat C. when I was fourteen?

I was so angry at him, so humiliated, I would have loved to have knocked him down but, no, I couldn't. He might have died. So many questions, so many feelings haunt me. *Why this? Why that?* I am so angry at him I can hardly see straight. The funeral is a blur.

The rest of the year I go inside myself.

"Do you want to play the lead in 'Dangerous Dan McGrew'?" the bandmaster asks me. It's the part in the band skit that had the audiences howling when I played it the year before. Dad was laughing so hard that even from the stage I could see him wiping the tears from his eyes.

"No," I answer. I play in the band. I get decent grades. I go through the motions. I don't want to be noticed, and no one does. Dad is dead and part of me is too.

— • • • —

Now, looking back, going through the feelings again, I find it hard to believe that Dad would place himself in such a vulnerable position—a man with diabetes and a history of heart disease, a doctor and a man of science, a man with a family he cared about so deeply, picking at a wart on the bottom of his foot with a dirty razor blade. That insatiable desire to pick away at things got him.

From this example we see that the rewriting process begins when I ask myself, "Am I in the picture? Are my feelings present?"

Then I ask myself, "Where does the story begin?" as I encourage myself to soften that critical voice of mine, the one that could so easily stop me from writing.

Then at the end of the second draft, I realize there is a point at which I have created distance from the experience—where I have gone off the track, perhaps where the event is too painful. This time I return to the event, keeping it close to my experience, no matter how painful.

This, then, is the process: Keep close to your feelings, hold your self-critic at bay, review the event to explore your actions and feelings more closely with each rewrite, and expand moments with dialogue and inner thoughts and feelings.

Keep a Checklist

As you review and rewrite, you need to keep in mind all of the things you learned earlier, while adding new items to the "stew." In fact, you might want to make a checklist of questions to ask yourself, as do pilots, who go through a list of procedures before takeoff and landing. At this point, your checklist might look like this:

Life-Story Writing Checklist

1. Is my story written in the first person and in the present tense?

2. Have I stripped the story of adult, intellectual language?

3. Are my feelings in the story?

4. Do the details and actions make the story clearer and more interesting?

5. Does the dialogue help tell the story and make the characters more interesting?

6. Have I kept to one well-focused incident at a time?

7. Are the characters interesting, perhaps unforgettable? Are their qualities evident?

8. Are my feelings about the events clearly expressed?

Rewriting now becomes easier because you know what has to be done and you have a variety of techniques with which to approach the task. At this point, look over the checklist, begin to visualize any changes you may wish to make, and then make them.

 EXERCISE

PART 1: MY MOST VIVID MEMORY BETWEEN TWELVE AND TWENTY
(FIRST DRAFT)

Think about something else that happened when you were young, something you see vividly in your mind. When you start writing, keep going until you finish. Don't stop for anything. Use the *present tense*. How do you feel about what happened? Include your *feelings*. Use *dialogue* if you can.

PART 2: MY MOST VIVID MEMORY BETWEEN TWELVE AND TWENTY
(FIRST REWRITE)

Now you will rewrite the memory you have just recorded.

Step 1: Form a picture in your mind of the memory you just wrote. Did you write it in the *present tense*? If not, rewrite it in the present tense. Did you add your *feelings*? If not, add your feelings. Does it contain anything that does not sound like the child speaking? If so, make the changes now. Did you add dialogue? If not, go ahead if you can.

Don't worry about spelling or grammar when you are writing. After you have finished your story, you can check your spelling.

Step 2: Ask yourself, "Am I clearly in the story as a character?" If not, make your character clearly visible. We do this by making sure the audience always knows what the narrator of the story is thinking, feeling, and doing even as he or she is listening to another person speaking.

"Go to the store," my mother says, "and pick up some eggs."

I shrug my shoulders. *Why do I always have to do the chores?* My head hurts and my stomach aches. I think I'm getting sick.

"Come on!" she demands. "Move those feet."

"Yeah, yeah," I mumble.

PART 3: MY MOST VIVID MEMORY BETWEEN TWELVE AND TWENTY
(SECOND REWRITE)

Read over your first rewrite.

Step 1: Ask yourself, "Am I clearly in the story?"

Step 2: If the answer is yes, ask yourself, "Is there a separation between what the *character knows* and what the *narrator tells us* through the dialogue of the other characters?" As an example, consider the following story:

I am playing with my train set on the floor in the living room. The train goes round and round. "Whee!" I laugh as it goes so fast that it falls off the track. I look up at Mama. She stands in the doorway, silent…looking down the street. There is a letter in her hand. I put the train back on the track and make it go faster this time. "Whoo Whoo!!" I laugh, making train sounds. In the background, I hear a car drive away.

"Get up, little one!" Mama whispers.

"Mama, I'm…"

"Get up right now." Her eyes are scared and full of tears. "We have to go."

Now in this scene, I — the child, the central character through whose eyes the story is being told — am not interested in anything except the train. I'm having fun. On the other hand, I — the writer — am creating a scene in which Mama has received terrible news of some kind and is reacting to the news. As the writer, I am responsible for building the scene, which includes the concerns of all the characters as well as anything that may be going on in the background, such as the sound of the automobile driving off.

As you rewrite the second draft of your story, see if you can create a separation between the interests and concerns of the central character (you) and the other characters, making their wants and needs as clear and powerful as your own.

Writing About the Inner You

"You want me to read first—in public?" asks Rebecca, the slim, bright, hip star of my Sunday workshop. A bewildered look crosses her innocent features. "I thought you were my protector, my mentor. Now you want to throw me to the wolves?"

"Now, now, it's not that bad," I reassure her. Behind that look is a hint of anger mixed with fear.

Rebecca and I and several other members of the group are sitting in a booth at a 1950s cafe, Delores' Restaurant, discussing the upcoming public reading of our work. My friend and student, Mar Puatu, has created a new anthology of stories entitled *Sojourns* and has asked me to enlist Rebecca in kicking off the afternoon of storytelling that will publicize the book.

"No, no, not 'that bad.' Much worse, thank you. I thought you liked me." She picks up her water glass and stares into it. "Mirror, mirror on the wall," she murmurs, "why is Rebecca the shyest of us all."

All of us who know Rebecca agree that she makes a terrific impression with her wit, looks, and graciousness. She loves being the center of attention, but she's not been ready for the next step—exploring her own work in public.

"Rebecca, Rebecca," I shake my head. "What am I to do with you?"

She chuckles, enjoying "Rebecca as victim, Bernard as tormentor." She says, "How about negotiating?"

"Your story is very funny, and you're so much better looking than the antique guys who've written the other stories."

She gives me another look, obviously not buying a thing I'm saying. "You want me to get up in front of a bunch of strangers *and* reveal the deepest part of myself. You want me to be that naked?"

"You didn't mind performing at the other public reading," I persist. "You told me how good it was for you."

"But I wasn't first," she squints at me. "I said it was good for *us*. Us in the general sense. I didn't say it was good for me. *You* said it was good for me. Remember how I hid behind all my hair. You could hardly see my face in the video."

Actually, I know very well what she means about feeling naked. When I read a story in front of people, even a happy story, I become very emotional. Tears usually fill my eyes and I do feel bare. *Why does that happen to me?* I wonder. I think back to a story I wrote about circling the Golden Gate Bridge in a single-engine airplane, the moonlight shining into the cockpit—my son, Jeff, and I flying—Christmas Eve—buddies. How much I love him and flying. I remember the tears when I read it in front of one of my classes. What is all this emotion about? Do I hate being a feeling person? Do I just not like people knowing that I have feelings?

"Well, OK," I sigh. "If you're not comfortable, we ought to go to plan B. We'll take the tarp off one of the antiques."

She smiles. "Ah, my mentor and my friend." There is a wicked glint in her eye, as if it's all just a game. "You're such a pushover." But I know her fear runs deep—and so does mine.

Composing

We will now discuss four additional ways of capturing feelings and getting them down on paper:

1. Use objects to convey emotion.
2. Use the five senses to convey your feelings.
3. Use inner monologue to convey your deepest thoughts and feelings.
4. Express inner emotion.

Use Objects to Convey Emotion

One of the most powerful ways to convey emotion in our stories without using words is to use objects and invest them with great personal meaning. For example, if a man is thinking about the brother he recently lost through death, it would be appropriate for him to look at old photographs of his brother as a remembrance of better times.

When such an object is described effectively, it can have a strong emotional impact on the reader or listener. This concept is similar in many ways to one of the exercises used by actors trained in the Stanislavski system, called "circumstances surrounding an object." In this exercise, the actor builds a past life around an object so that, when it is used on stage or on film, the audience will see and feel the connections to the past—the happy, sad, poignant memories connected with the object.

To give an example from my own life, the interior of the car I own, a 1964 Volvo, has a wonderful smell to it. It is a distinctive smell, one that everyone who climbs into the car notices. But only I know that it is a smell almost identical to that of my father's Packard, a car I loved, a smell that reminds me of a happy time in my life when I was small and my father was alive and showing me things in and around Detroit, things I was seeing and experiencing for the first time.

The little story that opens this chapter uses this technique: Rebecca picks up the water glass, seeking to find in it a clue to the origins of her shyness.

Re-Create Emotions by Exploring the Five Senses

In an earlier chapter, we identified certain emotions that we were able to put into a story. We added, for example, such phrases as "I am happy," "I am sad," and "I am nervous."

Now we can take our exploration of feelings to another level, incorporating the five senses into each moment of a story. Instead of writing "I am nervous," we can write "My hands are shaking," "My mouth is dry," and "My heart pounds in my chest." Use this technique whenever emotions are high, particularly as you approach the climax of a story.

Create Inner Monologues to Convey Emotion

One of the great advantages of the autobiographical story as a form is that the audience expects the author to write from his own point of view—"I" the storyteller. As part of this form, the author is expected to tell us his innermost thoughts and feelings.

For example, if a writer is frustrated with his marriage, he may pick a fight with his wife: "I don't want to go to the movies tonight. Why do we have to go out all the time? Can't we just stay in sometimes?"

This dialogue can be followed up with a more revealing thought or feeling: *Why do I (you) keep picking at her? She loves me (you) so much, and I (you) just keep finding fault. What's the matter with me (you)?*

When writing inner monologue, we usually set it off from other text and dialogue by putting it in italics. If you are writing on a typewriter or a word processor that cannot set text in italics, you can enclose inner monologue in single quotes to distinguish it from regular dialogue. Another common method is to use context—the way we phrase things—to alert the reader to the fact that we are writing inner monologue.

Questions are a very effective form of monologue because they bring the reader deeply into the writer's struggle to become aware of what is happening. *Why am I…? When will I…? What is happening…?*

I am often asked whether it is OK to invent inner monologue. The answer is, of course, yes. We do not ever want to violate the facts of a story, but there are no writing police around to say, "That inner monologue is not true!" So dig deep and invent.

Express Inner Emotion

In some stories, an event in the outside world triggers a flood of inner feelings, often conflicting ones. As with nonobjective paintings, such as those of Wassily Kandinsky and Jackson Pollock, the emotions may become detached from the object that inspired them. Or there may continue to be some reference to the object. In the late paintings of artists such as J. M. W. Turner (*The Fighting Téméraire, The Morning after the Deluge*) and Claude Monet (*Water Lilies*), there is always a hint of the object in the abstract swirls of emotion on the canvas.

Occasionally, the emotions of the inner world rise to the surface and appear as part of the outer world in a surprising and revealing portrait of the writer's own emotional landscape. Please read Stephanie Bernardi's story "My Mother's Death" (see page 285), a fine example of a strong awareness of emotions being part of the subject of the narrative.

To review, here are the steps to follow when "writing from within":

- Follow all the steps we have discussed up to this point to set clearly in your mind a story or incident that you would like to narrate.

- Review the story or incident that is in your mind, recollecting how you felt with each turn of events during the story.

- Recall not only your emotions and those of any other central characters, but also how other, specific people around you responded to the situation.

- Allow yourself to make your emotions—your sadness, pain, awe, amusement, fascination, and so on—the subject of certain episodes.

The following are some inner emotions that deserve attention:

- aloneness, as when my parents left me
- feeling naked, as when I did something very embarrassing
- exhilaration, as when I did something unique

- sadness, as when someone dear to me left, never to return
- frustration, as when something I tried and tried to do continued to be impossible to accomplish
- peace, as when some lengthy struggle finally came to a satisfying conclusion
- yearning, as when something I wanted very much became even more desirable than before
- awe, as when something I participated in took on a life of its own
- anger, as when forces beyond my control shaped the lives of those around me

———— • • • ————

*Now it is time for me to explore some events that hold some of my deepest feelings and emotions... I am traveling back over my sea of memories... I am beginning to see the moment... it is time to write... **now**.*

Reviewing

In reviewing your story at this point, you may find that you have more information to add to the story, information that the central character/narrator would not know. You can add such information at the end of the story in a P.S.

A P.S. is a postscript to your story. In it, you can add information that did not fit into the story, but is relevant, if only to the family—such as names, dates, places, or anything else you would like to add.

Particularly effective in the P.S. is information you wish the reader to know about the experience's effect on the rest of your life. If you detested spinach in the story and you never again ate spinach, the reader will probably enjoy knowing about this.

Conclusion

You now have the techniques you need to write your life stories, to express your inner feelings, as well as to describe people and events in the outside world. In your subsequent stories, try to achieve an effective balance of narration, dialogue, and inner monologue. Not every story requires such a balance, but most stories will be enhanced by it. And remember to use your inner thoughts and feelings, to "write from within."

Here is an updated version of the checklist introduced in Chapter 4:

Life-Story Writing Checklist

1. Is my story written in the first person and in the present tense?
2. Have I stripped the story of adult, intellectual language?
3. Are my feelings in the story?
4. Do the details and actions make the story clearer and more interesting?
5. Does the dialogue help tell the story and make the characters more interesting?
6. Have I kept to one well-focused incident at a time?
7. Are the characters interesting, perhaps unforgettable? Are their qualities evident?
8. Are my feelings about the events clearly expressed?
9. Have I created monologues to convey inner thoughts and feelings?
10. Have I improvised the facts where my memory has failed?

 EXERCISE

Journalists who write for magazines, newspapers and the like, generally use only narrative and dialogue to tell a story. Writers in personal journals generally use inner thoughts and feelings to convey their concerns. As life writers, we want to do both—give a picture of the outer world and also the inner world of our thoughts and feelings.

WRITING ABOUT THE INNER YOU

Step 1: Begin by taking yourself back to an event that holds within it some of your deepest feelings and emotions. When you have finished writing about the event, check your work to see that you have written in the *present tense*, added your *feelings*, and written some *dialogue*. If not, go ahead and do these things. Try to include inner *monologues* as well.

Step 2: Now it is time to write your feelings in an even more interesting and vivid way. Up to this point, you have been encouraged to add your feelings at each point in the story. "I am angry," "I am sad," "I am puzzled," and "I feel excited" are some of the phrases you may have used. These are good and helpful statements, and we will continue to use them.

However, there is a way of making such moments even more vivid for the reader, and that is to locate the feeling in parts of the body. Instead of saying "I feel angry," you can explore *where in the body that anger is felt*. For example, "I feel angry" becomes "My heart begins to pound," "My throat goes dry," "I clench my teeth," "My eyes burn." Heart, throat, teeth, eyes.

Here is another feeling: "I feel happy." To express this you may wish to explore other areas of your body, such as your legs, stomach, or toes. "My legs feel light," "My toes tingle," "The ache in my stomach has gone away." Explore what goes on in the various parts of your body when a feeling occurs.

Now, add these feelings to the rewrite of your story.

Step 3: When you have finished your rewrite you can begin to *edit* your story. That means checking *spelling, grammar,* and *punctuation.* You can use any kind of language you want in your dialogue, but you do want to spell and punctuate it correctly.

Cracking Open the Door to Your Past

"So many of my childhood memories seem to have disappeared," laments Arnold, a new student in my Musicians Union class. "I wonder what to do."

"Your past is like a refrigerator," I tell him. "Once the door is open, memories that are directly in front of you, the most vivid ones, will press themselves upon you. When you've finished writing about those, others in the back will come forward."

"Suppose I can't get the door open," he questions.

"There are more keys to unlocking that door than you can imagine," I say. "One such key is to concentrate on a place where vital, unforgettable things happened."

Composing

Particular places that we have visited, lived in and spent time at evoke vivid pictures in our minds as well as strong emotions. We want to take advantage of the strength of these recollections in order to write vivid stories.

Describe a Place Memory

Here is a process that may help you pry open the door to your past. First, imagine yourself floating over that place of significance. Next, ask yourself, "What sorts of things did I do there?" Try answering your question with *-ing* words, action words. "I found myself *exploring* the house…*wandering* the woods." Finally, write down the *-ing* words that surface, and allow them to help you find specific, vivid moments about which to write.

Try to find memories from your childhood first. You can begin by describing a place that generated experiences affecting you or members of your family.

One such vital and unforgettable place for me is the farmhouse my sister and I have up in Maine. My father bought it for my mother during the Depression, and restoring it was their life's project. I spent almost every summer there from the time I was six months old until I was eighteen. Even now I return almost every summer.

As I imagine floating over the house, a flood of memories comes back to me: *watching* Abner haying with his two-horse team, *reading* by a kerosene lamp at night, *exploring* our pre–Revolutionary War farmhouse, *celebrating* V-J Day near a lake where the ties of a forgotten railroad lay underfoot, *forming* my first band to play at church suppers, *holding* hands for the first time in the picture show, *seeing* Mom and Dad happy together in a way they never were in Florida, *taking* my wife and infant son to Maine and *creating* our second child on the dock at Songo Pond, *filming* my sons exploring the old railroad, *working* side by side with the boys for more than ten summers to clear the brush that had overgrown the meadows during my neglectful years.

Here are some places that may contain significant, vivid memories:

- places I lived as a child
- places I played as a child
- places I did something I shouldn't have done
- places I learned a lesson I have never forgotten
- places I saw or experienced things that changed my life
- the place Dad did his work
- the place Mom did her work
- the place Grandpa or Grandma lived when I was small
- the place I experienced my first kiss
- the place I worked for the first time

As we wander back through the years remembering the things we have done, particular moments from our past begin to reappear.

"But maybe I don't want to remember," you say. "My past was full of pain and I only want to get to the happy things."

The more deeply we write from within ourselves, the more fully we can capture an experience that may have been haunting us, find its meaning, and let go of it. This clears such memories, both positive and negative, from the front of our minds and allows us to explore previously hidden, but no less intriguing and vivid, memories.

———•••———

I'm getting ready to write what happened to me in a place of importance. I'm not going to get bogged down in details of the place…I'm ready to go back…way back…I'm going back to a vivid event in a special place…I'm going to begin writing… **now.**

Reviewing

As we come to the reviewing phase of our work, we will add two elements to our checklist:

- improvising with the facts when memory fails
- having concern for form and structure: finding the spine of the story

Improvise: Fill in the Gaps Where Memory Fails

As you continually unearth and confront your memories, you may begin to feel like something of an archaeologist. The brain is a magnificent and fascinating organ because it often yields what it wishes to give us, not what we think it ought to be giving us. Within its rich bank of memories you have undoubtedly discovered several fragments of recollections that seem to form a whole, but somehow you cannot complete it—the names, places, and times that are the links between the fragments appear to be lost. As a result, you may feel stuck and unable to write or complete a memoir.

The experienced archaeologist not only knows where to dig for artifacts of the past but, when they are in hand, also knows how to put them together in such a way that he can make educated guesses about ancient habits, customs, and beliefs. The past becomes clearer.

So, what does one do if one simply doesn't have enough evidence to create the links to complete the story that is lurking inside one's brain? Frustrating, isn't it? A paradox—to know that one's most interesting memory is the story one doesn't remember.

This is where we must operate not as a scientist but as an artist, not as an archaeologist but as a lover—in fact, as more than a lover.

Picasso once said, "Art is a lie that tells us the truth," and this is the sense in which we must become artist, lover, seducer, and Casanova. As a lure to bring out the truth we must be willing to invent, to lie a little. Oh, not to ourselves, or even to our readers, but to our brain. Invention is a creative right-brain strategy that we sometimes need to sneak past the guard of our critical left brain, which, for reasons of its own, is trying to hide the past.

So, as you move from the terra firma of one clear-as-a-bell memory to another equally well-grounded memory, if you suddenly find yourself sinking into the quicksand of forgetfulness, you can regain your footing by simply inventing parts of an episode until the clear memory appears.

Perhaps you don't like the idea of lying; perhaps this suggestion arouses in you the same enthusiasm that you had for castor oil as a child and curfews as a teenager. "I'm not a person who invents," a student will often protest. "If I wanted to write fiction, I would write fiction. I'm here to write my life stories." This is all quite true. But we are not dropping invented artifacts into archaeological digs and trying to pretend they are real—a Piltdown Man (a paleontological hoax) approach to life-story writing. Not at all.

Our purpose is to entice the brain into yielding the truth. So, once we have invented part of the story, we must rely on our intuition to let us know when something feels false, and then rewrite it, moving toward the truth as best we can.

Occasionally, the brain does not yield what we hope it will. In that case, simply preface the passage with a phrase such as "As well as I can remember…" or "My memory is a bit blank here, but I think the next part of the story goes something like this…." A disclaimer like that is all you need. No one can then hold you to the facts; you are off the hook. If a question you cannot answer arises in your mind, by all means deal with the question by responding "I don't remember" or "I don't know." Such a question is integral to the story and must be answered, even if the answer is simply "I don't remember." This way the reader will not continue to puzzle over the question and be distracted from the rest of the story.

Here are some simple guidelines for improvising:

First, when facts are available, stick to them. Do not invent facts just to make a better-sounding story. If you do, people will come to mistrust you and will cease believing your stories.

Second, allow yourself to re-create and improvise your own feelings. The reader wants to know what is going on inside you. Do not suppose what others' feelings are unless you can read the expressions on their faces, hear what they are saying, or read their body language. If you try to tell the reader what other people are feeling, your reader will not believe you.

Third, allow yourself to re-create dialogue using the truth of your intuition and feelings as a guide to what is believable. Readers crave dialogue as an alternative to narrative and inner thoughts and feelings.

And finally, if the facts as you remember them simply do not feel real somehow, write what does feel real and add a postscript explaining the difference.

Form and Structure (1): Find the Spine of the Story

Form is a tricky thing to talk about with writers. It is one of those things that all writers and writing teachers love to discuss. Knowledge of form is what makes a writer an expert, just as being able to fill cavities is what makes a dentist an expert. Or at least that is what writers like to believe.

Essentially, form gives one's work some definable shape, so that the readers or listeners know where they are going and can enjoy where they have been. A story about a duck needs to be about a duck. A story about an abortion needs to be about an abortion. A story about an uncle needs to be about an uncle. As a writer, this involves giving the reader or listener little clues about what to look for or listen for, a coherent thread, or even a running gag.

Sometimes a mood or an atmosphere running through a story can provide form. Stories can hang heavy with memory and emotion. This, too, is form.

Each story has its own emotional logic, its own concerns, and the line of that logic is the spine. Anything else should be left aside or saved for another story. Since the mind can hold just so many things in it at one time, we have to limit the mind's attention to those things that are related to the spine.

Let's suppose, for example, the beginning of our first draft is about taking a trip from Russia to the United States; the middle is about finding a house to settle in so that Mom, who is sick, can get better; and the end is about Mom's death and how everyone felt.

From the ending, we get a clue to the spine and the structure. In fact, the middle—Mom's getting sick—is also a clue. The beginning needs to relate to the end, so the beginning of the story needs to be about Mom's health or well-being. The trip from Russia is clearly a separate story.

Rewriting

For those of you who are continually working on rewriting your stories to make them more interesting and readable, other ways your stories can be rewritten to make them tighter and more effective are as follows:

- finding the beginning of your story
- creating a visual "look" to your story
- expanding the climax of your story

Form and Structure (2): Find the Beginning of the Story

Here are a few simple steps to follow to find the beginning of your story.

First, ask yourself, "What is the most powerful moment of this vivid memory of mine? What is the moment I remember most clearly?" Then ask yourself, "Can I start my story *just before* this vivid moment begins?" Usually, as writers, we give much more introductory information than the reader needs, information that can be left out or rearranged.

After you have finished your first draft, look over your story right away. Find that first line of dialogue or action. Often, the closer we get to the more vividly recalled moments in the story, the more dialogue we will naturally write. That first line of dialogue may be a clue to the beginning of the story—and to the spine of the story as well.

Don't worry about starting off the story with a perfect opening when you are writing your first draft. *Finding the beginning is strictly a rewriting task.*

Remember, writers have to warm up, and that's what the first few paragraphs of each draft are—a warm-up, until you rewrite them. The first line of dialogue or action is where you begin to hit your stride. By that time, you are in the story—and so are we, your readers.

The story that follows is an example of rewriting by locating the first line of dialogue and rearranging other paragraphs. Notice how sections 1, 2, and 3 of the story are rearranged in the second version for a better effect on the reader.

The Goose Story   *by Vera Mellus*   (FIRST DRAFT)

1   It was autumn. The leaves were turning red and yellow and it was a perfect day to take two little boys to the Los Angeles Zoo. I'm not familiar with the Zoo now, but then there was a barnyard where little children could pet goats and ponies, feed chickens, ducks, and geese. They could also see a cow being milked.

My daughter and I packed a picnic basket and set off with two eager little boys. We strolled by the bears, tigers and other animals, but it wasn't till we got to the barnyard that the boys really became interested and had fun. Here they could come in close contact with the animals.

It was a perfect place to take pictures. How great to snap the children feeding chickens and to get those happy smiles on their faces. I was so busy taking pictures I didn't notice a big, fat goose following me around.

2   I suddenly felt a hurtful pull and looked to see the goose had a tight grip on my big toe. He had braced his feet, stretched his neck to the last inch, and was hanging on.

3   "I can't believe this," I yelled. "Look, Dede."

"Mother, give him a kick," I heard her yell, as she was having a fit of laughter.

"I can't. He won't let go."

"I'll get a stick," I heard my grandson say.

By this time we were all laughing so hard watching this silly goose.

A few days prior I had fallen in the shower and had broken the toes on my left foot. They were so swollen I couldn't wear a shoe and so was wearing sandals; one toe was so swollen it was white, and to a goose it must have looked like a fat, juicy grub. He finally gave up seeing whether it was going to come off and I went home with all toes intact.

Vera Mellus   *Vera was in her nineties when she wrote "The Goose Story." She was born and raised in North Dakota during the wild years at the turn of the century. After the death of her father when she was very young, she recalls her mother running a tent hotel in Marmar. When her mother could not care for all the children, Vera crossed the country in a stagecoach and grew up in Glendale, Arizona, under the care of an aunt. She appeared in the first western movie shot in Glendale, in 1917, was educated in Los Angeles, married, and raised two daughters. Bright, elegant, and wise, Vera came to the class "to leave something to my grandchildren." She died in 1989.*

• • •

Class members suggested Vera look at the first line of dialogue or action to see whether that was where the spine of the story began. Here is her rewrite.

The Goose Story   (REWRITE)

3   "Oh, no. I can't believe this," I yell, shaking my foot, trying to discourage a big fat goose from trying to eat one of my toes. "Get away."

1, 2   My daughter, her two sons, and I are in the barnyard of the Los Angeles Zoo. The boys are feeding the ducks and chickens and having a great time. I've been so busy trying to get those happy smiles with my camera that I haven't noticed this goose.

"Get away. Shoo," I yell.

"Mother, kick him," I hear my daughter say, having a fit of laughter.

"I can't. He won't let go."

"I'll get a stick," my grandson says. "I'll make him let go."

By this time we are all laughing so hard to see this silly goose back up, brace himself, stretch his neck to the last inch and hang on.

I had fallen in the shower and the toes on my left foot are broken. I cannot wear a shoe and so I'm wearing sandals—and one toe is so swollen it is white and must look like a fat, juicy grub.

I brace myself and pull hard. He lets go. I limp away, then turn around. I'll never forget the look on his face. He stared at me—a look of triumph all over his face.

My two grandsons had a great day, but what really made the day was the goose.

— • • • —

Notice that the spine of the story is now very apparent: the goose's attack on Vera and the comedy that ensues. In the first draft, we had no idea what the story was about until we got to section 2. In the second draft, Vera drops much of section 1 and combines sections 2 and 3—the dialogue and the spine—together. Notice also that she has changed past tense verbs into present tense verbs.

Sometimes I am asked, "If you are writing in the present tense in one part of your story, how do you make the leap to the next part if it begins, say, a month later?"

You can leap ahead to the new time by explicitly writing "Now it is a month (week, day, hour) later, and I am waiting…" or some similar phrase. You may also wish to give the reader a little second-paragraph backstory of what happened between the time the first part ended and the next began.

Create a Visual Look to the Story

From the warm-up, we have created a wealth of material. From this material, we have found a first line of action or dialogue with which to begin the story. From the rest of this material we have constructed a second-paragraph backstory that tells us what has gone on in the past that is important to understanding the story.

At the same time, we want to be sure the audience can see the moment as if it were the opening of a movie: people acting within a setting of some kind, a distinct place where something is happening.

> I'm sitting in the Hollywood Race Track dining room on the second floor. In front of me is a small TV screen showing the horses outside. It is a miserable day. Sheets of rain are pouring down on L.A. The bitter wind is cold and blows through the grandstands, forcing the bettors inside to the dining room.

In this example, the writer gives us a strong sense of the place and the present circumstances. From the very first line we can see him in the story and what he is doing, "I am sitting…"

There are a number of techniques we can borrow from the painters and sculptors of the past to make our stories more visual. We can use color, perspective, texture, and space—but most of all we can use light, especially the interplay of light and dark.

The film noir movies starring James Cagney, Humphrey Bogart, and George Raft from the late 1930s and early 1940s were immensely popular, thanks in part to the wonderful black-and-white cinematography. The superb camera work and astute direction allowed characters to emerge from the darkness halfway into the light like primordial reptiles half in and half out of the slime of creation. These characters are often seen in silhouette or as shadows on a wall (as in Carol Reed's *The Third Man*) or with the shadow of a Venetian blind playing across their faces.

Much of the technique of such dramatic lighting can also be seen in the films and paintings of the early German expressionists. For example, Robert Wiene's 1919 film *The Cabinet of Dr. Caligari* showed us how an impression of macabre horror can be created if a face is lit from below, casting great shadows around the eyes.

Three centuries before, the Italian painter Caravaggio demonstrated the powerful impact of faces and figures emerging from darkness into light. Before him came such Renaissance masters as Leonardo da Vinci in the late fifteenth century and Masaccio in the early fifteenth century. In da Vinci's paintings, however, the play of light and dark is less for dramatic purpose than for illuminating the expressiveness of the body and face. For example, in the *Virgin and St. Anne,* the crosshatching of lines (especially evident in his sketches) gives each face and figure a depth and dimension never before seen in Western art, so that light and dark illuminate each person's feelings or state of mind.

We can do the very same thing in our writing, harnessing the drama of light and dark, as seen in the following excerpt.

Cricket *by J. D. "Dirk" Tousley*   (EXCERPT)

"Evening, Mr. Horner," I muster, still unable to see him through the screen though I do detect the odor of his cheap cigar.

"I brought you a Dutch Master," I say as I open the screen door and enter the porch. I can barely make him out in the dusk as he swings slowly back and forth in his porch swing.

"Trying to suck in with me, huh?"

I ignore the son of a bitch's remark, hand him the Dutch Master, and ask, "Is Cricket ready yet?"

He rolls the cigar between thumb and forefinger, testing its quality, before saying, "Why the hell you call her Cricket? Her name's Josephine. If I wanted her to be Cricket, I'd uh named her Cricket."

"Harry leave that boy alone," comes Mrs. Horner's voice from the darkest side of the porch.

"Oh, hello, ma'am. I didn't see you," I say, grateful for a champion in my corner.

"Well, I'm here. Don't pay no attention to him," she says as she rises and gropes her way through the gathering darkness to the living room door. "Gettin' kind of chilly for me," she adds on her way to the living room. But I know she's not chilly. It's hotter than hell. She doesn't want to listen to his badgering me again tonight, that's all.

A lamp in the living room goes on and casts its warm glow onto the porch through an open window. Now I can see Mr. Horner clearly.

There's no change from a few nights ago. Same white undershirt with shoulder straps. Same woolly chest hair peeking out. Same khaki pants.

Same high-top work shoes. Same bottle of Hamm's beer. Same crappy cigar. Same three-day beard. Same long black hair streaked with gray and combed back over the ears ending in a duck tail at the back of his head. Same suspicious look. I feel I'm dealing with a muscular forty-five-year-old man powered by the brain of a fifteen-year-old medieval peasant. How could God have presented this churlish man and his doltish wife with a cute, lively kid like Cricket whose only fault is saying "you was" rather than "you were?"

J. D. "Dirk" Tousley *Dirk makes his living writing books and newsletters on chiropractic matters. He yearned to be a writer from the time he was a teenager, when he traveled to Mexico, spending his time in bars until it was time to return to the United States. Now, some fifty years later, he has returned to his first love — writing.*

— • • • —

Notice how effectively Dirk uses light and dark to capture the mood on this porch: "'Harry leave that boy alone,' comes Mrs. Hattey's voice from the darkest side of the porch," and "she rises and gropes her way through the gathering darkness to the living room door," and finally "a lamp in the living room goes on and casts its warm glow onto the porch through an open window. Now I can see Mr. Horner clearly. There's no change from a few nights ago. Same white undershirt with shoulder straps...."

In our writing, we have to be very careful about spending time describing a place or a setting so that the description does not distract from or slow down the story. Where we place description is important, too. Making a story as visual as possible is especially effective at the beginning and during the climax.

Form and Structure (3):
Expand the Climax of the Story

"I wanted to know more of what was happening at the climax of your story," listeners often say to a writer. "It was so interesting, I just wanted more."

When you hear this kind of comment, I suggest you expand the dramatic moment when everything is coming to a head.

In films, for example, a dramatic moment of action or feeling may actually be done in slow motion or repeated in slow motion, from several angles. In one of the more memorable scenes from the film *A Man and a Woman* by Claude Lelouch, the camera circles the two lovers as they fall into each other's arms at the train station, as if spinning a web around them, sealing them off from the world outside, slowing everything so it seems these passionate moments exist out of time. Such cinematic techniques allow the viewer/reader/listener to understand and savor every fraction of a moment of such a wonderful experience. Similarly, baseball players, when they are hot, describe the ball coming to the plate as "large as a basketball and moving slowly...easy to hit." Everything is slowed down, and the moment when bat strikes ball is expanded.

This is not to say that you, as writer, are trying to slow down the action. Including more dialogue, more reactions from the minor characters, and more of a sense of changes taking place around the action has the effect of speeding up the action because the story becomes fuller, more complete.

Expanding the climax of a story is a subject that deserves considerable attention—attention that will be given in Chapter 8.

The following is an updated version of the checklist.

Life-Story Writing Checklist

1. Is my story written in the first person and in the present tense?
2. Have I stripped the story of adult, intellectual language?
3. Are my feelings in the story?
4. Do the details and actions make the story clearer and more interesting?
5. Does the dialogue help tell the story and make the characters more interesting?
6. Have I kept to one well-focused incident at a time?
7. Are the characters interesting, perhaps unforgettable? Are their qualities evident?
8. Are my feelings about the event clearly expressed?
9. Have I created monologue to convey inner thoughts and feelings?
10. Have I improvised the facts where my memory has failed?

(cont'd.)

11. Is the spine of my story clear?
12. Did I find an effective starting point? Did I begin with action or dialogue?
13. Is my story visual?
14. Did I find and expand the climax to the story?

EXERCISE

Now that you have written your memory of what happened to you in a place of importance, see whether you have included your feelings, have written in the present tense, and have used some dialogue and inner monologue.

Step 1. Now let's look at another step in the process, *finding the beginning.* Very often you can create a story by figuring out the climax to the story first. The climax of a story is the point toward which all the interest and emotion build. It is the point of greatest tension and greatest interest. It is probably what you remember most vividly. What is the climax to your story?

Step 2. The next step is to begin the story just before the climax, looking for the beginning by locating the first line of action or dialogue that directly relates to the climax. In other words, when you first start a story, you may give a lot of description of where it's taking place and why you are there. This is just a warm-up for your mind to get ready for the real incident. Don't include this in your revised beginning.

Locate the beginning by finding the first line of *action* or *dialogue* that leads directly to the climax. Below is an example.

> It's a real hot day and I was up late with my buddy Mauricio here in Houston, Texas, so I'm not with my friends this morning. I am fifteen years old.
> I'm tired so I'm going to go back to sleep. We were partying all night.
> "Don't wake me up if anyone comes to look for me, OK?" I tell my sister.
> A little while later she wakes me up and says, "Your friend's been killed."

Looking back at this piece, the writer searches for the first line of dialogue, "Don't wake me up," and makes it the first sentence of the story. He also drops the phrase, "so I'm not with my friends." Here's his next draft:

> "Don't wake me up if anyone comes to look for me, OK?" I tell my sister.
> It's a real hot day here in Houston, Texas, and Mauricio and I had been up late. I am fifteen years old. I am tired, so I'm going to go back to sleep. We were partying all night.
> A little while later she wakes me up and says, "Your friend's been killed."

This draft now has a better and more interesting beginning, doesn't it?

Step 3. This is where you will be *setting the stage.* You may bring in factual information later in the first, or even the second, paragraph, after beginning your story with action or dialogue.

Notice that in the revised example above, the stage is being set in the second paragraph: *It's a real hot day here in Houston, Texas, and Mauricio and I had been up late. I am fifteen years old. I am tired, so I'm going to go back to sleep. We were partying all night.* Notice also that we might take the sentence *We were partying all night* and add it to the earlier sentence to tighten the story: *Mauricio and I been up all night partying.*

Go ahead and rewrite, or better still, rearrange your first few paragraphs to find the beginning of your story and to set the stage.

Developing a Writing Strategy and Choosing Writing Exercises

"What should I write about now?" asks a young student when we return from lunch. "Should I begin writing in chronological order? I've already outlined over thirty memories."

I smile at her. "Always go with the memories that are the most vivid. You don't have to write anything in chronological order." Then I add, "But it is a good idea to write a vivid memory from each decade of your life, just to give you a sense of the arc of your life."

Developing a Writing Strategy

Once we have written and rewritten the exercises in the previous chapters and have written a number of vivid childhood memories, I suggest we all record a series of the most vivid moments of our lives, one for each decade. One way to do this is to note in a word or two, using index cards, the vivid moments in each decade of our life. Reviewing our cards, we will gain a powerful sense of what each moment is like without having to write the stories that come to mind. These are the *guide stories* through which the larger pattern of our lives will emerge.

Once we have recorded our decade memories, we can write three or four more vivid memories to fill in each decade. The most important decades to work on are the first two, from birth to twenty years. Later, after we have written each story, we can assess their impact on our lives, if we chose to do so, in a P.S. (see Chapter 5).

Please note that when I say "write a memory," I mean a *vivid* memory—not an ordinary, dull, repetitive memory. It is important that we seek out our vivid memories first, as well as the memories hiding behind the vivid memories.

Like tenpins lined up in a bowling alley, there is only room for a few in the first rows, but when we have knocked those down, we have a chance to see what is left standing in the back and at the corners. These are the hidden memories, which we will work with in Chapters 8 and 9.

Nancy, a woman whose beloved husband had died earlier in the year, came to one of my workshops intent on dealing with her grief. But for many months she found herself writing about her childhood and the pain and the pleasure of growing up, never once writing about her husband and their life together. She felt guilty for some time, but I assured her that she was handling the process the right way. Eventually, she said she was ready and asked what to do first.

"Should I write about his death?" she asked. The fear and pain in her eyes was evident.

"No," I said, "write about the wonderful times between you."

Little by little the richness of their life unfolded. After several months, she felt cleansed: Their happiness had been celebrated and now it was time for her to write about the end. At first she wrote in a clinical way, pushing away the pain and sadness. Her writing group quickly pointed out to her what was happening, and she began to tell us the story in a simpler, more vivid way.

"At last," she said, "I feel free."

We explore the memories we need to relive and put them to rest by fully experiencing everything that was in them to experience, including ways in which they remind us of old patterns from childhood, patterns that may or may not have served us well.

Choosing Writing Exercises That Meet Your Needs

You can easily tailor writing exercises to your own needs. You may wish to write more memories to see a shape to your life based on the memories you have been bringing to the surface. You may have a desire to develop your writing skill. Or you may want to write about your memories as an avenue to exploring your emotions.

The following series of writing activities will help you explore any or all of the above. They may be approached in any order, although I suggest you begin by writing one memory from each decade of your life and, if time permits, write at least half a dozen stories of memories from early childhood.

 E X E R C I S E

Occasionally we will find little tricks we can employ to stimulate the subconscious and shake loose some memories that have not revealed themselves for many years.

The following is one such approach we can use that is both very simple and very easy to employ.

PART 1: WRITE VIVID MEMORIES OF EACH DECADE

Working from the index cards on which you recorded a word or two to remind you of a vivid memory from each decade, now turn your decade memories into stories. As a collection, these *guide stories* will help you see some of the patterns that weave through your life, shaping who you are.

PART 2: HONE YOUR WRITING SKILLS

Step 1. Write a vivid memory to develop your ability to use dialogue. In this memory, let your characters interrupt one another. Also explore unusual speaking qualities, such as a Jamaican patois or a southern drawl; Latino, Yiddish, or black-vernacular phrases; and slang. Such language adds richness to stories and builds strong characters.

Step 2. Write a vivid memory in which each new, important character is introduced with a thumbnail description. For example, consider this thumbnail sketch of a newly introduced character:

> Uncle Eli walks in the door. Short, dapper, and quite small, he wears a faded dark suit and a sad smile on his face. There is a worn and yellowed handkerchief tucked neatly into his breast pocket.

This description tells us a lot about Uncle Eli—that he is a bit out of the mainstream, bent on keeping up appearances, but that life weighs heavily on his shoulders. It also tells us a lot about the writer—that she is observant and watchful.

> The guy runs by me. He is wearing something blue, a coat or a sweater. He's kind of youngish, maybe thirty. There is a sort of a smile on his face. It's kind of a scary, evil smile.

This thumbnail sketch works because it is fairly imprecise. It is believable as the point of view of someone who suddenly turns around and catches something out of the corner of his eye.

Now, try writing thumbnail sketches for your own characters.

PART 3: EXPLORE YOUR EMOTIONS

Step 1. Write a vivid memory in which you allow the central character to hold two differing emotions at the same time, such as happiness and confusion, love and disappointment, or anger and awe. Remember to use all five senses to convey these emotions.

Step 2. Write a vivid memory in which you turn inner thoughts and feelings told to the audience—*I wish he would be more truthful. It makes me angry when he lies like this*—to inner thoughts and feelings told directly to another character—*"George, stop lying to me!" I scream at him inside my head.*

This kind of direct but inner confrontation is even more effective when we allow the dialogue that comes from our mouths to be quite different from that we hear in our minds to be our normal speaking tone, which is often toned down. Consider another example:

> "I'll be back by six o'clock to pick you up," my son says to me. *I know he has no intention of being here by six o'clock or seven or eight. I won't see him for a long time. Why can't he just tell the truth?* "Okay," I say, my voice coming from a long way off. "Okay."

This passage can be revised by focusing the inner dialogue directly at the other character:

> "I'll be back by six o'clock to pick you up," my son says to me.
> "Bullshit," I scream at him inside my head. "You're not going to be here, are you? You're gonna disappear just like you did yesterday and the day before." My heart is pounding and my head aches. I'm so tired of this…so tired.
> "Okay," I say, my voice coming from a long way off. "Okay." I sit down, rubbing my forehead as he walks out the door.

Now, try this technique with a memory of your own.

Expanding the Climax
of the Story

During an advanced workshop, I welcome several faces from past workshops. Stephanie, a red-haired mother, for one, as well as Tamara, a whimsical young mother of two.

"Welcome to the second day of the workshop," I say. "It's good to see you all again."

"I'm glad I'm taking this workshop," Tamara says with a laugh. "It forces me to write. Otherwise, I just focus on my problems at home." The others nod their heads.

"It's not easy to tear myself away from small kids and a tired husband," says Stephanie, her broad smile and copper-colored hair lighting up the room. "I worked hard on this story."

I give her an encouraging smile, as I suspect she is about to dive into something important. "In this workshop, we are going to look at an important memory and see if there are places in each story, particularly in the climax, that can be opened up to reveal more of what happened than we remembered at first."

Each of the eight people in the workshop takes out the story he or she had written for the first night's work. One by one, they read and we make comments. Finally we get to Stephanie's story.

My Mother's Death
by Stephanie Bernardi   (FIRST DRAFT: EXCERPT)

My mother is dying. Cancer has eaten away at her once lush full figure. Today she weighs sixty-eight pounds. This has only added emphasis to her pale clear blue eyes. The eyes that always knew everything. She stares transfixed on the painting in the corner. His picture hangs over her chest of drawers. In every house, it always has. The icy blue eyes peering out from eternity and always calling to us, "I still am."

89

The thick knife strokes of paint fill in his cherub cheeks, rosy as that of all healthy blonde and fair three-year-olds. Forever three. My brother. The one I never knew.

His presence, though, in our family is as definite as any of the other seven siblings. It is just that we don't speak of him. Somehow, this has only added emphasis to his memory. Losing him into that cold silent death of drowning is still painful to speak of, even now thirty-five years later.

"What do you see, Mom? Is someone there?" I ask her.

"Yes," she says, "Gary." I don't doubt this. I just want to know more. She has not spoken for weeks. She drifts in and out. Occasionally she babbles. My father says it's from senility, from the cancer in her brain. I don't believe him. Something more is going on.

Stephanie Bernardi   *A mother of two small children, Stephanie assists her husband in his business and writes to keep her mind active.*

— • • • —

"This is a very beautiful story, Stephanie," says one of the group members. "But I wonder if I could be brought into it a little more?" Several others echo her thoughts. Stephanie looks a bit puzzled.

"Some of the language keeps us at arm's length, Stephanie," I say. "I suggest you take as much of your present, adult, reflective self out of the story as you can."

"Really?" she says. "I thought I had."

"Let's look at the first paragraph," I suggest. She rereads:

> My mother is dying. Cancer has eaten away at her once lush full figure. Today she weighs sixty-eight pounds. This has only added emphasis to her pale clear blue eyes. The eyes that always knew everything. She stares transfixed on the painting in the corner. His picture hangs over her chest of drawers. In every house it always has. The icy blue eyes peering out from eternity and always calling to us, "I still am."

"Some of that language, while wonderful, is a little difficult to believe. I sense you could carve some of it away and get more of a hard, gemlike self to emerge."

"Really?" asked Stephanie, shrugging her shoulders, unconvinced. "Well, I'll give it a try."

The next Sunday, the small group of writers reconvenes. Everyone is eager to hear what Stephanie has done. She takes out the story. "I don't think it's very good," she says. "I think I've pared it down too much."

My Mother's Death

My mother is dying. Cancer has eaten away at her. Today she weighs sixty-eight pounds.

As I sit and watch her, she stares off, fixed on the painting hanging in the corner. His picture hangs over her chest of drawers. It always has. His blue eyes catch me as they call out, "I still am."

The thick knife strokes of paint add depth to his three-year-old cheeks. He is rosy and animated and forever three.

My brother. The one I never knew. Thirty-five years ago he drowned. He is never spoken of. This has only added emphasis to his missing place in our large family.

"What do you see, Mom? Is someone there?" I ask her. There is no response, just that quiet. "Mom, is someone there?" I repeat.

"Yes," she says. "Mama is here."

I don't doubt this. I just want to hear more. She has not spoken for weeks. She drifts in and out. Occasionally she babbles. My father says it's from senility, from the cancer in her brain. I don't believe him. Something more is going on. In the hospital last week, when I sat with her, it seemed she was talking to someone, but when I asked her about it, I could get no response.

"That's wonderful, Mom. Is anyone else there?" I ask.

"Yes...Gary...and Helen." I am not surprised about Gary. But who's Helen? Helen...Helen? I think Grandma had a sister named Helen, I don't remember any special relationship though...at least she's never mentioned it. Maybe a childhood friend named Helen?

"What do they want, Mom?" I ask.

Of course, I know what they want. Here she lies in her suffering, shriveled up to nothing more than a faded memory of the mom she was. Her gestures are infantlike now. The fingers curled. And the hands. The part of her body that hasn't changed. I used to hate those hands. They were wrinkled beyond her age. My hands are the same. Now they are the only familiar part of her. I reach for them. Somehow, when I touch them and close my eyes for a moment, it is all forgotten: the feeding tubes up her nose, the diapers, the look of childlike innocence on her face that is pathetic from her. My once elegant mother even picks her nose and scratches herself.

Expanding the Climax of the Story

(The complete rewrite appears on page 285 in the "Stories" section of the book.)

— • • • —

"So you think this is an inferior draft, huh?" I ask. Stephanie nods. I laugh. The others do too. "Just goes to show what our self-critic knows."

Stephanie looks around. "You mean the rewrite is better?"

One woman in the group reaches over and touches Stephanie's arm. "It was one of the most powerful experiences I've ever had listening to a story. I cried all the way through." The others in the group echo her comments.

Stephanie is silent for a moment, then speaks. "Well, I'm glad I followed your advice, even if I didn't know it was working so well. But I see what you mean. Are there any other places?"

I have her read another passage from her first draft—

> His presence, though, in our family is as definite as any of the other seven siblings. It is just that we don't speak of him. Somehow this has only added emphasis to his memory. Losing him into that cold silent death of drowning is still painful to speak of, even now thirty-five years later.

—and I point out how effectively she has reworked it.

> Thirty-five years ago he drowned. He is never spoken of. This has only added emphasis to his missing place in our large family.

"Here you give us the action, the drowning first, then you tell us the impact on the family while getting rid of the purely intellectual concept: *His presence… is as definite as any of the… siblings.* This concept is one we as readers want to conclude for ourselves, and we do so by the end of the second rewrite."

"I see," muses Stephanie. "I guess it does work."

"But what's really impressive is the part that starts the climax, 'Mom, do you want to go with him?' Go ahead and read both versions."

Stephanie reads on.

My Mother's Death   (FIRST DRAFT: EXCERPT)

"Mom, do you want to go with him?" I ask.

A long pause. I know what her answer will be. I don't blame her. This is not a life. But I need to hear it from her.

"Yes," she whispers.

Her eyes remain transfixed on the painting. She appears to be listening to something. To what? I tell myself not to judge this moment and just be with her. I know he is here.

Now she reads the second version.

My Mother's Death

"Mom, do you want to go with them?" I ask. I know what the answer is. I don't blame them. This is not a life. But I still need to hear it.

"Yes, but they do not want…to steal the family," she tells me. This shocks me. But I don't know why it should. I mean, I clearly understand this. My mom is the center of this family and with her gone who knows what will happen…maybe we'll all drown.

Already my father and I are not speaking. He hates me. I do not agree with him. And he does not like that. I try to understand him, but I am angry that he does not treat her with respect. He lifts her roughly to put medicine on her bedsores. He talks in front of her as if she is not there. And worse, being a radiologist himself, he won't stop radiating this dying woman.

He says it's to keep her from pain, but the only pain I see is from the side effects. I just learned a new word today, "fistula." That is the hole that was just burned through her rectum into her vagina. Yes, I hate him too. Why won't he let this poor woman die? Forty-five years of marriage and he does not see what he is doing.

He is crazy with grief. Because I speak up, he has shut me out. He ignores me when I come to visit. I help take care of her in the day while he is working. I know she will not last much longer so I refuse to let him push me away. Last week I left him a birthday present hoping to make peace. It still sits in the entry unopened. He refuses to accept it. So there it sits for everyone to see his rejection of me. But I know she knows what's going on here and so do they.

"Mom, they're not stealing the family. Because of you, we're strong. We'll get through this. Your love will live on in all of us. We're all just scared right now but it will be OK," I lie to her.

"We must transcend this," she says.

Transcend? This is not my mother's type of word. I have never heard her use this expression.

— • • • —

I look around the room. "What is so stirring, perhaps mystical, even possibly mythical about this moment is not that she remembered more of the moment and wrote it in a simpler, more vivid way. What is remarkable is that she began to remember the whole story differently. At first she remembered her mother talking to her dead brother. But upon further probing she recollected that she had heard her mother doing something far more mysterious—talking to people on the other side—people whom Stephanie could barely picture—and

*Expanding
the Climax
of the Story*

93

Stephanie recognized that her mother was using the language of transformation, all difficult for someone steeped in religion to accept. But Stephanie's subconscious was beginning to let this information into her consciousness. This is remarkable writing and remarkable self-probing."

For the purpose of our self-discovery, it is important that every significant voice or person in a vivid moment be present, so we want to expand our climax wherever possible.

The truth of the event will gradually yield itself to the "path of the pen" as we rewrite the story. From time to time, as we reach the end of a story, we suddenly realize that our pen is telling us a different story from the one we had been writing. When this happens, we need to follow the path of the pen.

Stephanie's experience is a powerful example of this. Her mother was dying of cancer; Stephanie stayed with her mother most of that time. Where others shied away from intimacy, Stephanie drew closer. The experience was extraordinary but puzzling to her, though she didn't know quite why.

In the rewrite, we find that the climatic moment has been expanded. In the expanding, Stephanie began recollecting that the event actually happened a bit differently than she first remembered: Her mother was in the presence of a number of people she loved, not just Gary, her brother.

And a little later, as she continues to work her way through the climax, Stephanie opens it up even wider, giving us more of her feelings and her mother's feelings, and more of the mystery and the wonder of the death experience.

Expanding the climax of the story does three important things:

1. A fully fleshed-out climax creates intense interest in the reader. If the reader is ever to feel a bond with you and your story, it will come about through an intimate and vivid unfolding of the climax.

2. A better, more balanced story will appear. Most stories as they are first written tend to be heavy in the beginning—too wordy, too detailed— and too light in the climax. Stephanie's story is no exception. Better balance means that in rewriting, you may drop some things from the beginning while expanding your climax.

3. In locating the climax and fleshing it out, you may find that the story is actually about something other than what you thought it was about when you began.

While opening up the climax, Stephanie discovered that her story was really about the gift her terminally ill mother was giving her: a glimpse into the other side. Originally she thought the story was about her mother and her brother, which turned out to be the path into the story. The joy for us, the readers, is feeling each feeling, savoring each moment of this powerful episode in Stephanie's life: her mother's aiding Stephanie's transformation in becoming a more spiritual person.

Conclusion

As my students finish reading their stories and most of their questions have been answered, I commend them for their honesty, for the quality of their writing and their insights, and for their contributions to the cohesiveness of the group.

"Where do we go from here, Bernard?" asks Tamara. "This feels like just the beginning." I look around the room. Most of them are intent on my answer.

"Tamara's right," I reply. "Now that we know how to write in a powerful, vigorous style that is our own, we can explore a deeper, perhaps more shadowy, even more expressive side of ourselves, plunging into hidden memories and hidden meanings still to be unearthed. This is the ground we will cover in the next workshop."

Tamara nods her head in approval as do most of the people in the room, including Stephanie. As we shake hands and exchange hugs at the door, I feel like the pastor of some very unusual church. "Hmm," I smile to myself. "That's okay." I watch as the two of them walk out together. I wonder what stories will emerge next.

The last to leave is Arthur. "I've enjoyed this workshop, Bernard. I really have. I think I will wait before I take the next workshop. I need to just write for a while, see if I can use what you've been teaching. It is very interesting."

"That's as it should be, Arthur. Each of us has to go at this material at his own pace. Some of us need to do a lot of writing and re-experiencing before we plunge into the more soul-searching parts of the experience."

Arthur shrugs his shoulders and nods his head, still a bit mystified. He turns to leave, then turns back. "Is it because I am a man that I am having such difficulties getting back into my past as if I were a child?"

I put my arm around his shoulders. "It's not easy for us to be men and express ourselves openly, with feeling. Most of our stories are about actions because that is how we experience life. We have to work hard to know what we feel between our moments of action." He nods his head. "We have to have two sets of eyes: one that looks outward and participates in the actions of the world, the other that knows what we are feeling inside, physically and emotionally, each moment of our lives. It is not easy for us, as men, to do this. But we are making progress."

Arthur shakes my hand. "Thank you, Bernard."

"Hold on a second, Arthur," I say. "Come with me." We walk to my car and I rummage through my back seat, which is piled high with books and manuscripts. I take out a manuscript and look for a section called "Stories."

"These are good examples of men writing about their childhood with feeling, as well as action and dialogue. Read the stories of Sam Glenn and Eddie White. You'll see what I am talking about."

As I watch Arthur, I notice a sadness…and a hopefulness. Of all the people who will move on to the next phase of the writing process, I think Arthur is the one who needs it the most. Arthur, who still dwells unseen in the shadows of the closet, pushed there by three older, louder brothers who crave the spotlight in their family and get it. Will Arthur take the next step and step out onto center stage in his own life? I smile to myself as I see him lean against the car, already reading the first of the stories.

 EXERCISE

In every story we write, we must strive to create emotional highs and lows, culminating in finding and uncovering the climax of the story. If we do not do this, then our stories will look like unending links of sausage, each story looking like the previous one. Not a good thing.

HIGHLIGHTING VIVID MOMENTS

Locate the climax of one of your stories and expand it by doing any or all of the following:

- Add more dialogue, particularly if it is poignant, intense, and revealing.
- Expand and note a character's actions that reveal his or her qualities.
- Record more of your, the narrator's, feelings about the event.
- Add intense color or use dramatic lighting to intensify emotions.

The more of this you do, the more quickly the action will move and the more it will seem to suspend the reader in the middle of it, as happens in the famous sequence (if memory serves correctly) from Claude Lelouch's film *A Man and a Woman*, previously discussed in Chapter 6, in which Jean-Louis Trintignant hops off the train and sweeps up Anouk Aimée in his arms, the lovers rotate clockwise, while the camera circles them counterclockwise in slow motion, creating a web of intimacy and hunger sealed off from the outside world. Once you have expanded the climax of your story, note any ways in which it changes the story's meaning.

From Rewrite to Insight:
Uncovering Hidden Memories

In the middle of an in-service training I am giving at a Kaiser Permanente Chemical Dependency Unit, I suggest that the group begin the second assignment, writing a vivid memory from birth to twelve years of age. In the back of the room, I hear a mumble of some kind.

"I'm sorry, I didn't hear that," I say.

The person I thought had spoken looks embarrassed, as though I have caught him talking in school. "I said, 'How can I do that?'" he replies. "I was so drugged out, I didn't know who or where I was the first twenty-five years of my life.'"

Good point. If we don't remember who, where, and how we were, how can we take stock of our lives?

Like objects encrusted by coral far beneath the ocean's surface, our memories often lie hidden away. We have to pry off what surrounds them to uncover what lies beneath. Once that is done, we can begin to assess our lives. We must ask ourselves, *What is it that I know, that feels better remaining unknown?* How do we find the answer to this question?

The first step is to explore what we *do* remember. That is, if we remember nothing before twenty-five, we write a story about what we recollect at twenty-five.

Unearthing hidden memories is a bit like digging a mine. We sink a shaft where there is something we can dig into. Little by little, if we are willing to write as vividly as we can about the earliest things we remember, the memory will open up. If we are diligent, we will discover that somewhere in that memory is a clue to other memories.

There are any number of other techniques we can also try, such as writing with our nondominant hand, automatic writing, and hypnotherapy, to uncover hidden memories. I encourage exploring them all. These alternate approaches work well because each in its own way gets past the self-critic that keeps so much of our thoughts, memories, and yearnings tightly in its grasp. This is especially true if you are right-handed because the right hand is closely connected to the analytical, problem-solving, left side of the brain. The nondominant hand in a right-handed person—the left hand—is much more creative and less apt to be governed by the shoulds and shouldn'ts of the left-brained right hand.

The truth of this came to me very strongly some years ago. For a long time, I tried writing creatively, but without much success. Then along came the computer. At the keyboard I could type with both hands, correcting and moving things around almost as quickly as I could think. Sometime after that my sister asked, "Did you know you were left-handed as a child?" I reacted with surprise. "Dad didn't think it would be good for you to be left-handed," she continued, "so he had you changed."

As our memory begins to unfold, we need to keep writing stories that reach back farther and farther, to earlier and earlier times. The roots of the patterns of behavior we want to change lie in these early memories. At some point we may be able to see our behavior patterns, but until we see what they are rooted in, we will probably continue fighting with them, perhaps forever.

In a workshop I gave for the Los Angeles Actors Theater in the late 1980s, composed of the nine writers who gathered each Saturday for six weeks, one woman's stories showed remarkable changes from one week to the next. A trim, attractive, long-distance runner who was raised in convent schools as a young child, Lettie held us in shocked silence as we experienced her ever-changing story. As I listened, I noticed how powerful an experience it is for us as listeners to hear earlier drafts incorporated into the fabric of the storytelling experience.

Leaving the Farm   *by Lettie Watkins*   (FIRST DRAFT)

As we stepped out the door to the waiting car in the driveway, my mother turns to my brother and me and says, "Take a last look. We will never come back."

What does she mean? Never smell the sweetness of the alfalfa fields again? Never pick wildflowers again? Never roam the fields again on bare horseback? Never be lulled to sleep by the wind singing through the pine trees outside my bedroom window? Never see the countryside bathed in moonlight?

I accepted what my mother said, because I loved her. She would never, never do anything to hurt me, but a small part of me still rebelled. A large part of me hurt.

As my mother slid into the driver's seat I scooted over so that I could be close to her.

We backed out the driveway and she suddenly stopped the car. She looked like she wanted to say something. My brother and I sit dumbly staring at her face waiting for a sign of what to do.

Mother slowly took off her dark glasses she had been wearing. Her eyes were swollen shut. The swollen area is angry with red, blue, green and yellow bruises around them. I sit horrified. The only sound is the car motor and the drone of small insects. I look straight ahead at the dusty road which leads from our house to the highway. I can't bear to look at her again.

I heard her voice say quietly, "Your father did this to me. That's why we must leave." Something inside my head says, "No, no, no."

Lettie Watkins   *Lettie is a grandmother whose great passion in life is long-distance running. She writes in order to leave a legacy to her children.*

— • • • —

After writing her memory down on paper, Lettie began to realize that certain parts of it were inaccurate. As she went over the memory again, she realized that she had not first seen her mother's beaten face in the car, but earlier and somewhere else. Rewriting *in the present tense* helped her recall the truth of what had happened.

Leaving the Farm   (FIRST REWRITE)

Something woke me up. I turned and saw my mother standing in the doorway of the bedroom. She had on what she called a house dress, with pretty little flowers all over it. Mother always looked pretty and neat even when she was alone. She said to me many times, "We must always be ready for company. Be proud of ourselves and what belongs to us."

This morning she did not look very proud. Strange that she did not come in and sit on my bed as she usually did to give me my good morning kiss. I could feel her reaching out to me although she hadn't moved. I didn't know what to do so I said, "Good morning."

She still didn't move. I sat up so it would be easier for her to kiss me. She finally left the doorway and walked toward me. The one board creaking as I knew it would. The board was left that way on purpose. At certain times, it was a signal to anyone in the basement tending the still that he should stay there and be quiet.

As my mother got closer I saw her face more clearly. I thought I was dreaming. Her beautiful blue eyes, which she was so proud of, were slits. Her whole face looked like a stranger's. It was covered with ugly bruises— purple, yellow, green. Her lips were puffy and cut with little bits of dried blood on them. The thought went through my mind, "Oh, I hope she doesn't kiss me." I felt bad for having that thought because I loved her so much.

When she finally spoke, her voice sounded hard. "Your father did this to me and we are going to have to move, so he won't have a chance to do this again." I just stared at her. I could not think. I felt numb.

My whole world fell apart at that moment.

Why did Lettie's mind play tricks on her, putting the incident in the car rather than in the bedroom? Perhaps placing the event some distance from where it actually happened made it less painful.

After hearing Lettie's rewrite, the other members of the workshop sensed there was still more to be told. We all wanted to know more about how she felt as the episode was unfolding and more about her father's character—anything that would help her understand such a temper. In particular, we wanted to know what "my world fell apart at that moment" meant. We wanted to *see* it.

So in the second rewrite, Lettie changes the verbs from past to present tense so that the incident unfolds in front of her and the reader, a process that also helps her remember the incident more clearly. In the second rewrite, the new material is shown in italics.

Leaving the Farm   (SECOND REWRITE)

Something wakes me up. I turn and see my mother standing in the door- way of the bedroom. She has on what she calls a house dress, with pretty little flowers all over it. Mother always looks pretty and neat even when she is alone. She has said to me many times, "We must always be ready for company. Be proud of ourselves and what belongs to us."

This morning she does not look very proud. Strange that she does not come in and sit on my bed as she usually does to give me my good morning kiss. I don't know what to do so I say, "Good morning," *as though things are normal. She still does not speak or move. I suddenly feel cold. Something is not right. Maybe if I sit up it will be easier for her to kiss me.*

I wait. She finally moves from the doorway and walks toward me, one board creaking as I knew it would. The board is left that way on purpose.

Writing
from
Within:
The Next
Generation

100

At certain times, it is a signal to anyone in the basement tending the still that he should stay there and be quiet. *My daddy is what is called a Bootlegger. That means that he makes whisky and sells it to other people. This is against the law. I wish he would not do it.*

I hate making trips to the city with my mother driving the car, the rear seat filled with big cans of the awful-smelling alcohol. A big Indian blanket always covers the cans. Once a policeman stopped us and my mother thought for sure we would be caught. But we weren't, we just got a ticket.

As my mother gets closer I see her face more clearly. I must be dreaming. Her beautiful blue eyes, which she is so proud of, are slits. *She looks Japanese.* This is a stranger's face, the skin, the ugly colors—purple, yellow, green. Her lips are big with little bits of dried blood on them. I think, "Oh, I hope she doesn't kiss me." I feel bad for having that thought because I love her so much.

When she finally speaks, her voice sounds hard. "Your father did this to me and we are going to have to move, so he won't have a chance to do this again. *You and your brother will be living with Nona until I can find work. I promise we will be together again.*"

Her chin moves in a way that tells me she is going to cry. Sure enough the tears roll down her cheeks and are allowed to drop on her breasts. Outside, the sun dims.

Inside, the air is chilled. The silence is heavy—broken only by the quiet scratching of the horn toads in their sandbox. I want to squash them. The movie star pictures are crooked. I want to tear them off the wall. The buzzing of the bees gets on my nerves. I want to cry but I don't.

I just remain silent. But inside I am screaming, 'I don't care what the reason is! I don't want to leave. This is my home!!'

We move to the city. There is a divorce.

• • •

In the new draft of her story, Lettie has substantially expanded the last line, "My world fell apart." Her memory has yielded more dialogue: "You and your brother will be living with Nona." It also yielded vivid details of tears, sun, air, sounds, and her experience of feeling unable to handle any more stress. In Lettie's search for the truth of what happened, her story became much more artistically powerful.

Most of all, Lettie's story reminds us that the search for truth can go on within all of us if we encourage it—that the deepest layers of our inner selves can be reached if we make the effort. The process of writing draft after draft, uncovering bits of the truth each time, is our ally. Once our subconscious releases a bit of the truth to the paper (or computer) before us, it is free of that piece and will relinquish another to see if we can handle that information, too.

It is as if the memory has a mind of its own: If we handle what it reveals to us with reasonable skepticism and an honest desire for more, it *will* yield more.

For other examples of memories yielding hidden truths in rewrites, please review the changes that took place between the first and second drafts of the excerpts from Stephanie Bernardi's story "My Mother's Death" (see pages 89–93) and between the first and second drafts of my story "Dad's Death" (see pages 59–62).

 EXERCISE

If we choose to rewrite quite a bit, our memory bank will likely let go of long-concealed recollections, providing us with a truer and truer version of stories we may think we have recollected accurately. Writing a story and telling a story are two quite different things.

PEELING THE SKIN FROM OUR MEMORIES

Following Lettie's example, try now to rewrite one of your stories to see if any hidden moments emerge, moments you could not have predicted but that speak to you from deep within.

If you are not sure where to begin, ask yourself these questions: "What else would someone want to know about this incident?" "Is there anything important that I have left out of or censored from the story?" Pay attention to the gnawing feelings in the pit of your stomach, feelings that say "it didn't happen this way." If you know there is more but don't recall it, try improvising to see whether you can create something to which your subconscious will react—probably by revealing the truth of what happened.

You see, the subconscious *does* want you to know the truth, but since it is charged with keeping you on an even keel emotionally, it will reveal what is there *only* if it is sure you are ready to see, hear, and feel it.

Writing
from
Within:
The Next
Generation

102

Amplifying the Basic Steps in "Writing from Within": Narrative, Dialogue, and Inner Thoughts and Feelings

"Would you help my husband?" asked Jacqui Tousley, an attractive woman in her sixties, after a session of a life-story writing course I taught at the University of California at Irvine. "For more than fifty years, he has wanted to be a novelist but got sidetracked." She paused a moment.

Jacqui told me that as a young man, her husband, Dirk, went to Mexico to write, inspired by the life of Ernest Hemingway, but found himself more interested in drinking with the locals than in writing. Finally he returned to the United States with nothing written.

"I believe he can do it. I believe there is a novelist inside him," she continued. "I would be grateful to you if you would help him."

I wondered if Dirk really had the talent or will to write but agreed to start a private workshop in Playa del Rey for a few interested people, among them Karl Grey.

Dirk's first effort showed little that was remarkable; however, after I suggested he get rid of anything that sounded adult and focus on writing simple narratives with lots of dialogue, details, and inner thoughts and feelings, he returned with a story that demonstrated that Jacqui was right: He had a wonderful writing style, a terrific eye for detail and dialogue, and a strong desire to create.

● ● ●

Having explored the basic steps described in Part I and having written and rewritten several of your own stories using several advanced writing techniques, you are now ready to approach these steps in a more sophisticated way—to build on what you have done so far—so your writing becomes even more effective. As I indicated in the Introduction, in doing so, you will learn to better reflect the inner life and feelings of your characters, especially the main character—often you.

In telling a story, every writer has three essential ingredients to work with: *narrative*, *dialogue*, and *inner thoughts and feelings*. The way in which you manipulate these ingredients dictates the style that emerges and the pleasure the audience derives from the story.

Writing
from
Within:
The Next
Generation

104

chapter 10

Expanding Narrative

The word "narrative" is a fancy word for "story"; however, in the world of writing, narrative means telling the facts that move the story forward, sometimes without concern for the characters' particular qualities and the actions that emerge from these qualities.

When is narrative not narrative? For a great many writers and teachers of writing, narrative is interpreted as meaning a series of plot points that move the story from point A to point B to point C. If this is true, a world of writers' concerns such as backstory and character description exists in a kind of never-never land. Here is an example from an early draft of one of J.D. Tousley's stories, which eventually evolved into his novel, *Dangling in the Adios:*

> My life as a young pool hustler was about as sweet as life gets. In those days, long before MasterCard, when you could sit down at a nice clean lunch counter and get a bowl of steaming chili for a quarter, a slab of apple pie juicier than Mom made for a dime, and a steaming cup of coffee with free refills for a nickel, I usually carried at least two hundred bucks in my right front pocket and a couple of fifties hidden in my wallet. So I was doing all right.
>
> I'm telling you, business life couldn't have been sweeter, played out day by day on a rectangle of green felt four and one half feet wide by nine feet long. And I knew every inch of it.

In a way, this is good narrative (objective fact telling), but it is also *not* narrative. In fact, these two paragraphs are backstory to the story the writer intends to tell. The reader knows it is backstory because he mentions the present: "in those days, long before MasterCard...."

Here is the story after a few more drafts:

I've had it with stuck-up sorority girls. They act like they're too grand to do it, then when they finally let you in, they own you lock, stock, and barrel. Take Carolyn Forsythe, for instance, safely locked away from us college boys in her panty girdle. After we first met, I rolled around with her in the backseat of my convertible every night for two weeks, trying to pry her out of that medieval contraption, until late one night I got her to wriggle out of it on her own and start enjoying life. And it's been great. I never had it so steady before. But I'm paying for it with my freedom. Whenever Carolyn crooks her finger, I'm supposed to roll over and bark. You'd think she owned me. Now she's ragging me to quit playing nine ball so we can study together. Hell, I don't need study. That's what brains are for. And I'm not about to give up nine ball. Pool is my life, and besides, it brings in about thirty bucks a week.

How different with Cricket, my appreciative little drugstore clerk. On our second date I slid her skimpy panties down her bare legs and off her feet in a flash, what with no elastic wall, hooks, wires, or buttons to overcome. Panties off, and there it was. When we're not making love, she spends a lot of time in the crook of my arm, looking up at me attentively and asking questions I can answer.

I met Cricket a couple of weeks ago. She clerks at the drugstore around the corner from campus. One day I went in to buy a comb. Five minutes later, I had a new comb and a new girlfriend. Mostly I take her to drive-in movies and an out-of-the-way beer joint called Snookums in south Kansas City where I won't run into anyone Carolyn knows. Carolyn has gone home to St. Louis for a few weeks during summer break, which gives Cricket and me time to get acquainted.

Sex with Cricket is the best ever. Just thinking about her gives me a warm feeling inside I've never had before. Nothing's perfect though. Her father doesn't like me, and he's getting in my way. Just today Cricket reminded me on the phone that tonight is our seventh date. "Daddy raises Cain if I go steady," she said. "We'll have to find another way to meet before he goes berserk."

Writing
from
Within:
The Next
Generation

106

This excerpt is still narrative—that is, narrative in style, with no dialogue or inner thoughts and feelings. The narrative has transmuted itself into little pieces of action and backstory that do not move the story forward, necessarily, but do give a picture of the circumstances in which the central character finds himself. Already he's in a vise and he's being squeezed. The character qualities of Carolyn and Cricket abound: controlling, possessive, uptight Carolyn; spontaneous, innocent, carefree, adoring Cricket.

As the story progresses, the author brings the characters into greater focus through dialogue and inner thoughts and feelings:

It's nearly dark but still hot and humid as I park my car in front of Cricket's house, get out, and look around. My bright green Mercury convertible is definitely out of place in this working-class neighborhood of fading white frame houses and scrubby lawns. Though World War II has been over four years, some of the houses still display Gold Stars in their front windows.

I'm dressed in a navy blue polo shirt, white duck pants, and cordovan loafers, perfect attire for a summer night date with a cute girl. I'm feeling good and looking good, ready for a Saturday night blast with Cricket.

Looks like I'm in luck. Daddy isn't sitting on the porch steps as usual, and his old tired Studebaker is nowhere in sight. Hot damn! I won't have to face him tonight. But my high spirits are short-lived. As I mount the steps, his gravelly voice coming from inside the screened porch begins the challenge.

"Well, if it ain't Joe College." His cheap cigar smoke hangs in the humid air.

"Evening, Mr. Horner," I muster, unable to see him through the screen. But once I'm inside the porch, I make him out in the dusk, swinging slowly back and forth in his porch swing.

"I brought you a Dutch Master."

"Tryin' to suck in with me, huh?"

I ignore the bastard's remark, hand him the Dutch Master, and ask, "Is Cricket ready yet?"

He rolls the cigar between thumb and forefinger, testing its freshness, before setting it aside on the porch railing. "Why the hell you call her Cricket? Her name's Josephine. If I wanted her to be Cricket, I'd uh named her Cricket."

"Harry, leave that boy alone," comes Mrs. Horner's voice from the darkest side of the porch. "Evenin' to you, Tack."

"Hello, ma'am. I didn't see you," I say, grateful for a second in my corner.

In this brief paragraph, the author gives a picture of the scene as the character sees it: "dark…hot, humid…bright green Mercury…out of place…fading white frame…houses display Gold Stars…." The character is in the present, but Cricket's family and their neighbors all seem locked in the past.

Then the author gives a bit of character assessment through a description of how Tack is dressed: "navy blue polo shirt, white duck pants, cordovan loafers…feeling good and looking good…." He knows he's the wave of the future, and he knows that his cute little date, Cricket, will get that.

He follows this description with some inner thoughts and feelings: "in luck…old tired Studebaker…nowhere…Hot damn! I won't have to face him tonight." These feelings of elation are short-lived. "his gravelly voice…'Well, if it ain't Joe College….'"

In the short space of five paragraphs, the author has provided a description of the actions, attitudes, and circumstances of the central character, his taste for drama, his love of pool (nine ball), his careful planning of his appearance, his inner thoughts and feelings, and some good dialogue that tells the reader about Tack, Cricket's father, and Cricket's mother. The reader knows Tack plans to try to get away with something, and, sooner or later, he will have to confront both obstacles—Cricket's father and the sorority girl he also dates.

In this setup for the story he intends to tell, the author gives a full picture of the wants, desires, and intentions of this kid and the way he plans to get what he wants, even as the author describes several obstacles that the kid will have to overcome.

In a first draft it doesn't matter whether the narrative is flat or rich. In subsequent rewrites, Tousley's narrative becomes richer through the use of dialogue, actions, details, character qualities, setting, and backstory. None of these attributes necessarily moves the story along; however, they make the story infinitely more compelling, so as the story does move along, the reader cares more about the characters and the outcome. (For the narrative to move along, something has to happen very soon, and that something is the appearance of Cricket.)

For the purposes of this book, I suggest you consider narrative as anything other than dialogue or inner thoughts and feelings, for the simple reason that backstory, character descriptions, details, and imagery (visual motifs) all do move the story forward, at least indirectly.

Writing
from
Within:
The Next
Generation

108

Improvising Dialogue

In the original *Writing from Within*, I felt it sufficient to point out that moving a story from all narrative to some narrative with spicy dialogue would make the story better, more interesting, and more revealing of the characters who speak.

However, more needs to be said about dialogue. In the nineteenth century, such novels as those of Charles Dickens, William Thackeray, and Herman Melville contained long passages of all narrative. Dialogue was sprinkled in here and there. Theodore Dreiser filled his pages with cumbersome narrative and then punctuated the narrative with pungent, expressive dialogue. By the time F. Scott Fitzgerald emerged in the late 1920s, the characters speak more and more often with less narrative needed to move the story along. Ernest Hemingway and John Steinbeck in the 1930s and 1940s expressed themselves almost completely in dialogue and action.

What is the importance of dialogue? Dialogue is comparable to a two-shot in a motion picture (a shot with two characters in it). It provides a strong sense of relationship between or among characters. Using modern, lightweight cameras, and dollies, deft film directors compose the frames of their films so long shots, medium shorts (two shots), and close-ups occur within single takes. Writers can do the same thing.

The following is a short passage from one of my student's stories. Imagine this opening sequence as a filmed sequence employing establishing shots, two shots, and close-ups:

The Turkish Ambassador   *by Paula Moore Diggs*

"You know what a Turkish ambassador is, don't you?" Tom Rankin's deep-set blue eyes hold mine as he leans against the wall between the living room and kitchen at the Winders' home. Another English Department party. Our corporate benefactor, Dupont, gave the U. of Del. a huge endowment to bring big names on campus for a lecture series. The English Department got a chunk to bring famous authors here in hopes of putting Delaware on the cultural map. Sam, our department chair, explained to me that because I'm the youngest at twenty-six and best looking (which isn't saying a lot), I'd be one of the few wives included in the festivities. He didn't mention my cum laude degree... oh well. That invite didn't include lectures, just the parties where old guys run their hands up under my skirt at dinner.

"No, I don't know what a Turkish ambassador is," I tell him. Tom gives me a sly look. He was at the lecture that author James Dickey gave. Dickey's book *Deliverance* was just made into a film. He even played a part in it and strummed his banjo. A very big name. "Dickey told us a Turkish ambassador is sent in when the director thinks he may be losing the audience's interest," Tom tells me. "A guy walks across the scene, everyone says, 'Who's that?' Someone answers, 'the Turkish Ambassador,' music swells, and the audience is hooked, waiting to see what will happen. Dickey talked a lot about filmmaking, then he played his banjo." Tom smiles at me and leans further against the wall.

Next to him on a bookcase rests the Winders' son's fish tank. Fish are at the top gasping for air. The water needs to be changed. One fish floats slowly to the bottom. Gills pumping. Tom's mouth keeps moving faster, but no words come out. He slides noiselessly down the wall and sits, feet splayed out. Finally topples over on his side, mouth still moving. Cigarette smoke and the reek of alcohol rush into my face as this movement of his large six-foot frame disturbs the air. Sloshed.

If this were a film, the challenge would be to create in film terms all the backstory that the author has given. To do so using inner thoughts and feelings seldom works unless it's done very briefly and runs counter to the expressions and actions of the characters. Apart from that, imagine the camera focusing on the two characters in conversation, then recomposing to catch glimpses of other things, such as the fish gulping for air—a parallel to Tom's drifting down the wall, sloshed, dead for all intents and purposes.

Virtually none of this is narrative—that is, virtually none of it moves the story along in terms of plot. The writer provides backstory and, using dialogue, a sense of relationship between the main character and Tom as well as a sense of the pointlessness of the party itself. Taken together, the backstory, dialogue, and description of the texture and atmosphere yield a feeling of what the characters want to get away from, which is what happens as the story unfolds.

Writing
from
Within:
The Next
Generation

110

Creating Vivid Dialogue by Dropping Subjects and Verbs

The most vivid stories that are written or appear on screen as films and television programs often have colorful dialogue. A number of ways to create interesting dialogue exist.

Perhaps the simplest way to create vivid dialogue is to *eliminate the subject and/or the verb from the sentence.*

Here is an example from a story by another student, Dale Crum, in his story "Smoke Rings." Let's look at the first line of dialogue from his story:

"Stunt your growth," my dad used to say.

In this case, Dale dropped both the subject and verb ("It will"). The sentence becomes more effective because a lot of people do talk this way, with just a few words. The next line of dialogue:

Someone rattles the doorknob. Mama calls, "Dale, you in there?"

This time, Dale's mother drops the verb of the sentence ("Dale, [are] you in there?"). Once again, the sentence becomes livelier without the verb in it, because it accurately reflects the way real people talk.

Creating Vivid Dialogue by Having Characters Talk at Cross-Purposes

A second way of creating lively dialogue is for the people in the scene to talk to each other without entirely hearing or responding to what the other person is saying. This technique is called *talking at cross-purposes.* Here is another line from the opening of Dale's story:

I pick up the towel stuffed in the crack at the bottom of the door, spray air freshener all around, and unlock the door.
Mama rushes in. She comes out with a sniff. "Thought you quit."
"Yeah, going to college."
"Not what I meant. You got a good job at Boeing."

In this exchange, Mama nails Dale for smoking in the bathroom. He pretends she is talking about quitting school, deflecting her criticism of him and the smell of cigarette smoke onto a subject of greater importance. She immediately picks up on the new theme—going to college—and tries to argue with him in the sentence, "Not what I meant." In this sentence, the subject and verb have again been dropped ("[That is] not what I meant").

Interesting, huh? Well, this is how people do talk to each other—ideas move quickly from one person to the next without either speaker finishing thoughts or sentences, especially when one person tries to convince another to change his behavior, opinions, or both.

If a writer has characters speak expressively about themselves without talking directly about the thing that matters most to them, this type of dialogue is called "off the money." Alternatively, dialogue that says exactly what the character is thinking or feeling is often boring and lacks believability. This style of dialogue is called "on-the-money" writing. It takes a great deal of effort to become skilled at writing "off-the-money" dialogue, but the effort is always worth the trouble.

Creating Vivid Dialogue by Employing a "Hook"

A third approach to dialogue is to employ what might loosely be called a "hook." In this technique, one character says a line of dialogue, and then the character who speaks next repeats that line. For example:

> Janine shakes her head. "Tom, you're the most stubborn man I've ever met."
>
> Tom reacts with surprise. "Stubborn, me?"
>
> She laughs and hands him an apple. "Stubborn, me?" She shakes her head. "You seem so innocent."

In this brief exchange, the repetition of the lines of dialogue accomplishes several things. First of all, it is clear that Tom is really listening to Janine. Second, her line of dialogue nails a character quality in Tom that he has to deal with. Third, in handing him the apple, it clear that she likes Tom and may give him another chance to change, adjust, or do whatever he must to keep her interested.

As a writer, you may say, "Well, all of this is fine if you are a fiction writer, but I'm just writing life stories." In fact, all the techniques that I discuss are just as relevant to the palette of the nonfiction writer as to the fiction writer. If the life writer is skilled in the use of these techniques, he or she will begin to notice situations occurring in real life that reflect the techniques just discussed. So in the final analysis, the aim of these techniques is to help writers fine-tune their ability to listen to and observe life as it passes by.

Writing
from
Within:
The Next
Generation

112

chapter 12

Imagining Inner Thoughts and Feelings

Writing inner thoughts and feelings is a huge challenge for any writer. Writing or recording inner thoughts and feelings came at a late stage in the history of the development of writing. The first stage originated in ancient Mesopotamia, at a small village called Ebla, where clay tablets dating back some five thousand years have been found. These tablets were inscribed with symbols that indicated the recording of food stores and are the oldest-known records of writing.

The second stage occurred some five hundred to one thousand years ago, when storytelling began to be recorded in the epics of Homer's *The Iliad* and *The Odyssey*. These epics are told almost entirely in a narrative style.

The third phase occurred during the Renaissance, especially in England, but to an extent in Italy as well, where Niccolo Machiavelli and William Shakespeare demonstrated that dialogue could point the way toward a fascinating interplay of relationships, with an occasional foray into inner thoughts and feelings.

Over the next several hundred years, the novel in the hands of Richardson, Stendhal, Dostoevsky, and Melville included dynamic adventures (narratives) punctuated by poignant moments of relationship (dialogue). As mentioned in Chapter 4, often these narratives suggest a godlike point of view, as in Melville and Dostoevsky, in which a transcendent force still operates in the universe, although Dostoevsky looks more closely into the inner thoughts of the central character.

In the intensely masculine writing of Ernest Hemingway, the reader confronts a world in which very little narrative is present, suggesting no organizing force in the universe. Instead, interpersonal forces are in conflict, as reflected in revealing dialogue and occasional glimpses into the characters' inner thoughts.

Hemingway's approach to writing inner thoughts and feelings will be discussed more in Chapter 30.

When an author uses the third person to write about a character and the character's actions, the author may also use that third person to express intimate thoughts and feelings. If an author chooses to write the central character in the first person, then other choices become available when expressing inner thoughts and feelings. Here is a moment from a story entitled "The Garage" by a student of mine, Karl Grey (the complete story can be found on page 273):

"Please let me in! Please unlock the door." I can hear my mother on the other side laughing at me. I'm pounding on the door, and I'm sure the whole neighborhood can see me in my underwear. They have all come out of their houses and are standing in the dark street watching me like I'm on the screen at a drive-in movie. I can hear them laughing at me and my mother laughing at me and I can't stand the way I feel. I am so filled with panic.

I pound and pound on the door, but all I hear is the echo of laughing from both sides colliding on me. It's like this dream that I have over and over. I am walking on a sidewalk when all of a sudden I'm naked. I want to hide so that the other people on the sidewalk don't see me so I duck around behind the row of trees that is between the street and the sidewalk but the street is full of cars and all of the drivers can see me so I go back around the trees but then the sidewalk people can see me and pretty soon they have all stopped and all of the cars have stopped and they are all laughing and blowing the horns and saying, "Look at the naked fat kid. Does he even have a dick?" The sound gets louder and louder and I can't get away.

CRASH!

The kitchen door flies off the hinges and wood splinters as it hits the stove on the other side of the kitchen. I am in the house before the door hits the ground. My mother screams, and the scotch and water breaks on the floor. My stepfather has his belt undone by now and is pulling it through the loops of his pants.

I am running, into the den, into the cool…and my back stings, again and again, as I drop to the floor and roll myself into a ball and take it on my back. I'm safe now. I'm inside myself, and nobody can see me while he continues to hit me with the doubled-up belt.

"Thank you, ladies and gentlemen, it's been a really big shooooow tonight. Next week on this stage, Elvis Presley"…and the crowd screams and my back stings, but it's cool in here and nobody can see me.

By using the first person, the writer makes the sense of the character's pain all the more acute:

Writing
from
Within:
The Next
Generation

114

I am running, into the den, into the cool…and my back stings, again and again, as I drop to the floor and roll myself into a ball and take it on my back. I'm safe now. I'm inside myself, and nobody can see me while he continues to hit me with the doubled-up belt.

The reader feels the sting of the belt even as the character has withdrawn into a deep, remote place inside himself:

…roll myself into a ball…take it on my back…safe now. I'm inside myself…nobody can see me…he continues to hit me with the doubled-up belt.

Another interesting use of inner thoughts and feelings occurs when dialogue among two or more people is infused with the inner thoughts and feelings of the main character. The following is a simple example that illustrates this point:

Woman A: "Oh, darling, I love your hair. Where did you go to have it done?"
Woman B: "Thank you, dear, it's such a mess, but I'm glad you like it. Well, see you at bridge on Friday."

This sounds like typical, mundane, throwaway dialogue, yes? Now let's look at what happens when we add inner thoughts and feelings.

Woman A: "Oh, darling, I love your hair. Where did you go to have it done?"
Woman B: "Thank you, dear, it's such a mess, but I'm glad you like it." *Love my hair?! Love my hair?! I saw you at lunch yesterday with my husband — making eyes at him, you slut. You conniving slut. So he and I had an argument. So what! And you're going to lunch with him? I'll make life miserable for you. Oh, yes, I will.* "Well, see you at bridge on Friday."

Here the inner world and the outer world are at odds with one another. We, the readers, have a chance to see that woman B is perfectly content to hide her feelings from the outer world—Woman A—which is what many of us do, in fact must do, in life, in order to survive.

Note: You will have noticed that I have italicized the inner thoughts and feelings. Some books on writing style recommend the use of single quotes or no quotes to set off inner thoughts and feelings. My experience is that the use of single quotes or no quotes creates confusion. The use of italics creates a different feel and, to my eye, gives more of a sense of being "*inner*" than "outer." Use what works best for you.

Using the Basic Techniques with Challenging Subject Matter

You now have a wealth of writing techniques at your fingertips and, after several weeks, perhaps months, of working on your memoirs, have probably recorded quite a few memories from your childhood.

In fact, you probably have as much technique as you will ever need. Your style will improve as you learn to edit your work more carefully, and your dialogue will become sharper as you listen closely to the conversations of those around you. But, all in all, you have the basic techniques you need.

You are now ready to take on more complicated experiences. The memories of childhood are often distant and powerful, so they form wonderful stories almost by themselves. Adult life, on the other hand, is rather like a vast sea. A few things really stand out, but, mostly, our life is a series of larger and smaller ripples that spread out around us as we move in various directions.

For most of us, revisiting these memories may be painful as well as joyous. But remember that visiting a painful past may be one of the most therapeutic things we can do for ourselves. By putting the experience on paper, reading it aloud, and hearing our words, we can begin to let go of it. Or perhaps we could say that it lets go of us.

At the same time, the incidents may show themselves to be part of a larger narrative, and they will take on a different meaning for us. We will begin to see patterns in our lives.

Perhaps we view our lives as failures. We may find that an accurate retelling of the first episode of this "failure" could lead to a reconciliation with relatives and friends we long ago alienated in some way. Or perhaps we were headed in a dull, ordinary, or pedestrian direction when one of these "firsts" in our lives occurred, redirecting our lives, and now we understand the meaning and value of the experience.

Virtually every religion on this earth has, at its center, a person who has undergone a journey of some kind, who has been through a number of trials and emerged on the other side in some way transformed or reborn. That heroic journey, so well chronicled by mythologist Joseph Campbell, is not the sole province of great or important men and women. In one way or another we are all embarked on our life's journey, are tested by life, and have the opportunity to be reborn. Some of us will experience this rebirth in the process of writing our life stories, because only then will our lives make sense.

All of this is preparation for growing older. Most of us are fearful about this. We envision a state in which our faculties have diminished with age, our loved ones may be gone, and we are alone. But that is only one way of viewing aging. There are other ways, and we will discuss them in a later chapter.

When you feel you are ready for this voyage, step down into this little boat of creativity and journey into the vast sea of memory that awaits you.

"Right You Are If You Think You Are": Viewing Life from Different Perspectives

"OK," I say to the ten people gathered around me. "Let's write about an experience we have in common and see how our perceptions compare." Most of the five couples smiling at me have been married to each other for fifty years or more and are here for a little relationship renewal.

"That should be fun," says Ruth, a woman in her early seventies. "I know exactly what we will write about."

"You want me to put on paper how I ran across the pavilion and slid at your feet, just to ask you to dance," laughs her husband, Jerry. Ruth smiles at the thought.

We are gathered together on the second evening of this weekend workshop in beautiful, rustic Carmel Valley, California. The feelings among the couples are, for the most part, warm and filled with loving memories.

The next morning, however, one couple takes me aside. Younger than the other couples, in their late forties, they are perplexed. "We can't agree on what to write about," says Mary, a wry, thoughtful woman. "When I suggest one thing, Jeff says no."

"Yeah, and everything I think we could write about, Mary doesn't want to expose," chuckles Jeff, her handsome, boyish husband. "She even suggested we write about not being able to agree on something to write about."

"Well, why not write about that—the experience of not being able to agree?" I laugh.

The two of them look at each other. "Hmm, why not," laughs Mary. "We will write about last night."

So off they go to write about not being able to agree on anything to write about.

Their situation is not unusual. Oftentimes, particularly within families, we will disagree with one another about what took place. Our memories of the same event just don't correspond.

In fact, few events are ever experienced or remembered the same way by two people. Most of us argue incessantly that our version is more accurate than the other person's. Even so, some of us, in writing our life stories, actually modify our own remembrances by including facts and the memories of others with whom we shared the experience. "There must be one version of what has happened that is correct," we suppose. Someone has to be right and someone has to be wrong.

One of the more interesting challenges of the modern age has been to come to grips with the idea that there is no one universal, immutable truth that exists outside our own perception. There are only points of view about what exists. If many of those points of view agree, we conclude that those agreeing points of view constitute a truth, at least for the time being. Differing points of view might arise later on, but this does not make them wrong or false or unreal. There are only differing truths, particularly where it concerns our memories.

In drama, this was articulated most forcefully in the early years of the twentieth century by Luigi Pirandello. His plays *Six Characters in Search of an Author*, *Tonight We Improvise*, and *Right You Are If You Think You Are* provide us with unusual points of view, each argued powerfully, leaving the playgoers to decide whose version is correct.

If we also approach the writing of our life stories from the position that there are no "truths," only versions of the truth, then we can respect, admire, even enjoy someone else's version of events or experiences that seem very different to us.

For this exercise, find an event or experience that left a strong impression on you, one that you are certain a close relative or friend of yours viewed quite differently. Correspond with your relative or friend, reaching some agreement about the event you are recollecting. Then each of you write about it. Exchange versions, compare them, and then write a commentary about the similarities and differences. My guess is that this task will result in a lot of laughs or lead to a great deal more understanding between you.

Below are Jeff's and Mary's stories of the experience of not being able to agree on what to write about.

The Undecided Story   *by Jeff Thompson*

Mary and I are each lying down on our own bed, across from one another on each side of the room.

She says to me "O.K., we need to decide on what we are going to write about, or would you prefer to write your own story?"

"No," I reply, "I would rather do a story together."

"All right then, what's our story going to be about," Mary asks.

Looking back at her I try to think of a good story for us. "Let's see, after all these years together we should be able to think of something," I said.

Pause...couple minutes goes by and finally Mary speaks out....

"How about the time you sent me back to my parents in Michigan?"

I take a second looking back at her and then say..."Oh no, we can't write about that. Besides it gets way too involved and it really sounds negative, to me at least."

"No, it doesn't," says Mary. "That would make a good story."

Silence again.... Finally I speak up.

"We could write about the fun times we had remodeling a fixer-upper. Remember the insane times we had with the house in San Diego. We both nearly killed ourselves. I sanded the floorboards in the living room with an electric sander. A week later I ended up in the emergency room with severe pain in my side. It turned out to be a badly strained muscle. Man... did that hurt."

"Oh yeah," says Mary, "I sort of remember you being hurt, but we weren't living together then. Anyway, you living in LA kept me from knowing what was going on in your life at times."

Silence for a short while...We lay on our beds looking at each other and start laughing....

"There's got to be something we can write," says Mary. "How about the Concord Apartments fire. Now that was scary."

"Yeah...you're right, it was. Let me think about that."

"It's getting late," Mary interjects, "and we need to decide on a story, or would you like to write something on your own? You know you could put together something about the time you picked up your dad from Ford Hospital in Detroit, do you remember?"

"Not really. My memory of that is not very clear," I say, "and it would take me some time to describe all the events leading up to that time."

Several minutes go by....

"Here's a thought," says Mary laughingly. "Why don't we write about just not being able to agree on what to write about. What do you think? Anyway maybe by morning we'll know for sure."

We both roll over and fall sound asleep.

Writing
from
Within:
The Next
Generation

120

Jeff Thompson   *Jeff is a former banking executive who is exploring his creativity in midlife through computer-generated animation. He is a Vietnam veteran, and a number of his stories focus on his wartime experiences. He is married to Mary Molinar.*

The Undecided Story   *by Mary Molinar*

We walk into the room together. It's been a long and fun day of writing and playing. "What do you think we should write about, Jeff? Do you have any ideas?" I say. Jeff lays himself out on the bed, resting his head on his arm. We're both silent. "I can't think of a thing," I think.

It's Saturday night of a two-and-a-half-day weekend writing workshop. Bernard has assigned all the couples present to write about the same event from their own perspective. It sounded easy and fun. After all, we've known each other twenty-plus years. There should be plenty of events to write about. And Bernard always gives the caveat "or write anything you want" after he gives an assignment. The thing is, though, that he knows, secretly, that most of us won't feel free to choose that "out" of an assignment. I always take it up as "my next challenge."

"So Jeff, what ideas do you have?" A long silence. Damn, I'm always the one who comes up with the ideas, and then he feels trapped by ideas. I'll just wait for him. More silence. "Meow, meow," comes from outside. "Hey...the cat came to visit." I walk to the door to let her in. "Prrrr, Prrrr, Prrr," comes from this furry beast as she jumps on my bed. "Well, you could write about your side of the story of the dirt bike ride...you know... when I first realized I was physically attracted to you, but I don't have my story with me," I say. My mind drifts off to that memory and I'm lost in a time long ago, my body leaning into his. "Well, you don't have it with you, so we can't write that."

"How about when we decided to get married then?"

Jeff is very quiet. "I don't think I remember, so how could I write about that?"

"Oh, you know...it was 1984 in the fall...if I remember right I gave you an ultimatum." How dare he not remember such an important event, anyway. Damn, it must be an unpleasant memory he's blocked from his mind. Jeff rolls over on his back, staring up at the ceiling. "Well, I can think of some sexual escapades we've had, but that might be too X-rated for a writing group." I smile to myself and agree we don't want to tell that much of ourselves. "How about the night we first made love...not write about the actual 'doing it' but about that night then," I say. He rolls over and looks at me from across the room. "Now let's see, when was that... my mother's birthday, is that it? Mom and Bob were going out. That's why we were together that night, right?" "Yes, yes, that's right." "Well, I don't think that I can write that," Jeff responds.

The cat walks up to my face, purring loudly. "This is a very loud cat, who never stops purring." I pet her for a while as we drift off into our separate worlds, thinking of what to write. "Hey, how about when you kicked me out of the house," I say. "Now that's a story." No reply. Jeff sits up now as I roll over on my side. "No, no, Mary, no one would understand. Anyway, why would we want to write about such a negative event?" "But I don't think of it as negative because it was an event that forced me to look at myself and change." "Yeah, well, I don't think that's what he had in mind," Jeff says, turning toward me. "Anyway, it's much too complicated."

I get up and go into the bathroom, needing to move around. Jeff rolls onto his back again, eyes closed now. "Hey, Mary...I know...let's write about the fire." I walk back into the room. "Hmmm, that's a story. Actually there have been two fires. Remember when I lived on Long Branch, and the guy with the ammunition in his garage." "Yeah, I was there, but the other time was more scary." I smile to myself. "Well, O.K., I guess we could write that." Jeff and I look at each other, sleepily smiling. "Maybe we should write about how we can't decide what to write." Jeff laughs. "Well, that's an idea." We're both quiet for a while, drifting off. "Let's sleep on it and see what ideas strike us in the morning, honey." "Yeah, I'm tired now from all this thinking. Let's go to bed, Mary."

Mary Molinar   *Mary is a businesswoman who is devoting more and more of her time to writing. Her ambition in life is to write a children's book.*

— • • • —

In reflecting about which episode you wish to record, you may conclude that one of the stories you've already written would do just fine. If so, get in touch with the person in the story, who may have experienced the episode differently.

If you wish to begin a new story, remember that one of your objectives is to renew or revive an old relationship, so it is best to tread lightly if the subject is at all controversial or painful. But do not be reluctant to share your feelings as you remember them.

— • • • —

Let some vivid memories of incidents or experiences you've shared with others come to mind. Give the people involved a call; ask them to write out their version. Don't be daunted if someone says no. Find a person who says yes.

Writing
from
Within:
The Next
Generation

———

122

chapter 14

Confronting
Traumatic Situations

"Bernard, I have something I want to write about," murmurs Diane, an attractive woman in her early fifties. "It's been on my mind a long time. But I'm uncomfortable with the idea of writing about it."

"What's bothering you, Diane?" I ask.

"Well, it was pretty traumatic," she replies. "I'm not sure I want to relive the pain."

"It may be painful, I know," I answer. "But my experience is that once I write about a painful experience, I feel cleaned out." Diane gazes into my eyes with a great deal of concern. "You have heard me talk about my father's ill health and my mother's mental and emotional problems," I continue.

"Yes, I know." Diane turns and stares out the window of our classroom, pondering.

"Writing about it has helped me clean things out," I say, "perhaps to forgive, in a way. Certainly to lighten the burden."

She remains silent for some time. Finally, a flicker of a smile crosses her face. "OK, I'll give it a try."

Traumas may be genuine tragedies, intensely experienced, perhaps even caused by ourselves. Now is the time for us to view them clear-sightedly. Sometimes, they are the untimely deaths of people we love. Often, they are shocking injuries to someone we love, or even to ourselves. When writing about these experiences, there are four things we must do.

First, we must prepare for reliving the experience and writing about it; just as an athlete goes into training, we must go into training. And just as a part of training and conditioning is mental—"psyching up" for the task, visualizing good things happening—so we must encourage ourselves by

123

congratulating ourselves, telling ourselves what a good thing it is we are doing.

Second, we must finish the story once we have started it. Despite the tears and pain, we must keep writing.

Third, we need to maintain our objectivity. As the writer, our job is to make the reader see the truth, to describe to the reader what we see and experience and feel, so that the reader goes through that pain or feeling or experience.

Fourth, we need to resist the temptation to editorialize or moralize about what has happened. We are storytellers; we need to tell stories. Sometimes, at the end of a tragic or traumatic experience, we do come to certain conclusions about the way the universe operates. If this happens to us, it is appropriate to say something. And it is perfectly all right to express confusion and bewilderment at the nature and power of the Creator of us all. But keep it real. One honest observation is worth more than all the platitudes in the world.

These four points will help you through remembering and writing the painful episodes among your life stories.

The following is an excerpt from a story that describes such an experience.

Double Trouble   *by Diane Hanson*   (EXCERPT)

"OK, Gene, tell me what you know," I say over the dinner table at the Wagon Wheel restaurant in Ventura. He and my husband, Jack, have been selling cars together for over a year. It is early 1965.

Last night, I had called Valley Dodge to talk to Jack, but Gene answered the phone. "Oh, hi, Diane, Jack's not here. Did he tell you he was working late again?" he had said with a smirk in his voice. That alone added to my suspicions.

"Gene," I had said, "what are you implying?"

"I really can't go into it here and now, but I think we should talk," he responded.

(The rest of Diane's story "Double Trouble" can be found on page 289. You may wish to examine it closely to see whether it implements the four suggestions above, and whether the story is helped by them.)

After finishing her story, Diane went more deeply into it by doing a self-assessment.

Self-Assessment

What effect did this experience have on my life?
For a long time I was emotionally withdrawn and not trusting of men.

How did it feel writing this story and sharing it with others?
I was surprised at the depth of my emotions when writing and especially when reading the subject matter to the class. It brought back much of the feelings of the moment. My heart was racing and I felt fear. My hands were clammy and trembling. So much was still so real—even after twenty-five–plus years.

How did the "child" in me handle this experience?
As a child, I had been taught not to cause a scene—especially in public. These teachings overrode my instincts that told me I was in danger.

Was there a part of me that was a victim in this experience? How did that part of me handle the experience?
I was definitely a victim of rape by both my husband and his friend, as well as the "old tapes" regarding appropriate behavior. I was also a victim of a society where women are not to be believed when they cry rape.

Do I see a pattern emerging? What is it?
Trying too hard to please. Going along with the situation. Not speaking out about my feelings. Feeling wronged and victimized. Then getting angry. Releasing my anger in an unproductive way (screaming and yelling, becoming demanding, issuing ultimatums, feeling guilty and sulking).

What is the origin of this pattern?
I was told "Don't argue with your father. It doesn't pay. It just gets you more upset and him more angry."

So talking or arguing with a man has always been difficult. It has meant the loss of a close, emotional interchange with the men in my life. When there is strife, I close off. I don't share my inner feelings—especially if I think they will be perceived as negative. If I get angry, I take the risk of not being heard, not being understood, not being accepted. The other person will be even angrier and will reject me.

What patterns do you see emerging from this crisis moment in your life?
Certain patterns have revealed themselves to me over the past few years of my life (1987–1992). It hasn't been until recently (early 1992), through the Life-Story Writing Class and understanding that I have been "co-dependent" all my life, that I have been able to see the patterns.

These patterns have been in my personal relationships, especially with men, but also with women.

I will enter a relationship and at first the friendship grows and both of us are rather interdependent. The second step emerges when I convince myself the other person "needs me."

I like to be needed. They need me to "help them." This has usually been emotionally. I rarely have had enough money to help financially. A financial need would be more obvious to me that I was being used. Emotional giving was good to do.

Soon the other person would begin to "need" me and to "depend" on me. It would make me feel good to be needed and necessary to the other person.

I would give to the relationship until I became drained or exhausted. I would feel that I gave more than my share. That I was carrying more than half of the relationship.

Then I would get resentful and angry. I couldn't leave it, though, because the person still needed me and I enjoyed being needed. I also felt in control when the other person needed me versus me needing them. I just needed them to need me.

When it became too much for me, I would throw my hands up in disgust and run from the relationship.

Sometimes after a brief rest of a few weeks, or several months, I would feel guilty for having let my friend down. Most often I would relent and go back into the relationship and begin the cycle again.

When I finally gave up totally, I would become very independent. I would stay alone and begin to heal myself. I enjoyed the "being alone" and not having to worry about anyone else. I had a good job, a nice place to live, I paid my bills on time and always saved a little something. I felt emotionally relieved that I was not carrying around someone else's baggage, that I was not weighed down with another's problems. When I was alone, I had no real problems—at least none that I could not handle.

Then the loneliness and restlessness would set in. I would want another new relationship. One that would not end up like the last one. There was hope that it would be different next time.

Those were the patterns, and the cause was co-dependency, which was caused by the following:

1. I was raised in a co-dependent household. My father was the demanding, critical, hostile, and judgmental person, while my mother played the victim role and was passive-aggressive.

Writing
from
Within:
The Next
Generation

126

2. I was the oldest of six children and had a lot of responsibility toward them. Especially the youngest three who were 11, 12, and 13 years younger than I. I was a surrogate mother. I felt the responsibility to care for them and to help fix their problems.

3. I was raised in a strict, traditional church that preached putting the other person first. Sacrificing myself to others' needs.

4. I married young (18) to a man who had the same traits as my father and felt called to be a minister. This reinforced all the above.

5. I had my first child two weeks before I turned 19. Too much responsibility too soon. I accepted the "victim" role that had been handed down to me by my mother.

6. I had my second child by age 22 and felt locked in and trapped, thereby repeating the pattern taught to me by my mother.

7. My marriage continued until even I saw that my husband was too much like my father. He was beginning to criticize and demand things of my children that they were too young to deliver. He became verbally more abusive. I didn't want my children to grow up under those conditions. When the situation between my husband and me grew even worse, I divorced him.

8. After six years of marriage I saw some light and decided to break the pattern. I divorced my husband. Not getting any counseling and not even having heard about co-dependency, I struggled along as before. I had no new tools with which to make the change. So the patterns repeated themselves.

Is there another, better way?
Facing problems is facing reality. As soon as a problem arises, I go into a head-spin or shock. Then I regroup and reevaluate. I gather all the facts. I analyze the information and then, using my instincts and good judgment, I try to make an immediate decision. I decide on a plan of action and begin to implement it.

— • • • —

It is very important for us to face up to the traumas of our lives and write about them using all our skill and effort. As Diane's moving story shows us, getting them out of ourselves and into the open releases us from the burden of carrying around all the guilt and pain that has weighed upon us for so long. The more honestly we write about the event, the more fully we will release it.

Some of the very best work done in my classes has come from people who not only put their pain down on paper but put it down eloquently, not as a complaint but as an object for themselves and others to experience and contemplate.

By no means will the pain and anger of the past always result in painful, angry stories. Some of the funniest stories come from bottled-up anger: A few deft strokes of the pen, and a mean parent becomes a wonderfully absurd and short-sighted little person.

It also sometimes helps to work against the dominant side of oneself in writing. If we tend to be complainers about life in the present, it may help us to find the good and wonderful things that happened to us in the past. If we tend to be always rosy, it may be wise to look beneath the surface of our lives and confront some of the darker moments. Every life has them. We will find that the more of the one side we confront, the more of the other side will gradually emerge. The more the pain gets cleared away through writing, the more the pleasure of life will reappear. We will find that our memories will begin to return with surprising clarity.

But keep in mind that we don't want to *think* about writing. We want to write. Picking up the pen and simply writing, even if we have nothing specific in mind, is the strongest commitment we can make to getting our life down on paper. Once the pen moves, images will begin to come back. So keep the pen moving. Later we can find out where the actual story should start. When confronting trauma or any difficult episode, the best way to begin is to just begin. You can assess your own experiences by responding in writing to the questions in Diane's self-assessment.

— • • • —

Now it is time to relive once again some of the things you had hoped would remain hidden from view for the rest of your life. Congratulate yourself for your courage. You deserve it. Go ahead—jump in and start swimming. The results will amaze you. Believe me.

Writing
from
Within:
The Next
Generation

128

Writing Family Histories

Our efforts up to now have been directed toward creating writers where none existed before. Many people, however, for a variety of reasons, do not want to write their own life stories, yet they are interested in having their histories recorded or wish to record someone else's story. The techniques of writing these kinds of stories differ from those we have used and discussed previously.

There are essentially two ways of writing other people's life stories:

1. Writing down your experience of listening to your Mom or Dad, Grandma or Grandpa, or other family member telling stories of the past, while *capturing the relationship that existed between you and the story-teller at the time the story was told to you.* In our life-story writing classes, we call these *family histories.*

2. Recording a person's life on tape; then, using the techniques described in Part 1, transforming the narrative into intense life stories using dialogue, narration, inner monologue, and so on. After writing each story creatively, the writer checks back with the storyteller to be sure that what is written is as close to what happened as possible.

Writing Family Histories: Narrating Another Person's Story

Many of us who set out to write life stories are primarily interested in writing about the struggles and history of our parents and grandparents. "I want to tell my children about my parents and grandparents before it is too late," they say. Typically this kind of story is a simple narrative retelling of the past.

> My grandfather was born in the Ukraine. When he was sixteen he was forced to serve in the Czar's army. After a year he escaped and made his way to America....

While reading this sort of narrative, we, the readers, find ourselves asking a number of questions: How did the narrator hear about his grandfather? Who told him the story? How do we know it is true? How did the people involved (the grandfather and the narrator) feel about these events?

Out of a need to answer these questions, another, more authentic way of telling family histories has emerged, one in which the feelings of both the storyteller and the writer are evident while the story is unfolding.

"When writing this kind of family history," I tell my students, "let the reader know how you learned about the story." Were you sitting on Grandma's knee or taking a walk with Grandpa? Let the reader know what you remember Grandpa or Grandma doing or feeling while he or she is telling you the story. That way we get both the story and your relationship to the storyteller. We will believe it and feel it more fully. The next story is a good example of this kind of writing.

Family History   *by Lucy MacDougall*

My mother is dozing after lunch when I get to her room in the nursing home. Three nickels she won at bingo are still in her lap. She wakes right up at the prospect of an Eskimo Pie and her weekly copy of the *National Enquirer*, which she has told me at this point in her life she enjoys more than the Bible.

"How have you been?" I ask. "Fine," she says. At death's door, in the grip of gray depression or desperation, my mother always says fine.

I sit on the edge of her bed, scanning the state of her health in the wheelchair for myself as she bites into the chocolate covering. Will I be like that in twenty-five years, with occasional spurts of spirit and energy, living days the size and shape of postage stamps?

Her gaze, though, is intent still. She gobbles the Eskimo Pie while I stare at her. Now she is staring at me, impatient, ready to get on with it. I pick up my pencil and paper in a hurry.

"I was my father's favorite," she says right away.

My mother has been waiting patiently for days while I poke around in the past for her immediate ancestors. Now she is looking forward to being born and getting on with her own personal firsthand memories. Three other babies had to be born first. "Edward came first," she says, "then Albert and Percy, and I came next." Her mother named her Irene Jeannette Scherrer. 1883. The first girl.

Her face suddenly clouds. I know. It is going to be about Percy. It is always sad about Percy. Little Percy got sick with diphtheria and my grandmother and the housekeeper took care of him, but it was while Grandma was at work that he died. "Your grandma would never go back to work after that. She took care of us and did piecework at home. Percy was her favorite," she explains.

"But I was my father's favorite," my mother says again, anxious to make herself once more the rightful star of her own story. "Much more than Roma."

Here comes Roma, upsetting the order of the years. Here she comes, pushy little sister, on the scene in my mother's memory when my mother's barely gotten herself born yet. "Just like her," my mother says when I mentioned it, the surface of her placidity shaken even after eighty years by the appearance in the family of Roma with her dark hair, dark eyes, rosy skin, her fresh, demanding, little-girl ways, not taking any time to be a baby in my mother's memory.

"Eddie would ask her for a glass of water," Mother says, "and she'd bring it to the table and spit in it before she gave it to him."

"Wait a minute. That's later, when Aunt Roma's a little girl. She's not born and you're not even five yet."

"I don't remember anything until then," insists my mother stubbornly. "That's the way Roma was. But my father liked me more because I took after the Scherrers. They were very well-bred people, I told you that, and I took after that side of the family."

So my mother didn't want to be like her mother any more than I wanted to be like mine, or my daughters want to be like me. She had great admiration for her mother's fine qualities, but also seemed to feel a little above her. I ask her about this. She stirs uncomfortably. It is too late in life to bother to lie. "Well, a little," she confesses.

But my mother absolutely hated Roma. Probably because she felt my grandma spoiled Roma. "She let her get away with anything," mother complains now for the thousandth time. Since my grandma was a gentle, quiet person, she must have had it hard to keep Roma in line. I ask about Roma's terrible sins. My mother's anger is good as new. "My shoes," she cried. "I was saving them for best and when I went to wear them, she'd worn them out. And borrowing my best kid gloves from my bureau drawer, without asking, of course, and she stretched them." Roma's real sin, though, I can see, was taking center stage, struggling to take over princess position in the family.

To get her mind off Roma, I tell her my memories of what she had told me in the past. The old joys soften her grievances. Wearing a mulberry satin hair ribbon on the braids of her fine hair, ruffles on the dresses her mother sewed for her, carrying her roller skates from the hard-packed dirt of Watts Street to another village street, Mulberry, I think, where a man with a store had put in a stretch of cement in front. Roller skating for hours.

"I didn't go to school until I was seven. Your grandma taught me at home," she says. When she finally went to school, they put her in third grade.

"I was very smart," she says pridefully. "My brother Eddie and I learned piano. The German teacher rapped our knuckles for any mistakes. Eddie would practice for hours, but the teacher said I had more talent, even though I didn't practice." Her face warms at the thought of being able to top the brother at something.

"Talent needs practice," I point out, becoming the mother. She doesn't agree. "Eddie got the bicycle just because he was a boy. He got the camera. He went on day trips with my father. He got it all, just because he was a boy." She still resents it. She has to have something more and better than he does, so she's kept the teacher's remark deep inside for years to balance the books.

She's kept everything deep inside, that's her style. She never told Eddie or Roma or anyone in the family how she felt. "It made me sick. Roma and Eddie fighting all the time over who got what. I couldn't stand it. I'd crawl under the dining room table and hide there until it was quiet and I could come out."

Harold was the change of life baby for my grandma, a blue baby, my mother says. I remember Harold was always dear to her. I liked him, too. An agreeable moon-faced man when I was a little kid. He was born to my grandma when my mother was twelve. Harold Blessing Scherrer, named after some friends of Grandma's. Grandma liked to name her children after her friends to honor long associations.

"I brought him up," my mother says proudly. "I carried him around. I fed him and dressed him and changed his diapers." She'd told me that again and again, and what a help it was to Grandma, who hadn't counted on her last little blessing.

My mother gets a bit confused about this now. "I had this little son, Brian. He was my little boy."

"No, Mom," I say gently. "That is my son. He's your grandson."

"Oh. Yes. That's what I mean. It was Harold who was my son."

"No. He was like a son. Remember?" She shakes her head. She can't seem to get it right. "You were twelve or thirteen and he was your mother's baby. You took such good care of him," I add.

She averted her face. "Of course," she says, but I can tell she is embarrassed that she hasn't got that stuff straight.

She is tired. The past is pictures in her head and in mine, but it's more than that. The pictures fill our whole bodies, take them over. We are both tired.

That is enough for today.

Lucy MacDougall   *Lucy was born in Brooklyn. She married a writer shortly before World War II and moved with him to Los Angeles when he was hired to write* Objective Burma, *starring Errol Flynn. Always interested in writing, she began working at* LA Magazine *after her divorce. Life-story writing gives her the opportunity to force herself to remain creative. Once into the process, she began to see how it helped her review and understand her life's path.*

— • • —

As Lucy records her mother's story, we have an opportunity to get to know several relationships: Lucy's to her mother and vice versa, her mother's to the past, and Lucy's own views of her mother's sisters and brothers. The assignment was made easier for Lucy because she had recorded and noted many conversations with her mother over the years.

Notice the way the frame Lucy creates—the mother speaking to Lucy the narrator—helps us see and feel the mother's struggle to get the facts straight, and feel Lucy's patient yet amused concern for her mother.

Because Lucy's mother speaks directly to Lucy, we, the readers, experience the story through Lucy's eyes. It is important for us as readers or listeners to know through whose eyes we are experiencing events at every turn in the story. It creates belief in the story. It also increases our interest because writer and teller have a relationship to share with us, in addition to the subject matter of the story itself.

A hundred years ago we would not have thought to ask, "From whose point of view are we seeing the story, and is it to be believed?" Until the middle of the nineteenth century, writers like Poe, Dana, Scott, Thackeray, Hardy, Melville, and many others told their stories from a godlike, or omniscient, narrative point of view, and we accepted this point of view as truthful. But in the writings of Stephen Crane, Henry James, and James Joyce, and in the dramas of Pirandello, readers became more aware of the person through whose eyes the story was being experienced and seen.

So, as contemporary readers, we no longer take for granted the truth of a story unless we know something about who is telling it. By recording the relationship of the storyteller to the writer, we get a more authentic and believable view of the family history that is being told.

Writing
from
Within:
The Next
Generation

134

chapter 16

Writing Family Histories from Recorded Narratives

The second type of family history integrates "writing from within" techniques into an oral history narrative. The first step in this process is to record one's own story or that of a friend or relative on a tape recorder. Then, using the techniques described in Part 1, the oral narrative can be transformed into a series of separate stories that stand on their own.

An example of this second type of oral narrative is "Pool Hall," a story from the life of Ted Brown as told to and written by his former wife, Grace Holcomb. "It all started with those tapes," she says. "We got him a six pack, cracked it open, hit 'record', and let Ted go. The story I wrote might have been just a few lines on tape. I just took it from there.

"Oftentimes," she says, "what I did creatively might not have been accurate, but it got him to remember what did happen." She adds fondly, "It's all up there in that thick skull of his somewhere. I just had to shake it loose." With his input, she made changes, then brought the story to class, listened to more comments, reworked it, showed it to Ted one last time, revised again, and finally had a story. Here is an excerpt from her story.

Pool Hall   *told by Ted Brown; written by Grace Holcomb*   (EXCERPT)

Our town, Collbran, Colorado, only had about 300 or so people in the 1930s while I was growing up, and we had the usual assortment of stores in town.

By and large, the very best place in town to kids was the one and only pool hall. We loved it. As pool halls go, it wasn't much. Just a large room with a couple of big windows, usually dirty, and an inside toilet, one of the few we had. There was a bar all along one side of the room and beer and whiskey were sold, but not too much whiskey. Mostly everybody was a beer drinker. But if you wanted to just nurse a bottle of whiskey in private there were five or six tables and chairs. Men would just sit with the whiskey and a shot glass; they always drank it neat, and everybody knew enough to leave them alone. If they wanted company they would sit at the bar. The tables were mostly used for playing cards. The men played pinochle and pitch during the day and poker at night.

The pool hall was where the cowboys headed when they got paid and were in town to tie one on. Those poor bastards worked like dogs and pretty much lived like dogs too. They only got to town once a month when they got paid.

But the pool hall meant more to us than cowboys. Old Dewey Fitzpatrick hung around there too. He was an old man, must have been 50 or so, and he would spin stories for us.

"Dewey, please tell us again about how you lost your fingers?" we'd plead. "Well," Dewey would say, "sure you boys can take a bloody tale?" "Oh, yes, sir," we would answer. "You ain't agonna tell your mammas I done gave you bad dreams, are you?" he asked. "Oh, no, sir," we answered in chorus.

He then proceeded to tell us how he was fighting bears and this one bear was extra special mean. Dewey beat off the bear, of course, but just for damned orneriness the bear jumped up and bit off the ends of two of his fingers. He would then hold them up for us to inspect.

That old dope would go on telling stories about skinning buffalo and fighting Indians. We figured some of his stories could be true, he sure was old enough.

He just did odd jobs around town, and was the town drunk if he could afford it, but he always had time to spin a tale or two for us, and they were never quite the same except for the bear and the fingers. He never changed that story. He'd tell us about being in the middle of a buffalo herd and a whole company of Indians came at him. "But, Dewey," we would protest, "last time it was only a few Indians." "Well, hell, boys, think that only happened once? This was a different time," he said. "Shut up now, and listen or I ain't gonna tell you no more." We would all be quiet because you never knew what he was going to say each time.

One time Dewey was in the pool hall, pretty drunk, and went into the toilet. Fred Wallace wanted to go in the toilet and old Dewey wouldn't get off the pot.

Fred was the son of Bill Wallace, one of the biggest and richest ranchers around that area, and Bill Wallace was one of the meanest sons-of-bitches we had. He was built and looked like a pit bull and his son Fred

Writing
from
Within:
The Next
Generation

136

was just like him. Fred was about twenty when he was trying to get Dewey out of the toilet and it made him madder than hell. The other men heard the commotion in the toilet, but by that time it was too late.

Dewey was dead. Fred had dragged him off, then hit him so hard Dewey's head hit on the edge of the toilet bowl, killing him instantly.

Poppa was constable at that time, so he told us this story. Poppa came and told Fred to go on home—he would decide what was to be done later.

We had no courthouse or judge in Collbran, so Poppa and Fred drove into Grand Junction. Bill, Fred's father, was already in Grand Junction. Poppa came home the same day and so did Bill and Fred.

Poppa never did say what happened, and I never knew. All he would say was "Well, you know Bill Wallace has a lot of influence around here."

The town was pretty well divided over whether Fred should have gone to jail, but with time, it was forgotten. But the little boys of the town, of which I was one, never forgot it. We all wished we were bigger—we wanted to hang Fred ourselves. We all wanted to be the one to tie the noose. We missed old Dewey. He had been our friend. The pool hall was never quite the same with Dewey gone.

Ted Brown *and* **Grace Holcomb**   *Ted grew up on a sheep farm in Colorado during the Depression. The nearby town of Collbran was as rough and colorful as any western town in the 1880s. Part Native American, Ted spent a lot of time outdoors while growing up. He joined the army in 1940 and saw service in the Phillippines as a point man on patrol. His unit was the first to liberate Manila, and he saw firsthand the infamous death camps in the Phillippines. At the war's end he was hospitalized for jungle rot. Released from the army, he kicked around for some time, eventually heading west for the hardrock mining in Death Valley during the 1950s. Eventually he met and married Grace Holcomb. They had one child and were divorced. Ted and Grace have remained close friends over the years, and Grace came to class "so that we would be able to tell the grandchildren about Ted's life."*

• • •

The beauty of this technique is that you, the writer, are not in the uncomfortable position of asking questions and having the subject answering them, as if in numerical order. What happens is that once you have asked a question or two—"What is your most vivid memory from your days in the army?" "What is your most vivid memory from your early twenties?"—and have gotten an answer, you then return to the person being interviewed with a printed copy of the story for him or her to read. Even better, you can read it aloud to him or her.

In listening to the story, the person will almost always remember more. He or she will begin to add greater detail. If not, you can probe a bit: "Do you remember anything else that happened about this time?" Little by little, the person's memory will loosen up and reveal more and more.

Recently, I used the techniques described above to help a man in his seventies to write his life story. The grandson of one of the last important mandarins of Vietnam and the son of a wealthy industrialist who was kidnapped by the Communists in 1946, Jean Jacques had been a police detective in Hanoi in 1940, a soldier for the French in 1944–1945, and a diplomat for the French for forty years. On his own, he may never have written down his compelling tale.

Many writers who set out to write life stories are primarily interested in writing about the struggles and history of their parents and grandparents. Typically this kind of story is a simple narrative retelling of the past:

> My grandfather was born in the Ukraine. When he was sixteen, he was forced to serve in the Czar's army. After a year, he escaped and made his way to America.

While reading this sort of narrative, readers find themselves asking a number of questions:

1. How did the narrator hear about his grandfather?
2. Who told him the story?
3. How do I know it is true?
4. How did the people involved (the grandfather and the narrator) feel about these events?

Out of a need to answer these questions, another, more authentic, way of telling family histories has emerged in which the feelings of the storyteller and the writer are evident while the story is unfolding.

When they are working on writing this kind of family history, I tell my students "Let the reader know how you learned about the story. Were you sitting on Grandma's knee or taking a walk with Grandpa? Let the reader know what you remember Grandpa or Grandma doing or feeling while they were telling you the story. That way we get both the story and your relationship to the storyteller. We will believe it and feel it more fully."

John Strong's "How I Became a Rebel" is a good example of this kind of writing.

(**Note:** In this story, the narrator, the teller of the story, happens to be the writer, John Strong, and then the reader experiences a story-within-a-story. This kind of story—a touching, personal experience with a famous or important

Writing
from
Within:
The Next
Generation

138

person in history—might well be passed down within a family from one generation to the next.)

How I Became a Rebel   *by John Strong*

I am nine years old and in elementary school in Clymer, Pennsylvania. The year is 1922. One day the teacher tells us, "Class, we have a special treat today. We have two visitors...who fought in the War between the States. They are here to tell you about it."

A few moments later they walk in. Two of them. They are old. With beards. Today is Veteran's Day, so they wear their uniforms, blue tunics with blue pants. One has the bars of a lieutenant on his shoulders. They walk slowly and sit down.

I am eager to talk to them. On both my father's and mother's side of the family, I have relatives who fought in the Grand Army of the Republic, the Union Army.

At the first chance I get, I raise my hand. "Sir," I say, "could you tell us about being in the war. What it was like?"

The old man's eyes come alive. "I suppose you want me to tell you about the bloody battles, don't you?" I nod. He shakes his head. "I won't do that. War is hell. Absolute hell. But I will tell you a story about the war," he continues. He leans back in his chair. His eyes get a faraway look.

"The war was over. The bloodiest damn thing you ever saw. My best friend Joshua and I decided we wanted to go to college together. We were lieutenants in the GAR, the Union Army, and we wanted to stick together. So we chose Washington and Lee University."

The old man smiled down at me. His eyes were soft.

"We enrolled in classes there. General Lee—Robert E. Lee, the commanding general of all the Confederate forces—was the president of the university, but we didn't see him much. Occasionally a parade in the mornings. But he marched out of step, on purpose, to make himself ordinary, nothing special. But we admired him nonetheless.

"Almost all the other men there had fought for the South. After all, General Lee had been their commander. They'd've followed him anywhere.

"One day we got a note from the office of the president of the college asking us to stop by. When we arrived, the general was waiting for us. He was a soft-spoken man. A little shy. But powerful. I almost saluted him. He came right to the point.

"'Gentlemen, I suppose it has not escaped your attention that most of the boys at this here school were once under my command in the late war.'

"'Yes, sir,' I said, eager to say something.

"'Well, then, since you are the only two fellows from the Union Army enrolled down here, officers too, I wonder if you might tell me . . . why? Why did you come here?'

"I looked at my friend, and he looked at me. Finally I spoke up. 'General, sir, my buddy and me, we figured that you were the best general of any of 'em, North or South. Wherever you went, that was the place for us.'

The old soldier stops for a moment. He takes a glass of water and drinks. Finally he goes on.

"The general stood and looked at us, then nodded. There was a faint smile on his face. He shook hands with us both. We left."

The classroom is as quiet as an empty church. The old soldier looks around the room at each one of us. "Think about that, boys."

Notice that in the story, John speaks in the present tense, as if Clymer, 1924, were the present; but when the old soldier recollects the past, he speaks in the past tense. This is because the old soldier's recollection of 1865 is the past from the perspective of someone living in 1924.

John's soldier speaks directly to the reader as well as to him. The result is that the reader experiences the story through John's eyes. It is important for readers or listeners to know through whose eyes they are experiencing events at every turn in the story: It creates belief in the story, and it also increases interest, because the writer and the soldier have a relationship to share in addition to the subject matter of the story itself. It also gives the reader a sense of the subjectivity of the telling of the story.

For example, if you read a story told from the point of view of one sister who is obviously jealous of another, you know you are getting, in the telling of the story, other biases and other feelings, not the whole truth.

Contemporary readers are less likely than readers from the past to take for granted the truth of a story unless they know something about who is telling it. By recording the relationship of the storyteller (narrator) to the writer of the story, a more authentic and believable view of the family history is told.

Writing
from
Within:
The Next
Generation

140

chapter 17

Researching the Past

"Who am I?" "Where have I come from?" "Where am I going?" These enduring questions, whether asked consciously or unconsciously, remain important to all of us. Advances in modern medicine have enabled people to live a great deal longer than past generations, thereby allowing people to contemplate these questions in the midst of advancing age and good health. Advances in modern technology, specifically the Internet, have allowed unprecedented access to information about the past.

For many years, I thought the dominant influence in my life was my father's highly educated and accomplished German–Jewish ancestry. Fleeing the oppressive Prussian nationalism of the mid–nineteenth century, my father's forbearers settled along the East Coast (West Virginia) as farmers and then moved to Michigan, becoming—in one generation—successful merchants and attorneys. In my father's generation, they also became doctors and social scientists. For me, that knowledge always encouraged me to think for myself and to try to see clearly what was happening around me without being pulled into partisan arguments, affiliations, or dead end efforts. My mother's family had been sweet, kindly farm folks from Illinois, so far as I knew.

Then came the Internet. Thanks to it and a distant relative Bill, who sent a view of his snow-covered home in Virginia to members of the family, myself included, my view of my mother's family changed.

Bill and I began corresponding: His great grandmother was a sister to my great grandmother. For some time, he had been researching his family, the Clark family tree, utilizing the enormous resources online. (Ancestry.com has compiled and computerized a vast amount of information, enabling anyone to know who their ancestors were without expending a huge amount of effort.) Before long, my former wife, Gail, became interested in this research, along

141

with my first cousin, Mary Ellen. With a small army of cousins/researchers hard at work, we found a relative who had been a captain in the Union Army during the American Civil War: Bela Tecumseh Clark. Bela's middle name intrigued us because a general of the Union Army, William Tecumseh Sherman, shared the same middle name. What the link was, we did not know, but some day we would. A little more research informed us that Bela's father-in-law was one Colonel Sylvanus Thayer. The U.S. Military Academy's official website acknowledges Sylvanus Thayer as "the father of the U.S. Military Academy." That information surprised and even astonished us—to think that such an illustrious person was an important part of our family history without our knowing about him.

A bit more research told us that Sylvanus Thayer was an unmarried man. Thus we were on the wrong track—or perhaps not. Because they were both of approximately the same age (one born in 1798, the other in 1785) and both born in New England (Vermont and Massachusetts), we suspected they had a common ancestor. Researching that common ancestor we found a half-dozen Thayers who also fought in the Civil War, most from Illinois and Michigan. At long last, we found the grandfather of the two Sylvanus Thayers, as well as Col. William Clark, Bela Clark's great grandfather, who served as an aide to General George Washington during the Revolutionary War.

We found that many other relatives, such as the Grays, the Gowers, and the Culvers from this small area of Momence, Illinois, had also been officers and enlisted men in the Union Army. We found diaries and testimonials to their devotion to the career and politics of Abe Lincoln.

Gradually, I began to realize what impressive, free-thinking, hard-working generations of family lay behind my mother. I began to understand the impact my DNA has had on my behavior more and more fully, which helped me answer the questions "Who am I?" "Where have I come from?" and "Where am I going?"

The reason that I bring up the details of my family's ancestry research in a book about writing is that, ultimately, writing is about communication—usually about communication that moves from the writer to the reader, but lately, thanks to blogs, websites, social media, and the like, writing is about communication that moves back and forth, with lightning speed.

So in a project like this, a number of members of the family—Bill, cousin Mary Ellen, former wife Gail, and I—got to know each other a little better. My sister Mary Lee and cousin Tom reappeared too. Starting with a few facts, we have been able to piece together interesting fragments of life during the time when our family moved from the Eastern Seaboard westward through the Hudson River Valley and then the Ohio Valley and into the Midwest, in Illinois and Michigan. We have shared family photos and memorabilia and

Writing
from
Within:
The Next
Generation

142

analyzed and debated their significance. In several instances, the possessor of such memorabilia didn't know the significance, but other members of "the team" were able to identify who the subjects were in old photos. In fact, this group—Gail, Bill, and Mary Ellen—have given themselves a name: CHART—Clark Heritage Ancestry Research Team. (Hey, what am I? Chopped liver?)

The ongoing tasks—identifying photos, noting the signatures of guests at weddings, finding links between generations, preserving stories—create a wonderful bond among family members as well as lead to surprising connections with "outsiders." My sons, Jeff, an airline pilot, and Will, a Marine, are both fascinated by our link to the father of the U.S. Military Academy.

Through blogging and websites like Ancestry.com, more and more families will find common ancestors, stories, photos, and the like, creating ever-stronger family bonds. The history of every person's family is a miniature history of the larger events that have taken place over the centuries since the founding of our republic. In my case, I discovered that I count John and Pricilla Alden—among the first families of the original Plymouth Settlement in Massachusetts—as members of the family tree.

In this regard my family is not unique, as many hundreds of thousands of families can easily trace their roots back to such ancestors. Researching these roots is a fascinating task that offers many benefits, for writing your family history and for so much more.

Expanding and Managing
Your Creativity

Most of us would like to believe that we are at least somewhat creative. But we often suspect that we are not and that, in the great scheme of things, it truly does not matter whether we are or not. The truth is probably just the opposite. We are creative, all of us, and it matters very much.

Life, however, has a way of impinging on us, convincing us that its concerns are far more important than our real or imagined yearnings to create. To a greater or lesser degree we have to deal with life concerns, but we must also leave ourselves room and opportunity to create. A few years ago I was having lunch with a friend of mine, who had been a Hollywood production manager and line producer for more than twenty years. "Barry," I said, "how do you see yourself? What is it that you do, other than taking care of a multitude of nuts-and-bolts production problems? You've been at it a long time. You must get bored."

He grinned. "I do everything in my power to get things ready for the production—cameras in place, locations ready, cast and crew in position, sets dressed, lighting and sound all set for the flip of a switch—so that the director can do his creative best with cast and cameraman. Sometimes I get tired and frustrated, but not bored."

This is a great image for what we need to do for ourselves—*become powerful and effective production managers so that our director and creative team can do their best.* We need to surround ourselves with people who are supportive of our creativity, be our creative efforts artistic in the traditional sense or creative in some other way. Likewise, we need to give ourselves the time each week to create. Equally important, if we have emotional baggage that weighs us down and diverts us from creating (and many of us do), we must have the courage and intent to define that baggage, to find ways of letting it go, and to begin our creating and continue this creating. When we do this, we will find that many of life's cares become much less burdensome. Our lives have more focus and purpose. In this way, we can look forward to a path that is productive and fruitful until the day we pass from this earth.

After fifteen years in the film business, I made a short film of a Ray Bradbury story entitled "The Flying Machine." It turned out well. On a tiny budget it told a good story, was well acted, and transported people to a time in ancient China when a man who created a flying machine—the flying man—had to face his most severe critic, the Emperor, who feared the consequences of this burst of creativity. Yet another battle between critic and creator. The film project turned out to be an ironic exclamation point to yet another failed relationship in my life—this time with a woman I loved very much. It was the beginning of another long and difficult time in which I began to see that exploring something in life besides filmmaking was necessary.

One of the areas of life I needed to explore was reexamining my relationship to my parents; another was the arena of autobiographical writing. When I began, I was not a writer. I was a teacher and a director who knew something about contacting the actor's imagination. In the years since, I have overcome many of my own fears of writing, and have been able to do as I tell my students to do—take risks, engage my self-critic, believe in myself, write every day, and keep going.

Having listened to what I tell my students, I have come to enjoy putting myself on paper. It enables me to see my relationship to my parents in a unique way and to value myself as a child dealing with death and abandonment. It has helped me to develop the willingness, techniques, and peace of mind to tackle a large project—writing the life of a Renaissance prince, a seven-hundred-page novel I have had in mind since the age of twenty-two but never attempted because I didn't believe I would be able to devote years of my life to a single piece of work.

At the age of fifty-seven, I see myself as having cleared a path through much of the garbage, emotional and psychic, that overwhelmed me in my twenties and thirties. I went as far as I could as a filmmaker, but finally had to confront all the fears, anxieties, and craziness from the past, stuff I had avoided for most of my youth and young adulthood.

Whether my work is good is not the question. I would like it to be. I work hard for it to be so. But, more importantly, I have cleared a path so that I can create and help others create. The *tao* is visible. I have become a satisfactory production manager for my own life. I have given the *creator* in me the opportunity to create.

To me, the most remarkable consequence of my search for my own *tao* is the ironic fact that those who suffered most when I was lost in the "creative craziness" of my twenties and early thirties—my two ex-wives and my two children—are still close and wonderful parts of my life. My ex-wives are cheerful, wise, and supportive. My sons are boon companions—solid, insightful, purposeful, and humorous. Somehow, my suffering did not translate into lifelong suffering for them. For this, I am grateful.

The meaning I take from all this is that whatever our search may be, we can conduct it in our own way without being cut off from the love of others...and without their having to suffer forever just because we become unpredictable. There is plenty of room for quest and relationship. We must, therefore, *manage* our creativity.

Writing
from
Within:
The Next
Generation

146

chapter 18

Embracing Your Self-Critic

"My life is a mess!" laments Rebecca, a member of my Sunday afternoon writing group. In her early thirties and with a writing talent that sparkles, Rebecca ought to be sitting on top of the world, but she seldom writes.

"Mine too," echoes Diane, a wise and insightful woman in her fifties whose self-deprecating writing style is hilarious to all but her. Like Rebecca, Diane can barely get herself to her computer to write once every two weeks—just in time for the workshop.

As I look around the room at the other eight members of this writing group, I see agreement reflected on the faces of several of the most talented—particularly Dirk and Jackie, as well as a new member, David. Others, like George, who runs an art school and has extensive experience as an actor and artist, and Mary, simply go about their work, writing a little each day without a lot of agonizing.

Why do some of them have their creativity so well in hand while others struggle? I ask myself. What can I do to help?

One afternoon as we are reading our stories, Diane talks about how her self-critic is having a wonderful time dynamiting all her efforts. "'Diane, you're such a stupid idiot,' it says to me, 'thinking that anyone will want to read your writing.'"

"I would like to hear that voice in your story," says Mary. "It really is a very funny voice."

"Not funny to me," Diane grimaces.

"Maybe you need to put it down on paper so that you can hear and see the voice of your critic, rather than simply running from it," I suggest. "Let your critic have its own voice. And answer it with *your* voice."

Diane shrugs with indifference, but the next week she returns with the following story.

Them Boots Is Made for Walkin'   *by Diane Flor*

I drag myself upstairs to my bedroom, carrying the bags of clothes it took me three hours to accumulate. God, what a chore shopping is, getting dressed, undressed. There must be an easier way. Like have someone put the outfit together, bring the clothes to your house, and try them on for you. Yes, that's what I'll do someday when I'm rich, have somebody else do the shopping and trying on.

I'm anxious to see if the skirt I got goes with those multicolored boots that I haven't had much to wear with, so once again I get undressed and slip the skirt on. I swear, those mirrors at the store are rigged, I know my butt didn't look this big when I tried on the skirt there. Damn, no wonder I hate shopping. Oh, well, let's get the boots and see if they match.

That's funny, now where are those boots? Why aren't they here with my other boots? Let's see, maybe they're over here with my shoes, no... hmmmm, now that's really strange, what the heck did I do with them? This is really crazy.

No, you are really crazy, look at you looking on the shelf with the sweaters, like they would be sitting on top of a bunch of sweaters. Oh, yeah, that's good, why don't you look under those tennis shoes on the floor a few more times, or maybe move those slippers again, you never know... you might not have seen them hiding under those slippers. Or, wait, wait, maybe under the sandals, maybe you're looking right at them.

Right, or maybe you're losing your f___ mind! How the hell could you lose a pair of boots that you wore three times!

O.K., let's regroup. Where did I wear them last? Did I take them to Vegas when we went in January? Maybe I left them in the hotel room? Let's see, what clothes did I take to Vegas to wear? S___! If you can't remember what you did with the boots, how in the hell do you think you're going to remember what you took to wear?

Yeah, well, maybe I took them down to San Diego when Rick got married. Maybe I left them in the hotel room there, what with all the commotion that was going on. I wonder if I called them if they would know. Or if I did leave them there, would they still have them?

Oh, my God, I can't believe you said that! Are you nuts? What do you think, they're going to hold a pair of boots for six months, till some fruitcake like you remembers they forgot them?

O.K. Wait a minute, this is an easy one. I have pictures to help me out on this one. Now where are those pictures I took when we were down there? That will tell me if I had them there or not. Ahhh, here they are.

Well, that was good. At least you remembered where the pictures were. Oh, could you just shut the f___ up for a minute.

Writing
from
Within:
The Next
Generation

148

O.K. So, that settles that. We didn't take them to San Diego. Oh God, how the hell could I forget what I did with a lousy f___ing pair of boots.

Now I'm really getting mad, but I don't think that's what's making my heart race.

What's making my heart race is fear. Is this how Alzheimer's starts? Oh, I may joke about it a lot, but this isn't funny anymore. How could I not remember what I did with those boots? It's not like they were in my closet a hundred years, like some of the s___ I can't seem to throw out. I just got them six or seven months ago, for God's sake! So it's not like I just forgot that I gave them away three years ago, or something.

God, this is so scary I can't even believe it. Am I suddenly just going to forget where I put things? This is only a pair of boots, but what if it's something really important, and I don't have a clue?

O.K., now calm down. It isn't like I haven't remembered where I put something before, so why am I panicking? I've forgotten plenty of times where I've put things, and I eventually find them. Don't I?

But a pair of boots, how in the hell many places can you put a pair of boots?

It's not like a little piece of paper you've written a phone number on and stuck someplace. A little itsy-bitsy piece of scrap paper that you could have stashed anywhere. It's like a big thing! Not something you stuff in a drawer or mix in with some papers. I just can't believe I can't find them. I must be losing my mind, there is no other explanation.

The ringing of the phone startles me, making me jump. The pictures on my lap scatter to the floor.

"Hellooo...." comes my daughter's voice in a teasing tone. "Does there seem to be a problem?"

"What?" I say, thinking how incredible it is that we are so connected that she would just sense that I was having a problem.

"You called?" she laughs.

I called? Oh my God! I'd completely forgotten that somewhere in between looking on my sweater shelf and under the tennis shoes I had left her a message.

See what I mean, I can't even remember what I did ten minutes ago!

"Tami..." I say, trying to hide my panic, "you know those brown suede boots I got that matched that purse with the different colored patches on it? Did I loan them to you, 'cause I can't find them anywhere...."

"No," she says, "just that black one the time I had the cast on. Remember, I was going to wear it on my good foot...." Her voice trails off in the distance, as I stand in the doorway of my closet staring at the plain brown suede boots that have been sitting there all along. I had even taken them out and tried them on earlier, while I was looking for the multicolored ones.

Suddenly a light goes on in my head, both exciting and scaring me at the time. "Wait a minute," I say, cutting her off in midsentence. "Maybe it was only the purse that had the patches on it. Maybe these plain boots are the ones I got to match the purse."

"Yeah, Mom, the boots didn't have different colors on them. They just matched one of the colors on the purse."

"Oh my God, Tami, I can't believe what I just put myself through," I say as I tell her the story. "I swear to God, I really think I'm getting Alzheimer's. Either that, or I'm going crazy. I'm serious," I say laughing hysterically. "I mean I don't know if I'm relieved that the boots were here all along or not. What's the difference if I thought I lost them or I just forgot what they looked like?"

We hang up and I glance around the room. Let's see now, where did I put that article about the herb that improves your memory? Was it in the paper, or did I see it in a magazine? Did I cut it out, or did I throw it away by accident?

Or did I...wait a minute, hold on just one darn minute. I'm in no mood to go through that s___ again in one night. I'll just have to figure this one out tomorrow.

That is if I still remember tomorrow what it is I wanted to figure out.

Diane Flor   *Diane is the mother of two children and a former hairdresser. She came to life-story writing to recover memories of her childhood.*

• • •

From this burst of writing, it is apparent that Diane's sense of humor is intimately connected to her self-critic, which is also strongly connected to her deepest feelings: her uncertainty about the world, her vulnerability, and her ironic appreciation of life.

As I reflect on Diane's story, I am reminded that this powerful force, our self-critic—while so often turning us away from enjoying and pursuing our creativity—can become one of the most dynamic sources of our creativity.

I sometimes see that my students are annoyed with me for pushing them to confront their creativity. They often hold back these feelings, but every now and then they come out. Once they allow themselves to put this annoyance on paper—really an irritation with the raging internal battle between self-critic and creator—the creativity flows nicely.

Writing
from
Within:
The Next
Generation

150

 **EXERCISE**

Often we have to use our imaginations to shake loose thoughts and perceptions that lie far from our ability to see with our naked eye. Very often we can get the most out of our efforts by creating imagined conversations with different parts of ourselves. Here is one such imagined conversation.

WRITING A DIALOG BETWEEN YOUR CREATOR AND CRITIC

If you are intent on creating, but feel that you have apparently ground to a halt, write down all the hostile, angry dialogue going on in your head, dialogue that says, *You can't create, you don't want to, to hell with anyone who says you should create.* Sit quietly, and listen to how your inner dialogue responds when you think about creating. Write down whatever you hear, without judging it. When you are finished, read over what you have written, and see where it leads you — you may be surprised.

Then take a step backward and look at it again. All that negative stuff that has come rushing through can seem pretty funny when you gain some perspective. In fact, setting up a dialogue between your optimistic, creative side and your critical side can be quite humorous, even if it does not seem particularly funny when you are writing. So read your work to your writing group or friends. You may discover how humorous it really is — as Diane, Rebecca, George, and Mary from my Sunday writing group have all found out.

Handling Creativity
and Depression

We will now look at another source for our creativity grinding to a halt: the relationship between creativity and depression. There is a great deal of literature circulating in the larger world that says something like "creativity and depression go hand in hand" and that they are "unavoidable." In a recent documentary about creativity and depression that glanced at the life and work of American poet Anne Sexton, the academic narrator seemed intent on linking suicide and creativity as though they were partners for life. This is nonsense. The relationship between creativity and depression is active and alive, not inexorable and all-encompassing.

As a young filmmaker some thirty years ago, I created a documentary about life in the barrios of East Los Angeles. Although technically not of very high quality, it was raw, truthful, and compassionate. I was proud of my work. Soon a number of people in the film business and the Latino community were saying the same thing, including such documentary filmmakers as Haskel Wexler, whom I respected very much.

A few awards came my way, and I began to feel excited about my prospects as a filmmaker. "You are terrific!" I told myself. "Probably the next great documentary filmmaker." If I hadn't been arrogant enough already, I soon became impossible. I gave myself over to imagined press conferences, award ceremonies, and contracts for ambitious, well-financed projects. I imagined the film having a wonderful impact on the world around me—teachers, police officers, and social workers all changing their attitudes because of it. "Ah, you have opened my eyes," I could hear them saying.

I avoided work in the industry as a cameraman or editor for fear I would not be available when "the industry" came calling. Nor would I take any full-time teaching jobs lest I became "distracted" or unavailable for the next great documentary, which eager producers would be offering—soon, no doubt. My wife became impatient and bewildered by my Olympian attitudes.

Harsh reality soon began to take over. No fat contracts. No overnight success. No Academy Awards. If the film had a bit of impact, it was because I worked very hard to get people interested in it. I took it around to police organizations, teacher/parent groups, and community gatherings.

Waiting for something to happen, I fell into a void. For days at a time I felt depressed…empty…uncreative…listless…hardly alive. All this talent and nowhere to take it. Somehow, I thought, the world owed me recognition—and a living.

The listlessness into which I was falling was all the more scary because it reminded me of the pictures I held in my mind from childhood—pictures of my mother lying on her bed day after day, month after month. Pictures of her manic breaks—taking me and my sister out of school and leaving us with her brother while she disappeared—haunted me. "Is this what I am falling into?" I wondered.

My wife, Gail, was baffled by my behavior but probably not as bewildered as I was.

"I have to get out of this depressing, constricting, middle-class life we are living," I declared.

"I'm not leaving my house," she answered. That and the kids were as much certainty as she had in her life. Fortunately, in the four years and two children of our marriage, she had been solid and focused—graduating from UCLA, returning for a master's degree, and now teaching. So we parted. Now I had to deal with divorce and separation from my kids, as well as depression and an unfocused career.

In fact, I went on to make more films and to experience many more of the ups and downs of being a creative person in an unpredictable business. I lost another marriage, never made any money to speak of—and also did a few shorts that pleased me, had some wonderful moments, and learned a great deal about life, creating…and myself.

The arc I have described here is not unusual for creative people. A great number of the people I have talked to who are or have been in the film business have gone through the ecstasy of creating and then the postpartum depression of finishing a project and seeing no material rewards.

One of the things I have learned over a long period of time is that whatever one's strengths and weaknesses may be, the film business will highlight each…and propel us into unending heartaches until we have examined these attributes and made changes where necessary. To be able to make such changes, it would be helpful to understand the relationship between creativity and depression, for it is intimate and profound.

The Triangle of Creativity and the
Shadow Triangle of Depression

"I'm going to stop writing, just for now, while I get through my depression," says one of my students. Over the years, I have grown used to hearing this from some of the most creative people in my workshops.

Discovering that you are creative is an exhilarating and unsettling experience. For the most part you probably never knew you were in the creative cycle, except that in many ways you are unlike the people around you: You see the world quite differently from the way your friends see it, you have different goals, your learning process is different, your moods are different. Other than that you are quite normal, right?

Think about this next question, and write down your responses to it:

In what ways would you say you are different from most of the people you know?

When I was in college, I read the *Tao* of Lao Tze. For me, the most telling passage in this small book was an enigmatic poem, "The Tao" (The Path), which said something like, "when you are on the tao, you will know it, and when you are not on it, you will not know it." That one line has kept me on track most of my life and has proven to be profoundly true.

As a creative person, your unusual searching process, whether mental or emotional, is not easily defined by others. But by the end of it, your process is what allows you to feel as if you have found the path that Lao Tze speaks of. Accompanying that sense of finding the path is an exhilaration that can be very seductive—and perhaps short lived.

Now, think about this next question and, if you wish, write a story about what you discover:

Are you aware of a path—a creative process of uncovering and discovering—in your life? When did you first become aware of it?

Depression creeps quite easily into the lives of creative people early in their development because they have little or no control over when, where, and how they can regain the path when they lose it.

Scientists in the field of human behavior describe depression in a number of ways, including the following:

1. anger that wells up and is unexpressed

2. an event that goes badly, connected to other events that go badly, leading to the inner conclusion that *all* will go badly

3. a deep and prolonged anxiety about the future and one's ability to survive in it

Whatever definition we use, one thing stands out for us: When we are on the path, our mode of searching pays off; things unfold out of us without diffi-

Writing
from
Within:
The Next
Generation

154

culty, and often the world responds well to what is coming out. Usually we are elated. The opposite of this experience is depression.

There are a number of things we can do to make the path more evident and our depression less cosmic. The Triangle of Creativity shown below may help you find and maintain the path more and more often.

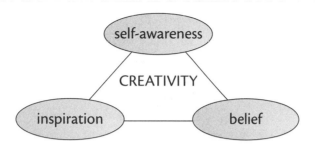

The Triangle of Creativity

When we are off the path for a long time and the path seems most remote, the Triangle of Depression shown below captures the spirit of what usually emerges.

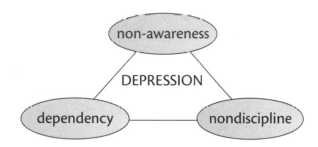

The Triangle of Depression

Where does one enter the Triangle of Creativity? you may ask. At the lower left-hand corner, at *inspiration*.

For the creative person, inspiration is a most misunderstood experience. "I am waiting to be inspired" is a phrase we often hear from artistic people. Linguistically, the word *inspire* means to *breathe in*. Well, breathe in what? Breathe in what is around us, that is, put ourselves in situations where we allow others to *inspire* us and to be *inspired* by us.

As a former college-, USAF-, and tournament-circuit tennis player, I have always played the game at a highly competitive level. As I grow older, the great pleasure in playing tennis on a high level is that anyone on the court who is having a really good day inspires the others to play better and better, opponent and partner alike.

Behind the act of letting others *in* (inspiring them, breathing them in) is our deep need as a creative person: to be able to believe that the world in which we find ourselves makes sense. True, the world is full of catastrophes of one kind or another—personal and cosmic. But what we as creative people (and I define *creative* as making something out of nothing) seek is an avenue into its "inner" order, an order that is there, but that each person must find for himself or herself. It is not available through the communal efforts of others, such as consciousness-raising groups, or even the solitary experience of meditation. It is available only through the actual manipulation of the materials through which we express our creativity—armies, if one is a general; babies, if one is a parent; students, if one is a teacher; pen and computer, if one is a writer.

With belief and a willingness to inspire and be inspired, we can begin to seek self-understanding, provided we are willing to do so in a self-disciplined way. This means that we contract with ourselves to manipulate the materials of our area of creativity, for a certain number of days a week, a certain length of time, *without fail.* What we accomplish is less important than our giving our creativity a chance to express itself.

Self-awareness means we have an understanding of the emotional baggage we bring to the table and a willingness to do everything possible to eliminate that baggage. It also means that we accept the limits of being a creative person.

A job is only a means of surviving and is not an end in itself. Our goal is to find high-paying work that affords us the opportunity to explore our areas of creativity with as much time to ourselves as possible. We must specify to ourselves the amount of money we can live on (minimally) each week and work toward achieving that level of income with the least expenditure of time and effort (without relying on others to do it for us and without depriving our children of the opportunities they deserve).

During my formative years at the University of Michigan, a cousin of mine, Bob Culver, was a powerful influence on my life. A watercolorist of great talent, he understood the relationship between work and career. When I met him, he was in his fifties, the father of two, and a draftsman at General Motors. Each year for the previous thirty years he had worked six months at GM, and then, with a little money in the bank, he would take off for northern Michigan and paint for six months. Each year he became a little more successful at painting than the last, and he amassed a huge collection of work. In my sophomore year in college, a gallery showing in Detroit brought him prominence and financial independence, enabling him to quit GM and work part-time as a teacher at Cranbrook Academy. From him I learned that I could live normally—have a family and work—while following my singular, creative path.

In our lives there are people who inspire us, are inspired by us, or are a part of our process of self-awareness, self-discipline, and creativity. *Everyone* in our

Writing
from
Within:
The Next
Generation

156

lives must become a part of this process: children, spouses, parents, business partners, and so on. And they can. James Joyce is known to have created numerous events in his life just so he could try out an experience before he wrote about it.

By allowing people who are not part of the Triangle of Creativity into our lives, we set up ourselves to enter and reenter the Triangle of Depression. It is as simple—and as challenging—as that.

 ## EXERCISE

Our imaginations can move us past what we perceive as "writer's block."

Very often this "block" is not a block but merely an indication that we must seek our path in a slightly different direction. At times, the block may in fact be an obstacle that a character in our story encounters and must overcome. Sometimes we must overcome the obstacle in our personal lives in order for our character to solve his or her problem.

FINDING YOUR WAY

If you find yourself and your creativity, both actualized and potential, subject to bouts of depression, I suggest you try this exercise. When you feel depressed, find a quiet place to think about and write answers to the following questions.

1. Would you describe your personal life as a *mess*? If so, what is making it a mess?

2. Are you a creative person? What do you do that is creative?

3. What do you do that is both creative and artistic?

4. What would you like to do that is creative, artistic, or both?

5. What voice tells you not to do the creative-artistic thing you would like to do—that says, "you can't," "don't bother," or similar things?

6. As you think about doing the creative-artistic thing you would like to do, what does this voice say? What is the dialogue in your head?

7. What could you do right now to pursue the thing you would like to do? (For example, my friend Marianne, who wanted to sing but had been too terrified to do so in public since childhood, signed up for a voice workshop.)

8. Write a story in which the voices in your head—the doubting, undermining, self-critical voices—become part of a humorous dialogue with other positive or practical voices. (For an example, see Diane Flor's story "Them Boots Is Made for Walkin'" on page 148).

9. Do you find yourself sinking into a depression when you think about creating or when you *finish* creating? Describe what happens.

10. What do you do to combat this depression?

11. Where do you enter the Triangle of Depression? What do you think this reveals?

12. What steps can you take to move from the Triangle of Depression to the Triangle of Creativity?

13. Are the people in your life inspiring and supporting your process of self-awareness, self-discipline, and creativity? Who is supporting it, and how do they do it? Who is not supporting it, and in what ways do they not inspire and support you? If you are not being inspired and supported, what steps must you take to ensure that you are surrounded by people who *will* do these things for you—no matter whether your creativity is expressed in artistic terms or in your professional or personal life?

14. Do you believe that creativity is important in your life? If so, how is it important? How well do you manage your creativity? What steps can you take to manage your creativity more effectively?

15. After you have explored your self-critic in several creative stories, have begun to move from the Triangle of Depression into the Triangle of Creativity, and have started to manage your creativity more effectively, write a story of how life feels under these conditions. Add a P.S. to your story in which you reflect on what the story says about you.

— • • • —

If the story and the P.S. have given you helpful insights into yourself and have helped you define your tao of creativity, refer back to this section of your writing if you sink into the more negative side of exploring and managing your creativity.

Writing
from
Within:
The Next
Generation

158

chapter 20

Experiencing the Story
as a Mirror of the Self

Up to now we have reviewed our stories by adding a P.S. at the end and by expanding them in a full-fledged assessment, as with the story "Double Trouble" by Diane Hanson (see page 289). Now, we come upon yet another way of looking at ourselves, one that is highly imaginative and fits into our new, more creative view of ourselves: experiencing the story as a mirror of ourselves.

As I have guided my students through the writing process, I have noticed that their stories often contain truly magical insights about the writers themselves. Sometimes the writers grasped these insights, sometimes not. Looking closely at the stories, I saw the process happening in several ways.

First, I could see that the "writing from within" techniques, particularly writing in the present tense, gave each writer a sense of innocence and freedom from criticism. The stories reflected this freedom, often yielding experiences on paper different from the ones the writers had carried around in their heads for most of their lives.

I noticed that the process of sharing a story often pointed the writer in the direction of moments in the story that needed to be expanded. In digging into the climax of the story, expanding and opening it up during the rewrite, the writer often uncovered a very different story. One such example is Stephanie Bernardi's story "My Mother's Death," which tells the writer something quite different about the experience as she expands certain moments (see the excerpts on pages 89–93).

In some instances, the rewriting process led to a completely different version of the story from what the writer thought he or she was writing, revealing what I call "hidden moments." For instance, in "Leaving the Farm" by Lettie Watkins, the first version yields to a second version that is much more complete and in which the truth of what happened is much less hidden. The third version reveals even more of the truth, a truth Lettie had kept hidden from herself for many, many years (see pages 98–101).

I also began seeing wonderful insights about the writers of some of these fine stories, even though the writers themselves were not yet seeing what the stories were telling them. When I asked the writers how they saw themselves, they often appeared inarticulate, confused, and off the mark in their answers. How could I help them to see what their stories were so clearly telling them about themselves?

My breakthrough came when I realized that most people are reluctant to take center stage in their own lives. Having been told that writing in the first person is self-centered and offensive, they leave themselves out of their stories by using "we" instead of "I" or by focusing on what others are doing. This is an effective way of not looking at one's own behavior. The "writing from within" process could and did bring out the behavior in a clear and truthful way, but it would still take some doing for the writer to see himself or herself with clarity and detachment.

I began my search by listening for stories in which the writer was in pain about some past or present event, but was writing with honesty and feeling about that event. I noticed that the event often revolved around the actions of parents, children, or a divorced spouse, and that the writer was feeling victimized and blamed the other for all that happened. When this occurred, I guided the writers back through the story, helping them to see how the characters were telling each other a truth that may not have been seen.

"Ask yourself, 'Who am I in the story?'" I suggested. "Use the story as a mirror of yourself. When we are in pain, we often cannot see ourselves very clearly. But a story is a mirror and it will tell us the truth, if we allow it to."

A few days after the Southern California earthquake of 1994, I was sitting among a group of older writers who had been meeting every Monday for five years. Everyone had been telling or reading stories about his or her experiences of the earthquake, such as stories about relatives and friends calling to inquire about the person's safety. When it came time for a good-natured, seventy-year-old German-Jewish refugee to read, the room grew quiet. Max Levin had been in considerable pain over the way he was being treated by his children. We wondered whether this story would be about that concern. He began to read in his soft, slightly accented voice.

Anya   *by Max Levin*

The phone rings. I pick it up. "Hello?" I say. "Are you OK, Papa?" I hear a voice say. "Anya, where are you?" I ask my daughter. "In Paris," she replies. "Paris??" I protest. "Your mother said you were in California." I hear silence from the other end. Then the phone clicks off. I am very unhappy. I have not heard from either Anya or my son in over a year. Their mother is turning them against me. I wait a few minutes then I call their mother's number. It rings and rings.

Finally, Anya answers. "Anya," I say, "why are you doing this to me? It has been a whole year since you and I spoke...what have I done that has...." "Papa, I am sick and tired of your negativity, always playing the part of the victim, the Jewish refugee from the holocaust. I'm tired of it." She slams the phone down. I feel crushed.

Max Levin   *Max became a child actor and appeared in several films. In the mid-1930s, his parents saw the need to get out of Germany and did so. Eventually, Max landed in Hollywood where he appeared in small roles in a number of films. During these years, he became interested in the restaurant business, owning and managing serveral well-known eateries, including Barney's Beanery, where he met Anya's mother.*

• • •

Max looks up at the group. Everyone is moved by the piece. The feedback from the group is that the story is honest and moving. Several listeners who have similar relationships with their children mention this to Max.

Max is tormented by the distance between himself and his grown children. What can he do to win them back? he wonders aloud. It occurs to me that by holding this story up to Max as a mirror, some answers may unfold.

"Max," I say, "what would you see if you held the story up as a kind of mirror of yourself?" Not quite sure what I mean, he doesn't answer. "Let's suppose," I continue, "that your daughter is telling you something she wants you to hear, and that you've done a very good job of getting what she says onto paper. Her words have a great impact on us. We feel them. So do you. Now, let's suppose she is speaking the truth. Is there a place in your life where you are behaving like a victim?"

"Well," he says, "my ex-wife is keeping them from me. She is poisoning them against me." Max looks hurt and sad.

"What I mean is, can you find a place in the *story* where you are behaving like a victim?" He looks at me with a blank stare. "Let's read the first couple of lines again."

The phone rings. I pick it up. "Hello?" I say. "Are you OK, Papa?" I hear a voice say. "Anya, where are you?" I ask my daughter. "In Paris," she replies. "Paris??" I protest. "Your mother said you were in California." I hear silence from the other end. Then the phone clicks off. I am very unhappy. I have not heard from either Anya or my son in over a year.

Max looks up, not quite sure what the words mean.

"Max," I say. "What voice is that saying 'Where are you?' and 'Paris? Your mother said you were in California'?"

Max's head begins to nod. "Yes, I see. It is the voice of the victim. Poor me. Right there in the story."

"That's the truthfulness of the story. But there is more."

He smiles. "Yes?"

"While you were writing those lines, do you remember any other voice wanting to be heard as you talked to Anya?"

Max leans back and laughs. "Yes, I wanted to say, *'Comment ça va?'*—how are you? in French."

The whole class laughs, realizing that he had almost chosen a light, pleasant retort to his daughter but instead chose the response that had so often been his.

"What is really interesting, Max, is that you almost wrote those inner thoughts, but didn't. You almost let yourself see that there was another, higher response in you, but you didn't quite let it out. But you did entertain it. It is pretty clear that everything you need to know about yourself and about why your daughter has been keeping her distance is there to see, in the mirror of the story." I stop to let the words sink in.

A slow smile comes over his face. "I understand better." He looks around the room. "Thank you. I will rewrite the story."

"We can see in this experience," I say to the group, "that everything Max needed to know is in his story. The thing he left out was the thing he needed to discover about himself, the playful, nonjudging voice that will help him establish a new kind of relationship with his daughter, one that has no burden of guilt behind it. But the voice was there all the time. It just needed to be brought out."

Writing
from
Within:
The Next
Generation

162

Writing Mirror Stories

We can see that the stories we have written may well turn out to be very helpful mirrors for us to see the things about ourselves we need to know, but that are normally hidden from us. Most of the time, our self-protective, critical mind keeps these insights safely from our view. But when the story is well and honestly told, it can become a prism through which the truth about ourselves passes into our consciousness without being filtered by our critic.

I wondered whether I could create an exercise using guided imagery to move some of my more advanced, searching students into a focused, meditative place. That way, they might begin to see themselves differently—not as they want to see themselves, or as they fear seeing themselves, or as others see them—but simply as they *are* in the story.

I ponder this as a student, Tamara Randall, reads her story.

The Beach   *by Tamara J. Randall*   (EXCERPT)

In the darkness of our *palapa* (beach hut), I awaken to the sound of the ocean waves crashing upon the beach. The air is rustling the palm leaves of our beach hut. I roll out of my hammock, landing upon my hands and knees in the soft sand floor.

Our hammocks are strung out from the center pole of the palapa like a Ferris wheel. I hear the brothers beginning to stir now. I have two brothers and three sisters. I am ten years old, the oldest in my family, and living in Mexico with my mother.

"Eric," I say, "help me open up one of the walls." Eric and I each grab one of the long forked poles that are used to hold the walls of the palapa open during the day. We spear the bottom corner of one wall with a pole and push it out and plant the poles in the sand. The ocean breeze rushes in and I can taste the salt in the ocean spray. The sea is blue green, edged in a clean white foam. The waves thunder down on the moon-shaped beach and I feel the earth shake with each wave.

(Please see page 297 for the remainder of the story.)

When she finishes reading, I look around the semicircle of students. Everyone seems eager for more. "Now is the time to improvise, Bernard," I say to myself. "Go ahead, take a risk." I want to do some guided imagery work, but am uncomfortable. This is not how I usually conduct my workshops. But I know it is what I must do.

"I would like you all to close your eyes," I say. "I am going to take you through a visualization that will help you see yourself more clearly in the mirror of your story. Wherever it takes you, you will then go ahead and write about that experience."

Once the students are comfortable, I begin the visualization prompt.

"I am imagining that I am in a desert. There are flames all around me. Ahead of me, I see a white light. I begin moving along a path that opens up through the flames, until I reach the white light. In the light, I see a mirror appearing. In the mirror, I see the story I have just written. As I look into the mirror, I begin to see a picture of myself in that story I have just written. Who is the person staring back at me from the mirror of the story I have just written? What do I see about myself that I didn't see before? As I see myself appearing in the mirror of this story, I will write about that person I see…*now*."

As soon as I am finished, my students begin writing. Tamara asks to read her self-assessment first.

The Beach: My Self in the Mirror   *by Tamara J. Randall*

I am a young girl and I am in my element, free, playful, giggling, laughing. I glisten and shine. I love the world. I love unconditionally. I am innocent, pure light and energy. I hold the world in my heart. I am sensuous, succulent, smooth, sharp, hard, soft, real, dreamy. Imaginary worlds are mine.

In the mirror I see many women old and young. I pick the one on the beach that day. She is precious to me. I love her and I want to keep her here with me always. She is pure sunshine, pure energy, pure love, pure freedom, pure child.

Tamara J. Randall   *Tamara's mother, a 1960s hippie, took her very young children to Mexico, where they lived hand-to-mouth for fifteen years. Tamara's stories are filled with the mystery of native religion and the folkways of Mexico. She is the mother of two children.*

● ● ●

When she finishes reading her mirror story, she wipes away some tears. "My marriage is in terrible shape," she whispers. "My husband is so critical. He sees nothing about me and the way I live my life that is of any value. He thinks I am just a child. I have a lot to give him, but he won't see it and won't accept it." She picks up a tissue. "This mirror or whatever you call it helps me…so much. I realize I am special." Again she wipes away tears. "I have a lot to give. It hurts so much that he can't see it."

Tamara wrote "The Beach" at a time when her marriage was at an end, when her highly critical husband could see nothing valuable about her and the way she lived her life. Resurrecting this memory and seeing herself in the mirror of that story has done a great deal to remind her of her essential worth.

Writing
from
Within:
The Next
Generation

164

 EXERCISE

You are now ready to look into the mirror of your own story. The best way to begin is to review any one of the stories you have written, and then ask yourself the following questions:

1. Who am I in this story? (Describe your qualities—courageous, vulnerable, broadminded, teasing, crowd-following, and so on.)
2. What do I see about myself in this story that I didn't know before?
3. What impact did this moment have on my life?
4. Along with the other stories I have written, what am I learning about myself in this story?
5. What are my feelings toward those close to me as revealed in this story?

These few questions, and our answers to them, will be important to us as we review our life's path. They will encourage the process of self-discovery. To ask them of ourselves is not to judge ourselves in any way. Our intent is simply to calm the waters of experience for a time so that we can see and savor who we were in those long-ago moments.

If it is difficult to get the self in the mirror into focus, use the visualization prompt to which Tamara and her writing group responded. Repeat it aloud to yourself, have someone else read it to you, or record your own voice and play it back just before you begin to write.

Now, write an assessment of yourself based on the person you see staring out at you from the mirror of one (or more) of your stories. (For more about Self-Assessments, please see Chapter 34, "The Benefits of 'Writing from Within,'" as well as my book *Character Consciousness*.

*Experiencing
the Story
as a Mirror
of the Self*

165

"Writing from Within": Advanced Work

As my students have acquired rather quickly the skills suggested in the thirteen-point checklist of *Writing from Within*, 3rd edition (1998), I have had to provide them with more and more sophisticated insights into the art of writing. Since many students are now writing novels, short stories, screenplays, children's stories, as well as life stories, the instruction I have provided them had to apply to these different forms of writing.

As a consequence, the thrust of my work over the past fifteen years has been to delve more deeply into the "art of writing." Much of this deeper writing involves observing and employing specific techniques such as "Hitchcockian recaps," visual motifs, backstory, denouements, and the like. However, beyond pure technique lay more sophisticated perspectives: understanding and employing the principles of art, creating subtext, developing interesting minor characters, and, most of all, separating the writer's voice from that of the central character.

Having written about these disparate elements of creative writing, I asked myself, "Is there anything that binds all of these techniques and perspectives together—a unifying principle behind this abundance of approaches to writing?" I thought long and hard about this.

Eventually two answers came to mind: First, my concern with helping writers move from writing a "good" story to possibility creating a "great" story—that is, creating a work of art. Second, my concern with undertaking the difficult task of exploring our inner thoughts and feelings in our writing.

The Evolving Story: Creating a Work of Art

Ours is a world energized with a desire to put thoughts and experiences, as well as the fruits of our imaginations, in print. Much of this writing may be interesting, even compelling. Characters may be vivid, narratives well crafted, and literary devices thoroughly planted. But their authors are not necessarily crafting works of art.

What mystical ingredients infuse a work and mold it into a work of art? The answer may not be entirely definable; however, one thing we can say is that a work of art does take us into another dimension in which our understanding of the world becomes richer and our appreciation, even awe, of the power of a human hand to craft such a work, grows. The works of Leonardo, Peter Bruegel, Picasso, Mozart, Ibsen, Strindberg, and Fellini all take us into another universe, one that enriches our understanding of the world in which we function.

Fine writing often provides the reader with interesting, quirky, well-drawn characters around which the reader will find a circle containing a spicy array of obstacles, minor characters, and well-crafted backstories suffused in a taut narrative.

Rising to the level of art are those works that contain a larger concentric circle—of concerns, characters, and obstacles that cause the major characters to do more than solve problems. They must reevaluate the world in which they live while at the same time coming to understand their inner lives, asking and answering fundamental human questions: What is real? What is illusion? What is the nature of man? Is he at heart good…or evil? How do we go about stripping away outer layers of who were/are (and who we appear to be) to get to the deeper layers of who we are?

Since 1998 I have seen certain students explore myriad techniques and perspectives that enable their work to move from "a good story" with interesting characterizations to a higher level that causes us to contemplate our human condition with unending fascination.

Exploring Inner Thoughts and Feelings in Your Writing

Uncovering inner thoughts and feelings has been a lifelong pursuit of mine— in my personal as well as my creative life. Following my father's early death (when I was barely sixteen), my mother's long bout with manic depression (especially when I was about twelve), and her early death (when I was twenty-two), I found a mass of confused, bewildered, sometimes angry, inner thoughts, feelings, perceptions, and ideas exploding inside me.

A friend of mine in college—an art student—often talked at length about her inner thoughts and feelings, especially her fears. Listening to her, I realized that people actually did talk about such concerns, although I was far from sure that I would be able to do so. In fact, I was quite certain that no one would want to hear me babble on about this inner world of mine.

Writing
from
Within:
The Next
Generation

168

At the same time, I had begun seeking answers to the questions: "Who am I? Where am I going? Where have I come from? Is there a God? If so, what does he/she/it look like? What is love? Is a good relationship possible? Why would a loving God take from me the person I needed most in my life, my father? Why would a loving God create so much misery for a good person, my mother?"

I sought answers in novels, plays, short stories, paintings, films, and music, and the answer I got was that the universe holds a multitude of answers, all beneficial to know, if one searches long enough and hard enough.

When I entered the arena of filmmaking—screen and playwriting and directing, as well as teaching people to articulate their life experiences as stories—I began to see that people's points of view about their experiences were often fascinating to me and my students. This was especially true as we delved into our inner thoughts and feelings.

As a teacher and writer, I found that allowing the outer world in which we live to unfold—the texture of the world around us, including the relationships we enter into—was a rich and challenging experience. But the real challenge lay in getting a hold of the deepest inner thoughts and feelings that all us humans have—but often don't know we have. These issues underlie all the books I have written, the screenplays I have created, and the films I have made.

While writing this book I repeatedly asked myself, "What is this book really about?" I began to see that a part of the techniques and perspectives outlined in the book had one purpose: to make as clear as possible how to express the fabric of our inner lives, the world of our inner thoughts and feelings, in the outer world of pen, paper, and computer. This meant both uncovering our inner thoughts and feelings as well as seeing the almost infinite number of perspectives that we humans have (and can share) about the nature of the world in which we live—especially the nature of the relationships that exist in our worlds.

Throughout my many years of teaching people to write their life stories and, more recently, to write creative stories, including novels and screenplays, this has become my primary goal—to help others give voice to the most fleeting of their inner thoughts and feelings, to help them put into words the things that they barely realize that they know.

This is what you, the reader, can look forward to in the remainder of this book: how to get the individual inner thoughts and feelings of your characters down on paper, while at the same time finding and creating characters who give voice to your own, personal, inner thoughts and feelings. You will acquire tools that allow you to express your sense of the world in which you and your characters live—good characters intent on surviving in an evil world or a world they never made; plodding characters, oblivious to their potential for a better, more-examined, more-meaningful life—to name just a couple of scenarios.

Advanced Perspectives
in Writing Creatively

The advanced perspectives in *Writing from Within: The Next Generation* build on the basic steps in *Writing from Within,* and it helps to know those well. Before you start in on the advanced techniques taught in this book, be sure of the following:

- You are familiar with, and quite comfortable in using, the basic steps described in Part I of this book, which were also outlined in *Writing from Within,* 3rd edition.
- You are familiar with the feedback process outlined in the Appendix to this book.
- You understand and embrace the concept of rewriting as many times as you feel are necessary before coming up with a final version.

Note: If you have already had experience as a writer and are looking for additional ways of enhancing your writing, these advanced perspectives may be helpful to you without first absorbing the basic steps of "writing from within."

A good way for you to start building the creative knowledge needed to grasp the material provided in this first section is by learning to recognize how others use these techniques. At a certain point in each chapter, I give you a picture of how I see these methods being used in the stories at the end of the book. I strongly suggest that you go to the end of the book and read these stories (and also go to www.WritingFromWithin-Stories.com, where more stories are found), and then look for the uses of the techniques in each story before I discuss them in depth. By reading the stories and noting the use of these techniques in the stories in advance, you will be able to compare your perception of the advanced techniques in the stories to mine. Keep in mind, though, that it is not necessary that you agree with my perception. It is only necessary that you do the work on your own and have a perception of how and where the techniques are being employed in each story.

By reading the stories over and over, you will come to understand the advanced techniques and perspectives in order to make them your own, like a jazz musician who plays a tune again and again, making changes until the melodic line becomes his own original expression. I urge you to read these stories in their entirety before proceeding.

Note: From time to time I refer to writing (and filmmaking) techniques that appear later in the book. When I make such references, my intention is not to digress but to give you, the reader, a sense that many of the techniques discussed in this book are deeply intertwined. Likewise, I often mention films and musical and theatrical pieces. On first glance these discussions or mentions may seem to be digressions, but they are not. No matter the medium of expression, the production of creative work is always somewhat similar. As a lifelong musician, photographer, play and film director, screenwriter, and novelist, I have come to see the remarkable similarities that exist so strongly in the many art forms that I have explored.

Using Short Sentences, the "Objective Correlative," and the "Hitchcockian Recap"

"Hi, I'm Dale Crum," grins an amiable, older gentleman as my new adult-school, life-writing class gets together in Woodland Hills, California, for the first time. The year is 1998.

For some fifteen years, I had been teaching my life-story writing classes on the west side of Los Angeles, not far from my home in Venice, California. With my kids grown, however, I wanted to live in a cozier, more rural space, so I moved up to Topanga Canyon in the Santa Monica Mountains. Shortly afterward, I began teaching my writing classes in Woodland Hills and Calabasas, California.

From 1998 to 2012 Dale absorbed the original steps of "writing from within" without difficulty, integrating them into his stories with ease. The skill with which he did this prompted me to look into and teach more subtle and effective ways of telling a story. At every step along this path, Dale absorbed and integrated the new material with unusual clarity and depth of understanding.

Here is the beginning to Dale's story:

Smoke Rings   *by Dale Crum*   (EXCERPT)

My cigarette smoke drifts toward Mama's open bathroom window. I smoke two packs of Camels a day and crave nicotine early. Sunshine splashes on the pink shower curtain. Multicolored gold fish fluoresce among its folds.

Reminds me of tame Calicos, orange Orandas, and Bubble Eyes in the Marshall Islands. They swam close to my navy face mask in the coral reefs only three years ago. Wish I were there, now. These rainy Seattle streets depress me.

I stand up and look in the mirror. Out-of-focus wallpaper surrounds bloodshot eyes and scruffy whiskers. Eeeyoo, my breath smells rotten. My tongue feels like sandpaper. I hate these cigarettes! Or, rather, I hate myself for liking them.

"Stunt your growth," my dad used to say.

But he said that about playing with myself, too.

Someone rattles the doorknob. Mama calls, "Dale, you in there?"

I yell, "Won't be long" and reach for the Listerine. Oh, didn't think she would get up before seven o'clock. Too cold to go outside and smoke. I pick up the towel stuffed in the crack at the bottom of the door, spray air freshener all around, and unlock the door.

Mama rushes in. She comes out with a sniff. "Thought you quit."

"Yeah, going to college."

"Not what I meant. You got a good job at Boeing."

"Just made up my mind. Talked to Elsie about it."

She frowns, "Oh, her? You like her?"

"She's a college sophomore in California. She'll show me around."

My B-50 flight control rigger's job only pays one dollar and ten cents an hour. That's union swing-shift wages, too. Boeing hired me a year ago for seventy-five cents an hour. Maybe Harry Truman here in the beginning of his first full term can kick-start the peacetime economy.

I sold my 1941 Buick sedan for eleven hundred dollars. Bought a cream puff '37 Chevy sedan for only four hundred. The G.I. bill will pay for my college tuition. With a part-time job, I can have fun in the sun and learn something, too.

(Please see page 275 for the remainder of the story.)

This opening to Dale's story incorporates a number of techniques that we will now discuss.

• • •

Having mastered the basic steps of "writing from within," you are able to write a very credible story. The present tense brings the story into sharp focus. Simplifying the language enables the writer to reach the reader's heart and gut. Incorporating feelings glues the story to the reader's heart. Dialogue brings relationships to life. Inner thoughts and feelings bring the reader even closer to the central character. Beginning the story with action or dialogue brings the reader into the story immediately.

Now I want to focus on several other things you can do to give the story even greater impact. For one thing, you can focus on writing short sentences, often dropping the subject and verb in the sentence to add a faster pace to the

Using Short Sentences, the "Objective Correlative," and the "Hitchcockian Recap"

173

story without losing clarity. Then, as you begin rewriting, sharpen the characters' character qualities: Every action characters take in pursuit of what they want comes from a quality they have. Finally, in the second paragraph (more or less), you will learn to slow down the action and to give the reader a glimpse of what has gone on before the story opens—what battles, resentments, quirks of fate, and foolish actions have shaped the main character's life.

Using Short Sentences

Where possible, use short sentences, especially in the descriptive passages. This technique moves the story along as fast as possible, allowing the reader to see what is going on rather than being told what is happening.

Here is an example of the effective use of short sentences from Dale's narrative at the beginning of his story "Smoke Rings" (for the complete story see page 275). The story begins with action, transporting us to another time and place, at least for the moment:

> My cigarette smoke drifts toward Mama's open bathroom window. I smoke two packs of Camels a day and crave nicotine early. Sunshine splashes on the pink shower curtain. Multicolored gold fish fluoresce among its folds.

The second paragraph continues to use short sentences:

> Reminds me of tame Calicos, orange Orandas, and Bubble Eyes in the Marshall Islands. They swam close to my navy face mask in the coral reefs only three years ago. Wish I were there, now. These rainy Seattle streets depress me.

This paragraph, which gives the reader a glimpse of what happened before the story opens, is called *backstory*. The short sentences enable the reader to get a quick, vivid picture of what is going on in the character's mind as well as what takes place around him.

Here is another example of the use of short sentences from the work of Sam Glenn, a musician friend of mine.

The Board   *by Sam Glenn*   (EXCERPT)

I'm leaving for college tomorrow. Freshman year. Leaving home. Gotta go through my things.

"Sam, I think I'll set up my sewing machine in your room." Mom's

Writing
from
Within:
The Next
Generation

174

voice sounds like she might start crying as she leaves my room and heads to the kitchen.

What to throw away? What to take with me? What to store?

Oh, there's my work board. Should I throw it away? I've had it since I was nine years old. Wow, what a lot of memories. Look at these cut marks—every direction—hundreds, maybe thousands from X-ACTO blades, razor blades, my Boy Scout knife. Crisscrossing the grain of the wood. And my name burned into the corner. Old English–style letters, SAM. Used my wood-burning kit. There's a little bit of solder embedded over on this edge. That's from when I built my Heath kit stereo receiver. And all those clamp marks. From the C-clamps I borrowed from my dad's toolbox.

How many model planes did I put together on this board? Those really neat ones with wings made of thin balsa strips, covered with colored rice paper, then dampened, stretched, and glued so it was tight like a drum-head. Rubber-band powered. Sounds simple, but everything had to be just right. They didn't all fly well, but when one did it was heaven. My favorite was a British biplane from World War I. It was blue. Like the kind that fought against Manfred von Richthoven—the Red Baron.

(The complete text of this story can be found at www.WritingFromWithin-Stories.com.)

The short sentences in this opening give a punch and immediacy to the writing. Sam uses incomplete sentences—"Freshman year. Leaving home."— to add more punch and immediacy to the writing. This approach to writing makes the narrator sound youthful and energetic, a no-nonsense person. In this way, the style of writing—short, immediate, sometimes incomplete sentences—conveys a sense of the character's qualities and moves the story forward at a rapid pace.

For more of Sam's work, please go to the "Stories" section of the book (see page 284) and also www.WritingFromWithin-Stories.com.

Two other techniques allow writers to add clarity to their stories: the objective correlative and the "Hitchcockian recap." Each one enables the writer to keep the audience on track with the story, avoiding questions that might break the sense of being on a wonderful voyage, which is what the writer hopes is taking place.

The "Objective Correlative"

The "objective correlative" is a rather technical-sounding term made famous by T.S. Eliot in the early years of the twentieth century. Eliot was appalled at the excessive emotion that nineteenth-century Romantic writers created in their stories when, in fact, there was no objective reason for all the excitement. (This overabundance of emotion is readily visible in such works as the operas of Verdi and Wagner.) Eliot suggested that if emotion is to be present in a novel, play, opera, or short story, readers or viewers have to be able to see what caused the emotion and to judge for themselves whether the cause warranted the emotionality. He called the actions or circumstances behind the emotion the "objective correlative." It is no accident that the flamboyance of the nineteenth-century romantic novel and opera, as found in Stendhal's *The Red and the Black* and Verdi's *Aida*, gave way to understated but intense realism in drama such as Ibsen's *Hedda Gabler* and Strindberg's *Miss Julie*, and continued into the twentieth century with films such as in Elia Kazan's *On the Waterfront*.

What is the relevance of the objective correlative to your interest in writing effective life stories? Writers sometimes make the mistake of asking the reader to believe there is a reason for a high state of emotion in a character during the concluding section of a story even when the reason for that high state of emotion has not been explained convincingly in the beginning of the story—that is, a *defining motif* (a recurring pattern) in the story is missing. (For a more complete discussion on motifs see Chapter 23.)

A good example of a well-placed motif—an objective correlative—appears in David Lean's classic film *Dr. Zhivago*. Midway through the film, Lara is about to leave Zhivago—for him, a searing departure. The music ("Lara's Theme") swells. Does the audience know why her departure means so much to him? Indeed it does. In the beginning of the film, a young Zhivago stands at the grave of his mother as her coffin is lowered into the ground. Zhivago's sense of longing and loss are echoed in the music that swells upward ("Lara's Theme") as a panoply of flowers and snow drifts upward along with the spirit of Zhivago's mother. So when the audience witnesses Lara about to leave, sees the sunflower in the corner of the frame, and hears "Lara's Theme," it understands that Zhivago is experiencing profound loss—his mother, as well as Lara—in this scene. In this way, the objective correlative plays a huge part in the audience experiencing Zhivago's feelings.

In Dale's story "Smoke Rings" (see the complete text of this story on page 275) he provides numerous examples (objective correlatives) for his suspicions that he shouldn't trust Elsie—she is too naïve. Her smoking is a tipoff that she is young, inexperienced, and hungry for experience. Later, when she throws out the ashes, she reveals herself as "gauche," like Dale at an earlier time. Then when she plows through the mud, the reader sees that she is messy. So, inexperienced, gauche, and messy—not a woman for Dale to trust. Of course, the pleasure of the story—the "aha," the epiphany—is that she reveals herself to be far more calculating and aware than Dale ever expected.

Writing
from
Within:
The Next
Generation

176

The "Hitchcockian Recap"

Alfred Hitchcock created any number of techniques in his films to keep viewers glued to their seats. One of the most effective was his use of the "recap"—that is, retelling what has happened in the film up to the moment when the recap begins. However, this recapping of the events is not mere exposition—in which themes, motifs, and concerns in a story are laid out—but a subtle reviewing of what has been happening mixed in with some distracting action.

In a famous and oft-quoted moment in Hitchcock's *Rear Window*, James Stewart, playing an invalid with a broken leg, has been watching what happens in an apartment building across the courtyard. He sees a salesman, played by Raymond Burr, argue with his bedridden wife, and a little while later the wife disappears. Stewart tells the stunning Grace Kelly—his love interest in the film—that he suspects foul play. She pooh-poohs his observations, trying instead to interest him in her. At the end of the scene, Kelly goes out to run errands. While she is out, a number of significant things happen across the courtyard. When she returns, Stewart recaps what has gone on in her absence. Kelly, who is far more interested in nudging their relationship forward, is all seduction and pouting displeasure. Far more interested in the gorgeous Ms. Kelly, the audience barely pays attention to Stewart's recap.

Nevertheless, Hitchcock accomplishes his goal: reminding the audience of what has happened in the story up to that point in the picture. He uses this technique over and over in his films, always with good results. The audience may not be aware that information is being fed to it, but the recap tells it just what it needs to know to avoid being lost in any way. (This scene from *Rear Window* is also an excellent example of the dialogue/action of one character working at cross-purposes with the dialogue/action of another character.)

This technique is one that you can use in your stories as well. In "My Sister's Shadow," another story by Dale Crum (see the complete text of this story at www.WritingFromWithin-Stories.com), Dale meets up with his friend, Milt, and recaps what has occurred in the story from his point of view. Milt has a totally different take on what Dale has observed. Without the recap from Dale's point of view, the story would not have a great deal of impact. Dale's use of the recap solidifies the reader's grasp of what has happened and, at the same time, leads to an interesting moment when Milt provides Dale with a totally different way of interpreting Dale's sister's actions.

Developing Character Qualities, Backstory, and Denouement

One of the most important aspects of creating stories is developing interesting characters. In a dramatic film, such as *On the Waterfront* with Marlon Brando, the audience finds itself caring about the characters to the degree that it wants to see them succeed against great odds to attain something they care about. *How* characters go about pursuing their dreams, their comebacks, and their goals is what the audience cares about in a story.

Are Character Qualities Evident in the Story?

Every action characters take stems from the *character qualities* they possess, even though the characters may not know they possessed those qualities in the beginning of the story.

Examples of basic character qualities that get people through life are honesty, humor, dedication, adaptability, persistence, ingenuity, passion, and the like.

For example, in *On the Waterfront,* Brando's character has been knocked around the boxing ring for so long, he can't think straight. When his brother, who hangs out with the local mob run by Johnny Friendly, tells him to do something, he does it, no questions asked.

But when he encounters an upstanding woman (Eva Marie Saint) whom he desires, a woman who wants to find her brother's killer, Brando's character finds himself torn between loyalty to his brother and the mob and loyalty to his new love. The character quality that rises to the surface is *emotional honesty.* Brando may not tell his love interest the whole truth in the beginning, but he doesn't lie to her, and he finally admits that he knows who killed her brother… and even that he had a small part in the killing. He risks her rejection in favor of telling the truth about his involvement. Later, he risks his brother's love by going to the government with evidence against the mob.

Note: If you are interested in knowing more about character qualities, a fuller discussion is found in my book *Character Consciousness.*

In writing a life story, in the first draft you need to focus on purely getting the story down on paper, without worrying about such concerns as whether the characters' qualities are visible. However, from the second draft on, sharpening these qualities must become a primary concern. For example, whatever actions a character takes in the development section or the concluding section of your story must be planted, as a motif, in the setup—the introductory section—of your story. Generally speaking, writers get into trouble by having characters take actions late in the story that are not suggested in the setup of the story.

When done well, the incorporation of character qualities gives the reader a sense of knowing a character well, of being able to anticipate how they will handle a situation and whether they will find new inner qualities with which to handle new obstacles. (Please take a look at Bill Rempel's story on page 234 about creating *At the Devil's Table* for a probing look at the character qualities of a very interesting man.)

Creating Backstory to Inform

One of the most effective ways of giving the reader some context to whatever is going on when the story opens, while also giving dimension to certain characters, is to provide some *backstory* to the event that is taking place.

Very often this backstory occurs in the second or third paragraph of the story. The first paragraph is often devoted to an "attention getter" that takes the reader out of their boring, humdrum life and thrusts them into the action of an exciting story.

However, in the second or third paragraph, an effective writer weaves some history relevant to what's going on into the unfolding narrative. Here is Dale's second-paragraph backstory in "Smoke Rings" (see page 275 for the complete story):

> Reminds me of tame Calicos, orange Orandas, and Bubble Eyes in the Marshall Islands. They swam close to my navy face mask in the coral reefs only three years ago. Wish I were there, now. These rainy Seattle streets depress me.

From this information, the reader learns that the main character is not some rebellious teenager but a veteran of World War II who has likely acquired

*Developing
Character
Qualities,
Backstory, and
Denouement*

179

habits similar to those of others his age, such as a desire to move along in life, to get educated, and to make something of himself.

Effective writers also provide the reader with backstory gradually, as the story progresses, rather than giving it to us all at once.

In Dale's story, a few more sentences of dialogue reveal that Dale is thinking about leaving his parents' home in Seattle and heading for college in Southern California:

> My B-50 flight control rigger's job only pays one dollar and ten cents an hour. That's union swing-shift wages, too. Boeing hired me a year ago for seventy-five cents an hour. Maybe Harry Truman here in the beginning of his first full term can kick-start the peacetime economy.
>
> I sold my 1941 Buick sedan for eleven hundred dollars. Bought a cream puff '37 Chevy sedan for only four hundred. The G.I. bill will pay for my college tuition. With a part-time job I can have fun in the sun and learn something, too.

Another helpful example occurs in the story "In the Beginning…," by Roy Wilhelm:

In the Beginning… *by Roy Wilhelm*

The plaque on the wall near the front entrance says that this state youth prison was built ten years ago in 1962. How many times have I looked at that plaque in the last half hour as I paced back and forth? This time as I stop to stare at it, a voice interrupts my thoughts, "You sure read slow. You've been studying that plaque the whole time I walked through the parking lot from my car."

I quip, "I have a bachelor and master's degree, but I still read slowly."
He laughs.

"Actually, I was deep in thought." I continue, "You know how it is waiting for a job interview. The receptionist said it will be awhile until they call me. I'm so nervous, I had to take it outside here to get fresh air."

He replies, "Well, it sure is a great place to work. Good luck to you." He walks inside.

Man, I want this job so bad. I'm forty-one years old, and for twelve years I've studied, trained, and had various jobs that would qualify me to be a California state institutional chaplain. Three years ago, they interviewed me, but they hired somebody else. I'm thoroughly frustrated.

My wife and I drove from Phoenix, Arizona, and stayed last night at the home of my friend, Rev. Dan Berth. He told me, "Roy, I visited Ventura School in Camarillo a year ago. It's like a high school campus. I think the Lord made you wait and prepare yourself this long so you'd be well quali-

Writing
from
Within:
The Next
Generation

180

fied to help those young people." He patted me on the back. "I'm sure you'll get the job."

Notice that the third paragraph describes what has happened in the past, enabling the reader to understand what getting the job means to Roy and how much is riding on getting this job—that is, how high the stakes are.

Most effective stories employ backstory to give a rich sense of where the central character has come from, as well as the minor characters. That is the value of backstory.

The Denouement

Well-developed stories depend on the use of certain artistic principles such as balance, variety, repetition, tension, and release (these are explained in greater detail in Chapter 24). A skilled writer who understands the need for balance supplies something more after the climax of the story to make sure the story ends in an emotionally satisfying way. This resolution is called the *denouement*, a French word meaning "falling off"—literally "untying a knot."

Here is the ending of Dale's story "Smoke Rings." Pay close attention to the denouement in his story:

Smoke Rings   *by Dale Crum*   (EXCERPT)

We reach Los Angeles late the next day. I park in back of the women's dorm, shake out the kinks, and open the trunk. I turn with Elsie's bag and bump into a guy. He hugs Elsie and asks her, "Drive nonstop from Seattle?"

"Nope. Willie, this is Dale," she replies. "Stopped in southern Oregon." He persists, "Side of the road?"

"Nope. Motel."

She swivels her body away. Willie's face turns color. He slobbers into his red bandana handkerchief. I steel myself for his next question. In the same room?

He makes choking noises. No words come out. They stand nose to nose. I set her bag down, back out of the lot, and light up a cigarette before he clobbers me.

I've seen riled up Cajuns in the navy. They hold both hands together in a giant fist and slam down on someone's head. Pole-axed, they call it.

Four days later I sit near Elsie in the cafeteria. She waves her left hand at me. A large rock sparkles on her ring finger.

She giggles, "Me and Willie."

I give her a big epiphany smile of admiration. "Congratulations."

She outsmarted both her mother and me. Made Willie jealous enough to pop the question. I feel relieved. For once I don't need another cigarette. Any more may drive me crazy, may drive me insane.

The climax occurs when Willie shows his emotions at the thought of Elsie and Dale sleeping together. Perhaps Willie will tee off on Dale. The wonderful twist to the climax is the moment when Elsie shows Dale the ring that Willie has just given her. This is the moment of greatest tension…and release. Dale's realization that his take on Elsie has been wrong—that she has not been trying to hook Dale at all—constitutes a satisfying denouement to the story.

Writing
from
Within:
The Next
Generation

182

chapter 23

Creating Visual Motifs, Minor Characters, and Form

Sophisticated use of visual motifs (strong visual images, often repeated, that underscore certain messages or themes), minor characters, and form abound in the work of fiction writers. However, these techniques are also available to the writer of nonfiction life stories.

This does not mean that as a life-story writer, you invent what is needed, as a fiction writer does. On the contrary, you learn to look at your life and see the things that happen to you as potential parts of your stories. Minor characters throw into high relief the struggles of the central character. Visual motifs underscore the meaning, themes, and plights of the central character. Finally, you want to be sure that any motifs you create—character motifs (actions and the like) or visual motifs—occur in the setup to the story (the first third), unfold in the middle, and pay off at the end of the story. This is what *form* means.

Creating Visual Motifs

One technique that writers and filmmakers use to underscore messages/themes is to employ a strong visual image that resonates in the audience's mind or heart. This visual image or motif is simply a recurring theme of some kind. For example, in John Steinbeck's *The Grapes of Wrath*, the Joad family makes its way to California in a beat-up old truck. In the middle of the road, under a hot, desert sun, a turtle moves across the highway, ever so slowly. The Joad vehicle flips the turtle on its back, leaving it to bake under the hot desert sun, unable to right itself. This image of the turtle is the writer's way of giving a clue as to the fate of the Joad family—a creature struggling to survive, out of its element (the farms of the Midwest dust bowl), helpless under the cruel, hot sun.

As writers of life stories, you can do the same things. All around you, visual images echo the struggles of the central characters. To effectively use these images as motifs in stories they should occur at least three times: You should include them in the setup of your story, again in the development section, and then again in the conclusion.

In Dale Crum's story "Smoke Rings" (see the complete story on page 275), the cigarette is a visual motif that signifies different things. In the beginning of the story, his cigarette symbolizes his independence from his family, his worldliness and impatience with their way of life. Early on, in the hands of cute little Elsie, it's an expression of innocence seeking worldliness. Later, when Elsie flicks the ashes off her cigarette onto the ground, her casual attitude about her messiness makes Dale wonder if she might also be casual about protecting Dale's well-being. Here is what Dale says about creating motifs in his stories:

> I don't think "motifs" per se when I start a story. But by the time I write the first page, natural motifs, which were there all the time, pop up in my memory—a cloud, a blue sky, a baby's cry. The feel of her hand. Smells of the river. A taste of honey. Then I add them, starting near the top of the story. They work best when scattered throughout.

Visual motifs are a powerful tool for a writer. If the motif is central to the character's actions, the audience will *feel* it through the power of the image. For example, in Shakespeare's *Macbeth* the prophesy—that order will be restored "when Burnham Wood comes to Dunsinane"—connects the motif of the restoration of order and an image of the movement of Burnham Wood in the reader's or viewer's minds early in the play. But the audience thinks little about it until the end, when McDuff's forces emerge from Burnham Wood, concealed beneath brush and trees, as they crawl toward the castle of Dunsinane. When Lady Macbeth sees the prophesy coming true visually, the impact of it makes her—and the audience—gasp.

Often, visual motifs gain significant power from their representation of a moral or God-given order in the universe. The turtle's struggling to right itself or Burnham Wood's coming to Dunsinane suggest a moral order in which the turtle ought to be allowed to right itself and Burnham Wood ought to come to Dunsinane. In an age when the certainty of a moral order is open to question, the presence of powerful visual symbols reassures the audience that a moral order may exist.

It hardly needs to be said that one person's moral order may look like tyranny to another person: Witness the variety of symbols, such as the swastika, that provoke all kinds of emotion in people. So as you search for arresting visual symbols in your stories, you also need to consider the use of false symbols by nonheroic characters in these same stories.

Writing
from
Within:
The Next
Generation

184

Creating Three-Dimensional Minor Characters

The quality of your storytelling will become substantially better if you allow minor characters to react to circumstances that bedevil the major characters.

Very often, minor characters fall into certain types: the mentor, the playboy, the innocent, the martyr, the trickster, the villain, the mystic, the adventurer, the old wise man, and the like. These "types" often exist in life, and a knowledge of them allows you to recognize them when they cross your path in real life.

In Dale Crum's story "My Sister's Shadow" (the complete story can be found www.hunterhouse.com), Dale is uncertain about whether he really ought to be trying to protect his sister. Therefore, he seeks out Milt, a friend who advises him to let well enough alone. But Milt does more than that. He levels a certain amount of criticism at Dale for being naïve. In doing so, the character of Milt reveals himself to be something of a trickster—an impish, mercurial type of person whose unpredictability serves the main character well by saying things to him that others might not be willing to say aloud:

> "Cleo doesn't go with church guys. Claims they're too sissified."
> (Milt) sneers, "Sounds like what my sisters might say about you, Dale."

The reaction of minor characters is often what governs the actions of major characters and can also support the mood the writer wants to convey. In motion pictures and television shows, such reactions are vital to the progress of the plot.

In the old *Gunsmoke* series, Marshall Dillon inevitably winds up in a gunfight with the bad guys. In and of itself, this might not alarm the viewing audience. However, when the audience sees Chester, Doc, Festus, and Kitty start to react with fear or concern, then the audience begins to do so as well. In film parlance, this is called "coverage"—making sure the director has filmed plenty of reaction shots so the editor can cut away from the main action to another angle.

Creating a Sense of Form

The human mind cannot hold in its memory bank very much of what it receives. Therefore, the artist must create a form that allows the audience to make sense of what it receives and to remember what it understands. The principles of art (which we will talk about next) help in establishing this sense of form. One of these principles—balance—comes into play by creating a shape to the story, usually a beginning (called "a setup"), a middle (called "development"), and a conclusion (sometimes called "a recap").

At the beginning of a story, or the setup, authors often introduce motifs, which are small, powerful images or sounds that contain the seeds of all the dramatic material to come. Later, in the middle of a story, these motifs are developed into full-blown themes. In the conclusion section, the conflicts related to these motifs/themes are resolved in some way.

Note: In many stories, a motif or motifs may gradually transform into, and predict, a developing theme. A visual motif may not reappear as a motif but in the reader's mind an inner "alarm button" is created, which is then set off as the larger theme begins to take shape. The following is an example of a visual motif that morphs into (and predicts) a larger theme to follow:

Recall that at the beginning of *The Grapes of Wrath*, Steinbeck introduces a turtle motif. He shows the creature, upended on a highway leading from the dust bowl of the Midwest to California, struggling to survive, roasting under the hot sun, with no way to right itself. Later, in the development section, the members of the Joad family struggle terribly with the poverty into which they have been thrust, with no apparent way of coping with their situation. In the conclusion, they find ways of coping, of righting themselves, and of surviving.

These concepts are explored more fully in the next chapter, "Employing the Principles of Art and Subtext."

Writing
from
Within:
The Next
Generation

186

chapter 24

Employing the Principles of Art and Subtext

For a writer's work to make sense to the audience and for it to remember what the writer is talking about, the writer has to employ certain artistic principles. The writer must compose a story in the same way that a musician or a painter uses composition to create the desired impact. Composition, in this context, means manipulating the elements of an artist's craft by using artistic techniques and following certain principles of art—repetition, balance, symmetry, variety, contrast, tension, and release—that are used by all artists at all times.

Some of the most memorable works of art and literature are those that rise above the literal: In other words, what the story *seems* to be about may not be what the story really *is* about. We call this additional meaning subtext.

Employing the Principles of Art

The human mind can only retain a small amount of the information it receives, a small portion of the stimuli that the eye perceives and the ear receives. For a viewer to accept and retain any portion of that stimulus, the artwork must be shaped into palatable chucks of information. At the same time, the viewer does not want to retain that which he has previously seen, so information must be shaped in new packages to keep the viewer alert and stimulated.

As a consequence, artistic endeavors throughout the history of mankind have relied upon certain principles that can be found in all works of art, though the shaping continues to vary from one work of art to the next. They apply to each of the elements within a work separately and to all of the elements collectively.

Dramatists such as Ibsen and Strindberg, filmmakers like Billy Wilder and Orson Welles, as well as composers and arrangers from Beethoven and Monteverdi to John Williams and Quincy Jones use these same principles of art. In fact, artists at all times and places, working in a variety of mediums, use these principles to channel the viewers' or audience's or readers' perceptions and thoughts.

As life-story writers, you, too, can use these principles of repetition, balance, variety, and the like—but how?

Primarily, you must create a motif (pattern) in the beginning of the story, change and develop it in the middle section of the story, and make its meaning clear as you resolve the story. These principles become clearer via an examination of Dale's story in the next section.

The principles of art are as follows:

1. repetition

2. balance

3. symmetry

4. variety

5. contrast

6. tension and release

7. unity

Balance, Symmetry, Repetition

The single most fundamental principle of art is that of balance. Nature, including the human body, exists because of a basic balance to the way things are. Every leaf on every tree in nature has a balance of capillaries that shoot outward from a central vein giving it a balance that allows the leaf to grow. Every tree has a balance of branches that spread outward in all directions seeking light from every direction. The human body is similarly balanced—a right leg and arm on one side; a left leg and arm on the other; each foot with five digits; each hand with five digits. This is the fundamental balance of nature.

When the left and right sides of something like the body exists we call that *symmetry*. The object is symmetrical. If the right and left sides are exactly the same, we call that *bilateral symmetry*.

Writing
from
Within:
The Next
Generation

188

The leaf of which we spoke earlier has a number of tiny capillaries that spread out from a central vein and feed the leaf. When we look at the leaf, we notice its function (to feed the leaf) but also its form—its symmetrical form. This symmetry is achieved by means of veins reaching out, one after another, in a repeated hierarchy of tiny capillaries. This repetition is what gives the form of the leaf its beauty. As we look at the leaf, our eyes are immediately drawn to the repeated patterns of tiny veins and capillaries that reach out from the spine of the leaf to the outer edges of the leaf. Just as a musical phrase in a Mozart composition is repeated, so too are the veins of the leaf.

During the Italian Renaissance, artists made every effort to create the illusion of three dimensions by using artistic techniques that create a sense of perspective on the surface. These artists drew lines that converged at a single point, often in the middle of the painting. The viewer's eye is led into the deep distance, as in Leonardo da Vinci's *The Last Supper* (see page 55) or Peter Bruegel's *The Fall of Icarus* (see page 56). These converging lines create a sense of balance, even as they create an illusion of three dimensions.

By contrast, modern artists often try to arouse emotions by creating strong visual accents on the surface of the painting. Nevertheless, these artists are still governed by the principles of art—repetition, balance, symmetry, variety, contrast, tension, and release. For example, in Matisse's *The Joy of Life*, rounded shapes colored in red, which we interpret as dancing figures, create an illusion of motion and energy through the repetition of the shapes. Colored red, these shapes stand out against (in contrast to) the blue of the background.

In writing, these principles are most evident in stories where the beginning of the story bears a resemblance to the ending of the story. In "Smoke Rings" (see the complete story on page 275), the story opens with Dale's cigarette and the smoke it creates. The cigarette continues to weave in and out of the picture throughout the story and reappears at the end of the story.

Variety and Contrast

If we look closely at the aforementioned leaf, we notice that while the tiny veins and capillaries are more or less symmetrical, nevertheless those on the left side of the leaf are not exactly placed nor are they the size of the veins and capillaries on the right side. For the eye, this is pleasing, because the lack of exact repetition gives us some relief from what could be monotonous. This variety gives the leaf added dynamism. We feel its aliveness, seeking a route to light that will keep it alive.

In circumstances where the variety we see opposes the original motif, then we use the term contrast. In a tree, we might see a number of green, healthy leaves, but we might also see contrasting leaves that are dead or dying. In fall, maple trees are rich with color, often contrasting colors ranging from green to red to yellow, all degrees of health.

The visual arts present us with rich examples of variety and contrast. The sixteenth century painter, Caravaggio, in a painting such as *The Calling of St. Mathew,* paints a room filled with people. He imagines that the room is in darkness until the light of God pierces that darkness, partially illuminating the faces and figures of those surrounding St. Mathew. In this painting we have dynamic contrasts of light and dark.

Three hundred years later, filmmaker Orson Welles, in *Touch of Evil,* gives us a similar light and dark rendering of space in the opening sequence of the film. Shot as if it is night, the film pelts us with images of a bomb planted under a car, then an image of Charleton Heston and Janet Leigh in their car illuminated by momentary flashes of light from surrounding buildings and from lightning and thunder, then an explosion—all connected by an uninterrupted, unifying tracking shot. Welles' tour de force opening sequence keeps tension high while introducing all the elements of the story that the filmmaker is about to tell.

The same elements of contrast, especially in lighting, are present in the extract from J.D. Tousley's story "Cricket" on page 80. As Tack approaches the porch on which Cricket's father is sitting, Mr. Horner is sitting half in the light, half in darkness. This presents a sense of mystery and foreboding, much like that created in film noir movies.

Tension and Release

Most works of art that unfold over a period of time, such as music, theatre and the novel, depend on alternating series of tensions, and release from tension, to hold the interest of the audience. Some analysts of motion picture plot and story lines, such as Syd Field, have gone so far as to insist that plots/story lines should turn in an unexpected direction (an increased tension) on page 33 and again on page 66 of 100 page scripts. In fact, film producers do often look for these "turns" in the plot on these pages.

However, tension and release can take many forms, not just turns in the plot. The writers of 1940s film noir movies created significant tensions by introducing the "bad guy's" backstory. Two thirds of the way through *This Gun for Hire,* Alan Ladd tells Veronica Lake about the abuse he experienced as a child. Not only does she suddenly come to care about him, the audience does as well. No one wants to see anything bad happen to him.

Vittorio de Sica's *Bicycle Thieves* is filled with tensions and releases from tension. Shortly after WWII comes to an end, the protagonist—a poor head of a small family—finds himself desperate for work. His family flirts with starvation. A job comes his way, but he needs a bicycle. (First tension.) His wife agrees to pawn precious linens to get his bicycle out of hock. (Tension increases.) A happy man, he sets out for the job with his son (Tension releases.) While he is on the job, the bicycle is stolen. (Tension increases again.) Searching for the man who stole the bicycle, he catches a glimpse of the thief. (Tension releases.) He and his son pursue. (Tension increases.) He gets angry at his son for a small incident. The son wanders off, heart-broken. (Tension increases.) He finds his son and asks forgiveness. (Tension diminishes.) He finds the thief and accuses

Writing
from
Within:
The Next
Generation

190

him of the theft, but cannot prove it. (Tension increases.) He leaves, laughed at and humiliated. (Tension increases.) Desperate, he steals someone else's bicycle. (Tension increases.) He is caught. (Tension increases again.) The policeman lets him go (Tension diminishes.), but he is no longer the hero in his son's eyes. (Tension increases again.) The film ends on this sad, ambiguous, heartfelt note.

From the ups and downs of this plot line, the orchestration of the tensions and releases in a film becomes one of the primary concerns of the writers, directors, editors and producers of any film.

Dale's story "Smoke Rings" provides a very nice sense of tension and release throughout the story. The stakes are high: Will Dale get caught in the web of intrigue the Elsie seems to be spinning—trapping Dale in an unwanted marriage or embroiling him in the conflict between Elsie and her boyfriend? The tension heightens as Dale and Elsie arrive in Los Angeles. The tension releases when Elsie shows Dale the engagement ring on her finger—her intended object from the beginning of the story.

Unity

Unity is the final principle of art that brings together the entire ensemble in an enjoyment-producing, stimulating way. Modern artists find a great deal of pleasure in creating a unified canvas. Dutch painter Piet Mondrian, in paintings such as *Broadway Boogie Woogie,* plays with small blocks of reds, yellows, blues, and greens to create abstract movement that echoes the energy to be found in the streets of New York.

Likewise, filmmakers strive to find the subtle balance of writing, acting, directing, editing, and filming that makes a film work. However, motion pictures that place too much emphasis on just one or two of the elements of filmmaking, such as too much action and not enough characterization in films like the 2002 remake of *War of the Worlds,* result in films that feel lopsided.

Films of the 1930s often appear to have excessive dialogue and not enough action. Preston Sturges' films, other than *Sullivan's Travels,* often appear to suffer from this defect. For example, *Unfaithfully Yours,* a delightful film in many ways, plods along through thirty to forty-five minutes of dialogue before the film leaps into Rex Harrison's worried fantasies about what his wife, Linda Darnell, may or may not be doing. Thus, its laborious opening scenes have weakened the unity of this film.

Modern audiences, particularly audiences of young people, are quick to grasp the subtleties of filmed drama. Their eyes and ears take in much more stimuli than older audiences, as is the case with the popularity of the *Matrix* series. Thus, classic films such as *Casablanca* and *Citizen Kane* may appear to be sentimental or slow to younger viewers. In *Casablanca,* the circumstances in which Rick finds himself may be too obscure for younger audiences to appreciate. *Citizen Kane*'s "Rosebud" ending may have the look of pop psychology about a man who doesn't interest modern audiences.

All of these problems have to do with a lack of unity that may not have been apparent to audiences of the past.

Developing the Subtext of a Story

Creating subtext is one of the most difficult yet rewarding tasks that the writer of creative stories undertakes. In a play or a motion-picture screenplay, the writer provides the text—that is, the actions taken by the hero/heroine and minor characters as well as the dialogue.

Interpreting the dialogue so that believable relationships occur is the objective of the director and actors as they work on a screenplay. In a novel or short story, the writer must supply the subtext (the implicit or metaphorical meaning) by supplying dialogue, actions, and inner thoughts and feelings that may conflict. Here is an example: In "Smoke Rings" (see the complete story on page 275), the subtext emerges little by little. Here are the narrator's lines that provide a picture of what is going on:

> I can't leave my good friend, Vera, a divorcée who works in the blueprint room.... Nor Joanne, the Catholic girl I sometimes go out with. Joanne's parents don't like Protestants. I really like Betty and Rosemary from our church. Mama does, too.

From this description, the reader sees that the narrator likes girls and dates quite a bit.

> She beams, "Mom says I can ride down to L.A. with you."
>
> Whoa! Her mother is a straight-laced woman from a straight-laced church. Takes two days to get to L.A. Unless you want to switch drivers and speed nonstop on that narrow, winding Highway 99.
>
> Elsie stops in her driveway. Her Mom, Mary, rushes to the car. "Oh, Dale, I'm so glad you decided to go. I trust you with Elsie. I know you will have an enjoyable trip."
>
> I think most mothers want to marry off their daughters by the time they're twenty years old. Wait a minute. Something's going on here.

From what is said, it looks like Elsie wants to go on a trip with Dale, and her mother hopes they get involved so they will wind up married—none of which is to Dale's liking.

Writing
from
Within:
The Next
Generation

192

"Huh-oh," this time I say under my breath. Takes only a second for the picture to develop in my mind. Mary wants me to take her daughter alone to California. She knows Charlie will find out. Poof! There goes Charlie.

I leer like Groucho Marx, "Long drive with me."

Elsie stares at me for a long time, then takes a cigarette from my package. I hold my Zippo lighter up, and she moves to the flame like a moth to a backyard barbecue. She inhales a little bit, coughs, and waves the smoke away from her face.

Here it appears that Dale sees Willie as no threat, and he makes a "we might have a night in a motel together" kind of a face. She appears to be thinking it over. In taking a cigarette from his packet of cigarettes, Elsie appears to be signaling that she is ready for a new experience.

Soon they arrive at a motel along the way and prepare to spend the night:

The bored clerk looks up from her *True Romances* magazine. She spits out of the side of her mouth, "Six dollars."

"Give me two adjoining rooms."

Her eyes flicker. She looks out the door before she hands me the keys. She makes me feel weird. Why spend the extra six dollars?

I carry the bags and balance on the bricks while Elsie splashes down the middle of the muddy walkway. After I plop down her bag, I move to the door.

She gives me the same quizzical look I saw on the clerk's face.

Now the reader sees that Dale plans to play it safe—no sex with Elsie. He doesn't want to risk winding up with her, just what her mom hopes will happen. No, he's going to outsmart them both.

We reach Los Angeles late the next day. I park in back of the women's dorm, shake out the kinks, and open the trunk. I turn with Elsie's bag and bump into a guy. He hugs Elsie and asks her, "Drive nonstop from Seattle?"

"Nope. Will, this is Dale," she replies. "Stopped in southern Oregon."

He persists, "Side of the road?"

"Nope. Motel."

She swivels her body away. Willie's face turns color. He slobbers into his red bandana handkerchief. I steel myself for his next question. In the same room?

He makes choking noises. No words come out. They stand nose to nose. I set her bag down, back out of the lot, and light up a cigarette before he clobbers me.

Now the reader thinks that Dale feels pretty good about himself. He has outsmarted Elsie and her mom in their desire to lasso Dale into early marriage. And he has not done anything to make Willie mad at him. Good for Dale.

> Four days later, I sit near Elsie in the cafeteria. She waves her left hand at me. A large rock sparkles on her ring finger.
> She giggles, "Me and Willie."
> I give her a big epiphany smile of admiration. "Congratulations."
> She outsmarted both her mother and me. Made Willie jealous enough to pop the question. I feel relieved. For once I don't need another cigarette. Any more may drive me crazy, may drive me insane.

Now the reader realizes that Elsie had a whole different take on what was supposed to happen than Dale did, and her take turned out to be the true take. Careful Dale, sure he had outsmarted another calculating woman, realizes he has been too careful: He could have had a good time with Elsie without any consequences, because she was focused on making Willie jealous and getting the ring whether Mama liked it or not.

The *text* of this delightful story is that despite his lusts, Dale avoids the snares of a calculating mother and her lustful, carefree daughter. He may have lust in his heart, but he is too careful, too smart, to fall for mother and daughter's plan to trap him into early marriage. The *subtext* is that women have agendas of their own, and no man is smart enough to figure out all the angles when a woman knows what she wants.

Dale uses the motif of the cigarette throughout the story to underscore its meaning. In the beginning, the cigarette makes him an alien, an unwanted person in his mother's home, something of a fallen angel. In the development section, Elsie takes the cigarette from Dale and coughs, a sign that she is still an angel but is willing to be initiated. Dale, however, is suspicious of her motives (and her mother's), so he does not seduce her and feels elated that he did not. In the conclusion, the reader sees that Elsie is no angel but a temptress. Whether Dale seduced her or she seduced him, she played the seduction card with her fiancé and got what she wanted—the ring. In this way, the repetition of the cigarette motif leads the reader to believe Dale's interpretation of events would be the tune that would be played, but, in fact, her version of what was happening, her tune, was the one that she wound up playing—"Here Comes the Bride."

In this way, the motif of the cigarette builds slowly into a theme (will Dale initiate the "uninitiated" girl?) However, by the end of the story, we see that this girl has turned everything her way, allowing us to see that subtext of the story: The young girl controlled the situation all along. Motifs developing into themes are very often the route by which subtext unfolds in a story.

Writing
from
Within:
The Next
Generation

194

Separating the Writer's Voice from the Central Character's Voice

This last perspective on writing perplexes writers more than any other. Writers of life stories find it especially difficult to grasp. Fiction writers know that to create interesting central characters, they must also create interesting contexts (circumstances, settings, obstacles, and minor characters) within which the central characters function. Without these elements, their stories will have little appeal.

On the other hand, the life-story writer often feels that because they sketch things that have really happened, all they must do is simply record accurately what took place.

The appearance of this task as "simple recording" is an illusion. We know that the human mind plays tricks all the time. In Part I, we discovered that a sibling will rarely recollect shared experiences the same way you remember them. Additionally, many forgotten experiences lie in your subconscious, waiting for you to become ready to deal with them before they emerge.

A writer using their life experiences must create an interesting central character and a context within which the character operates, just as the fiction writer does.

Very often this means that a writer of life stories must look hard for certain characters—that is, minor characters—who cause the central character to act decisively, revealing themselves more fully in the process.

Distinguishing Between the Narrator's Voice and the Central Character's Voice

In "Smoke Rings," Elsie is a fully realized character who has her own agenda in life and fools Dale and her mother. Dale is forced to admit that although he thought he was in charge of the situation, he was wrong; young Elsie was in charge. The laugh was on Dale.

Karl Grey's story "The Garage" (see the complete text of this story on page 273) gives us a picture of a kid who doesn't have much going for him, a situation made more difficult by an indifferent mother and a brutal stepfather. Any action or movement on Karl's part becomes an opportunity for the insensitive parent to retaliate. So what can Karl do? What will he do? Eventually, he finds a place deep inside himself where no one can reach him, no one can touch him, a place of dignity and safety. At this moment, the reader likes Karl. In his own way, he has triumphed over oppression.

When you write life stories, you know the disposition of the central character—the character's wants, needs, goals, and hopes and dreams. Readers want to see that character struggle to achieve his or her goals, not wallow in despair.

Consequently, you must make the minor characters that appear in the story more vivid than you might remember them initially. This does not mean that you should falsify them. But you do have to take a close, hard look at them and get behind their wants and needs, just as you would if you were writing fiction.

Often my students will say, "Well, at the time, my character didn't know these things. Yes, I know them now." (For example, the many types of abuse a woman may have endured.) But the fact is, someone in the picture *did* know about the abuse and probably said something, even though it was ignored, making that person a significant minor character in the story. (So often in life, guides exist who know what is good for us but, at the time, we didn't understand what the person was saying or we chose to ignore what they might have been saying.) All these minor characters must have a voice when you write.

Or in other circumstances, a minor character may be the voice of convention, wanting the central character to behave the way everyone else does. The central character can only define him- or herself by heading off in his or her own direction. Thus in Dale's story, his mother disapproves of Dale's decisions—quitting college, going to Los Angeles, bringing Elsie along, smoking cigarettes. But Dale's independence can only occur if he goes against his mother's wishes for him to lead a conventional life. This arc of his progress is made more difficult for him because he does love and respect his mother. Once again, a minor character helps defines who or what the main character is.

When asked what has helped him become the skilled writer he is, Dale had this to say:

> Sounds mundane, but switching to the computer screen years ago expanded my ability to see what my stories needed on first revisions. Seeing a whole page at once on the bright screen highlights the character/writer concerns, conflicts. Shows a panorama of what's missing, or included.

Writing
from
Within:
The Next
Generation

196

(Some students) amaze me with good writing using pen and paper. As good as they are, I think they could improve if they applied your "Art of Seeing" and "Character Consciousness" to a computer screen.

To me, after a few paper cross-outs and marginal notes, needed things get lost in the fuzziness. (Also, you have mentioned the better use of left/right brains in two-handed writing.)

Your instruction to get behind the protagonist/antagonists' feelings with their dialogue/actions has helped me the most. My self-centered inner thoughts and feelings [and] narration limited a story's appeal.

Another way of expressing this concept would be to observe that on the one hand, a central character has a series of concerns (problems) that they want solved. In most stories, they either fail or succeed. On the other hand, the writer's concerns may be something quite different. They may very well be concerned with making a statement about the way the universe works and not so much about the success or failure of the central character, who may or may not be an heroic figure.

James Joyce's *Ulysses* demonstrates the distinction between the central character's concerns and the writer's concerns. In this novel—a recreation of the Greek myth in which Ulysses, the warrior, returns home to find his wife entertaining other suitors—we spend most of the novel with Bloom, the eternal wandering Jew. He knows he must stay away from his home because his wife, Molly, is entertaining Blazes Boylan, her lover. Bloom wants his wife to be his and to have a true identity. Molly, on the other hand, luxuriates in the knowledge that she has the best of both worlds—Bloom's devotion and Boylan's complete, if momentary, affections—all available because of the power of her sexuality. What goes on in Bloom's head is only one aspect of the novel. Joyce, in fact, has a much larger concern—the fate and condition of his beloved Ireland: compromised by its history, its identity uncertain, its future torn among competing factions.

*Separating the
Writer's Voice
from the
Central
Character's
Voice*

197

Exploring Character
Through Rewriting

Like Michelangelo who spent countless hours chipping away pieces of marble in order to reveal the image he had in his mind, we writers must chip away at the countless words in our mind in order to find the ones that properly create a story. This chipping-away process is what we call rewriting. Some of the pictures in our mind are clichés that we have heard and seen somewhere else. We have to chip away such clichés. Some of the pictures in our mind lack detail, so we must chip until the details emerge. Sometimes our characters' actions do not seem to be rooted in any similar past behavior, so we must create the character's past (backstory), finding similar behavior in that past.

Writers often talk about the importance of rewriting to produce the best possible finished product. However, to beginning writers the concept of rewriting may seem bewildering. For those of us who are a bit long in the tooth, rewriting in school often meant finding spelling and grammar errors in our written work. If I remember correctly, that's how I approached my academic papers, even in college—not much actual rewriting but a lot of proofreading.

For creative writers, the rewriting process is both murky and essential. Of course, no two creative writers rewrite in the same way. Writers like myself create bland structures in the first draft, hardly more than sketches. In fact, I used to criticize myself severely for the inefficacy of my first drafts. Over time, I realized it didn't matter what the first draft looked like, so long as I continued to rewrite with a sense that it would all work out. Writers like my student Dale Crum will go through as many as eight to ten drafts before the final draft is realized. Other writers, like my friend Karl Grey, may not rewrite at all. Karl continuously adds layers and details to the version of the story he has in his head so when he sits down to write, what comes out the first time is well crafted.

Wonderful writing has four main characteristics:

1. The writing style is so rich that the reader can practically taste its quality and deliciousness. The reader feels elevated just savoring how the writer strings words together.

2. The writer's characters are so complete and multifaceted that the reader feels as if they know them well and may share some qualities with them.

3. The storyline grabs its readers forcefully and takes them into another world.

4. The writing gives the reader a sense of the shape of the world—perhaps even the universe—the character lives in. Sometimes it may show the character's life as if the reader is watching events from a great distance.

This unit discusses how to develop an intimate sense of character through the elaboration of inner thoughts and feelings and the delineation of a character's actions and reactions.

Developing Confidence in Your Rewrites

How do you develop confidence that your rewrites are on the right track? Perhaps the most effective way is to work with a writing group that has been trained in how to give helpful, positive feedback. In fact, it is a virtual "must" for every writer to do this. Professional writers, such as Bill Rempel, author and veteran investigative reporter and editor (see Chapter 31), may rely on editors and friends who are writers for feedback. Too often, however, feedback in writing groups is either simplistic ("My, that was nice") or too critical ("Frankly, I was bored by that opening"). I have experienced both extremes as a young writer, and the overabundance of "helpful criticism" I received at UCLA's film school set me back decades in my efforts to write. What each of us needs is insightful, nonjudgmental feedback that focuses on the reader's experience of the story; that is, the feelings that they find have been aroused by the story. Guiding the discussion of the writer's use of techniques is best left to the leader of the group, who is hopefully an experienced professional writer. For more about this process, please see the Appendix, "Creating a Supportive, Noncritical, yet Insightful Writing Group."

Revealing Character:
Rewriting Inner Thoughts
and Feelings

Over the course of my life I have met numerous interesting people, one of whom happens to be my former wife, Gail. During our brief marriage, she finished her bachelor's degree, acquired a master's degree, began a career as a teacher, and had two children.

Having her tell stories of her experiences after our marriage ended has been illuminating for me, especially as Gail is quite adept at revealing her inner thoughts and feelings about her experiences as a woman.

The following is an excerpt from her story "A Normal Life?" (see the complete text of this story on page 279). This excerpt illustrates the importance of finding important, perhaps critical, moments in a story and opening them up through exploring inner thoughts and feelings. (Please note: Gail's references to her "husband" have to do with her second husband, whom she met soon after our separation.)

A Normal Life? *by Gail Field* (FIRST DRAFT: EXCERPT)

My husband stands over me holding my hand while I lie waiting on the gurney just outside the delivery room. "It's a boy," I say. "We'll name him Martin and call him Marty, just like you."

Marty grips my hand even tighter, his long fingers circling my hand. He swallows hard, blinking, not saying anything. For the first time ever, I see tears moisten his face. He swallows again. "Good job." His voice cracks, and he looks away. I have never felt his hand so tight in mine.

The roses that Marty sent me grace the windowsill in my private room overlooking the entrance to the UCLA Hospital maternity wing. Outside on the narrow patch of green along the driveway entrance, a bed of asters swoon and sway, bending their heads in the slight August breeze, inviting me to take a long look. I, too, was born in the fall, and asters have always been my favorite flower. They bloom just when the weather is changing, just when the cool air comes to surprise us with its announcement of fall. The roses in my room are lovely, romantic, beautiful. But the asters signal a change. Something mysterious and yet inviting. I smile as I think of the change that is coming for our family. This moment, this day, this outcome is what my husband has wanted ever since we met and, I would guess, for long before that.

It was my mother who convinced me that having a baby with Marty was the right thing to do. "He hopes it would be a boy," I began. "I am not sure I am ready, since Jeff and Willy are still in preschool."

Outside my hospital window, the sun is setting now, and I fall into the bed, tired from the labor and from the months of waiting for this day. Now, at age twenty-six, I am a new mother for the third time.

So many times I have taken just one step, without resisting, and things have turned out all right. Like the time I didn't push Marty when he told me he wanted to go out every Friday night to be with his gay friends. Perhaps my reluctance to resist has brought my husband closer to me—has helped him see the value of family and of a traditional lifestyle. So different from what he thought he wanted to be, and maybe, just maybe, what the deepest part of him wanted all along.

Members of our writing group gave high marks to Gail for the sensitivity and deeply felt emotion that her story revealed. When they finished, I added my thoughts and observations—that at the critical moment when she reflects back on her mother's words, we need to see and to feel more of her concerns (that is, more of what the issues are that she has to deal with—the interruption of her teaching career to please her new husband, her concern for the well-being of the two children she has already borne, her uncertainty about her new husband's sexuality and fidelity, and how her mother might handle the latter if she knew).

Gail agreed that the story would be better if she worked on these aspects of the story. Here is the story with the inner thoughts and feelings that occurred at the critical point in the story expanded. (The new material appears in **bold italics.**)

A Normal Life?   *by Gail Field*   (REWRITE: EXCERPT)

A bluish shaft of light from the hospital ceiling illuminates the side of my husband's face—setting off his sparse beard and the almost undetectable quiver in his strong square jaw. My husband stands over me holding my hand while I lie waiting on the gurney just outside the delivery room. "It's a boy," I say. "We'll name him Martin and call him Marty, just like you."

Marty grips my hand even tighter, his long fingers circling my hand. He swallows hard, blinking, not saying anything. For the first time ever, I see tears moisten his face. He swallows again. "Good job." His voice cracks, and he looks away. I have never felt his hand so tight in mine.

The roses that Marty sent me grace the windowsill in my private room overlooking the entrance to the UCLA Hospital maternity wing. Outside on the narrow patch of green along the driveway entrance, a bed of asters swoon and sway, bending their heads in the slight August breeze, inviting me to take a long look. I, too, was born in the fall, and asters have always been my favorite flower. They bloom just when the weather is changing, just when the cool air comes to surprise us with its announcement of fall. The roses in my room are lovely, romantic, beautiful. But the asters signal a change. Something mysterious and yet inviting. I smile as I think of the change that is coming for our family. This moment, this day, this outcome is what my husband has wanted ever since we met, and, I would guess, for long before that.

It was my mother who convinced me that having a baby with Marty was the right thing to do. "He hopes it would be a boy," I began. "I am not sure I am ready, since Jeff and Willy are still in preschool."

My mother leaned forward, her soft eyes settling on the neat and clean kitchen counter, the flowers in the window, the pictures of family in silver frames on the cabinet tops. She must have been surprised at this orderliness compared with the way I kept my room as a girl, clothes piled high on the rocking chair, dolls scattered about the house. She smiled and lowered her voice.

"You know," she said, her tone soft yet strong, "a good wife does what she can to please her husband. And I know how much Jeffrey and Willy mean to you."

I didn't want to hear this. I preferred to make these decisions myself, without input from my mother. She didn't know the whole truth, and there was no way I was going to tell her. Instead, I nodded as if in agreement and said I understood. I felt like a teenager again, half listening to her, not objecting, then making my own decisions in secret silence.

If she knew Marty spent every Friday night out with his gay friends, doing God only knows what, then she would certainly have an opinion. Then I would have to grapple with that, too, as if I were a child trying to please, caught between the desires of Marty, my parents' wishes, and my own sense.

Outside my hospital window, the sun is setting now, and I fall into

Writing
from
Within:
The Next
Generation

202

the bed, tired from the labor and from the months of waiting for this day. Now, at age twenty-six, I am a new mother for the third time.

I am wondering what my mother would say now, thinking of what I would tell her if I were willing. I'd tell her that I am not really sure whether my decision to give up the birth control pills and have this baby was out of wanting to please my husband or whether I thought I could change him, whether I could make him love us more. Whether I wanted to rescue him from a lifestyle I thought would lead to misery for him and for me. Whether I feel I know what's best for him and for me. Feeling that I could make it all right, like it says in the psychiatry books in Marty's office. I wish I could tell her everything and have her understand without judging.

I would tell her that so many times I have taken just one step, without resisting, and things have turned out all right. Like the time I didn't push Marty when he told me he wanted to go out every Friday night to be with his gay friends. Perhaps my reluctance to resist has brought my husband closer to me. Has helped him see the value of family and of a traditional lifestyle. So different from what he thought he wanted be, and maybe, just maybe, what the deepest part of him wanted all along.

As I read Gail's words, I sense the fullness of her uncertainty. I am drawn into this world of her sensitive, aware, twenty-six-year-old efforts to see clearly what the uncertain future holds. All the threads of her dilemma are well sketched out.

During these years, when Gail was married to Marty, her second husband, she and I were doing battle, sometimes weekly, often daily. But in later years I came to see, to experience, and to benefit from the deep well of love from which all of Gail's actions stem.

Gail began to write these stories for her son Marty III, who has grown up to be a fine, wise, loving young man, as are Gail's and my two sons. It is a gift to Marty to see what it is like to have a mother who loves everyone and a father whose lifestyle is quite different from that of the average father. It is also a gift to me to be able to see events from a point of view other than my own and to help her express her innermost thoughts and feelings, the ones that she seldom puts into words.

As I mentioned in the Introduction to this book, my primary goal in teaching over the past decade has been to help my students give voice to the most fleeting of their inner thoughts and feelings, to help them put into words the things that they barely realize that they know.

What makes this task easier is that each draft of a story has a life of its own. When you finish that draft, it will call to you in a certain way, and a path toward its final realization will begin to open up. When writers allow each draft to speak to them in its own way, then they allow themselves the most growth, the most awareness, the most understanding of the inner world that many of us inhabit and/or struggle to reach.

Self-Assessments: Gaining Access to Self-Knowledge and the Inner Life

Over the past few years, I have become increasingly interested in how to gain access to one's inner life—my own and that of others. What prompts us, enables us, to look inward and to dig around in our innermost feelings? Gail's story "A Normal Life" tells the reader that she has a rich inner life and that she has access to it. Not everyone has an interest in doing so, but for those who do, Gail's story may prove to be an interesting guide.

The unveiling of deeper levels of inner thought and feeling often occurs at a critical point in a story—the beginning of the "development" section. This is the point in a story where all the important issues have been laid out for the reader (which is the purpose of the "exposition" section of a story). At the beginning of the development section, the central character must often make a difficult decision regarding the direction they will take. Opening these inner thoughts to the reader provides them with an intimate sense of the character at this early point in the story.

From the beginning of *Writing from Within* almost thirty years ago, I have suggested to my students that they add a P.S. at the ends of their stories if they have additional information they wish to convey to the reader. Over time, I became aware that this P.S. could easily become a place of self-assessment, a place where the writer could look into the mirror of the story and gaze upon their strengths and weaknesses.

Exploring the self-assessment phase of a life story became the focus of a subsequent book, *Character Consciousness.* In this book, I explore an almost infinite number of questions that a writer could ask themselves in the self-assessment phase of writing, such as "Who am I in this story?" "What are my strengths and weaknesses?" and "What character qualities show up in the story that I didn't realize I had?"

These self-assessments have been helpful to a number of my readers and students. They provide a reliable look at their inner lives—their concerns, fears, hopes, dreams, and past history—all based on something objective, the story. Through the medium of unfolding self-assessments, I have been able show students a path into the subconscious, a path that requires neither a PhD in psychology nor the help of an expensive therapist to explore. Please see page 247 for more information about writing self-assessments.

Writing
from
Within:
The Next
Generation

204

chapter 27

Unraveling Character: Rewriting Action and Details

In general, writing done by men and women unfolds in quite different ways. Female writers generally provide their readers with a whole host of inner emotions, very much like the story that Gail Field provided in "A Normal Life?" (see the complete text of this story on page 279). The depth of her emotions as she considered various life options gives the reader a glimpse into her character as a woman.

Men, on the other hand, usually provide their readers with telling glimpses into a character's actions that reveal character qualities, often with strong visual elements against which the character's actions may be seen. Just such a scenario occurs in Bill Rempel's "Front Page to Hard Cover" (Chapter 31 of this book), the story of how he wrote *At the Devil's Table*.

The depth of his story may be seen in several drafts of one passage, which unfolds as follows:

> Without question, the biggest challenge in the book was capturing the real Jorge Salcedo. He held high rank in the biggest drug syndicate in history, yet he never trafficked in drugs. He was close to the richest crime bosses on the globe, yet he never got rich. He supervised bodyguards and associated with paid assassins, yet he never harmed anyone. After six and a half years in the company of ruthless killers and traffickers, his biggest crime—and prosecutors considered it a felony under U.S. conspiracy laws—was protecting the security of cartel godfathers and the lives of their families.

> To the extent that *At the Devil's Table* succeeds in creating a complex portrait of Jorge, all I can say is: Thanks especially to Will Murphy, my editor at Random House, and to Halpern and friends at the Robbins Office in New York. They battered and abused my pages until the character

of Jorge finally shone through in all its enigmatic and ultimately heroic glory. Forty years of journalism may have helped. Not because it taught me how to write, so much as it taught me to embrace prepublication criticism. Good editing is a lifesaver. I crave it.

As I read over this passage, I asked Bill to give me more details about this moment in the story, especially the interaction that must have taken place between himself and his publishers/editors. Here is his second draft. (New material appears in ***bold italics***)

> ...after six and a half years in the company of ruthless killers and traffickers, his biggest crime—and prosecutors considered it a felony under U.S. conspiracy laws—was protecting the security of cartel godfathers and the lives of their families.
>
> ***"But he's too good," Will Murphy, my editor at Random House, complained more than once. The brevity of the original newspaper story had allowed only for the most superficial examination of Jorge's character. It did show how he got recruited into the cartel to help kill trafficking rival Pablo Escobar, Colombia's Public Enemy Number One, how the Cali bosses rejected Jorge's resignation after Escobar died, and how orders to kill a colleague finally drove Jorge to contact the DEA and risk his life to quit the cartel. But the book had to go further—using his actions and often-impossible choices—to show Jorge descend deeper and deeper into the criminal organization. He came out of that process still a good man, but a much better character.***

My eyes opened wide with interest at the lines: "But the book had to go further—using his actions and often-impossible choices—to show Jorge descend deeper and deeper into the criminal organization. He came out of that process still a good man, but a much better character."

I thought Bill was definitely on the right track, but I still wanted more details regarding the "actions and impossible choices," so I asked Bill to provide me with more details of what had taken place. Bill complied:

> "But he's too good," Will Murphy, my editor at Random House, complained more than once. The brevity of the original newspaper story had allowed only for the most superficial examination of Jorge's character ***and a handful of key moments. He was recruited into the cartel with an appeal to his patriotism, to help the rival traffickers kill Pablo Escobar, Colombia's Public Enemy Number One. The newspaper story also detailed how the Cali bosses rejected Jorge's resignation after Escobar died and how Jorge finally was driven to risk everything and reach out to the DEA after being ordered to help assassinate a potentially damaging cartel witness. Those***

Writing
from
Within:
The Next
Generation

206

were important moments, but the book needed much more. I had to show Jorge descending deeper and deeper into the criminal organization, defining him by the ethical and difficult choices he faced.

Jorge answered all of my questions, and without apparent hesitation. But, remember, I was learning new details about his cartel years with virtually every interview. Specific elements of his character came into focus well after the first draft and after Murphy's early complaints that Jorge was "too good."

Gradually, that changed. In interviews spanning several months, Jorge detailed over and over his duties with the cartel, adding detail as we dug deeper. He had first designed radio communications systems that served the cartel's business and security interests, but did no one any harm. Later, he was involved in more sinister projects: a blackmail scheme to compromise an anti-narcotics military official. He also bugged phones and earned favor when he once sounded an alarm to protect a multimillion-dollar cash shipment from seizure.

And then there were the paid assassins who considered Jorge a friend. They sometimes told him about plots and murders that he could do nothing to stop without risking the lives of his own wife and children, a seemingly impossible choice. A more imperfect Jorge emerged on the pages of my later drafts—bloodied, haunted, and regretful, but still a good man... and a much better character.

To the extent that *At the Devil's Table* succeeds in creating a complex portrait of Jorge, all I can say is: Thanks especially to Will Murphy, my editor at Random House, and to Halpern and friends at the Robbins Office in New York. They battered and abused my pages until the character of Jorge finally shone through in all its enigmatic and ultimately heroic glory. Forty years of journalism may have helped. Not because it taught me how to write, so much as it taught me to embrace prepublication criticism. Good editing is a lifesaver. I crave it.

Now I understood what a terrifying, morally compromising position Jorge was in. With each step ("he had first designed radio communications...that did no one any harm..."), I could see, feel, taste, and believe each deeper rung of the hell into which Jorge Salcedo descended.

As a skilled, professional writer, Bill provided me with an ever-more-precise and action-filled picture of Jorge Salcedo. In less than half an hour, we moved from first draft to third draft, e-mailing the various drafts back and forth.

In the real world of storytelling—the world of the journalist—character is revealed through action. Bill and I worked this moment back and forth until Jorge Salcedo's actions revealed how "bloodied, haunted, and regretful" the hero had become by the end of Bill's summary of *At the Devil's Table.*

My editorial comments to Bill ("more detail") reminded me of the film (and novel) *The Andromeda Strain* by Michael Crichton, in which "something" from outer space turns the blood of residents of a small town into dust. Eventually that "something" is traced to the inside wall of a vehicle from outer space, which remains invisible until the powers of the camera lens are amplified by a series of "diopters" that magnify the "toxin" until it can be seen, probed, analyzed, and understood.

This process is similar to the way in which investigative writers like Bill Rempel probe the world of their characters, looking for clues to the qualities of their characters in the actions the characters take, a process no different than that used by life-story writers probing their past experiences.

Writing
from
Within:
The Next
Generation

208

Leaping into Longer Work

Writing life stories often has an interesting impact on us as writers. As we become more sure of ourselves, give ourselves up to the task of rewriting over several drafts, and grow skillful in observing and putting into words the actions and thoughts of major and minor characters, we want to do more. "What would it be like if I tried a longer work, perhaps a fictional work? How would I go about it?" we ask.

Writing a novel-length story or work of nonfiction or creating a screenplay may appear to be a daunting task. At one time or another, most people who attempt such a project get bogged down, not knowing where to go, and give up. The key to starting and finishing a large project is to start small. When Leonardo da Vinci conceived of his monumental works—*The Adoration of the Magi, The Last Supper,* and *The Equestrian Monument of Francesco Sforza*—he started small. A few sketches of characters around the Madonna and Christ. More sketches of horses. He allowed his concepts to unfold from the characters he observed and created.

Most writers, artists, and musicians draw inspiration for their larger works from smaller works they created earlier in their lifetimes. Picasso's *Guernica* is the product of many, many sketches that evolved over time into the concept he wanted to express: the horrors of the Fascist bombing of the town of Guernica in 1936. It took time for his images of distortion to find their full expression.

In the same way, if you intend or hope to write a novel, you will generally find the inspiration you need in characters you have already explored in writing life stories. The following stories illustrate how two of my students came to write novels based on characters they created, or re-created, during the time they were in my classes.

209

One of the most interesting and exciting events that occurs in a writing class is the moment when instructor and student realize that they have just been witness to the creation of a truly fascinating character, one that appears to be so interesting that they deserve to be "set in motion," as we say. In other words, what would this character do in other, even-more-challenging circumstances? How would they react to a different set of obstacles?

That is what took place with J. D. Tousley's character of Tack, which eventually resulted in his novel, *Dangling in the Adios.* It is also what happened when in class we first read about Paula Diggs's impossible, nine-year-old heroine, Suzanne, whom Paula was able to use as the main character in her novel *New Shooter.*

• • •

Over time I have learned that "writing from within" stories—really, sketches from life—can take a writer in many interesting directions. These skills make other kinds of creative writing much easier, whether it is inventing personal myths from classic mythic tales or developing an ease in storytelling that enables an academic person with numerous college degrees to write effective stories for children. One example of such a story is "Molloko, the California Condor" on page 217, which is an excerpt from *Creative Stories* by Inés Horovitz, PhD, a mammalogist.

This story is also is an excellent example of how this writer uses her imagination to come up with a unique perspective from which to tell a story. Many people may have passed through school and done well or poorly without ever using their imaginations. Sometimes it occurs in childhood but becomes redirected toward academic work; sometimes it only occurs in later years or not at all. In your future, I want to encourage you to cultivate your imagination as much as possible. Your relationships will improve, your pleasure in creating will develop dramatically, and your satisfaction in life's pleasures will expand.

Writing
from
Within:
The Next
Generation

210

chapter 28

Turning Life Stories
into Novels

Most writers find the prospect of writing a lengthy work of fiction, such as a novel or a screenplay, quite daunting. I know I did when I began writing many years ago. In fact, throughout my years as a filmmaker, I found it almost impossible to tackle a project longer than a few pages. My uncertainties and insecurities got the better of me.

Eventually I began to see that it could be done, and I advised some of my students to take their short life stories into the realm of fiction. I found out that all you need is a *good character*.

If such a character can maintain the reader's interest and can overcome substantial obstacles in a short story, that character can do the same in a longer work of fiction. "Give the character more substantial obstacles and see what happens," I said to my students.

Here is one such character, created by Dirk Tousley, a student of mine for a number of years whom I have mentioned previously. Dirk had been something of a rebel as a youth. He went to college on a hope and a dime, keeping himself flush with cash thanks to his local pool hall skills. His first story looked like this:

> This doodling is an UNFINISHED TREATMENT of a short story or maybe a film I couldn't seem to get a hook on several years ago, but the character undoubtedly morphed into Tack in *Dangling in the Adios*. The story is autobiographical only in my dreams.

The Sweet Life *by J. D. Tousley, author of* Dangling in the Adios

211

My life as a young pool hustler was about as sweet as life gets. In those days, long before MasterCard, when you could sit down at a nice clean lunch counter and get a bowl of steaming chili for a quarter, a slab of apple pie juicier than Mom made for a dime, and a steaming cup of coffee with free refills for a nickel, I usually carried at least two hundred bucks in my right front pocket and a couple of fifties hidden in my wallet. So I was doing all right.

I'm telling you, business life couldn't have been sweeter, played out day by day on a rectangle of green felt four and one half feet wide by nine feet long. And I knew every inch of it.

I was strictly my own man, too. No alarm clock kicking me out of bed at six in the morning. No cranky boss to kiss the ass of. No measly paycheck creating resentment. Instead, I played pool for a living and usually came out ahead. Usually, but not always.

That's when my plucky little blonde girlfriend would rise to the occasion. Sugar loved me dearly and I loved her, loved to hold her in my arms, squeeze her, and feel her quiver in a giggle. Most of the time she had some kind of job, maybe waiting tables, maybe clerking at a drug store, maybe pounding a typewriter in some small office, but always showing up Friday nights with a few tens and maybe a twenty hiding out in a little brown pay envelope. Yet as scant as her pay might be, Sugar was always willing to share if need be. It seems what you may have heard about pool hustlers was occasionally true even of me: chicken one day, feathers the next. But I loved that little gal, and on those rare occasions when I tapped her for a loan, I always paid her back in a day or two, you can be sure.

The opening of this first draft is reminiscent of Dirk's earliest stories of his life as a pool hustler while he was in college. Notice that his first draft is all narrative. Interesting narrative to be sure, but narrative all the same.

Eventually, his life experience as a pool hustler morphed into a novel of a young man's experiences:

Dangling in the Adios   *by J. D. Tousley*

Chapter One

I've had it with stuck-up sorority girls. They act like they're too grand to do it, then when they finally let you in, they own you lock, stock, and barrel. Take Carolyn Forsythe, for instance, safely locked away from us college boys in her panty girdle. After we first met, I rolled around with her in the backseat of my convertible every night for two weeks, trying to pry her out of that medieval contraption, until late one night I got her to wriggle out of it on her own and start enjoying life. And it's been great. I never had it so steady before. But I'm paying for it with my freedom. Whenever Carolyn crooks her finger, I'm supposed to roll over and bark.

You'd think she owned me. Now she's ragging me to quit playing nine ball so we can study together. Hell, I don't need study. That's what brains are for. And I'm not about to give up nine ball. Pool is my life, and besides, it brings in about thirty bucks a week.

How different with Cricket, my appreciative little drugstore clerk. On our second date, I slid her skimpy panties down her bare legs and off her feet in a flash, what with no elastic wall, hooks, wires, or buttons to overcome. Panties off, and there it was. When we're not making love, she spends a lot of time in the crook of my arm, looking up at me attentively and asking questions I can answer.

The following provides another example of a short life story turned into a novel. The author portrayed herself as precocious and impossible, always a step ahead of everyone else, but her mother's exasperation was always evident. This created a fascinating, self-centered, but creative and intriguing character. I suggested she turn this character loose in a story, perhaps a mystery, and see what happens. Here is Paula's original story, followed by the beginning of her novel:

Mañana Is Good Enough for Me   *by Paula Diggs*

I don't want to eat tomato soup again on Saturday, but here it is, and I have to clean my bowl. "As the ships go out to sea, I push my spoon away from me," I say to my little sister Kathleen.

"Show off," Kathleen says. She is only three and doesn't know how to eat soup properly. Since I am nine I have good manners, even though sometimes Mother says I show off and that is a bad thing to do.

Miss Hansen ate her tomato soup properly yesterday when I brought her home for lunch. She is my fourth grade teacher, and she is just beautiful. She has two big braids that she winds around her head. Her fiancé was killed in the war we are having overseas with the Germans, so everyone is trying to be extra kind to her. Mother let me bring her home for lunch. We had tomato soup and cottage cheese on Mother's special clear green plates. I got to walk back and forth from school with my teacher. She is wonderful. She told Mother I am very imaginative and talented. She told Mother that I organized a group of girls to put on plays at recess. I like to make up the plays. Mother said she's not surprised, I like to show off. I guess I can't help it, but I try not to. The plays I make up are about a princess who is captured by an ogre and has to escape. I am the princess, and my friend Sarah is the fairy godmother. There are lots of other parts for elves and fairies. My boyfriend, George, gets to play the ogre and the prince because he wants to play with us even though we are a girls' club.

Sarah is my best friend. She has dark curly hair like Mother's and a happy round face. Mother said she would be pretty if she didn't look so Semitic. Mother likes to use big words. Sarah is thin like me, so I guess that is what it means. Mother told me I would be attractive if I weren't so thin.

Lunch was almost over when the phone rang. I listen and Mother says, "I don't know if she can come. I'll have to ask her father. Thank you for calling."

"Who?" Daddy Don says. "Mrs. Stein, Sarah's mother. They are having a birthday party for Sarah. Do you think I should let Miss Big Ears go?"

"That's very nice of them," Daddy Don answers.

"It's nice, but...."

"But what?" says Daddy Don.

"Well they are Jewish and so ostentatious. The party is at suppertime, and there will be games after. We don't do that sort of thing."

"I don't know what you mean," Daddy Don says. "This isn't Kansas, and 1944 isn't the dark ages in this country."

Ostentatious is a word I don't know either, and I read a lot. Sarah's house is beautiful. It is big with lots of rooms. It smells good, like lemons. Maybe that is what it means, something like fancy. Her father has a department store. They have pretty plates with flowers on them and long lace curtains. I went to her house two times. Her brother, Aaron, has good manners for a boy. He is twelve years old and shook my hand when we were introduced. He is nice and quiet and is always reading. When I went to Sarah's, we read our Nancy Drew books and made up plays where we were the detectives and solved mysteries. I love Sarah's house.

Mother said Sarah can't come here because she would be uncomfortable because we are Christians. I am happy that I got to go to Sarah's house. She is my best friend ever. I am always comfortable with her.

Now I am going to get to go to Sarah's birthday party because my little sister Kathleen let her friend Joanie, who is two, take my darling turtle Sweetie out of its bowl and stepped on it and squished it all over the place. When I saw what happened to poor Sweetie, I started screaming until I thought I was going to faint. Mother said I could go to Sarah's birthday party if I would just calm down. So I did.

In the story, the reader sees that this little girl loves attention, loves to use big words, loves to shade meanings to her advantage, gets into trouble, and pretends not to know why. It is easy to see what a handful she probably is to her devoted but exhausted mother, who is not nearly as broad-minded and observant as is this little girl. The reader delights in this character because, even though she is based on Paula's own person, the writer does not shy away from

Writing
from
Within:
The Next
Generation

214

showing the character's many flaws, include her love of showing off and the way it annoys those around her.

At my suggestion, Paula decided to create a fictional story around this child. Because the child in real life liked to play detective, I suggested that she allow this child to become a detective, at age nine. The result is shown in the following section.

New Shooter   *A novel by Paula Diggs*

Chapter One: Just Listen to Me

A huge slobbering Doberman Pincher clamps his jaws on the little dog's throat. Blood shoots out and splatters all over me. A swarm of bats flies at my eyes. I can't see. Run and climb a tree to get away. Climb higher and higher foot slips and start to fall. Falling and falling down, down, down.... Below me a large bug stands on home plate, his bat in position to swing as I fall in front of him. A hand touches my shoulder and grabs me. "Help," I cry, "help, help me, please!"

"Calm down, Suzanne. It's all over. No one's going to hurt you. You're dreaming." Daddy Don and Mother stand by my bed.

"No," I tell them. "Out there on the street. I can hear them."

"It's only crickets, Go back to sleep. You're nine years old, a big girl, stop imagining things. Nothing's going to hurt you now."

Those bad dreams keep bothering me. Things without heads follow me around. They try to make me eat stuff that smells bad. Spam. Poison. It makes me gag. Sometimes I throw up in my bed. Last night was the worst ever.

So when I come down for breakfast the next morning, Mother tells me I look like something the cat dragged in. What does that mean? I couldn't get back to sleep at all. Ideas of dark things jumped around in my head. All night. A claw grabbed me. It held on. I had to stay awake, or they would get me. I was alone. Really alone. All by myself. No one would help me.

"I cried in my sleep all night, Mother. I thought they were coming to get me. I could hear their feet." Mother takes things in and out of the drawer. Over and over. Everything nice and tidy.

If writers have at their fingertips a character who can maintain the interest of the audience, then writing a novel becomes much less of a burden. What makes an interesting character? Every character must have a goal, an objective that they intend to pursue. The more noble the goal, generally the more interesting the character, although this may not always be the case. This is also true for the antagonist and the minor characters.

Writers often talk about "the stakes," as in, "How high are the stakes?" In Hollywood films, the stakes often involve saving a life, or perhaps all of civilization. In more subtle films and novels, the stakes are often matters of identity, self-worth, and unrealized dreams from long ago.

When a character's goal is clearly defined (even though it may change in the course of the novel), the obstacles they face become important. The greater the obstacles, the more interesting the conflict.

With the goal and the obstacles in mind, the writer must create character qualities in the central character and in the minor characters that make overcoming the obstacles possible.

Conflicting qualities often make for an interesting character. In Paula's story, the nine-year-old detective knows a great deal—about a lot of things that don't matter. And she often knows nothing about what's going on around her. Sometimes this disconnect can contribute to a wonderful sense of fun, even absurdity.

Backstory contributes to the audience's understanding of what has happened before the curtain comes up on a story and is essential to most, although not all, novels. In Dirk's novel, *Dangling in the Adios,* his second-paragraph backstory gives the reader all the information necessary to understand Tack's predicament.

The main difference between a novel and a short story, such as a life story, is in the arc of the story. A short story generally has only one climactic scene followed by a denouement. In a novel, the writer must create smaller climaxes and denouements that culminate in a final, climactic scene.

Writing
from
Within:
The Next
Generation

216

chapter 29

Writing Creative Stories

Writing life stories is to a writer as sketching is to an artist. It is a first step to creating something bigger. Leonardo da Vinci filled up many, many sketchbooks with ideas before he created *The Last Supper*.

Creating sketches from life based on your life stories will help you do other kinds of creative writing. One kind of writing is called "creating personal myths."

In this kind of writing, you choose a legend, folktale, myth, or fable and look for the meaning behind that myth or legend. Then, find a moment in your own life that also illustrates that meaning or message. If you cannot find it in your own life, make up or imagine what is necessary.

The following is an example of a highly creative story. After writing a few life stories to acquire the skills of using narrative, dialogue, and inner thoughts and feelings, the writer created a series of stories about mammals and wrote each story from the point of view of the baby coming into the world, growing up and learning to fend for itself:

Molloko, the California Condor   *by Inés Horovitz*   (EXCERPT)

I can hear the wind blowing through the pine trees. It's sunny outside, and I am waiting for my mom or my dad to bring me some food. I live in a cave high up on a cliff. It's a little scary: I almost fell off a few times. I am also a little scared that a golden eagle will find me. My mom told me to watch out for them. I think I can hear my mom or my dad now: There's a hissing sound.

"Hi Molloko, good morning!"

"Hi Mom! I love it when I hear the hissing sound because I know you or Dad is near. How do you make it?"

217

"It's the wind going through our wing feathers."

I'm really hungry, so I'm very excited to see her! She smells really clean. I can tell she took a bath. I would love to take baths too, but I have to learn to fly first to get to a bathing place.

I flap my wings as hard as I can to let my mom know I can't wait for my food anymore. She stands beside me and opens her bill over my head, so I stick my head in it. Some food comes out of her throat. It's been in her tummy and it's a little digested already. I take the food in my mouth. After I swallow it, more food keeps coming. When we're done, I try to get my head out of her throat but I'm stuck. My mom puts her foot on my neck and pushes me down to the floor of our cave so my head comes out. What a relief! I can breathe now!

"What food was that, Mom?"

"It was a dead weasel I found on a big boulder. It probably fell off the cliff above."

"Have you ever caught any animals, Mom?"

"No, dear. We don't catch animals. We just find dead ones."

"But I like to play I catch things, Mom. I will catch animals when I grow up."

"You like to play that way because a long, long time ago, our great, great, many times great grandparents were different from us, and they hunted for their food. But we condors and vultures have changed over millions of years to just eat carcasses, dear. Our babies still play that way because you are born with the need to learn that skill, but you will lose the need to use it when you grow up. It's okay to play that way, though— it's fun, isn't it?"

A few weeks later I start walking out of our cave onto a narrow ledge, and I wait for my parents from there. I am a little afraid of flying still, but I have been flapping my wings inside our cave to practice and get stronger. If I fell off the ledge, I think I would be okay: I could flap my wings hard enough that I would not hit the rocks below too hard, I hope.

"Have you preened your feathers this morning?"

"Yes, Mama."

"They look shiny! I can tell you've been taking good care of them. Just a few spots need a little preening. I'll feed you, and I'll preen those spots after," says my mom.

I love it when she does that. I feel a little ticklish. Sometimes I preen her feathers, too.

"Molloko, you should start flying off into the canyon. We've had five full moons since you hatched. You are old enough now, and your feathers look great! You should start using them! I'm off to find more food now. See you later!"

Writing
from
Within:
The Next
Generation

218

I am feeling good now that my mom fed me. They don't feed me that often anymore: Some days they don't feed me at all. I can see some birds flying by from my ledge. It looks like so much fun! Maybe I could try flying off. Maybe I am ready to do it now. My heart is beating so fast, it feels like it's going to take off before I do. Here I go.... One, two, three! Weeeeeee!!!!!!

I'm off, and I flap my wings as hard as I can. They sound loud! At first I am going straight down, but then I manage to fly forward for a short stretch, and then my wings get tired and I start going down again. Mom, Dad!!! Anyone around???? Help!!!! There's a tree coming straight at me!!! "No, no tree, out of my way, move, move!" But it won't move. I crash right into it. OUCH!!!!!

I hold on to a branch for a while until I recover from my emergency landing. I'd love to get back to my nest! But I'll have to do it little by little. I'll try to get to a nearby sequoia tree as my first stop. It's not far. Maybe I can do it! I take off and lose height at first but manage to fly up a little and ahead!

"Here I come, sequoia! Stick out a branch for me!!!!"

But the sequoia won't listen. It just stays still, and I have to find a branch myself. It's hard, though! I can't really aim at anything to land on, I can't fly that well yet. I finally crash against a branch. OUCH!!!!

— • • • —

This unit has explored other ways that writers can profit from "writing from within."

Additionally, don't forget that the world of your creative imagination is as fertile a breeding ground for stories as any other part of your life experience. Practicing life-story writing as a regular part of your weekly routine gives you confidence and the momentum to explore fascinating, off-to-the-side, almost-out-of-view dimensions of your imagination. Such people as engineers, doctors, and academics with a plethora of degrees (indicating their left brains operate well) may be surprised to find that they have active, creative, right brains that can be as fertile with imagination as those of any writer, actor, or painter. It just takes a little patience and openness to a new process to find the wonders of the imagination…and the ability to go ever deeper into mysterious places within yourself.

Creating Screenplays from Short Stories: Hemingway's "The Short Happy Life of Francis Macomber"

(**Please note:** This section is a portion of a chapter from my book *The Art of Seeing: Appreciating Motion Pictures as an Art Form and as a Business.*)

Writing a motion-picture screenplay is a subtle art form and a maddening craft. By their very nature, screenplays are incomplete in the same way that plays are incomplete: They provide only the text with which the actors and director must work. Creating subtext that breathes life into the screenplay and the finished film or play is the job of the actor and director. However, a skilled screenwriter can give strong indications to the actor and director about what the subtext should look like. A good script means nothing until the screenplay gets to the screen, so any indications of subtext may enlist the interest of a producer, director, and/or actors.

As I described earlier in this book, every writer—whether novelist, short-story writer, playwright, or screenwriter—has three basic tools with which to work: narrative, dialogue, and inner thoughts and feelings. The novelist or short-story writer must be skilled at narrative and good with dialogue. Both have the advantage of being able to express inner thoughts and feelings directly. The screenwriter must be skilled at creating narrative that can be communicated through action and dialogue. Their success, however, derives from the way that they handle inner thoughts and feelings that can seldom be expressed directly.

There are, of course, many ways for screenwriters to fail (or succeed) in translating a novel or short story to the screen. Eliminating the author's use of inner thoughts and feelings may be one of those failings. Misunderstanding and changing a character and their qualities is another place where screenwriters go astray. Sometimes a slavish devotion to the external events of an author's work may create a bed of quicksand from which the screenwriter cannot free him- or herself.

Adapting Ernest Hemingway to the Screen

Because many scripts are adaptations of novels, short stories, and plays, let's take a look at a classic American short story to see how it was adapted to the screen. I have in mind Ernest Hemingway's "The Short Happy Life of Francis Macomber." An example of American short fiction at its best, "Macomber" was one of Hemingway's favorites. The short story was also made into a 1947 movie, *The Macomber Affair,* starring Gregory Peck. The story is typical Hemingway: Every moment in the story is a test of a man's manhood.

In the short story "The Short Happy Life of Francis Macomber," a handsome, athletic, very rich, rather naïve man goes on safari in Africa, accompanied by his wife and their guide, Wilson. Let's look at the opening:

The Short Happy Life of Francis Macomber
by Ernest Hemingway

It was now lunch time and they were all sitting under the double green fly of the dining tent pretending that nothing had happened.

"Will you have lime juice or lemon squash?" Macomber asked.

"I'll have a gimlet," Robert Wilson told him.

"I'll have a gimlet, too. I need something," Macomber's wife said.

"I suppose it's the thing to do," Macomber agreed. "Tell him to make three gimlets."

This seems like idle conversation, yes? Except for the phrase "pretending nothing had happened." What does this line mean? Hemingway goes on:

Francis Macomber had, half an hour before, been carried to his tent from the edge of the camp in triumph on the arms and shoulders of the cook, the personal boys, the skinner…he had shaken all their hands, received their congratulations, and then gone into his tent and sat on the bed until his wife came in. She did not speak to him when she came in and he left the tent at once…to sit in the shade.

So the public perception of Macomber is that he has done something to be proud of, but Mrs. Macomber doesn't share that view. Next, Hemingway describes these characters:

Mrs. Macomber looked at Wilson quickly. She was an extremely hand-some and well-kept woman of the beauty and social position which had, five years before, commanded five thousand dollars as the price of en-dorsing, with photographs, a beauty product which she never used. She had been married to Francis Macomber for eleven years.

"He's is good lion, isn't he?" Macomber said. His wife looked at him now. She looked at both men as though she had never seen them before. One, Wilson, the white hunter, she knew she had never truly seen before. He was about middle height with sandy hair, a stubby mustache, a very red face, and extremely cold eyes with faint wrinkles at the corners that grooved merrily when he smiled. He smiled at her now.

Francis Macomber was very tall, very well built if you did not mind that length of bone, dark, his hair cropped like an oarsman, rather thin-lipped, and was considered handsome. He was dressed in the same sort of safari clothes that Wilson wore except that his were new, he was thirty-five years old, kept himself very fit, was good at court games, had a num-ber of big game fishing records, and had just shown himself, very pub-licly, to be a coward.

Ah, so there it is: Macomber has shown himself to be a coward. What kind? Because this is a safari—probably a wild animal hunt—the reader can suppose that Macomber ran from a lion or a rhino. If so, what will the consequences be?

Early in the paragraph Hemingway damns Macomber with faint praise: "if you didn't mind the length of bone" (gangly), "thin-lipped" (unsensual), "good at court games" (a too-civilized form of mano-a-mano competition).

> "Here's to the lion," he [Macomber] said. "I can't thank you enough for what you did."
>
> Margaret, his wife, looked away from him and back to Wilson.
>
> "Let's not talk about the lion," she said.
>
> Wilson looked over at her without smiling and now she smiled at him.
>
> "Hadn't you ought to put your hat on, Mr. Wilson . . . you have a very red face."
>
> "Drink," said Wilson.
>
> "I don't think so," she said. "Francis drinks a great deal but his face is never red."
>
> "It's red today," Macomber tried to joke.
>
> "No," said Margaret, "It's mine that's red today. But Mr. Wilson's is al-ways red."

From this we see that Macomber has done something to be ashamed of, apparently something cowardly, such as running away from danger. In all like-lihood, Wilson saved his life and shot the lion. Macomber tries to joke about

Writing
from
Within:
The Next
Generation

222

his cowardice, as if it's a small thing—and maybe it is to Macomber. But it's a big thing to his wife. She is ashamed. Or is it something else? Perhaps they have a relationship in which each struggles for power and now Mrs. Macomber has the power on her side. It seems that way, from the way she flirts with Wilson.

The two men talk about the natives, Wilson allowing that a good beating every now and then keeps the natives in line. Macomber replies, "We all take a beating every day, you know, one way or the other," a line suggesting that Mrs. Macomber has been indulging herself in exercising her power over her husband quite often. Moments later, Macomber says:

> "I'm awfully sorry about this lion business. It doesn't have to go any further, does it? I mean no one will hear about it, will they?"

So now we see that Macomber is ashamed of his actions and he doesn't want the world to hear about them. Or is he? It is an odd line, so "on the money" (see page 112 for an explanation of this term).

If the reader repeats the line, remembering that Macomber is a very rich man, they get the impression that he is more concerned about the annoyance of having failed at this sport than the shame. He certainly sounds more matter-of-fact than deeply wounded. Wilson is put off:

> "'You mean will I tell it at the Mathaiga Club?' Wilson looked him coldly. "No, I'm a professional hunter. We never talk about our clients. Supposed to be bad form to ask us not to talk, though."

Hemingway follows with several lines of Wilson's inner thoughts and feelings:

> He had decided now that to break would be much easier. He would eat by himself and could read a book with his meals. They would eat by themselves. He would see them through the safari on a very formal basis—what was it them French called it? Distinguished consideration—and it would be a damn sight easier than having to go through this emotional trash. He'd insult him and make a good clean break.
>
> "I'm sorry," Macomber said. "I didn't realize that. There are a lot of things I don't know."
>
> So what could he do, Wilson thought. He was all ready to break it off quickly and neatly and here the beggar was apologizing after he had just insulted him. He made one more attempt. "...you know in Africa no woman ever misses her lion and no white man ever bolts."

A moment later, Macomber says, "I bolted like a rabbit." We might expect him to feel humiliated by his lack of courage, but he's strangely forthright—not ashamed, just nonplused. Hemingway reveals more of Wilson's thoughts:

Creating
Screenplays from
Short Stories:
Hemingway's
"The Short Happy
Life of Francis
Macomber"

223

Now what in hell were you going to do about a man who talked like that, Wilson wondered.

Wilson looked at Macomber…[who]…had a pleasant smile if you did not notice how his eyes showed when he was hurt.

"Maybe I can fix it up on buffalo," he [Macomber] said. "We're after them next, aren't we?"

Here, the exposition comes to an end. Macomber has shown he is a coward but not a blustering, silly coward—just a matter-of-fact coward, not a man for whom Wilson can summon any contempt.

Mrs. Macomber, however, enjoys her husband's vulnerability to the fullest, savaging him like a picador teasing the bull before sticking the sword in its shoulders:

"Why not let up on the bitchery just a little Margot," Macomber said.

"I suppose I could," she said, "since you put it so prettily."

So, Robert Wilson thought to himself, she is giving him a ride, isn't she? Or do you suppose that's her idea of putting up a good show. How should a woman act when she discovers her husband is a bloody coward? She's damn cruel but they're all cruel. They govern, of course, and to govern one has to be cruel sometimes. Still, I've seen enough of their damn terrorism.

Before going on to the development of the story, Hemingway takes the reader into a backstory that allows them to experience and to feel every bit of Macomber's cowardice in facing the lion.

Returning to the present, Hemingway begins the development section of the story by having Margot continue Macomber's humiliation by sleeping with Wilson.

Yet Macomber does not go to pieces. Like one of the animals being stalked, he's wounded and hurt, but not crippled. Despite her infidelity—which has taken place many times before—he is alert and ready for the hunt. (For a more complete analysis of this story, please see my book *The Art of Seeing: Appreciating Motion Pictures as an Art Form and as a Business.*)

Writing
from
Within:
The Next
Generation

224

Adapting "The Short Happy Life of Francis Macomber" to the Screen

How might a writer translate parts of this story into the language of the motion picture? Let's look at the beginning, this time cast by me in motion-picture script format. (Note: "EXT." is the abbreviation for "exterior," "INT." for "interior.")

The Short Happy Life of Francis Macomber

```
EXT. AFRICAN DESERT-TENT-DAY

On a vast plain of the Serengeti Desert, sev-
eral small tents dot an oasis. Two Land Rovers
sit behind the tents, as the "beaters" eat
their lunch at some remove from two men and
a woman who sit beneath the fly of the dining
tent.

EXT. UNDER THE TENT FLAP

A tall man leans back in his chair. He is
Francis Macomber, rich, wealthy, mid-forties.
A sportsman. Next to him sits his wife, Mar-
got, a once-beautiful woman, now a bit lined
in the face. Across from them sits the guide,
Robert Wilson, middle height, and red-faced
from living outdoors all his adult life.

                    MACOMBER
          Will you have lime juice or lemon
          squash?

                    WILSON
          I'll have a gimlet.

                    MARGOT MACOMBER
          I'll have a gimlet, too. I need some-
          thing.

                    MACOMBER
          I suppose it's the thing to do. Tell
          him to make three gimlets.
```

— • • • —

This is the scene almost exactly as Hemingway wrote it. The physical descriptions, the dialogue, everything. Except that it means nothing. The most pregnant phrase in the beginning—"they were all sitting under the double green fly of the dining tent pretending that nothing had happened"—has not been dealt with in any way. Consequently, there is no opening.

*Creating
Screenplays from
Short Stories:
Hemingway's
"The Short Happy
Life of Francis
Macomber"*

225

Ask yourself what each character wants. According to Hemingway, Macomber is there to shoot lions. But in reading the story, the reader learns that he's there for some other reason. His wife taunts him as she has done in the past, so he's looking for a way to get past her taunts. And perhaps her taunts serve a purpose—to goad him into facing what he has never faced: his basic cowardice.

So that's what he wants: to gain his manhood.

And that's what she wants: to remind him of his smallness, his insignificance, his impotence. Is that what she wants, really? No, the author has something else in mind.

What does she really want? To feel powerful.

Having used her beauty all her life to get what she wants, she knows her power lies in her face and her figure. But now that both are fading into middle-aged wrinkles—and knowing that her husband looks a hell of a lot better than she does, she must find some other way to feel powerful. How does she go about it? By reminding Macomber of his impotent insignificance. Thus he will stay close because she's smarter and stronger. Uh-huh, that'll work.

What does Wilson want? The reader knows from the story that he loves the opportunity to match wits with and to test the mettle of wild animals. He also loves bailing these "sporty" fellows out of trouble and bagging their wives, if the occasion warrants, as his bounty for saving their skins. So he wants to feel superior to these rich people. But if a man who has shown himself to be a cowardly sport suddenly turns out to be ready to test his mettle in some earnest way, Wilson will give him all the credit in the world. So his secret desire is to help men become men, as would a top sergeant who brings his infantry troops to the front lines for the first time.

What does he want? To free men of their cowardice.

So if Macomber wants to find his manhood, running away feels bad, feels like a defeat, or perhaps he's trying to overcome some inability to focus when panic surfaces. How would a writer express this in action and dialogue?

—•••—

Writing
from
Within:
The Next
Generation

226

EXT. UNDER THE TENT FLAP

Francis Macomber leans back in his chair. Rich, wealthy, midforties, a sportsman with a surprising innocence about him. His smooth cheeks and bright eyes suggest a man who has not been out in the sun more than necessary. Next to him sits his wife, a once-beautiful woman, now a bit lined in the face, who has been out in the sun too often.

Across from them sits the guide, Robert Wilson, middle height, and red-faced from living outdoors all his adult life, coupled with a pint of whisky at the end of each day.

A servant brings them vodka gimlets, frosted, out here in the desert.

                    MACOMBER
               (raising his glass)
          A toast.

                    MARGOT MACOMBER
               (giving him a look)
          How you do love your toasts.

                    WILSON
          I'm in.

He lifts his glass, just barely. Macomber clinks his glass against his wife's.

                    MACOMBER
          To Mr. Wilson. A crack shot.

                    MARGOT MACOMBER
               (eying Wilson)
          Umm, yes. A crack shot. Put it right
          where he wanted it. I suppose you're
          always pretty much on target, aren't
          you, Mr. Wilson?

Macomber's eyes narrow as he gives her a look. Wilson catches their look.

                    WILSON
          Paid to do it, Mrs. Paid to do it.

                    MARGOT
          My husband's a crack shot, aren't you,
          dear?

Macomber eyes her, holding back something.

> MACOMBER
> *(shrugging)*
> No one's perfect, my dear.

Margot leans toward Wilson.

> MARGOT
> A perfectly wonderful shot, Mr. Wil-
> son. Yours, I mean. A work of art I
> should say, you-standing there wait-
> ing-until the last moment. Then pow!
> The crack of the rifle. Down it goes,
> poor helpless, frightened beast.

She gives Macomber's arm a patronizing pat.

> MACOMBER
> *(shrugging)*
> Helpless, eh?
> *(looking up)*
> Tomorrow, Mr. Wilson?

He clinks Wilson's gimlet glass.

Wilson who has closed his eyes to the two of
them, awakens with the slow rattle of a snake
uncoiling.

> WILSON
> Tomorrow, Mr. Macomber? I should have
> thought you might want to wait a day.
> Gather yourself.

> MARGOT
> *(laughing)*
> Oh, you know how we Americans are.
> Fall off a horse, get right back on.
> We're taught that from birth.

Wilson, fully awake now, sizes up the two of
them. He downs his gimlet.

> WILSON
> If you'll excuse me.
> *(getting up)*
> Tomorrow, eh?

Writing
from
Within:
The Next
Generation

228

He gets up, taking his gimlet glass with him, walks over to where the "beaters" are eating, and tosses the glass to an elderly black man who washes dishes.

>   SERVANT
>   (laughing, showing rotten teeth)
>   Americans, boss?

>   WILSON
>   (shrugging)
>   Americans. They say the women all have
>   one breast-so they can draw back the
>   bow string a little better.

He motions as if to draw a bow string across his chest and shoot an arrow then swings around as if to send it into the servant's heart. They laugh.

• • •

As you evaluate the job done on this section of the story, consider six questions:

Q: Is it faithful to Hemingway's intent?

A: It has established what each character wants: Macomber to test his manhood again; Margot to make him pay for all the ways in which he has failed her, imagined or not; and Wilson to play a waiting game.

Q: Has it found a way of keeping the inner thoughts and feeling of the characters present through dialogue and action?

A: Wilson's inner thoughts and feelings are difficult to reveal in a story such as this, so they must be externalized somehow. Thus the moment with the elderly African-American man — "Americans."

Q: Has it managed to keep the dialogue interesting — that is, does the dialogue avoid being too much "on the money" (obvious)?

A: The excerpt keeps alive the sense that something went wrong and these people are reacting to it, trying to make everything normal, as happened in the story, but on the other hand Margot is not going to let an opportunity like this go by unchallenged.

Q: Are the character qualities of the actors faithful to the author's intent, and do these qualities still work to make the story interesting?

*Creating
Screenplays from
Short Stories:
Hemingway's
"The Short Happy
Life of Francis
Macomber"*

229

A: The excerpt keeps alive Macomber's sense of innocence, his singular focus on getting his manhood back "tomorrow." It keeps Margot's sly bitchiness in sight as well: "Always on target, Mr. Wilson?" Wilson remains slightly contemptuous but open to possibilities—to Margot's in-your-face infidelity as well as to Macomber's intent on righting his ship and proving he's a man.

Q: If changes have been made, do they work on behalf of the original story?

A: The changes made have been in the direction of shortening the dialogue while keeping Hemingway's sense of characters in conflict. A film has a life of its own, so being too faithful to a book or story can be a drawback. But if the script moves too far away, it loses the feel of Hemingway's life experience. The goal is to find a happy medium.

This excerpt is a script from which actors and directors can draw upon their talents to bring the conflict into focus. At the same time, it is visual enough and sufficiently readable that a producer will be satisfied that it will serve their purposes: to raise money and to encourage talent to want to work on the project.

Hollywood's Bizarre Recreation of the Hemingway Story

Now let's look at the 1947 Hollywood version of the story starring Gregory Peck, Joan Bennett, and Robert Preston, and directed by Zoltan Korda. The first frame reveals a wholly different film in which Wilson (Peck) and Margot Macomber (Bennett) have boarded a Ford Trimotor returning to Nairobi, Africa.

The Macomber Affair

```
INT. AIRPLANE

Wilson, a tall, good-looking American, leans
over to Margot Macomber, a trim, attractive
brunette, and touches her face with affec-
tion.

                    WILSON
          Don't worry, you'll be alright.
```

Writing
from
Within:
The Next
Generation

230

```
EXT. LANDING STRIP

The plane lands. Wilson and Margot debark.
Newsmen and police await them.
```

This scene indicates that Hemingway's surprise ending has been obliterated and a love story inserted. Hemingway's intention—to show a man, Macomber, who finds his manhood and pays the price for it—has been subverted in favor of a Hollywood love story, a triangle, if you will.

A few moments later, Wilson tells the police inspector:

```
                    WILSON
        He was just unlucky-

                    INSPECTOR
        Gored by a buffalo?

                    WILSON
        No, shot in the back. Accident.
```

Wilson looks deeply troubled by this report. He appears conflicted. Later, he is given a form to fill out, a questionnaire about the "accident." The screenwriter takes the opportunity to include a flashback that begins with Macomber (Preston) meeting Wilson (Peck) in the lobby of the hotel.

How Screenwriting and Casting Can Betray a World-Class Short Story

A film can only be as good as the screenplay upon which it is based. For a screenplay to be "good," the character's qualities as discussed earlier in this book must fit the novelist or short-story writer's delineation of the character and then the producer must cast the parts in accordance with these qualities, as laid out by the screenwriter. In this film, the screenwriter got the qualities all wrong and thus the casting was also all wrong. (**Note:** The demands of the film business being what they are, the availability of a star often requires perfectly good screenplays to be rewritten so that an available star—not necessarily the best one for the part—can play it.)

Let's look at the qualities the screenwriter gives to the characters as well as the casting based on these qualities.

Preston is a short, compact, extroverted sort of man—a quick-talking, friendly man. Margot (Bennett) is pleasantly outfitted in feminine garb as if waiting for a garden party to begin.

Peck is tall, soft-spoken, genuine—an American archetype.

Already this interpretation of the story is in trouble. The original story calls for a too-tall sportsman type to play Macomber, someone like Peter Graves, who starred a few years later in *Stalag 17* (1953) and later in the television series *Mission: Impossible.* Graves has deep-set, rather haunted eyes that could communicate the fear that Macomber experiences.

Bennett seems to be miscast as well. The original story suggests that Margot should be played by a great beauty whose gorgeous appearance is fading, leaving her desperate to regain some power. Therefore, the film calls for a woman with transcendent beauty—Rita Hayworth, Ava Gardner, or Lana Turner. All would have been terrific. All could have been sufficiently bitchy—as the part required—especially Lana Turner. But Ava Gardner would have trumped the other two—a woman whose beauty could drive men crazy. Peck is the most completely miscast of all. When Wilson is called upon to bed Margot Macomber, the turn in the script is completely unbelievable. Peck's most enduring quality is his loyalty and fidelity to a cause or a mission. Recall his performance in *Twelve O'Clock High* or in *To Kill a Mockingbird.*

Wilson is an observer of life, even as he does his job extremely well. He is all man, with contempt for humans generally and Americans in particular, especially American women. He has contempt for unmanly Americans, but he's open to seeing them change their stripes. Thus Wilson needs to be a tough guy, preferably an Englishman, or an English version of Hemingway, whose values are flexible—not a big guy, not a great-looking guy, but certainly a fellow who has been in combat, preferably an Australian or an Englishman.

Why not Richard Burton? Or someone like Burton—perhaps Robert Shaw—who has the depth to convey the inner thoughts that Hemingway writes into his story.

Up to this point, the screenwriters have failed to capture Hemingway's theme—regaining manhood—turning the focus instead onto an implausible love story.

They have failed to catch Wilson's wonderful inner monologues on women, on hunting, on Americans, trying instead to create a story through dialogue that would interest audiences—not Hemingway's audience, mind you, but large audiences who remembered the bitch Joan Bennett played in *Scarlet Street* (1945) with Edward G. Robinson. Sadly it didn't work, but the failure of the film to work underscores my point, which is that screenplays often live or die with the degree to which they can recreate the inner life—the inner thoughts and feelings—of the main characters.

Writing
from
Within:
The Next
Generation

232

● ● ●

This chapter has explored some of the problems and solutions facing the writer who adapts a story written in one medium into one written for the screen. The successes are so few that those receiving Oscars for film adaptation usually deserve the award many times over.

Two things make the Hemingway short story a fine piece of writing: (1) the themes that a man can always redeem himself, no matter the circumstances, while a woman can only control a man so long as he is governed by fear and weakness; and (2) the quality of the inner life of these characters—Macomber reveals his inner life in his actions, and Wilson reveals his inner life in a few brief lines of inner thoughts and feelings. The screenplay turns these rich themes into Hollywood fluff—silly romantic conflicts of no consequence—and it cannot figure out how to bring the rich inner life of the characters to the surface.

In creating a screenplay from another medium, the screenwriter must find a way for the characters' inner thoughts and feelings to be visible. Very seldom does it work for a character to say openly what he thinks and feels. Film works by indirection, so characters have to speak "off-the-money" dialogue—speaking at cross-purposes to what they feel and think (see explanation on page 112)—and their actions often need to be at cross-purposes with what they say, as Dale Crum writes in his stories "Smoke Rings" (see the complete text of this story on page 275) and "My Sister's Shadow" (see the complete text of this story at www.WritingFromWithin-Stories.com) and J.D. Tousley writes in *Dangling in the Adios.*

For writers of life stories, the lessons of this chapter are many. First and foremost, if you, as a writer, depend on narrative and an interesting narrative style, that way of telling a story must be transmuted into something else—primarily into action and hard-hitting or spirited dialogue. If you depend upon dialogue in your stories, you must find ways of building subtext through characters speaking at cross-purposes and actions that tell a producer, director, and actor clues about the subtext. If your story depends on deeply revealing inner thoughts and feelings, as does Gail Field's "A Normal Life?" (see the complete text of this story on page 279) then you will have to give the characters bits of action that work at cross-purposes to their dialogue. That is the film way of working: It must be visual.

"Front Page to Hard Cover": Bill Rempel's *At the Devil's Table*

by William Rempel
Author, *At the Devil's Table*

At the Devil's Table began as a featured article published in the *Los Angeles Times* in February 2007. As a newspaper story, it received extraordinary treatment— front-page display with a photo spread inside along with another one hundred column inches of what writers admire most: beautiful gray type. Still, the story of Jorge Salcedo and his incredible life in the Cali drug cartel had to be drastically abridged to fit even those generous limits. Thankfully, Random House would step forward to provide bounteous book-length space. What I soon discovered, however, was that taking a 3,700-word newspaper account to a 100,000-word book manuscript would require much more than additional nouns and verbs or expanded anecdotes and details. I would also need loads of patience, a marathoner's stamina, an appreciation of criticism, and a healthy dose of ruthlessness to slash good material for the greater good of the big story.

First, some background: This was an unusual project from the start. It took more than eight years of reporting, and waiting, to finally publish those initial 3,700 words. Debriefing Jorge was not a simple matter. He and his family were hiding somewhere in the Federal Witness Protection Program. I had no idea where he was and no phone contact information. Rules of the U.S. Federal Witness Protection Program discouraged such sharing. And because I could not call him, I had to wait—days, weeks, months, and sometimes even years—for Jorge to call me. Contacts occurred entirely at his discretion. He called when he had the time and felt safe. And sometimes, Jorge acknowledged, he had second thoughts about telling his story to the world.

We first met in the fall of 1998 in a Miami federal courtroom. I had been tipped by a news source and flew out to Florida on short notice to attend a morning court hearing. I stepped into the public seating area a few minutes early and realized that I was the only member of the public in the room. No other spectators, no media. Down in front, inside the courtroom railing, assorted officials seemed busily engaged preparing for the next hearing while waiting for the judge. Off to one side, near the vacant jury box, two beefy U.S. marshals in dark business suits chatted amiably with a tall, distinguished-looking Latin man. Jorge Salcedo was easy to spot from across the quiet chamber. I have no idea what I was expecting, but he didn't look at all like the chief of security for the Cali drug cartel. He didn't look the least bit dangerous. Indeed, he appeared almost professorial, more like a math teacher than an organized-crime operative.

I already had introduced myself on the phone to his lawyer, so Jorge was expecting me.

"I'm so pleased to meet you," he said in perfect English, offering a warm, firm handshake when I introduced myself at the railing. He was instantly likeable. He also had been thinking about telling his story. I happened to be the first journalist he met since stepping into witness protection.

• • •

Telling Jorge's story in 3,700 words required plenty of detail. But making the tale read like a 100,000-word novel with detailed scenes and real dialogue, three-dimensional characters, and dramatic pacing required detail on a cosmic scale. I needed Jorge to call me two or three times a week. In between those calls, I worked ten- and twelve-hour days at the keyboard, roughing out the first draft. I often found myself writing scenes that needed more detail than I had in my notes. Typically, I would write a temporary version based on my imagination, making up the missing descriptions pending the next conversation with Jorge.

Once, I was laying out a bribery sequence in which the Cali cartel was about to pay off a Salvadoran colonel to acquire military bombs on the black market. I wrote the scene describing crime boss Miguel handing over the $500,000 to Jorge, his courier, in a black leather briefcase. As usual, on matters small and large, reality turned out to be far superior to my imagination.

In this case, when Jorge called, I learned that the Cali boss had personally gift-wrapped a large shoebox-sized block of wrapped U.S. currency, disguising it as a birthday present. Not only that, but Jorge described the boss as a meticulous artist, neatly folding each corner and finishing off the wrapping project with a handsome bow. I asked the obvious: What color was the paper…and the ribbon? And suddenly a rather ordinary scene came alive in red and gold trim, along with unexpected insights into a quirky mob boss.

Given that it took about eight months to gain access to the DEA agents, it was a good thing that, as characters in my story, they did not show up until the final third of the book. The interview load increased, too, but Random House liked the new material as much as I did—and my impossible summer deadline for a first draft shifted to the end of the year.

•••

Without question, the biggest challenge in the book was capturing the real Jorge Salcedo. He held high rank in the biggest drug syndicate in history, yet he never trafficked in drugs. He was close to the richest crime bosses on the globe, yet he never got rich. He supervised bodyguards and associated with paid assassins, yet he never harmed anyone. After six and a half years in the company of ruthless killers and traffickers, his biggest crime—and prosecutors considered it a felony under U.S. conspiracy laws—was protecting the security of cartel godfathers and the lives of their families.

"But he's too good," Will Murphy, my editor at Random House, complained more than once. The brevity of the original newspaper story had allowed only for the most superficial examination of Jorge's character and a handful of key moments. He was recruited into the cartel with an appeal to his patriotism, to help the rival traffickers kill Pablo Escobar, Colombia's Public Enemy Number One. The newspaper story also detailed how the Cali bosses rejected Jorge's resignation after Escobar died and how Jorge finally was driven to risk everything and reach out to the DEA after being ordered to help assassinate a potentially damaging cartel witness. Those were important moments, but the book needed much more. I had to show Jorge's descent deeper and deeper into the criminal organization, defining him by the ethical and difficult choices he faced.

Jorge answered all of my questions, and without apparent hesitation. But I was learning new details about his cartel years with virtually every interview. Specific elements of his character came into focus well after the first draft and after Murphy's early complaints that Jorge was "too good." Gradually that changed. In interviews spanning several months, Jorge detailed over and over his duties with the cartel, adding detail as we dug deeper. He had first designed radio communications systems that served the cartel's business and security interests but did no one any harm. Later he was involved in more sinister projects: a blackmail scheme to compromise an anti-narcotics military official. He also bugged phones and earned favor when he once sounded an alarm to protect a multimillion-dollar cash shipment from seizure. And then there were the paid assassins who considered Jorge a friend. They sometimes told him about plots and murders that he could do nothing to stop without risking the lives of his own wife and children, a seemingly impossible choice. A more imperfect Jorge emerged on the pages of my later drafts—bloodied, haunted, and regretful, but still a good man...and a much better character.

To the extent that *At the Devil's Table* succeeds in creating a complex portrait of Jorge, all I can say is: Thanks especially to Will Murphy, my editor at Random House, and to Halpern and friends at the Robbins Office in New York. They battered and abused my pages until the character of Jorge finally shone through in all its enigmatic and ultimately heroic glory. Forty years of journalism may have helped. Not because it taught me how to write, so much as it taught me to embrace prepublication criticism. Good editing is a lifesaver. I crave it.

My first draft came in at 120,000 words and would take nearly one year to revise and rewrite into a final draft. From his first read, Murphy suggested lots of deletions. I quit counting how many times he scribbled "bland...too slow...boring...do we need this?" and assorted other notes that a more fragile writer might regard as devastating insults. One of my favorites: "This sucks— improve!" There is nothing more frustrating than a demanding editor—and nothing more valuable.

If something "sucks" or doesn't make sense to Murphy or Halpern or anyone else, it might not work for Joe Average Reader, either. If the pace seemed to sag for my editor, it very likely sags for others, too. A writer has to be ruthless in defense of his story—but also ruthless with himself. Many a nice turn of phrase never made it between the covers of this book. Of my first 120,000 words, I probably deleted close to 50,000 in the first revision. In one typical edit, a provocative 1,500-word description of a murder that embarrassed the godfathers was cut to barely 200 words—focused only on what it taught Jorge about his bosses.

No story element, regardless of how colorful or telling, is worth preserving if it threatens the dramatic pace. I know. As a schoolboy, I fell asleep whenever Herman Melville put aside the chase for Moby Dick to examine in numbing detail the whale oil business. I don't presume to suggest a Melville rewrite, but as a newspaper editor I've seen too many writers fight to protect favorite lines that are really sure cures for insomniacs. It seems obvious that every writer's first rule should be: Don't put your readers to sleep.

To that end, I cut out page after page—including an entire chapter representing well over three weeks of work. It simply didn't move the story along. The excised chapter came early in the first draft, a colorful, even outrageous, tour of the Colombian jungles with Jorge and a group of British commandos as they secretly plotted an assault on a guerrilla outpost. The Brits were great characters, full of swagger. Unfortunately, their anti-guerrilla mission was never launched. There was no dramatic payoff. The episode took place months before Jorge had anything to do with Cali cartel bosses and revealed more about the British mercenaries than about Jorge, the main character. Most of the original three-thousand-word section vanished in a *click* of my "Delete" key.

Yes, I cringed at the time, but I have no regrets. It improved the story, just as a thousand other cuts did.

A colleague and friend of mine for many years at the *Los Angeles Times* was a revered writer and editor, part of an elite team of long-form journalists affectionately known as "The Poets." Words mattered to Rick Meyer—they mattered a lot. But his philosophy of research, writing, and editing could be summed up in a short sentence: "It's all about the story." By that, he meant that all efforts, all motives, and all words—even the poetic ones—must first and foremost serve the greater good of the story. It's that simple—and that demanding.

Of course, the one thing that eases the pressures of deadline and keeps the tedium of cutting and polishing in perspective is having a great tale to tell. For that, you'll have to find your own Jorge Salcedo.

• • •

Bill's experience in expanding a news article (which, in this case can be seen as a life story of his experiences with Jorge) into a book holds many valuable lessons for those who write life stories. First, it illustrates the enormous patience it takes to get "deeper" into the story. Without such patience, Bill would never have seen the project through to the end, no matter how much confidence he had in his abilities. After all, finding the truth of things depended on Jorge's willingness to surface, a willingness that Bill could not predict.

Second, it shows that Bill could not have gotten anywhere alone. His network of contacts made it possible for him to hear of Jorge in the first place, and his genial personality and work ethic put him on the good side of a host of people who could help him—DEA agents, FBI personnel, literary agents, editors, and the like. For life-story writers, this means going about your tasks in a similarly professional way—committing yourselves to establishing a regular pattern of writing, getting feedback, and putting your work—sharing your work with others as well as seeking out publication—without being discouraged.

Third, Bill is always looking for "actions that matter"—that is, actions (and obstacles) that reveal the character of Jorge in an ever-more-telling way. The longer he is involved with the cartel, the greater his challenge to retain his soul. These are the heroic qualities of which Joseph Campbell speaks in *The Hero with a Thousand Faces*—descending into the hell of the drug cartel's activities, undoubtedly feeling lost and alone, adrift, ruled by forces larger than himself. Finally, as he devises a plan to bring down the cartel—a plan that works—he is reborn, spiritually.

Fourth, Bill seeks the points of view of minor characters, such as the DEA agents whose voices play a significant part in the drama as well as other "players" on this dramatic stage.

Writing
from
Within:
The Next
Generation

238

Fifth, the experience offers a glimpse of a "cosmic" view of the world through Bill's and Jorge's eyes: a world of chaos and madness within which a good human can easily become lost and destroyed. However, resilience, patience, and focus eventually provide an opportunity for "good" to have its day. This is also important for the life-story writer who, too frequently, sees only the very small world of their own actions as being important. Seeking a sense of how the universe works and recreating it in your stories is an important consequence of going "deeper within" your stories and yourself. This effort reminds me of the arc of *Pan's Labyrinth,* a fine Spanish film in which a woman who experiences a number of wrongs done to her finds the strength to do the "right" thing by first diving deep into her inner life and imagination.

The final chapter of the previous unit, "Separating the Writer's Voice from the Central Character's Voice," demonstrates how to do this in your life stories. It examines the distinct worlds of the writer's voice (the creator of the universe within which all action takes place) and the central character's voice (the smaller world of the protagonist's story, or arc).

In his book *At the Devil's Table,* Bill is the creator of this world of action and events that has behind it a view of the cosmos as beneficent (God exists and works on humanity's behalf) or antipathal (God either does not exist or is furious with humans and works against our well-being). The reader has to decide which view Bill takes in his book. Jorge, of course, speaks for himself, the central character in his own drama of good and evil.

For the Future

Over the past thirty years, I have explored the many ways in which *Writing from Within,* and now *Writing from Within: The Next Generation,* can be used to affect people's lives in a positive way, by bringing to the surface unexpected creativity and previously unexpressed feelings. From the beginning of *Writing from Within* in 1982, I suspected this writing method held untold potential for influencing people's lives; it was up to me to explore this idea further.

At first, I found a welcome home for *Writing from Within* in the senior population with which I dealt. Older adults wanted to write and write well as a means of leaving something for future generations. Many of them, especially the younger oldsters, found a welcome opportunity to review their lives in the stories they wrote about their long and usually fruitful experiences.

I then offered my services to various agencies that work with recovering addicts, such as Kaiser Permanente, and, again, found a welcoming response. The groups that I worked with at Kaiser were filled with men and women who had vast resources of untapped creativity but who, for one reason or another, had strangled the expression of their thoughts and emotions. One young man in particular made an impression on me. He wrote about the moment when his father died: "I had been playing guitar and heard a noise from my father's bedroom. For a moment, I thought about stopping, but I continued playing a while longer. A few minutes later I stopped, went into my father's bedroom, and found him dead. I was horrified, filled with shame that I could be so stupid, so uncaring. I stopped playing the guitar and never went back. That was twenty years ago." I suggested that perhaps it was time to forgive himself and to go back to being creative. He agreed.

Many of the older men in my writing classes had gone through World War II as servicemen. A number of these combat veterans found a great deal of solace in writing about their experiences. One veteran, Chuck Woolf, had been on the destroyer *Morrison*, which went down in the Pacific in 1943. Chuck spent the better part of three years working on his life stories, every few months revisiting the painful moment when the kamikaze attacks caused the *Morrison* to flip over on its back and sink. Chuck described finding himself underwater, going down with the ship, and then suddenly seeing a shaft of light that he followed to the surface, where he and a small number of the ship's crew floated in the oily waters. Fewer than half the crew of 1,500 men survived.

Back on land, Chuck found himself haunted by nightmares of the incident for the remainder of his life. When he finished his book, I asked him how it felt. "I had a good night's sleep for the first time since 1943," he smiled.

As a former USAF officer and believer in the importance of a strong, enlightened military, I have wanted to bring *Writing from Within* to veterans' hospitals. However, that door has never opened. It remains one of the unresolved frustrations I have experienced.

In one of my writing classes located in the Fairfax area of Los Angeles, I found that a number of my students were Jewish survivors of the death camps in Poland and Germany during World War II. Most of those survivors found that by writing about what had happened to them, they experienced a sense of release from the pain sharply etched in their memories. One such woman, Joanne B., had been an unsung hero of the Polish resistance. Because she spoke fluent German, her Nazi captors often used her to translate orders from them to their captives. Joanne soon found that brutal orders enunciated by angry, contemptuous, and often ruthless Nazi guards could be softened if she repeated the orders back to the guards "to be sure [she] got it just right." After this process ran its course, the guards usually softened their orders.

Joanne saved hundreds of lives during the time that she was imprisoned in the Warsaw ghetto and in the camps in Poland. Initially she was a secretary for a Nazi sergeant who recorded the names and types of medical equipment rounded up from the Jewish Poles. The resistance asked her to leave the window of the office open one night so they could obtain her boss's rifle, which she did. In a second audacious move, they asked her to suggest to her boss that he should be pedaled around Warsaw in a rickshaw, as happened with others of his rank. A very convincing woman, Joanne persuaded him to do this, and two resistance workers built the rickshaw with a secret compartment in it. Every time Joanne's boss left the ghetto in the rickshaw, the resistance fighters who pulled the rickshaw filled the secret compartment with medical supplies to be dropped off after the Nazi officer had been carried home. In a third monumental act of heroism, Joanne witnessed a group of professional printers being sent off to a death camp against the orders of the German commander in that region. Since the Nazis highly valued skilled printers, Joanne decided to take her chances saving these men by making her way to the commander's quarters, getting his signature on a release form, commandeering a German staff car, stopping the train, and seeing to it that the group of one hundred highly skilled printers was rerouted to the duty of printing.

This fascinating story has never been told publicly, because Joanne wrote it simply to let her son know that her life was not worthless. She did not want her story published except at the hands of her son.

Over the years, my students often said to me, "Mr. Selling, what do I do if there is more information I want to put in my stories about the effects of the trauma I experienced?" As I mentioned in Chapter 5, after giving the matter some thought, I advised them to write a little P.S. at the end of the story.

• • •

When the riots of 1993 occurred in Los Angeles, I asked myself, "What can I do to be of service to my city, so torn apart by anger and frustration?" My answer was to offer a writing class at the Musician's Union of Los Angeles. As a musician myself, I have long known the wonderful bond that exists among musicians of all races and genders. As the class grew, a parade of top-notch musicians passed through the class: jazz great Buddy Collette and his friends Jackie Kelso and Eddie White; Latin jazz great Bobby Rodriquez; virtuoso violist Dave Schwartz; Jerry Velasco, one of the top accompanists for Lena Horne and Quincy Jones; and many others.

Buddy's stories of his drive to integrate the Black Musicians' Union and the White Musicians' Union in the mid-1950s were particularly moving, as were Eddie's stories of growing up in rural Louisiana as a young boy, listening to such legendary singers as Blind Lemon Jefferson.

A man of vision and compassion, Buddy made an effort to bring my work to the attention of a wider audience. At the time, he had been working with a private arts agency connected to the Los Angeles Unified School District. He recommended that it work with me in some capacity. That group, the Learning Tree, submitted a request for a grant to the State of California, and with the funds appropriated, we began a series of workshops in which my seniors, in groups of six or eight, read stories to entire grades—fourth through sixth—in San Fernando Valley schools and would then offer writing workshops to the students, if they desired. In this effort, we were quite successful. Frequently at least 50 percent of the more than one hundred student listeners at a reading would sign up for the workshop. Each senior reader led a table of six to eight students. The school's teachers later reported that after the workshops their students were writing stories more quickly, more fully, and with greater ease than ever before.

Writing
from
Within:
The Next
Generation

242

In one surprising moment, one of the women in my senior group read a story of experiencing her father's death when she was only five years old. I was a little unnerved by this choice, as I had expected her to read a different story, one that was not so personal. After she read the story, a young girl came up to her with tears in her eyes: Her father had died earlier that week, and she didn't know what to feel or what to say to people. The reading gave her permission to feel what she needed to feel and express what she needed to express. The girl and my senior reader hugged for a long time.

From these many experiences in and out of the classroom, and from looking deep within myself when I wrote my own stories, I know that eventually the educational system will need to recognize storytelling (in an intimate and personal way) as a legitimate skill to be taught. I also know from the faces of rioters in 1993 and from my experience as a documentary filmmaker in the 1960s that rage and pain need an outlet: People need to be able to look into their own experiences and find paths out of despair and frustration. And so I now look at possible places where *Writing from Within* will lead me and my readers in the months and years to come.

For the Future

"Writing from Within" and Schools

Teachers of academic writing often find their tasks to be daunting if not overwhelming. First of all, most students, it seems, do not especially want to learn how to write a good analytical paper in school. Secondly, the amount of grading that an academic writing teacher has to do is often overwhelming.

Can learning life-story writing skills help the beleaguered writing teacher?

At first blush, one might think the skills gained in learning to write life stories is 180 degrees away from the skills needed to write a quality analytical paper. But that is an illusion.

In what way can these skills help? Let's first look at the difficulties facing the teacher of academic writing and then ask, "How can life-story writing skills help?"

The difficulty for teachers of writing in an academic environment is that they must teach two very dissimilar skills: 1) *analytical skills* that produce logical arguments, well-defined objectives, and the use of a number of rhetorical skills, while at the same time teaching students 2) *entertainment skills* to be found in arresting first paragraph "teasers" followed by well-described examples, characterizations, quotes, and the like.

This process is made much easier if the students in question are first exposed to the craft of writing life stories. In the course of doing so, student writers develop a great deal of skill in learning how to create stories that have considerable appeal to audiences. Creating arresting first paragraphs, vivid pictures, three-part structures, believable dialogue and convincing climaxes to ones stories develops a person's writing skills in a significant way.

When students learn these skills by writing their life stories, they can then apply these techniques to their academic papers. They have learned the "entertainment" skills that come with understanding and appealing to their audiences.

In those situations where students develop these skills in the less demanding arena of life-story writing, the teacher can then concentrate on teaching the analytical skills that are so in demand in today's society.

—•••—

This process certainly sounds good, at least in theory, but has it been tested in actual school environments? The answer is yes. Over the course of some thirty years as a college and adult-school academic writing teacher as well as a teacher of creative writing, I have introduced this method to my writing students on all levels—some as young as eight and nine. Again and again my college writing students let me know that becoming skilled at life-story writing was a great help in tackling academic writing.

Note: *One interesting and unique way to excite student interest was to have a group of senior citizens read life stories to students, as I did with an entire fourth grade at a local elementary school, and then have the senior citizens lead life-story workshops for the young writers.*

Likewise, I tested this method with classroom teachers over a two-year period when I conducted teacher-training workshops up and down the eastern seaboard, from New Hampshire to Florida, and then along the gulf coast, from Biloxi, Mississippi, to Houston, Texas. The response was very enthusiastic. Teachers especially liked the potential carryover from life-story writing to academic writing.

This writing method has also been used with low-achieving students in charter schools in Los Angeles, California; in Los Angeles County juvenile detention facilities; and within the academic curriculum of the entire Division of Career and Adult Education in Los Angeles, California. In each case, results far exceeded expectations.

Yes, despite its successes, "writing from within" has barely scratched the surface of its potential to assist students to become motivated, high-achieving academic writers. The future holds great promise in this direction.

"Writing from Within" and the Human Potential Movement

Storytelling skills can have an abiding impact on relationships. Often, couples having relationship trouble begin and end with accusations and blaming ("you should; you shouldn't"), where a good story might help solve the problem by allowing one person to see the other person's point of view more clearly.

Eventually, in writing my own stories, such as "The Jewish Wife," (see the complete text of this story at www.WritingFromWithin-Stories.com) I realized I had a lot to say about the growth I experienced as a result of the incident I had chosen to write about. My training in the Stanislavsky Method of acting as taught by Lee Strasberg, Jack Garfein, and Harold Clurman reminded me that virtually all relationships are about character and the actions we take as a result of the character qualities we possess. As I wrote more of my own stories, I began to see my own worthwhile character qualities coming into focus.

Years earlier, a critical point in my life made me face up to some difficulties I had been having in personal and professional relationships. After examining my own behavior, I realized that in everything I had done throughout my life I had exhibited creativity, and that, in not recognizing this trait in myself, I had been limiting my goals and opportunities. Once I accepted this perspective and began to see and promote myself as a creative person, many new opportunities began to surface.

Little by little, I began suggesting to certain students that they look at their stories as mirrors of who they were and how they behaved in life. If they felt they needed to make changes, I counseled, "Write a story about an incident that relates to the change you feel necessary, then look at your story as if it is a mirror in which you can see character reflected, qualities you may not have previously known or appreciated. Once you see your own best qualities, you will see how to make the changes you think necessary." The one thing I did know about human behavior, having taught writing for such a long time, is that most people do not value themselves for the many good qualities they possess. A change in behavior means looking at our best qualities, for those qualities are what we rely upon in times of stress.

Over time, I put these observations together in a sequel to *Writing from Within* entitled *Character Consciousness*, which establishes a path through which everyone can come to recognize their best qualities by observing their behavior in many different life circumstances. The essence of this process is a series of questions that writers must ask themselves: *Who am I in this story? What are the qualities that get me what I want in this story? Am I the victim of some trauma of the past that has caused me to want to hide certain events of my life? What do I need to do to stop hiding those events?*

Here is what psychiatrist Douglas Caldwell had to say about this process in the Foreword to *Character Consciousness*:

> Selling's *Character Consciousness* encourages us to see ourselves as capable of growth by changing our perceptions of ourselves. His first profound, heartfelt book, *Writing from Within*, nudged us toward the childlike part of ourselves—the innocence that deserves to be seen and felt, showing us how to find and nurture this part of ourselves. *Character Consciousness* moves the work inward. By exploring early traumas through writing and rewriting them in closer and more intimate detail, we break through and recover heroic aspects of our experience that we have forgotten, ignored, or overlooked. In this way we begin to reframe our experience of trauma.

What this means for the average person is that self-knowledge and self-awareness are important aspects of each person's growth as a human being and that the responsibility for teaching growth need not fall solely in the hands of trained professionals—psychologists, therapists, counselors, and the like. The potential of much of this growth and awareness can be seen in our own experiences if we choose to pay attention, and life stories are an excellent first step toward paying attention.

An example in my own life occurred many years ago, shortly after my first divorce. I had told my wife that I needed to be free of the bonds of marriage. Of course, now she had a lot of power in her hands, such as the power to decide when, if, and how I would see my children. Thus began a five-year, deeply unsettling dispute, not unlike that which many couples with children face: Love is gone, and the struggle for power begins. Here, from the first few pages of my book *Character Consciousness,* is the brief story of how this struggle for power changed into a life-long friendship.

Defining My Turning Point Behavior and Finding Its Origins   *by Bernard Selling*

From Character Consciousness – *Chapter 9*

Most of us struggle in our lives with the question, Can I ever really change? Can I turn it around? At the core of existential philosophy and literature in the '40s and '50s was the assurance that, yes, we can change. At the same time, the dominant force in psychology—Behaviorism—suggested it was really quite hopeless for us to try. We were all victims of the forces of something larger—authoritarian political movements, supernatural forces, Big Brother, brainwashing, and the like.

During my darkest moments, I adopted a philosophy of life-as-trickster—that is, just as we are about to get what we want, the universe, the divine trickster, will pull the rug out from under us. I don't know that this point of view served me well—I felt helpless and out of control, Sisyphus-like, condemned to making the same mistakes over and over—many of us have felt this force.

Yet for most of us, there are moments when we have acted well even in the midst of our darkest times. Eventually, after we have rooted out the painful memories and understand how the past has held us captive, we can turn and look at those moments when we have acted well to find the roots of those actions in our early years. Gradually, we can turn things around and see ourselves in the middle of a surprising history of taking positive risks that turn out well. We can trace the origins back to moments of courage, insight, independence.

For example, if I were asked to write my single most important "turning point" memory for the past three decades of my life, it would be the following:

Winning   *by Bernard Selling*

"I'm not going to sit here and listen to you run me down anymore," yells Gail, my ex-wife. She is fuming. "It's just like when we were married." She picks up her purse and marches out of the counselor's office.

The counselor gazes at me for a moment. He is tall, thin, rather serious-looking, and quite young. Maybe thirty. About my age. Gail is twenty-five. We have two kids and have been divorced now for a year.

"Gail's pretty angry at you, Bernard," he says, leaning forward.

"Yeah, she is, huh," I reply.

"Any idea why?" he asks.

"She doesn't like me telling her what to do. She doesn't like me telling her what's good for the kids.... She doesn't like to hear me remind her that the kids are mine as much as hers. I deserve, and I'll get, equal time with them if it kills me," I mutter. My teeth are clenched.

"Bernard. Think about it. You left her, right?" I nod. "So she's getting even. You've been a good father, yes?" Again I nod. "Her only weapon is the kids…and she uses it." Again I nod. He leans back for a moment, then forward. "…and she always will, as long as you keep on this way."

"This way? What does he mean by that?" I wonder.

He looks at the clock. Time is up. He looks at me again. "If you want to have the kind of relationship with your kids that you say you want, you'll have to stop trying to win."

I start to protest but then decide just to let it sink in. Stop trying to win? Is that what I'm doing?

Over the next few weeks I think about this a lot and decide he may be right.

Several times Gail does things that would normally bother me, but I become more polite, less antagonistic. I begin to compliment her for things she is doing, particularly for the kids.

"You wimp!" hisses Kathy, my wife-to-be. She hates to see me being nice to Gail, giving in to her requests.

"Believe me, I know what I'm doing," I say.

———— • • • ————

After several years, Kathy and I go our separate ways. But Gail and I become better friends. No longer does she try to get even with me. My regard for her grows.

Assessment

Now thirty-five years after our divorce, Gail and I are the best of friends. We have raised the children in a nonpossessive way. We spend holidays together, the four of us. In fact, we celebrate the holidays together even when the kids are not in town. There have been occasions where Gail and the kids and Kathy and her husband and my girlfriend and I all share a pre-Christmas glass of good cheer.

As I look back on that moment in the counselor's office, I am surprised that I was able to act so well and take the good advice that was offered me. I was in the middle of a very hard and lonely time in my life. I was in a great deal of pain and guilt over my failed love relationships and very confused and frustrated about my career as a filmmaker. Yet somehow I was able to calm myself a bit and reduce the level of anger between Gail and me. It opened the door for what mattered most: our children growing up happy and well-adjusted, feeling their parents cared about them and respected each other and were in their lives, day to day, week to week, year to year, forever.

I befriended my enemy and found her to be a human being like myself. As distant as we were to each other as husband and wife, so we became equally open to each other as parents.

No easy task. I acted well where I could have easily acted in a small, petty, selfish way.

Where did I get that? I ask myself sometimes. Where did it come from?

———— ••• ————

As I look back on my youth I see myself as mostly a wimp until I began to grow into my adolescent body in the eighth grade. I recollect one Saturday afternoon that year talking to a girl at a local swimming pool when I glance down and see a toddler sinking to the bottom in eight feet of water. I dive down, pull the baby up, and give it to its mother. The baby is gasping for air but it is okay. So I go on talking to the girl. No big deal. Not bad, Bernard.

Perhaps it is my awareness that my father, despite his illnesses and his rages, never wasted an opportunity to take a trip with me to explore something historical—a railroad, a battlefield, a ship, a museum, a restaurant serving hamburgers on model trains. As far back as I can remember my father does that, giving me a chance to learn. And I know that I will give those same chances to my two sons, no matter what the obstacles.

These moments in life are very important. They are the moments when we enhance our sense of self-worth, when we touch the nobility that lies within us. Even at our darkest and most confused moments, the seeds of our better selves are at work. Most of us do act well at various times in our lives but do not value ourselves the more for it.

By writing your life story and reflecting back on the person you are, the person you have been, and the person you can be, you set in motion a more positive future for yourself and your family.

———— ••• ————

When I wrote this chapter in *Character Consciousness* some five to ten years ago, I had not yet experienced the pleasure of being a grandfather.

At the age of seventy-two, I can look out on the family I created all those years ago. My sons are productive and engaged in life. They love me, they love their mother, and they love their stepmother, my second former wife, Kathy.

Writing
from
Within:
The Next
Generation

250

When we divorced, she was saddened at the thought that her relationship with my sons, then ten and eleven, would end. I assured her it wouldn't: "You'll have whatever relationship you want to have." She wasn't sure that would happen, but over the years, Will and Jeff never failed to spend time with Kathy and Ben, her husband. And Isabel and Max, my adorable grandchildren, spend weeks at a time with Kathy, Ben, Gail, and, of course, my daughter-in-law's mother, Dorothy.

Yesterday, my six-year-old grandson spent the day with Grandma Gail as passengers in the turbo prop airplane that my son flies for Skywest Airlines. Gail couldn't wait to relate all the fun that she and Max had riding on "Daddy's airplane."

None of this would have happened had I not listened to the good advice given to me some forty years ago by a young therapist. Writing and reflecting upon my stories has forced me to slow down the way I respond to things. Impulsive, emotional, knee-jerk responses are a thing of the past. Knowing my best character qualities enables me to allow things to happen around me.

Sometimes you just have to get out of your own way, as the saying goes, and allow things to happen.

The Benefits of
"Writing from Within"

Writing from within ourselves, going beyond the facts and into the moment-to-moment feelings of our lives, can be scary but also deeply liberating. Done honestly and diligently it can help clarify our lives, allowing us to value our strengths, forgive ourselves and others for real or imagined hurts, and release events or people who have confused, angered, or weighed upon us. We can then embrace more fully those who have given us love, support, and guidance, and can look forward to that which is ahead of us.

How can we get the most from the "writing from within" that we have done? One way is to ask at the end of each story, "What did I learn from this experience back then? What am I learning from the experience now? What am I holding back that I could express?"

Healing from Within: Handling Loss Creatively

At a certain point in our lives, people we care about deeply begin to physically or mentally fail. Perhaps they are still living but need care we cannot provide and must be placed in an appropriate facility. Perhaps they hardly recognize us. This can make us feel very alone. Our sense of loss affects us deeply, and our self-esteem is often badly shaken. Our resolve to write, our discipline, may also be shaken: We don't want to write; we dwell on the object of our loss, excluding all else.

Writing about that special person may be difficult, but it is necessary for us and for them. Writing of the sweet, happy times is good. Writing of the struggles is good, too, as is writing about the absurdities and ironies of our relationship. And sometimes the results are quite surprising.

A student of mine had been having a hard time writing during the first few months of class. Her stories were short, factual, and very limited in what they revealed. When I asked her what was happening, she replied, "My husband is in the hospital with Alzheimer's disease. It's very hard to think of anything else." She was trying to avoid thinking about him by writing stories that had little to do with their relationship or the human or humorous side of the man. He had been a prominent physician, and she couldn't help but see the difference between the way he had been and the way he was when she visited him. "He's only conscious five minutes out of the hour," she said. "Even then, just barely."

I suggested she do the difficult thing—take the bull by the horns and write about their relationship. She was younger than he, a devoted wife, awed by his place in his profession, content to write about the trips they had taken around the world traveling from one professional meeting to another.

"Write the stories of your life together," I suggested. "The growing-up years, the struggles, how absurd he could be."

She laughed. "Oh, he could be. Maybe I should write about the time he was drunk in Paris and got propositioned right in front of my eyes." The class laughed and began clapping, wanting this stuffed shirt unstuffed.

An Evening in Paris   *by Helen Winer*

"Show me the way to go home.
I'm tired and I want to go to bed..."
Lou is singing as we walk along the boulevard in Paris in June of 1954. He had lectured at the university that afternoon on his specialty, dermatology, and we had stopped to have some wine after his talk.
"...oh, I had a little drink about an hour ago
and it went right to my head..."
Barbara, our college-age daughter, has been getting more and more disgusted with her father and so she steps back to join me and her sister, Marylee, who is fourteen. Lou keeps on singing.
Just then a very pretty floozy walks up to Lou and says, "You want to come home with me?"
"No," says Lou, waving his hand toward us. "I've got my wife and daughters with me here and I'm just singing. Say," he says, looking at her face, which is very close to his, "I'm going to send you to the best dermatologist in Paris. Tell him to treat you. You've got some bad-looking moles on your face. You don't want to have your pretty face spoiled by these moles, do you?" She looks at him in complete surprise. "Say Helen," he turns to me, "Do you have Jean Civatte's card in your purse? Give it to this

girl." I give the card to her. "Now run along kid." He turns to me. "Come, walk with me instead of with the girls." He smiles and begins singing. . . .

> "Wherever I may roam, on land or sea or foam
> You can always hear me singing this song..."
> Barbara and Marylee and I join in as we walk down the street.
> "...show me the way to go home."

Helen Winer   *Helen grew up in Minnesota where she met her husband when she was nineteen and he, an already prominent dermatologist, was twenty-nine. They moved to Los Angeles, and she raised her family while her husband achieved international fame. She came to class to begin memoirs for her grandchildren, memories of her beloved husband who was hospitalized with Alzheimer's disease.*

— • • • —

The class was delighted to see a different, informal, human side of their relationship. They were pleased that Helen could look at this dying man, the man she loved and adored, and see his imperfections and absurdities and laugh at them even as he lay dying a few miles away.

"Take this story and read it to him," I suggested.

She looked at me as if I were an idiot. "He's not conscious," she said. "He can't even speak and he can't hear anything." She shook her head, almost in tears.

"Whether he seems conscious or not, read it to him," I insisted. "Believe me, he'll hear it. And he'll love it. Just hold his hand. Whether he says anything or not, you'll be able to feel in his hand that he is hearing you."

"If you say so, I'll do it," she answered, unconvinced.

The following week she came to class with a story of her experience at his bedside.

I Read My Story to Lou   *by Helen Winer*

Writing
from
Within:
The Next
Generation

———

254

As I enter Crescent Bay Convalescent Hospital, I notice one of my friends, a patient, coming toward me in her wheelchair. "Do you wish to hear my latest story?" I ask. "My teacher said I should read it to Dr. Winer and see his reaction."

"Ya, sure. I like your stories. I'll listen even if he doesn't," says Mary, "because he probably is only half here." We go into his room and he is half-awake. I start my story.

"Show me the way to go home.

I'm tired and I want to go to bed..."

Lou stiffens. I can see he hears my voice. I take his hand. As I read he begins to smile. By the time I read about the floozy girl who tried to pick him up, he is grinning from ear to ear. "It's OK honey, I never looked at another woman. Just you!" Lou says and then dozes off. I smile at Mary and put my story in my purse.

I go home and hug myself.

• • •

We can learn a number of things from Helen's experience. If we have relatives or friends who are seriously ill or near death, we need not give them up as lost. They may not be awake, but they are accessible. Talking to them when they are in an unconscious state will be good for them whether they seem to respond or not. Writing about an experience that has been shared, bringing back the good times of the past, and reading the moment to them rather than merely talking about it is all the more powerful because we have taken the time and energy to shape the experience artistically.

When someone is a long way away and we intend to make contact with him or her, we can write about the experience we wish to share. The more vividly we write, the more deeply our loved one will be touched.

The healing power of "writing from within" is enormous for the writer. The power of the story can push deep into the unconscious of even those who are very sick and infirm. Likewise, if we can awaken searing memories from the past, as does Joanne Baumgart with "Christmas 1944" (see the complete text of this story on page 301), bringing the story to life as vividly as possible is a way of removing it from the part of ourselves that is haunted by the past. The more fully the story is written, the more complete the release from our past and, therefore, the greater the possibility of healing ourselves from this terrible wound. (Remember Diane Hanson's story "Double Trouble" [see the complete text of this story at 289]—and why she wrote it.)

A Profitable Merger: Fiction Writing and Life-Story Writing

Although a number of my writer friends consider life-story writing to be a poor stepchild to the high art of writing fiction, some of them have changed their minds after taking my writing workshops. "Writing my life stories brings an honesty to my work that I can't seem to get anywhere else," says Mar Puatu, a novelist and screenwriter. "There is a grittiness, a texture to my life stories that I am able to get into my fiction only when it is based on some kind of life experience."

Over the years I have noticed that when my life-story writers attempt fiction (and I encourage only those who are skilled at "writing from within" to do so), the first few efforts don't ring true. They often overwrite, embrace clichés, or write from their heads rather than from their guts. Gradually, I bring them back to the simplicity of life-story writing, to the directness of feelings and the focus on physical sensation, and their fiction becomes more honest and believable.

Most of the skills learned in life-story writing translate directly into the fiction medium, such as the way we uncover character in "writing from within" by stressing the very real difference between the narrator's concerns and the character's concerns. If the character is a young child and his or her innocence must be respected, then the narrator must lay in details in such a way as to establish rather than to undermine the belief in the character's understanding of what goes on.

Another crossover skill is using action to portray character. Too often in fiction we see a lot said *about* the characters by the narrator. Too seldom does the writer simply *allow* the character's actions to reveal who he is.

These techniques, when practiced in the writing of our own life experiences, will help us write more authentic, more believable (and more salable) fiction. At the very least, the sketches we create when writing life stories enable us to draw accurately from life. Even if our sketches are nothing but short, single-page vignettes of people we know, they become the source material for longer, richer stories.

On a visit to the British Museum some ten years ago, I was fascinated to see how many half-size sketches for his famous "A Sunday Afternoon on the Island of La Grande Jatte" impressionist painter Georges Seurat created before he did the final work. In sketch after richly colored sketch, each tiny point of pigment creates a sense of the life at the river's edge. That's just what we do when we write and rewrite our stories. In each moment, we find a changing color…and a different quality of honesty or grittiness as our light passes over the surfaces of our characters and their struggles.

Bringing the Family Together

This book began with a brief statement about the way in which our society has developed a certain rootlessness over several generations. Fortunately, our society has turned its attention once more to the stabilizing influence of family and roots in preserving and developing some of the qualities that lead to fulfilled lives: a sense of belonging, enhanced communication, freedom for growth, and the need for support and encouragement.

Life-story writing practiced "from within" can be one of the factors that leads to a more harmonious family life. Writing one's most vivid early memories brings many members of the family into the arena of one's life. Writing about significant characters gives unusual members of the family the opportunity to be seen and understood. Writing from several points of view allows family members to compare notes about important moments and to experience events each in his or her own way, knowing that most of the family will disagree about both the facts and the meaning of any given circumstance. Pursuit of family history allows family members to glimpse stories from the past and the relationships out of which those stories have come. Additionally, this pursuit serves to help those who are shy know how important such revealing is to other members of the family. In sum, life-story writing allows the many points of view within a family to be heard.

The actual process by which stories are exchanged may be a fascinating story in itself. Distant families in which little sharing takes place can begin to dissolve some of the barriers that keep them apart. Closer families in which bonds are stronger may develop more of a sense of who each family member really is.

Life-Story Writing and Values in the Twenty-First Century

The United States is an increasingly pluralistic and multicultural society. Our schools, legal, judicial, and welfare systems strain under the unfamiliar customs, habits, and language of those coming into our systems as well as the poor, homeless, and drug-damaged dwellers in our urban areas.

What common ground do all of these people have? How can we as a society work toward common goals with such diversity around us?

Seventy years ago the goal of every immigrant was to learn the language, customs, and habits of this country and to melt into American society while keeping some traditions alive. This is not the main goal of most immigrants today, nor of the poor and the homeless. America's money, power, political freedom, and material opportunities are still desired. Its ideological and judicial elasticity are quite puzzling. Its humanistic concern for a highly developed, personal ability to grasp ideas and express them vigorously is little understood.

Storytelling is one thread that can weave all these diverse needs and desires together. The poorest and wealthiest touch one another through stories of struggle, humor, suffering, and compassion.

Storytelling cuts across all boundaries. Religious fundamentalist and existential humanist alike communicate through stories. Older adults touch the lives of children not through insistent and didactic moralizing but through stories of life's mysteries.

Every child in every classroom across the country can learn to tell and to share stories of his or her significant experiences in life. These stories are as significant to the child as a substantial bank account is to an adult. Each child needs to know how to put stories in and take stories out of his or her memory bank. For too long, storytelling has been forgotten as a part of our educational system. From the lower grades through college, storytelling through life-story writing will help build positive values and enhance self-esteem. (For teachers who wish to employ some of what we have been exploring in this book, please see my book *In Your Own Voice* [Alameda, CA: Hunter House, 1993].)

I recently spent several months working with a group of people in recovery from alcohol and drug abuse. I introduced them to the idea that perhaps each of them carried inside a creativity that had gone undiscovered or neglected over a lifetime. Almost everyone responded strongly to this idea and wrote vivid, expressive life stories. It became clear to me that these former addicts (mostly young men who came from lower middle class, very macho families in which the fathers were highly critical and contemptuous of creativity as too feminine) yearned for that which would allow them to be more creative in their lives, and not be criticized for it.

In subsequent conversations with their counselors, I learned that several of those with whom I had worked were, in fact, further exploring their life stories and were apparently much more focused on their recovery than before I began working with them.

Every segment of society profits by the ability to tell stories effectively. The homeless win refuge, abused children win safety, teachers win community support, and the disenfranchised win representation. Stories told well support each person's claim to truth and importance and win for each storyteller growing self-esteem.

Plato tells us that everything we need to know already exists and that our job is to penetrate through to our awareness of the truths that lie within. A central question asked by one of the popular human-growth-potential organizations is, "What is it that you know that you are pretending not to know?" Parsifal, the great warrior-knight of the Grail Quest of the middle ages, was on this very path. His name (sometimes spelled Perceval) means to pierce through or to see through. His is the story of the warrior who sees through conventional definitions of what a warrior must be and discovers compassion in order to be reunited with his father. Family stories remind us of such values, conveyed in an entertaining way, without insistence.

The stories of our personal past, even if we are small children, form the mythic path we are to follow for the rest of our lives. Some family stories lead

Writing
from
Within:
The Next
Generation

258

to family traditions of compassion, dedication, self-sacrifice, and idealism. Others lead to family traditions of honest public service. Personal and family stories help produce citizens who are not molded by popular culture alone. A society in which personal and family stories are developed is a society in which survival values are strong.

I hope we will return storytelling to a place of honor within the family and in the classroom.

Conclusion

Over the thirty years I have been doing this work, I have heard thousands of stories—some wonderful, some self-centered and egotistical, some simple and lyrical, some anguished. Those that stand out, the ones that remain in my memory for decades, wed an interesting character to a situation, setting, or circumstance that included panoplies of fascinating minor characters. These stories weave major characters into an intricate pattern of human relationships and concerns—as intricate as any pattern woven into a Peruvian tapestry from the pre-Columbian era. Such a storytelling tapestry or web of relationships tells us about ourselves through a story that happened long ago and far away— the sounds, sights, thoughts, and smells from eras that have passed away but remain fresh through the stories we tell.

Writing our life stories gives us the opportunity to approach events and experiences creatively, perhaps for the first time. We have learned that writing is not so magical a thing that only a few can do it. We *can* create. We *can* write. By softening our critic, seeking helpful feedback, and becoming aware of our own writing process, we can continue to grow as writers and storytellers. Little by little we are discovering our own authentic voices as writers. By first looking at life through the innocent eyes of the child who still dwells within us, we can write stories in a way that is fresh, direct, visual, and emotional. Our inner critic rests.

Beginning with writing the stories of our lives, we progress to other, more challenging kinds of writing—sometimes creative, imaginative and fictional— often searching through our understanding of who we are and, at times, changing our perceptions of ourselves and the way we interact with other people.

This journey has been a fascinating one for me. The thirty years have whipped past me as if in the blink of an eye. So many writers, so many new friends, so many stories, so much learning, teaching and interacting. All worth it.

I hope you, the reader, will embark upon your own writer's journey with this volume beside you, alert to the twists and turns of your own path of self-understanding and self-expression.

Stories

Now you have arrived at the end of this small journey. You have absorbed the techniques of "writing from within," of writing in an authentic voice. You have reflected on the experiences and stages of your life, worked on your stories, and read a number of other stories that may have served as models for your own writing and rewriting. You have explored your own creativity—your ability to express what you have seen and felt in life—and have experienced the pleasure of writing well.

Perhaps you have also come to view the difficulties you've encountered in your life in a new light, gaining a new understanding of their meaning and a new respect for the ways in which you handled yourself in the circumstances. In the course of writing your life's stories you may also have given a great deal of pleasure to and provoked considerable thought and feeling in your readers and listeners.

Keep writing, and encourage those you love to do the same.

— • • • —

The following are a number of stories that will give you some insight into how this process is incorporated into writing actual stories. Additional stories can be found at www.WritingFromWithin-Stories.com. The stories on the website are:

Bernard Selling—"The Jewish Wife"
Bernard Selling—"Mom's Trip North"

• • •

Eddie White   *Eddie is seventy years old. He grew up in rural Louisiana in the 1920s. The family moved to Cleveland, Ohio, and eventually Los Angeles where Eddie worked at odd jobs, played the saxophone, and became friends with jazz musicians Buddy Collette, Eric Dolphy, Jackie Kelso, Chico Hamilton, and Charlie Mingus. He tried his hand at boxing but at 5'5" he had a short career. After thirty-six years working for the post office, Eddie retired and now writes much of the time. He wrote this memory of a time when he was seven years old.*

The Overhead Bridge   *by Eddie White*

I love to walk to the post office and pick up our mail. The post office is about two miles from Granny's house in downtown Ruston, Louisiana. Our box number is Box 107. I remove the mailbox key from the string around my neck and open our mailbox.

"Ahh, Ooooweee!" I yell to myself. I count to myself. "Granny has a lot of mail today." Because my mother is a school teacher and helps me with all of my school work along with her two youngest sisters, Baby Lowell and Sally Brooks, I learned to read very good and I have a very good knowledge of words and a better-than-most-kids understanding of the language. With three good teachers any kid can learn fast, at least something. Since I was three years old, I read better than most kids. I am seven now.

"Oh! Here is a letter from my Mother Dear; wonder if she has any money in it for Granny and me? One is from Aunt Brooksie, another from Baby Lowell. I bet they want something. They are away at school, college or something!"

"Ooooo, here's one from Aunt Anna. She hasn't written in a long time; this one is from Aunt Tee. (Lucyellen). I don't know why we call her 'Aunt Tee.' And here is the last one—a letter from good old Uncle Charlie, Granny's oldest son." This should make my grandmother happy, six letters in all, but I know what she will say when I get home. "Sonny, we didn't get no mail from Little Brother." Everyone calls Uncle John Glover Harvey either Little Uncle or Little Brother or the Baby Boy. Lawd! Lawd! Why don't he ever write just to let me know how he is getting along. I keep so worried all of the time wondering if something has happened to him. My baby got his leg cut off riding them freight trains when he weren't but nine years old, and has been a-hoboin' ever since, just ridin' the rails all over this land. He's been in every state in the country I 'spect. Lawd! Lawd! Have mercy!"

It seems that Granny would know by now that Little Uncle only writes to her

Writing
from
Within:
The Next
Generation

264

or anyone else when he needs some money or something. We see him once in a great while. One day Little Uncle will come home for a day or so, then he will leave just like he came, like Santa Claus. Only Little Uncle won't bring anything but himself. "I just cain't stand to hear a freight train whistle blow. I just have to put on my travelin' clothes and go." That's what Little Uncle tells everyone.

"Hey there, boy!" One of the mail clerks hollers at me as I am walking out the door of the Post Office, "Tell your grandma that sure was a good chocolate cake she mailed to her daughter. Be sure to tell her to make a bigger cake next time so everybody in our post office can get some." He laughs real loud. "Heh! Heh! Heh!" I turn and look back at him. He kind of throws back his head a little. He has a very red face, a big throat, and he is the one I have seen up close with the wrinkles in his neck like a turkey.

I say nothing as I wonder to myself, "Is he one of the kinds of people that the rich white people call 'cracker trash'?" I am getting close to the old overhead bridge. It is made and shaped like a big rainbow. I have to cross the bridge going to and from the post office. Trains going out of and coming into town pass under the overhead bridge.

Sittin' on an old cane-bottom chair at the bottom of the crossing of the bridge is a very old, gray head white man. He is talking to a very big white boy as he kind of rocks back and forth in his chair.

As I get near them I see that the boy is about Baby Lowell's age, around seventeen or so, and he is not old and ugly looking like the old man. The boy is bareheaded. His hair is short, light-colored, and sandy-looking. The old man has on a dirty pair of raggedy-looking overalls and an old straw hat that has a hole in it. Neither of them have any shoes on, just like me. Because both the old man and the boy are poor-looking, I think that they must be nice and not mean white people, like that old post office clerk who ate up Baby Lowell's chocolate cake that Granny had baked and mailed to her.

As I walk by the two, the old man and the boy, I kind of smile at them, thinking they are nice people.

"Wait a minute!" shouts the big boy real mean and ugly-like. "Whatchall en you hanes?" He drawls out nasty and slow.

"It's mail for my Granny," I whisper, kind of scared but not too much because the ugly old man is nearby.

"Gimme dat dare mail," he drawls, snatching the mail from my hand. I look kind of long at the ugly old man and wait for him to make the big boy give me back our mail. Being little and the boy being big, I know that the ugly old man will be on my side and will make the boy give me back my mail. The mean old gray-headed man just grins his toothless grin and watches me. Tobacco or snuff spit drools down the corner of his ugly mouth which seems to sit almost in the middle of an ugly, odd-shaped face. He has greenish birdlike eyes that shift from me to the big boy. He reminds me of a chicken hawk.

The big boy begins to open my mail. He takes his time and reads the letters very slow to the old man, and they laugh at anything they think is funny. Because Granny cannot read or write, all the family members know that I read her mail to her. They write large and clear, and are sure to use words I can understand.

The big boy stumbles across a word that he cannot pronounce. It is an easy word, at least for me. He begins to stumble and spell out the word. "Let me see," he stumbles, "Ppp-rrr-o-gram? Prigrin-UH! Wonder what the hell is that?"

"It's not prigrin. It's program. Don't you know what a program is?" I ask him.

"Listen heah! You shut up, nigger! Don't you every dare to make a fool out of a white man! Do ya heah me, nigger boy?"

"Yes!" I answer.

"Whatta you mean yes. Don't you know you be talkin' to a white man? Yo folks better teach you yo manners 'fo you grow up an gits lynched. We love ta have neck tie parties for you smart uppity niggers. They want ta teach you to grow up right and respect white folks! You heah me, boy?"

"Yes sir," I answer. Tears begin to run down my face to the hot ground. It is not the word nigger or saying yes sir that makes me cry. It's the reading of our mail—our mail—granny's mail.

He puts all of the mail in the right envelopes. I think he is trying to let me know that he can read as well as I can, but I know that he can't. He gives the mail back to me.

"Now you git! I wantcha ta git! Git ta runnin'! Don't ya dare look back!" He slaps his hands hard and loud, and kicks at me. I jump back. He misses. I run almost all the way home. I am mad and scared as I run home. Two miles is a long way for a seven-year-old, so I run some but trot most of the way. I think of the old man and the big boy. How they stink. I think it is a very hot day and both of them are mean and stinking. But "the ugly old man stinks worst than the boy," I say to myself. "Maybe it's because the old man has been meaner and stinking longer than the boy." There is a difference between the postal clerk and the mean two. The postal clerk must be what rich white people call "cracker trash," and the mean two must be what rich white people call "poor white trash."

Granny works for a real rich white lady sometimes, and Granny tells me that when Mrs. Satterfield leaves her home for any reason, she tells Granny, "Now Lucinda, effen any niggers at all come by heah a-beggin for food while I'm gone, I want you to be sure and feed the niggers, but effen any poor white trash come by heah for anything at all, I want you to call Sheriff Thigpen and get them the hell away from my premises. Don't give THE TRASH a damned thing! Let the trash starve to death! That's what they deserve. They been free all their born, no account days. Now do you heah me, Lucinda?"

"Yes'm, I heah you, Niss Satterfield."

Writing
from
Within:
The Next
Generation

266

One day I asked Granny, "What do you do when the beggars come by, Granny? Do you do what Mrs. Satterfield tells you to do?"

"God don't love ugly, chile. I just feeds them all who comes by begging for food. I feeds them all, black and white alike."

I am finally home. It seems like I have been gone all day. I hurry into the house. Granny can tell I have been crying, and I am a little out of breath. "Why what's the matter, chile? What's the matter? Tell your Granny."

I tell Granny all about it. The South bein' what it is, nothing can be done about what happened to me. Granny pulls me to her and whispers, "We will just have to take it to the Good Lord in prayer. He will wipe away all tears and he will wash away all sorrow. Let us try and forget about it. God changes things, Sonny."

I think to myself just before getting ready to go to bed, "Granny is right. Granny is always right. My Granny is always right? There are no tears, and no sorrow and no anger."

Now I look back and laugh at it all—but how can I forget?

— • • • —

Florence Mayweather *Florence spent much of her life in the rural south where her father, mother, brothers, and sisters lived as sharecroppers for most of her young life. The family dreamed of one day leaving the farm, but sharecropping did not provide them a way out, at least not until this story took place. Eventually Florence found her way out and made it to Los Angeles.*

Leaving the Plantation *by Florence Mayweather, age 72*

"It's feeding time," I can hear my father yell after he comes home from working the fields. My younger brother and I tag along to help care for the animals. Milking cows, feeding chickens, and slopping hogs is just another job to be done as part of our daily farm life.

We grow ever so tired and weary of working the plantation from sun up to sun down. Oh, how we long for a better life. My father and brothers often complain of getting overheated in the corn crops, or having to plow the fields in the heat of the southern sun. Time and time again things become almost unbearable and my brothers talk of leaving the plantation, one by one. We can always make ourselves feel better by vowing to save enough money to buy our very own house.

Poor crops and the low price of cotton make this almost impossible, because all sharecroppers are paid at the end of each year.

For many years my father is given a drink of whiskey and a pat on the back and told, "Sorry, Henry, but you did not make it out of debt this year."

"Those words would always make my heart ache," my father says.

The land owner attempts to pacify him by saying, "Now, Henry, if you and your children work hard, I am sure you will make it out of debt by next year."

My father tries to explain to him the things that we need just to be able to exist.

"Don't worry about a thing," the land owner says to him. "Haven't I always taken care of you and your little colored children? I have made arrangements at the general store and you can get a few things that you need there."

My father says, "Yes sir, Mr. Temp."

Mr. Temp places a big cigar in his mouth, unscrews the cap on the whiskey bottle. "Have another drink, Henry," he says. "I look forward to drinking with you good colored folks at the end of the year."

Sometime during the early forties, just when we think our dreams are never going to become a reality, farmers all over the South have a good year, crops are excellent, the price of cotton goes extremely high. There has been some talk among the share-croppers that absolutely no one is going to be left in debt this year.

They are right. The land owner comes and pays my father more money than we have ever seen in our lifetime. We have more than enough to buy our own house in the little country town of Keo, Arkansas, located twenty-five miles away from our home, where we are sure to live a more progressive lifestyle.

Now that we have the money, I am waiting for my parents to say that we will soon be moving any day. We know that my father is a bit hesitant, but we do not know why.

Then one day without warning he comes home with a big car—long, black, shiny, and new.

He has a big smile on his face. When we see that big car we have smiles on our faces, too. My mother meets him at the door with no smile on her face.

"Henry, what is this?" my mother asks.

"Well, Florence, as you can see, it's a car," my father answers.

"What about our house?" she asks.

"We can get our house next year," my father replies.

Somehow my mother is able to contain her tears, but she is not able to maintain her sanity.

"I can't wait another year!" she shouts and glares at my father. "If it's left up to you we will never get off this plantation."

Writing
from
Within:
The Next
Generation

268

My mother starts running around kicking chairs and pounding on tables. Many angry words flow from her lips. By now any smiles that we have had on our faces about that car have faded. Spellbound, we sit, watch, and listen, as our mother verbally fights with our father over spending the money on a car that we were going to use for our house. She accuses him of being afraid to leave the plantation. She tells him that he had to have received encouragement from the overseer to do such a thing. My father has little to say in defense of himself. I don't think there's anything he can say.

When it is all over, my mother has succeeded in painting such a clear negative picture of my father even we can see it. She has made him look as if he has less than a bird's brain. We sit without movement, looking at him with big sad, glassy eyes, feeling little or no sympathy for him. It is obvious whose side we are on.

The next few days at our house are sheer gloom. The gloom is lifted when my mother takes matters into her own hands and announces that along with the leftover money we are going to sell the animals to help make payment on our new house. My older sister and brothers are happy. My younger brother and I are oh, so sad, because we grew up with most of those animals that she is talking about selling and to release them isn't going to be easy.

These animals that are being sold are like members of our family. For example, Old Rose, our brown and white cow. She is gentle as a lamb. She had never kicked over a bucket of her milk in her life. Old Rose is first to go. Then there is Fat Sam, the hog. We had raised Fat Sam from a little pig. Sam is so greedy he used to slurp all the slop from the other hogs and squeal long and hard if we did not give him more. As much as we complain about him we cannot hide the pain when it is Fat Sam's turn to leave. Tears roll from my face as I say goodbye to most of the animals I have known as a child. I have these same uncontrollable tears when it is time to close the front door on the old plantation farm house that had been my birth place and the only home I have ever known.

—— • • • ——

Liz Kelly   *Liz Kelly was seventeen when she wrote this story. Shortly after the incident described in this story, which occurred when Liz was sixteen, she dropped out of school, left Wyoming, and came to Southern California where she began working as a live-in housekeeper. On her one morning a week off, she would come to one of my life-story writing classes.*

Tank Top   *by Liz Kelly (age seventeen)*

With my limited wardrobe, I don't know how I am ever going to dress cool. It's hard to get noticed being only a sophomore, and I don't want to dress like a geek. I stare into my closet; same old shirts, same old pants, same old skirts. I've worn every combination of clothing possible, and this morning I don't know what I'm going to put on.

I glance out the window. It's a dark gray morning blanketed in soft white snow. It looks so quiet and peaceful. I turn back into my room and cross over to my dresser. I open the middle drawer of the old antique and absentmindedly search through the muss of clothing for a possible outfit. An idea strikes me as my hand passes over a dark gray tank top. I reach back and grab the top from the pile.

"Okay, I'm on a roll now," I think to myself. I slip the top over my head and stride back over to my closet. I take the dark brown cords from their hanger along with the light purple oxford. I'm dressed within seconds, and I open my door and step into the hallway. I can smell the coffee and toast coming from the kitchen.

I hear the showers running, and I know that everyone is up. I look at myself in the full-length mirror that hangs on the rough wood wall. "Not bad. Definitely different, but not ugly," I think. I tuck in my shirt and unbutton the top buttons so that the gray tank shows. I go back in my room to find my old high tops. I want to look casual. I pull my laces tight and then go in search of breakfast.

In the kitchen I run into my older brother, Pat. He's a year older, and we don't get along all that great at times. "A bit revealing, isn't it?" he comments on my shirt.

"No. I'm not showing anything," I shoot back at him.

"Just a little cleavage." He turns back to pouring his milk on his cold cereal. I stand on the other side of the big counter and concentrate on making myself some toast.

"Good morning," says Dad as he comes in and pours himself a cup of coffee.

"Good morning," we respond simultaneously.

Dad looks at me. "Is that what you're wearing to school?"

"Yes," I say.

"She's setting a fashion statement," Pat chimes in.

"I wear it today, everyone else wears it tomorrow," I laugh.

"Go change," Dad says. Pat and I stop laughing. (Pat looks away. If he needs to stand up for himself he does, but otherwise he tries to steer clear of Dad.) I look at Dad's face, searching for a clue to what's going on. I'm not sure if he's really angry. His face is serious, and his brow is furrowed.

I don't wait to hear him yell at me so I take off to my bedroom to change. I hear his heavy footsteps in the hallway. I study the closed door of my room, the planks so carefully put together yet not even touching, the smooth black handle and the solid bar that latches the door shut.

The latch raises sharply, metal clanking on metal. The unforgiving wood creaks at me in warning. "Oh, God," I think. "Why did I have to dress this way? Why didn't I know better?" I watch, unmoving, as my father gives the door one hard push and it sails open, slams into the far wall, and slowly bounces back to its resting place, quivering violently all the while.

In three long strides my father is across the room, and he grabs me by the arms. I'm flung from the window to up against the bunk bed.

My head cracks soundly against the old wood frame of the upper bunk, but I dare not reach my hand up to try to soothe away the pain.

"You are not wearing that to school," he screams. "Don't you have any god-damn decent clothes?"

Writing from Within: The Next Generation

270

"No," I want to scream back. "I'm trying to make do with the little that I have," but I don't scream it. I know I have to take his shit. He points his finger at me. His hand is becoming worn with age, but I know how strong that hand still is. He jabs me forcefully in the chest.

"This is my house! I make the rules, and if you are going to live here then you better damn well follow them." His finger is the only thing that keeps his fist from hitting me again and again as if trying to stay in beat with my pounding heart.

"I won't cry," I tell myself. I bite my lip and hold back the tears. "I'll change my clothes, and I'll follow his rules, and I'll take his shit, but he is never ever going to see me cry because of him." I look him in the eye and listen to every word he says. I ignore the shaking of my legs and the tears welling up in the back of my eyes. He gives me one hard shove, and I sit down hard on the bottom bed.

"No daughter of mine is leaving this house dressed like a whore!" he says with finality and storms out of the room. I sit on the bed not daring to move, still shaking like a leaf.

"I am not crying," I say to myself over and over. "It's okay." I take a deep breath. "I'll leave. I'll go live with someone else. I'll run away. I will get out of here somehow, some way." I bring myself to my feet and walk to my closet. "He doesn't care. He never has and never will. Just wait 'til I'm gone."

I grab a different shirt from its hanger and change the shirt I have on. Then I take off my shoes and change my pants for jeans. Off in the distance I hear a door open and then slam shut again. "Good. He's gone to school," I think. I open my door and step into the hallway to check myself in the mirror. Pat comes from the kitchen and watches for a moment as I straighten myself in the mirror.

"The shirt really was revealing," he says.

"It was not that revealing," I argue.

"Liz, if I was Dad, I wouldn't let you dress like that either. You let your boobs hang out, and you'll have every redneck in the school staring at your chest," Pat tells me.

"I am not that big," I say.

"You have big boobs," he says and walks past me into the bedroom.

"Some free country we live in. I can't even dress the way I want to. I was hardly dressed like a whore. Dad can say what he wants and do what he likes, but as soon as I'm gone, I'm never speaking to that bastard again." I talk to myself tough, and I act tough, but my insides feel like spaghetti. I go back to the kitchen, acting as normal as I possibly can.

I eat my toast, trying to keep from choking. My younger brother, Michael, looks at me from across the table with his big brown eyes and just shakes his head. He's three years younger than I am but smart for his age. He believes in keeping his nose clean. He reads his books and does his homework.

I finish getting ready for school and step out the door into the icy cold morning. I slide my feet across the frosty porch and down the slippery wooden steps. Crunch, crunch, crunch. My footsteps are the only sounds in the snow. Thud, thud, thud. In my mind I hear his finger banging into my chest.

"Damn it. I am not going to cry. I have my pride and if I let this little incident get to me then I'm never going to survive the real world." The school isn't too much farther. The gray paved road stretches forever though, right up to the gray sky. When I reach the school door, I take a deep breath, trying to calm my shaken nerves.

"I pray to God I don't run into him," I tell myself. "It really sucks that my dad teaches at the high school, but I don't see him." I dump my stuff in my locker and go to join my friends in the hall hangout. I see my friends, Lori and Joszi.

"Hi, guys," I say.

"Hey Liz, how's it going?" they ask.

"Fine," I reply. Lori gives me a funny look. I'm trying as hard as I possibly can to hold back the tears that seem to be forming in my throat.

"Liz, what's wrong?" Lori asks.

"Nothing," I say as I turn and quickly walk away so they won't see me crying. I only take a few steps, then I dry my eyes and turn and walk back.

"Liz, there's something wrong," Lori says. She puts her arm around me and guides me into the counselor's office. Mr. Cothern, the counselor, gives me a knowing look. I've been here before. Lori sits me in a chair, and I put my face in my hands and cry.

Lori leaves to go to class, and Cothern and I go into discussion.

"I can't live with my father anymore," I tell Cothern. "I can't handle it."

Cothern gives me a serious look. Well, as serious as his looks ever get. Mr. Cothern is a tall man who reminds me of a character out of a cartoon strip. His eyes are always laughing, and I don't think he takes me seriously.

"Cothern, I'm serious," I try to convince him.

"Liz, your dad isn't going to move out, and if you stick around things are going to get better. You can work them out."

"Fine," I say.

I sit and listen a while longer, then I go back to class. I know, only too well, that things are not going to change.

P.S. I began to see that my father wouldn't change so I had to. I dropped out of school and moved to Los Angeles from Wyoming. On my day off, I took Mr. Selling's writing class. I sent my stories back to my family. They began talking about all the things that had happened in the family. My father's rage and the alcoholism that triggered it were part of the discussion. They've been getting help.

Writing
from
Within:
The Next
Generation

272

Karl Gray   *Karl grew up in Texas, the son of a band leader of the 1920s and 1930s (and later a booking agent for Jelly Roll Morton and others) and the singer in his father's band. Karl's father barely knew his son and died when Karl was very young. His mother later married, but maintained dreams of celebrity, style, and status. Karl was a hindrance to her, and she never let him forget it.*

The Garage   *by Karl Grey*

If I hold my breath just like I do when I shoot and brace my arm against my leg just right, I can paint the chrome strip on my model car so good that nobody will be able to tell it's painted by hand. I love building model cars. I love painting all the detail on them that I can, because nobody else I know can do it as good as I can, and that's what has won me trophies for the last two summers at Mrs. Sherman's Lakewood Hobby Shop.

The sweat on my leg—with my arm braced against it—is starting to make me slip, but if I can hold on long enough I can finish this strip down the side panel of my '55 Chevy convertible. Man, is it ever hot. It'd sure be a lot better if she held these contests in the wintertime, then I wouldn't have to sweat so much when I'm painting. I guess I could wait until it's a cooler time, but right now all I want to do is paint my '55. Besides, a summer night in Texas is about as cool as it's going to be for a while anyway.

In the background I can hear the sound of the air conditioner in the window in the den and the TV turned up too loud so that my mother and stepfather can hear it while they are washing the supper dishes. The door from the den to the kitchen is shut so the den will stay cool, but they want to hear *The Ed Sullivan Show* until the dishes are done. My mother washes, and my stepdad dries, and they have their drinks, scotch and water over ice, until they're done. My stepdad tells her all about what went on during the day at work, and she says, "Uh-huh."

I have all my windows open, but I keep the curtains shut so that nobody can see me in my room at night. The only way I can stay cool enough is to sit in my underwear. I wouldn't mind if somebody saw me in my underwear if I wasn't so fat. In fact, if I wasn't so fat, I would probably walk around in my underwear in front of people. If I wasn't so fat, the sweat would roll straight down my body and make me look better, like the guys in *Strength and Health* magazine. My sweat just gets caught in the creases between the rolls of my fat, and then it mixes with whatever dirt is on my body to make "fat mud," which isn't too bad until I stand up. When I stand up, I look like I have stripes on my body. My belly button really gets the worst of it, but nobody can see that. I just have to make sure I dig it out when I shower, otherwise it smells bad.

The model contest is a week away, and because I'm such a good painter I think I can win a first-place trophy this time. The other kids use model putty to make some pretty neat-looking custom cars, but none of them can paint as good as I can. Crap! The paint's running. What caused that? Now I have to take all the paint off and start over, and that can make the plastic look bad if I don't get it off right. There it is, a little piece of molding overrun on the chrome strip. Why didn't I see that when I was shaving it with my X-ACTO blade? Too late now, all I can do is take it off and start over.

I can hear the sound of the locusts outside, the whir of the air conditioner in the den, and the faint sound of conversation in the kitchen. I have to go to the garage to get my trimming blades. I wish I hadn't left them there, but Billy Pike wanted me to carve notches into his six-shooter, and my mother won't allow him into the house.

"Billy Pike is not the right kind of person to be in my house. He'll mess things up, and then you won't clean it up. You never do."

So I had to take my blade kit outside. At least I'll get to cool off when I go through the den. As I stand up, the sweat in the folds of my fat rolls down my body and catches in the waistband of my underwear. As I open the door to the den, the blast of cool air hits my wet skin. Ahh, that's more like it.

"And now, tonight, on this stage—"

I pause to see who is going to be on *Ed Sullivan* and to get as cool as I can. Buddy Hackett. I keep walking, through the other door from the den to the kitchen. There they are, my mother and my stepfather. Their backs to me, facing the window over the sink. She is washing with her drink off to her left, and he is drying with his drink off to his right. I bet they don't even hear me. My mother removes her hand from the suds, picks up her drink with the sudsy Playtex Living glove.

They hear me. She says, "Close the door! Do you think we're trying to air condition the whole house? Where do you think you're going like that?"

"I'm just going to get something in the garage," and I open the door. Shit! The outside garage door to the street is open, and I already shut the kitchen door. I don't want to go all the way back to my room to get something else on . . . I'll just turn off the light. I know just where the X-ACTO kit is. I can just run out and grab it and run back in and nobody will see me.

I hit the light switch, run into the dark, and grab the X-ACTO kit. Slam! Click! All of a sudden, the lights are on, and I am exposed to the neighborhood, standing in the garage in my underwear.

Panic seizes me. I feel ashamed and embarrassed. Through the door I can hear my mother laughing. I drop the kit and start to pound on the door. I'm pulling at the handle and hitting the door.

"Please let me in! Please unlock the door." I can hear my mother on the other side laughing at me. I'm pounding on the door, and I'm sure the whole neighborhood can see me in my underwear. They have all come out of their houses and are standing in the dark street watching me like I'm on the screen at a

Writing
from
Within:
The Next
Generation

274

drive-in movie. I can hear them laughing at me and my mother laughing at me and I can't stand the way I feel. I am so filled with panic.

I pound and pound on the door, but all I hear is the echo of laughing from both sides colliding on me. It's like this dream that I have over and over. I am walking on a sidewalk when all of a sudden I'm naked. I want to hide so that the other people on the sidewalk don't see me, so I duck around behind the row of trees that is between the street and the sidewalk, but the street is full of cars and all of the drivers can see me, so I go back around the trees, but then the sidewalk people can see me and pretty soon they have all stopped and all of the cars have stopped and they are all laughing and blowing the horns and saying, "Look at the naked fat kid. Does he even have a dick?" The sound gets louder and louder and I can't get away.

CRASH!

The kitchen door flies off the hinges and wood splinters as it hits the stove on the other side of the kitchen. I am in the house before the door hits the ground. My mother screams, and the scotch and water breaks on the floor. My stepfather has his belt undone by now and is pulling it through the loops of his pants.

I am running, into the den, into the cool...and my back stings, again and again, as I drop to the floor and roll myself into a ball and take it on my back. I'm safe now. I'm inside myself, and nobody can see me while he continues to hit me with the doubled-up belt.

"Thank you ladies and gentlemen, it's been a really big shoooow tonight. Next week on this stage, Elvis Presley"...and the crowd screams and my back stings, but it's cool in here and nobody can see me.

— • • • —

Dale Crum   *Dale grew up on a farm during the Great Depression, a hard time in Arkansas. Both his father and mother were solid, God-fearing people, although his teacher/father was a big fan of F.D.R. Tired of his small-town roots, Dale joined the navy just before WWII. After the navy, he followed his parents to Seattle where they had moved during the war. Dale got an education through the G.I. Bill and went to work for Boeing in Seattle. Later he met the woman of his dreams and they settled in Southern California.*

Smoke Rings   *by Dale Crum*

My cigarette smoke drifts towards Mama's open bathroom window. I smoke two packs of Camels a day and crave nicotine early. Sunshine splashes on the pink shower curtain. Multicolored gold fish fluoresce among its folds.

Reminds me of tame Calicos, orange Orandas, and Bubble Eyes in the Marshall Islands. They swam close to my navy face mask in the coral reefs only three years ago. Wish I were there, now. These rainy Seattle streets depress me.

I stand up and look in the mirror. Out-of-focus wallpaper surrounds blood-shot eyes and scruffy whiskers. Eeeyoo, my breath smells rotten. My tongue feels like sandpaper. I hate these cigarettes! Or, rather, I hate myself for liking them.

"Stunt your growth," my dad used to say.

But he said that about playing with myself, too.

Someone rattles the doorknob. Mama calls, "Dale, you in there?"

I yell, "Won't be long" and reach for the Listerine. Oh, didn't think she would get up before seven o'clock. Too cold to go outside and smoke. I pick up the towel stuffed in the crack at the bottom of the door, spray air freshener all around, and unlock the door.

Mama rushes in. She comes out with a sniff. "Thought you quit."

"Yeah, going to college."

"Not what I meant. You got a good job at Boeing."

"Just made up my mind. Talked to Elsie about it."

She frowns, "Oh, her? You like her?"

"She's a college sophomore in California. She'll show me around."

My B-50 flight control rigger's job only pays one dollar and ten cents an hour. That's union swing-shift wages, too. Boeing hired me a year ago for seventy-five cents an hour. Maybe Harry Truman here in the beginning of his first full term can kickstart the peacetime economy.

I sold my 1941 Buick sedan for eleven hundred dollars. Bought a cream puff '37 Chevy sedan for only four hundred. The G.I. Bill will pay for my college tuition. With a part-time job I can have fun in the sun and learn something, too.

But, when the sun shines, how can I leave Seattle? All shades of green mixed with azaleas, rhododendrons, lilies, peonies, roses, black-eyed Susans, tall fir trees, deep blue sky, pure oxygenated air, and seventy-degree temperature. Can I leave my parents again and their extended family of loving church people?

I cough and spit out nicotine phlegm. Hush up, my brain throbs. It rains all the time here. I sit still in Mama's rocking chair and rethink what I just thought. I can't leave my good friend, Vera, a divorcée who works in the blueprint room. Yeah, I can. She has two little kids that her rich mom takes care of in Portland.

I stopped there once when they were all together. Her mom called me gauche because I refused a pair of her late husband's pajamas and slept in my underwear. Mama doesn't know about Vera.

Nor Joanne, the Catholic girl I sometimes go out with. Joanne's parents don't like Protestants.

I really like Betty and Rosemary from our church. Mama does, too. But Betty's father, Walter, doesn't like me. We went out for breakfast once. I put ketchup on my sunny-side-up eggs. Most everyone does that in the navy. Walter snickered, called me a hick, and used the word gauche, too.

Writing
from
Within:
The Next
Generation

276

Can I leave my playground basketball team or fast-pitch softball team? I'm the pitcher, and we're in first place in the "A" league. Man, I gotta have another cigarette and run to my car.

Elsie double parks her mother's car beside me. I stub out my cigarette and jump in the seat beside her.

She beams, "Mom says I can ride down to L.A. with you."

Whoa! Her mother is a straight-laced woman from a straight-laced church. Takes two days to get to L.A. Unless you want to switch drivers and speed non-stop on that narrow, winding Highway 99.

Elsie stops in her driveway. Her mom, Mary, rushes to the car. "Oh, Dale, I'm so glad you decided to go. I trust you with Elsie. I know you will have an enjoyable trip."

Mary, a former Alaska school teacher, holds my interest more than Elsie. I could talk to her all day. I think most mothers want to marry off their daughters by the time they're twenty years old. Wait a minute. Something's going on here.

Elsie drives to a soda fountain. The jukebox plays, "Cigarettes and whiskey, and wild, wild women. They'll drive you crazy, they'll drive you insane."

Elsie smiles, "I like chocolate."

I pinch off her straw sleeve. "How about Willie?" I think he's still her hot-headed Cajun boyfriend.

"Willie? I don't know."

"Crazy about you, I recall."

"Finishing up summer school, I think."

"Uh-huh," I grunt. "Pretty possessive?"

She frowns, "Mom doesn't like him."

"Uh-oh," this time I say under my breath. Takes only a second for the picture to develop in my mind. Mary wants me to take her daughter alone to California. She knows Willie will find out. Poof! There goes Willie.

I leer like Groucho Marx, "Long drive with me."

Elsie stares at me for a long time, then takes a cigarette from my package. I hold my Zippo lighter up, and she moves to the flame like a moth to a backyard barbecue. She inhales a little bit, coughs, and waves the smoke away from her face.

"This your first?"

"Yes, first time I inhaled."

For a whole week Mama walks around with a quizzical look after I tell her, "It's to save money. Share expenses."

I keep moving, too. I don't sit still long enough for her to quote the Bible or other proprieties to me.

We get on the road and run out of things to talk about after about two hours. Elsie takes over and drives to Eugene, Oregon, with me still awake. When I take over, she empties the ashtray on the parking lot. The word "gauche" comes to mind again. I hope I don't need those butts if I run out of cigarettes. She falls asleep with a hip pressed into mine.

That old Marine at my teenage filling station hangout pops up. He cautions, "Millions more babies would be born every year if men didn't exercise what little restraint they have." He says that while he watches the backsides of pretty women wiggle by.

Elsie's body pushes harder into mine. She stirs me. I can't drive anymore and pull into a rustic motel with a "Vacancy" sign. A light mist falls.

I shake Elsie half-awake. "Got any money?"

She hands me a twenty-dollar bill. Narrow rows of flat bricks line each side of a muddy walkway. I teeter back and forth on the bricks and run straight into the lobby with dry feet.

"How much for a room?"

The bored clerk looks up from her *True Romances* magazine. She spits out of the side of her mouth, "Six dollars."

"Give me two adjoining rooms."

Her eyes flicker. She looks out the door before she hands me the keys. She makes me feel weird. Why spend the extra six dollars?

I carry the bags and balance on the bricks while Elsie splashes down the middle of the muddy walkway. After I plop down her bag, I move to the door.

She gives me the same quizzical look I saw on the clerk's face.

She mumbles, "Wait, where are we?"

"Grant's Pass, Oregon. Good night."

She raps on the thin wall between us. "When do we get up?"

"Early," I holler and run water in the sink.

We reach Los Angeles late the next day. I park in back of the women's dorm, shake out the kinks, and open the trunk. I turn with Elsie's bag and bump into a guy. He hugs Elsie and asks her, "Drive nonstop from Seattle?"

"Nope. Willie, this is Dale," she replies. "Stopped in southern Oregon."

He persists, "Side of the road?"

"Nope. Motel."

She swivels her body away. Willie's face turns color. He slobbers into his red bandana handkerchief. I steel myself for his next question. In the same room?

He makes choking noises. No words come out. They stand nose to nose. I set her bag down, back out of the lot, and light up a cigarette before he clobbers me.

I've seen riled up Cajuns in the navy. They hold both hands together in a giant fist and slam down on someone's head. Pole-axed, they call it.

Four days later I sit near Elsie in the cafeteria. She waves her left hand at me. A large rock sparkles on her ring finger.

She giggles, "Me and Willie."

I give her a big epiphany smile of admiration. "Congratulations."

Writing
from
Within:
The Next
Generation

278

She outsmarted both her mother and me. Made Willie jealous enough to pop the question. I feel relieved. For once I don't need another cigarette. Any more may drive me crazy, may drive me insane.

• • •

Gail Field   *Gail was a junior at Colorado College when she met her first husband, an instructor at the U.S. Air Force Academy in Colorado Springs, in September 1964. By June 1965 they married and headed for California, where her new husband (me, Bernard Selling) intended to get a degree in film and work in the industry. Gail finished her degree in Spanish, got a master's degree, and had two children during that time. She began her teaching career in the fall of 1968. Within a year, they divorced. Gail met and married her second husband not long after, had another child, divorced, and began a career in business, all by age thirty. She retired in 2008 after twenty years at WellPoint (Blue Cross) as its beloved and highly respected director of Human Resources.*

A Normal Life?   *by Gail Field*

A bluish shaft of light from the hospital ceiling illuminates the side of my husband's face—setting off his sparse beard and the almost undetectable quiver in his strong, square jaw. My husband stands over me holding my hand while I lie waiting on the gurney just outside the delivery room. "It's a boy," I say. "We'll name him Martin and call him Marty, just like you."

Marty grips my hand even tighter, his long fingers circling my hand. He swallows hard, blinking, not saying anything. For the first time ever, I see tears moisten his face. He swallows again. "Good job." His voice cracks and he looks away. I have never felt his hand so tight in mine.

The roses that Marty sent me grace the windowsill in my private room overlooking the entrance to the UCLA Hospital maternity wing. Outside on the narrow patch of green along the driveway entrance, a bed of asters swoon and sway, bending their heads in the slight August breeze, inviting me to take a long look. I, too, was born in the fall, and asters have always been my favorite flower. They bloom just when the weather is changing, just when the cool air comes to surprise us with its announcement of fall. The roses in my room are lovely, romantic, beautiful. But the asters signal a change. Something mysterious and yet inviting. I smile as I think of the change that is coming for our family. This moment, this day, this outcome is what my husband has wanted ever since we met, and I would guess for long before that.

It was my mother who convinced me that having a baby with Marty was the right thing to do. "He hopes it would be a boy," I began. "I am not sure I am ready, since Jeff and Willy are still in preschool."

My mother leaned forward, her soft eyes settling on the neat and clean kitchen counter, the flowers in the window, the pictures of family in silver frames on the cabinet tops. She must have been surprised at this orderliness compared with the way I kept my room as a girl, clothes piled high on the rocking chair, dolls scattered about the house. She smiled and lowered her voice.

"You know," she said, her tone soft yet strong, "a good wife does what she can to please her husband. And I know how much Jeffrey and Willy mean to you."

I didn't want to hear this. I preferred to make these decisions myself, without input from my mother. She didn't know the whole truth, and there was no way I was going to tell her. Instead, I nodded as if in agreement and said I understood. I felt like a teenager again, half listening to her, not objecting, then making my own decisions in secret silence.

If she knew Marty spent every Friday night out with his gay friends, doing God only knows what, then she would certainly have an opinion. Then I would have to grapple with that, too, as if I were a child trying to please, caught between the desires of Marty, my parent's wishes, and my own sense.

Outside my hospital window, the sun is setting now, and I fall into the bed, tired from the labor and from the months of waiting for this day. Now, at age twenty-six, I am a new mother for the third time.

I am wondering what my mother would say now, thinking of what I would tell her if I were willing. I'd tell her that I am not really sure whether my decision to give up the birth control pills and have this baby was out of wanting to please my husband or whether I thought I could change him, whether I could make him love us more. Whether I wanted to rescue him from a lifestyle I thought would lead to misery for him and for me. Whether I feel I know what's best for him and for me. Feeling that I could make it all right, like it says in the psychiatry books in Marty's office. I wish I could tell her everything and have her understand without judging.

I would tell her that so many times I have taken just one step, without resisting, and things have turned out all right. Like the time I didn't push Marty when he told me he wanted to go out every Friday night to be with his gay friends. Perhaps my reluctance to resist has brought my husband closer to me as I helped him see the value of family and of a traditional lifestyle. So different from what he thought he wanted be, and maybe, just maybe, what the deepest part of him wanted all along.

When it's time to leave the hospital, we wrap up tiny Baby Martin and set out to pick up the boys, Jeff and Willy, before heading home. I hold this baby tight, this baby with the big nose, brown hair, and soft, smooth skin scrunched in a ball. Smooth, scrunched in a ball. So tiny. So much hope.

I put the baby on the backseat so that I can greet each of the boys with a big hug before they see the baby. The boys, Jeff, five, and Willy, four, run out of their father, Bernard's, house and rush to the car. Willy gives me a hug then opens the back car door and jumps inside, not seeing the baby and barely missing landing right on top of him!

Writing
from
Within:
The Next
Generation

280

"Willy! Watch out! That's your new brother!"

Willy looks at the small bundle of blanket and baby. "Oh, oh!" he says and slides to the far side of the car. Now warned, Jeff gets in more carefully, and we take off for our home.

Once we settle into a routine, husband Marty is cheerful and helpful. "Let's go to the movies and take the baby," he suggests. So we bundle him up and take him to see *A Clockwork Orange*. "Won't they complain if we take a baby in?" I ask.

"Nope," says Marty with a sly smile. "We'll wrap him up like a present with a peephole in the blanket. They'll never know!" We laugh about our private joke, and I am happy to have my husband back on Friday nights with the family.

I see that he is more attentive, more engaged with me and the boys. We go to Magic Mountain, to Acapulco, to pony rides, and to the park. We pack the baby in the car and go on Sunday drives. We are family, and it feels good.

"We should move to a bigger house," says Marty. "One with room for Baby Martin and more room for Jeff and Willy, too."

We settle on a house in the upscale neighborhood of Brentwood with bedrooms for the boys, a room for a live-in maid, and even an office in front with two exits where the previous owner, also a psychiatrist, saw his patients.

The widow who is selling us the house must love asters, too. The front yard is abloom with them, in yellow, sunny orange, and golden brown, vibrant with new life. I breathe the crisp air blowing through the tall trees in the front yard. Fall is here. Winter will soon follow.

"Marty," I say, pulling in my arms against the fall breeze. "I'll be signing the boys up for their new schools. We'll find the post office and the grocery store and the good restaurants. So much to do to adjust to our new life. It's exciting and a little intimidating."

"Uh-huh," he says slowly as he bends down to pluck a flower. The petals of the golden brown aster are beginning to fade. Marty squeezes the flower and lets it drop to the ground. He turns to me slowly and puts his hand on mine. He looks at me with the same look he had on the day Baby Martin was born. It is a look I'll remember always. "Yes," he says. "A new life."

Mother would be happy for me, for us. "I'm happy, too," I say silently to her. "I know things change, and if they do, I'll be ready. Thanks for listening."

• • •

Eddie White   *Raised in Louisiana, Eddie came north to Cleveland, Ohio, with his family in the years after World War II. He studied music and tried boxing. At five feet four inches, he decided he was a bit undersized for a pugilistic career. Arriving in Los Angeles, he befriended many of the greats of jazz including Buddy Collette, Charlie Mingus, Eric Dolphy and Chico Hamilton. He retired after working for the post office some thirty years.*

Blind Lemon Jefferson Sings the Blues   *by Eddie White*

"But I thought for sure that Blind Lemon Jefferson was born in Shreveport, Brother Johnson."

"Naw, Suh! Naw, Suh! Blind Lemon was born in Wortham, Texas, in 1897. They say he was born with a guitar in his hand, and he weren't a-bawlin' for milk, he was bawlin' the blues, Brer Jackson. Blind Lemon was born singing the blues and pickin' that mean guitar."

"Yes, Lawd! Heh! Heh! Heh!" laughs Brother Johnson.

The word is being said all over Ruston that Blind Lemon is gonna stop off in Ruston on his way to Monroe, Louisiana. Everyone is looking forward to seeing and hearing Blind Lemon Jefferson sing the blues.

My Granny says that, "It ain't the kind of music I just like to hear, but it is so filled with something—I just have to hear that poor man sing."

Time passes. It seems like Blind Lemon will never come.

"Granny, is Blind Lemon Jefferson ever going to come to town?"

"I right 'spect he will, chile. I right 'spect he will, effen it be the good Lord's will."

We work and wait. We wait and wait. "Granny, do you think it's gonna rain, it's so cloudy looking?"

"Naw, Suh! I don't think so. Just kinda looks like that."

"Granny! Granny! Listen! Don't you hear somebody singing? It's a long way away, Granny, but it seems like I can hear somebody singing."

"Shhhhh! Shhh! Chile, I believe that must be Blind Lemon Jefferson. That must be Blind Lemon." Granny takes off her apron in a hurry, and puts on her bonnet.

"Come on, Sonny, come on," she tells me.

I hurry outside. It seems like a stampede, a wild horse stampede. The people are running, just running running to see and hear Blind Lemon Jefferson.

We children join the grownup chase. We can't keep up, but we are not far behind. I can hear Blind Lemon real good, but I cannot see him. "Hey, Lawdy Lawdy," he moans and strums his guitar. "Since you been gone—I BE SO LONE-SOME AND SO ALONEOWN! But one day WO-O-MANNE, you AIN'T go worry my life NO MO!"

Blind Lemon sings like he knows what the weather looks like on this cloudy, rainy-looking afternoon. Blind Lemon throws his head back and howls.

A big tall man looks down at me, picks me up and puts me on his shoulders. "I want you to see and hear something that I hope you never forget," he tells me.

Blind Lemon howls so sad; it's almost like a funeral.

"YOU TREATS ME MEAN-and aruh so low down. Sometimes Ah feels lak I ON DE EH groundHOUND, but someday WO-O-Manne-DAS RIGHT!" he shouts. "YOU AIN'T GO WORRY MY LIFE NO MO!"

It's one day in May 1927 I will never forget! Blind Lemon has on a dusty-looking brown suit. His shoes look new but they are dusty-looking too, as they should be. Paved roads are few, and the few paved roads are mostly for white people. A few white folks have come to hear and see Blind Lemon Jefferson, but they stay way in the back because white folks and colored folks are not to get too close together. That's against the Law. When the white people go to see Grambling College play football, they stand on the tops of their cars on the nearby highway. I look back, way back, and see some white people standing on the tops of their cars, seeing and hearing Blind Lemon Jefferson.

One day, white people will learn to sing and play the blues because they sure do listen to them. One day I will think—if one does not like the blues they must be dead. Granny goes to church but she likes Blind Lemon.

A young man stands near Blind Lemon. They say that he is some kin to Blind Lemon. The young man also leads Blind Lemon Jefferson around. A tin cup is at the end of Blind Lemon's guitar. It will be passed around to pick up whatever money the people can afford to give.

I hear one person say, "He sho goin' to make a heap er money when he go to Monroe, and I sho hope he do!"

Many people witness and say soft-like, "Sho do hope so! SHO DO!"

Another says, "Even if he ain't blind, he sho do deserve all the money he can make—because that man, Good Lawd, Good Lawd! Blind Lemon Jefferson sho nuff sing the blues."

Twilight is coming on. Blind Lemon has stopped singing. I guess he is going to go on to Monroe now. Everyone is kind of silent and quiet-like now. It is a feeling as though we have just come out of church. The Doxology and Benediction have been read, Amen! Amen! With each head, it seems, a little bowed, we begin our journey home with silent thoughts.

The sun has set. Nighttime comes in a hurry to a small country town. The nightingale and whippoorwill sing their blues in the night, while a few lightening bugs try to make us feel not so blue.

As we walk along, Granny and I hear two men talking loud. At first we think they might be angry at each other.

Then we hear them laugh.

"They don't mean no harm, they just joshing with each other," Granny tells me. We listen. Oh, it's the voices of Brother Johnson and Brother Jackson.

"Weren't that sho nuff something, Brer Jackson?"

"Sho was, Brother Johnson! Sho was!"

"It were like the singing of angels on wings of thunder and lightning, Thunder and Lightning!"

"Right! Right! You right as rain, Brother Johnson."

"It just seemed like the stars were gonna fall right down outta the sky," Brother Johnson continues, "the heavens resounded! Can I get a witness?"

"I'm right HEAH!" yells Brer Jackson.

"The moon, the sun, and the stars turned to silver and gold," Brother John-son throws back his head and hollers—"Heh! Heh! Heh!" and raves on in a sing-song voice—"and the silver and gold turned into diamonds, and the diamonds became a lake of fire! And the lake of fire became rubies and pearls—and the rubies and pearls are placed on the necked breast of a whole heap of colored virgins, fifty thousand ebony maidens whose warm black thighs have advised them that the time done come! Come enter in and let your soul find its moon mad bliss when Blind Lemon Jefferson sings the blues. Let no soul stand still. You gotta be moved out, inside-outside-inside because the TRUTH done come! The soul Truth done come!"

"And you sho' ain't wrong, Bro' Johnson!" shouts Brother Jackson. "You sho' ain't wrong!"

"Sonny, I hope you tried to turn your ears from all that wild talk of Brother Johnson and Brother Jackson," Granny says.

Granny goes on, "Everybody thought that Blind Lemon is mighty fine, but the way those brothers carry on it's a shame before the Lord, Uh! Uh! Uh! I won-der if Brother Johnson and them have been drinking some of Grandma Brad-shaw's moonshine? Uh! Uh! Uh! It's a shame before the Lord!"

* * *

Sam Glenn *Born in Texas, Sam moved to Washington, D.C., during World War II, where his father worked for the Army Corps of Engineers. Developing into a fine musician, Sam made a living playing around D.C. while still in high school. Later, he attended the Curtis School of Music, played in a unit of the U.S. Army band, and eventually moved to Los Angeles to pursue his career as a jazz musician. A unique improviser, Sam's solos "swing," yet they retain the complexity of a Bach fugue. In Los Angeles he fell in love with and married a woman with two children and later with his wife had a child, Tammy. Today, at seventy-three, he is a fixture in many fine big bands around the Los Angeles area.*

Epiphany   *by Sam Glenn*

Mr. Wigent nods his head. His bald head. I return the nod. Ready. I'm sitting next to the Baptismal. Clarinet in hand. He's next to the altar. Seated at the or-gan. To think not so many years ago when I was nine, this is where I was bap-tized, where I became a Methodist. But now I'm sixteen. He seems far away. I look up. Up toward the high vaulted ceiling and to the back of the church. The tall, narrow windows. Stained glass. Rainbows of light stream angle above and across a sea of people. There in the balcony, at the railing she stands. Mary Es-ther. Like an angel. In her blue robe. White collar. Her black hair held in place

Writing
from
Within:
The Next
Generation

284

with a silver headband, framing her face. Her flawless face. She's home from college for spring break.

Another nod from Mr. Wigent. From the wall of organ pipes, so capable of making thunder and making the floor vibrate beneath my feet, comes a simple melody. I count my measures of rests and now my turn to play the melody. The organ lays down a cushion of notes. Seconds or is it an eternity later, Mary Esther's voice, lyrical, joins us like a triangle. The organ, the clarinet, her voice. The words. "Panis Angelicus." Repeats—"Panis Angelicus."

I glance over at a woman in the front row pew. She dabs her eyes with a white lace handkerchief. Her husband bows his head as if in prayer. A hundred faces, no, hundreds of faces. A tapestry of lives gathered together. I look over at the minister. Soon he will give his sermon. He looks at me over the top of his glasses. Is that a glimmer of approval? That I'm playing okay. The organ, the clarinet, and the soprano. All three weave in and out. Sounds and words. To inspire, console, enrich. To give meaning to all of our lives. Yes. To be a musician. That's what I want to be.

— • • • —

Stephanie Bernardi   *A mother of two small children, Stephanie assists her husband in his business and writes to keep her mind active. Earlier drafts of this story appear on pages 89–93.*

My Mother's Death   *by Stephanie Bernardi*

My mother is dying. Cancer has eaten away at her. Today she weighs sixty-eight pounds.

As I sit and watch her, she stares off, fixed on the painting hanging in the corner. His picture hangs over her chest of drawers. It always has. His blue eyes catch me as they call out, "I still am."

The thick knife strokes of paint add depth to his three-year-old cheeks. He is rosy and animated and forever three.

My brother. The one I never knew. Thirty-five years ago he drowned. He is never spoken of. This has only added emphasis to his missing place in our large family.

When I was eleven, our family dog was hit by a car. As I sat on the beach sobbing in front of our house my mother came slowly down the steps. She told me she was worried about Dad. He was crying. I guess she thinks girls cry all the time because she didn't seem to even notice my tears.

"I have never seen him cry since Gary drowned thirteen years ago," she says.

Not to cry for thirteen years. I am afraid of the pain that caused this.

"Mom, how did you ever get over it?" I once boldly ask her.

"You don't ever get over the pain, you just learn to live with it," she replied. End of conversation.

And now today, as she lies dying in this rented metal hospital bed continually staring at the painting, I am aware that we are not alone. In the silence between us, I can feel his presence. It surrounds us. It always has.

"What do you see, Mom? Is someone there?" I ask her. There is no response, just that quiet. "Mom, is someone there?" I repeat.

"Yes," she says. "Mama is here."

I don't doubt this. I just want to hear more. She has not spoken for weeks. She drifts in and out. Occasionally she babbles. My father says it's from senility, from the cancer in her brain. I don't believe him. Something more is going on. In the hospital last week, when I sat with her, it seemed she was talking to someone, but when I asked her about it, I could get no response.

"That's wonderful, Mom. Is anyone else there?" I ask.

"Yes . . . Gary . . . and Helen." I am not surprised about Gary. But who's Helen? Helen . . . Helen? I think Grandma had a sister named Helen, I don't remember any special relationship though . . . at least she's never mentioned it. Maybe a childhood friend named Helen?

"What do they want, Mom?" I ask.

Of course, I know what they want. Here she lies in her suffering, shriveled up to nothing more than a faded memory of the mom she was. Her gestures are infantlike now. The fingers curled. And the hands. The part of her body that hasn't changed. I used to hate those hands. They were wrinkled beyond her age. My hands are the same. Now they are the only familiar part of her. I reach for them. Somehow when I touch them and close my eyes for a moment, it is all forgotten: the feeding tubes up her nose, the diapers, the look of childlike innocence on her face that is pathetic from her. My once elegant mother even picks her nose and scratches herself.

However the antiseptic smell does not hide when my eyes are closed nor does the sound of the plastic mattress cover the sound of her thick breath.

"How does Gary look, Mom?" I ask.

"He looks wonderful because of his beginning and the place he is in," she says.

His beginning. He didn't get very far did he? So untouched. I know the place must be heaven. Where else would a three-year-old be? I am curious.

"Mom, do you want to go with them?" I ask. I know what the answer is. I don't blame them. This is not a life. But I still need to hear it.

"Yes, but they do not want . . . to steal the family," she tells me. This shocks me. But I don't know why it should. I mean, I clearly understand this. My mom is the center of this family and with her gone who knows what will happen . . . maybe we'll all drown.

Already my father and I are not speaking. He hates me. I do not agree with him. And he does not like that. I try to understand him but I am angry that he does not treat her with respect. He lifts her roughly to put medicine on her bedsores. He talks in front of her as if she is not there. And worse, being a radiologist himself, he won't stop radiating this dying woman.

He says it's to keep her from pain, but the only pain I see is from the side effects. I just learned a new word today, "fistula." That is the hole that was just burned through her rectum into her vagina. Yes, I hate him too. Why won't he let this poor woman die? Forty-five years of marriage and he does not see what he is doing.

He is crazy with grief. Because I speak up, he has shut me out. He ignores me when I come to visit. I help take care of her in the day while he is working. I know she will not last much longer so I refuse to let him push me away. Last week I left him a birthday present hoping to make peace. It still sits in the entry unopened. He refuses to accept it. So there it sits for everyone to see his rejection of me. But I know she knows what's going on here and so do they.

"Mom, they're not stealing the family. Because of you, we're strong. We'll get through this. Your love will live on in all of us. We're all just scared right now but it will be OK," I lie.

"We must transcend this," she says.

Transcend? This is not my mother's type of word. I have never heard her use this expression.

"Mom, I want you to tell Gary that we don't blame him for wanting you now. We've had you all these years. Now it is his turn. Tell him how much we've missed him in our lives and how much he's loved by all of us. We just wish things had been different...he could have been here."

"Every family has a beginning and he was our beginning," she says.

I grab a pencil and paper and take notes. No one will believe this. I've got to put down exactly what she says so I don't forget it or reword it. Her phrasing is odd but the power in her words...it's like I've got this window through to the other side. Gary being the beginning? He was not the first child; he was the second. So his death was a new beginning? Is that why they had five more kids?

"Just give me twenty more minutes," she is begging.

Now what's going on? What is she talking about? To live? To keep this communication open? Don't die! We're not done yet...I'm not ready.

"Mom, what's going on? Are you OK?" I ask. There is no answer. She is talking within herself. "Mom...Mom, are you still with me?" I ask.

Slowly, I see action return to those eyes. She is coming back.

"Unfortunately I have to translate for us, and that's why, it is difficult to translate these things," she says.

To translate things? What is the form of communication? Just keep going. Say everything you need to say, Stephanie.

"Mom, I want you to tell Gary something else. I've always felt specially close to him because of being born on the same date that he had died. I also think the reason I was a girl and not your fifth boy was because of his help. He made that sad day a special day for you and it's always made me feel special," I tell her.

She is studying me. What does she see? So often I hide my sadness. I don't even wear makeup to visit her anymore; too often I leave with black eyes. I wonder, does she notice? I know she hates the perms. Always says it looks healthier without one . . . I think she sees my strength. That's what she sees.

"You are special, because you have chosen the source," she says.

The source? Mom has never said that word either . . . referring to God as the source is not from her Catholic thinking. And calling me special because of choosing the source. Amazing.

"We've learned a lot together haven't we, Mom? It hasn't always been easy, has it? But look how far we've come. How close we've gotten . . . I love you," I tell her.

"The chance to learn is the only point we have in life. And we are only given one chance to learn it," she says. What is she saying? Learning to love, is that what it's all about? Her words are confusing but the feelings are clear.

"Mom, you still haven't told me yet, do you want to go with them?" I ask.

"Yeah," she says as she looks at me. Am I imagining the relief I sense in her with those words? It's probably my own selfish relief that this won't keep going on week after week . . . "But something is holding me here," she says.

"Who? Me?" I ask.

"No."

"Is it Dad?" I say.

"No," she says. There is quiet. Then, "The whole bunch," she tells me.

She is right. It's all of us. The name on our boat for the past twenty years has been *The Wild Bunch*. She even signs her Christmas cards that way. She is looking tired. I don't blame her. We're a big group to worry about. She's got to let go and so do we.

"Mom, it's like I said. We're just scared, that's all. It doesn't mean we want you to stay on suffering like this. It's OK for you to go, Mom. The only thing you need to know is how much you are loved and that we will be OK. Alright? We will survive," I say.

I feel strong and I am proud. If I can say this so clearly and without tears, then I know it's true. And if Gary and her mom are waiting for her, then won't she be waiting for me, too? There is relief in this.

"Will you be there for me, Mom, when I die?" I ask. She giggles. Her curled fingers flex as she studies them. She reaches for the tiny stuffed dog that hangs from the metal pull-bar over her. He has the St. Augustine medal pinned to his neck, the saint that is supposed to help get us safely to the other side. She bats at it like a three-month-old. She cannot grasp it, but it fascinates her. Now I understand why. She knows its red-and-white checked bow around its neck, its barking happy expression that tells her not to be afraid.

"How can it be? That would make me one hundred and eighteen?" She smiles slyly. Her sense of humor never really leaves. I wish she would be serious.

"No, I mean like Gary is there for you, Mom. Will you help me cross to the other side?" I am crying. She smiles. I wait. "Yes, I will," she whispers. "Yes, I will... but now it is my turn," she says. I can hardly hear her.

Her arms try to reach me so I help wrap them around my neck. Her hands flop on me as she tries to stroke my hair. I climb in bed with her. We cuddle, my mom and I, something we've not done in years. Just my mom and me. For this moment, I am her baby again.

Out the window the day is crystal clear. The bay water is oily smooth. The large tree is no longer bare of leaves. Winter has ended here and, for the first time, I am aware of the early signs of spring. Those branches, that were so empty and cold to look out at, are turning green again.

Inside my head, while wrapped in my mom's still-warm body, I am rapidly calculating that my mother, my supposedly senile mom, has just figured out that I will be eighty-eight when I die. Does she see the future in this state, too? She tries to tell me something about my father's red Porsche and about the estate, but they are not clear. I am losing her now. I won't know until I die if she saw the future or not. But what I do know is someday she and I will be together again. Also, I now know, someday I will finally meet Gary. And then there will be no more sad goodbyes, just hellos.

———— • • • ————

Diane Hanson   *Diane was married young to a ministerial student with whom she had two children. Initially, she came to life-story writing classes to write about the experience of living through the death of one of her sons due to cancer. She later married a dentist.*

Double Trouble   *by Diane Hanson*

"OK, Gene, tell me what you know," I say over the dinner table at the Wagon Wheel restaurant in Ventura. He and my husband, Jack, have been selling cars together for over a year. It is early 1965.

Last night, I had called Valley Dodge to talk to Jack, but Gene answered the phone. "Oh, hi, Diane, Jack's not here. Did he tell you he was working late again?" he had said with a smirk in his voice. That alone added to my suspicions.

"Gene," I had said, "what are you implying?"

"I really can't go into it here and now, but I think we should talk," he responded.

I hesitated. I didn't want to spend time with Gene, but I did want to know whatever he knew about Jack's affair. "OK," I said. "Where and when? Remember I still don't drive. I don't have a driver's license and we have no car. Also, Newbury Park is 40 miles from the dealership in Van Nuys."

"Hmm, let me think a minute...." he said. "Why don't we go to dinner tomorrow. Jack has a dealer trade and will be out late—maybe all night," he adds with a sneer. "We need privacy to discuss this, so we shouldn't meet at your house with your kids around."

My curiosity was peaking. "Well, OK. Can you be here at 7:30 p.m.?"

"Sure, I'll see you then, I have to go now. We'll talk tomorrow night," he had said and then hung up.

"Well," he says now, playing with a spoon on the table, "I'm sure that you suspect that Jack is having an affair and want more details or you wouldn't be having dinner with me."

"Gene," I say, "I need specifics, something strong enough to confront him with, so that he can't lie his way out of it." I stare at Gene.

His eyes divert while he says, "I know that he is seeing some secretary, I think her name is Eileen, from one of the other Dodge dealerships. I'm not sure which one. It has been going on for several months. Other than that, I don't have any real details. He's been tight-lipped about it. I guess he thought since my family and I had visited you on a few occasions that I might say something. Therefore, he's been careful not to say too much around me. The other guys don't like him much, so he doesn't confide in them."

I sigh. This is not what I had hoped for. Now I feel like the whole evening was wasted. The information he has given me isn't enough to confront my husband of six years with. I want stronger grounds for a divorce than "mental cruelty."

"Look," says Gene, "I know that you're disappointed and must be angry but surely you know that he's playing around on you. I understand this isn't the first time either."

I nod, "You're right. It's not the first time. The first time was when he was still in Bible School and I was pregnant with our second child. It probably won't be the last time either. The divorce will be easier and faster with evidence."

"Are you really going to divorce him?" he asks.

"Yes," I answer, "but his unfaithfulness isn't the complete reason. He's just a lousy father and husband. He's constantly criticizing and demeaning me, and now he has started to do it to the boys. He ignores the kids. He never takes me out. He's never home to spend time with us. When he is around, he just yells and complains. There seems to be a big emptiness inside him, which he tries to fill by having affairs. He can't provide for us financially. Last month, his commission was $7.00. We have nothing but bills that we can't pay. He spends his money on his girlfriends, on silk suits and Italian shoes so he will look successful to his

Writing
from
Within:
The Next
Generation

290

clients. Meantime, his kids need clothes and new beds." I sigh. "I'm only 24, and I don't want any more of this."

There is a lot of anger in my voice. I look up at Gene, who is staring at me. He didn't know how I felt. But then, how could he? The only times we have been together was when he and his wife and three kids came to visit, or when he rode his motorcycle on his day off and stopped by our house. Jack always monopolizes the conversations. I never get to say much, much less what's on my mind.

"Look, Gene," I continue, "thanks for whatever you are trying to do, but I had better get home. I have to pay the baby sitter out of my grocery money, so I can't stay out with the meter running. Thanks for dinner. It's the first time I've been out in months."

"All right," he says as he reaches to pay the check.

Once in the car, Gene says, "Let's take a little drive. It's still early."

I just want to get home but I say, "OK, but not a long drive."

We head north. The ocean is on our left. The moon glistens on the water. It seems so peaceful, especially in comparison to my life. No matter what happens, the ocean continues its own pace unknowing or caring about a man or woman's troubles.

I feel the silence in the car, a growing uneasiness. I look over at Gene. He is just driving. His prominent Italian profile and dark hair are outlined in the light of the oncoming cars.

"I need to get some gas," he says.

I feel tense and nervous. What? After a few minutes drive, we see a gas station and he pulls in. There is a telephone booth there. I sit in the car and watch as Gene talks to the attendant and then goes to the men's room. I feel so uncomfortable and I don't know why. I glance again at the phone booth. I have the strongest urge to call Beverly and tell her to come get me, but I'm not even sure where we are. "This is foolishness. What do you think will happen?" I can't answer myself, but my hands feel clammy and I want to run, but I don't know where. Gene returns to the car and we leave the station.

We continue the drive in silence. I want to talk to break this dreadfulness, but I feel so uneasy that my throat is closing up. My heart is beating fast. Gene is also quiet. "What is happening here? Why do I feel this way?" I ask myself again, and still get no response. Then Gene drives off the road. I can feel the tightness in my spine and my stomach jerks. We are on a dirt road near the oil wells in Ojai.

"Gene, where are we going?" I ask anxiously, but he doesn't answer. He drives over the bumpy road, passing a worker's shack, and then stops and turns off the car. It is dark, and I can't see anything.

"Gene, what are you doing?" I'm really scared now. "Gene, I have to get home!" I feel panic. My armpits are prickling.

Gene turns to me and says, "I'm going to rape you now." His voice is controlled and calm. I am stunned into silence. He begins to move towards me. He grabs me and starts to tear at my clothes. I begin to struggle with him. I have worn a white dress with pink polka dots and a jacket to match. Also a girdle with stockings and high heels. It was my Easter dress last year. I do not want him to tear my dress. I clutch at it and stare at him with terror in my eyes.

"If you don't help me, I will hurt you," he says in a firm, angry voice. I go numb. I do not believe what is happening.

"Gene, why are you doing this?" I plead with him. He slaps me and pushes me down on the seat. Maybe I should kick him in the groin. There isn't much room in here to get at him or away from him. Could I overpower him? If I could, what would I do then? I don't drive. I don't know how to handle the car. If I got out of the car, where would I go? We are in the middle of a dark oil field! In these heels, I could never run fast enough to get away. The buildings I noticed on our way in appear to be empty, but if they have men in them would they help me, or would they rape me too? Gene is ripping off my stockings.

"Gene, please don't do this, please I beg of you." His mouth comes down on top of mine. I try to push him away. I want to bite him. What if I hurt him just enough to make him madder? What will he do then? The struggle is exhausting me. I lie still and try to catch my breath. I try to get my bearings, try to decide what to do. He is pulling on my girdle. "That should keep him busy for a while," I think.

"You had better help me or you'll be sorry." I hear the anger in his voice and feel his frantic hands tugging on my girdle. I become very calm, and my mind drifts. If I go along with him, it will be over in no time. I don't think he will beat me and leave me here. I decide to help him to take off my girdle. I feel a coolness come over me and a detachment from my body.

What is happening to me? It is like I am floating outside myself and I feel no pain or fear. This is nice. I like this floaty feeling. I do feel the pressure of Gene's body on mine, but it seems a far distance off, like my whole body is filled with Novocain. It sorta feels like when I gave birth to Jimmy and got a spinal. I was numb from the waist down. I could feel pressure but no pain. This is the same—kinda. This is really crazy, I think. Then I notice that Gene has stopped moving and is beginning to sit up.

"See, it's over," I tell myself. I sit up too. I stretch and begin to look for my clothes. Gene is leaning over the steering wheel. His head is resting on his hands. I get all my clothes back on and wait for him to say or do something. I must wait and see what his mood is so that I do not anger him.

He raises his head to look at me. "I feel so terrible. I don't know how I could have done that to you. You of all people," he says with a sob in his voice. His head is back on his arms.

Writing
from
Within:
The Next
Generation

292

I am shocked. What shall I do? What shall I say? "Oh, God, don't fail me now," I pray. "I know that you are there God. I know that you are always with me. I don't understand why this is happening to me. Please help me." I still feel unusually, unnaturally calm. "Gene, it's OK. Just take me home now. I must get home to my kids," I say calmly, like nothing happened.

"I feel so terrible." He begins to cry.

The panic is returning and I want to get out of here, but I need him to do that. "Gene, it will be all right. Please just take me home." I plead, while trying to keep the panic out of my voice. What will happen to my boys if something happens to me?

"Are you sure?" he asks. "I really care for you. Do you know that?" He stares deeply at me. "Do you think that I could see you again?" he asks.

I go rigid. Certainly, he is crazy. What will I do? How should I handle this? I wonder. "Gene," I say, "we both have had a rough night. Let's get home. Get a good night's sleep. Why don't you call me tomorrow and we'll talk?"

He brightens and visibly relaxes. I feel better. I have to get out of here before I lose it. I feel the panic rising from my stomach into my throat. My insides are trembling. I feel so close to screaming, but I can't. This man is on the edge, he could do something really crazy. I must remain very calm, very cool, very in control. "Do you think that it will be OK? I really want to see you again," he asks.

"Sure, Gene," I say in what I hope sounds like a cheerful voice.

"Good. I feel a little better now. You do forgive me, don't you?" he asks in a little boy voice.

"Sure, Gene, it'll be OK. You'll see...let's just get home now. After all, you have a long drive even after you drop me off." I force a smile at him and he starts the car. My heart leaps for joy along with the engine. I hold my breath, anxious for us to get closer to civilization. I can't wait until we are on the freeway so we can go faster. I want to get home to my kids, and I want to get there fast. We are off the dirt road and back on the paved street. I feel so much better. Gene glances over at me. I look at him. My face is stiff and a smile won't come. He drives on and reaches the blessed freeway. As he gets on it, my blood soars. "Faster, faster," I think. He is watching me again and I feel the tension returning in him.

"I can't face what I have done," he says as his voice grabs. "It would be better if we both die." I wait, I say nothing. What can I say? God, where are you? Tell me what to say! I have a crazy person here. My body is beginning to tremble. One minute I am calm, the next I begin to shake and shiver but I must hide it from Gene.

"I think that I will kill us," Gene says. Panic rushes through me and then the calmness again. I look at him. Still no words come. His face is stuck in a grim expression. "Do you know what I am going to do?" he says with the voice of a sleepwalker. My mind is blank. It is like I have no control and don't care. I am numb and cold. He looks at me, I look back at him. All is quiet, then he says, "I am going to get the car up to 120 miles, then I am going to drive it into the free-way overpass."

Everything seems to go gray but I am still silent. No words come to mind. He begins to accelerate. I watch the speedometer. It begins to climb. We are at 85 mph. I feel excited. The faster he goes, the faster I will get home. I just have to time this right. I watch the road quietly. Then I look at the dial again—we are going 100 mph. We are going very fast. I love it. I will be home soon. I want him to go faster. I must be getting crazy too.

"We are at 110," he announces. Then he says, "There is a freeway overpass coming up. That is the one I will drive into." I glance at the dial, we are almost to 120 mph. I look at the ramp coming closer. "There it is," he says again as he looks at me. "I am going to drive right into it. Do you want me to do that?"

I watch it coming closer and closer, my eyes are glued to it. I want to get home fast, so I want to go fast as long as possible. Slowly I move my eyes to look at him. "Shall I do that?" he asks.

"Gene, I don't think you really want to do that," I hear myself say. The voice is so calm, it doesn't seem to be mine. Our eyes meet and I do not blink. I slowly look back towards the road. We have passed the overhead ramp and Gene's foot is getting lighter on the pedal. I feel a long breath leave my body. The crisis is over...or almost.

We drive in silence. The silence makes me uneasy. I feel the panic beginning again. "How can I keep myself together until I get home?" I wonder. I must say something to him to keep his mind occupied, but what? Panic is in my mind and belly. Then I hear..."Gene, it would probably be best if you dropped me at the corner of my street. I don't want the sitter to see you," I say in a conspiratorial tone.

He smiles and says, "OK." He seems less tense. He drives to the Wendy Drive off-ramp for my house. I feel so relieved. I could hop out and run from him, but I don't think I will have to. He is going to behave. I can hold on—it won't be much longer. He stops at my corner. I grasp the door handle. I must not rush out, or he will get upset again. I must remain calm. I am almost home.

I must say something—what? "Gene, thanks for dinner. You will call me to-morrow, won't you?" I say with a smile like I had ended a date. That should keep him calm.

He smiles and says, "Sure, I'll call you. Early." I get out of the car, turn and wave. I even stand there awhile as he drives off.

On unsteady legs I turn and stiffly walk to my house. I am shaking so badly I can't get the key in the lock. As I fumble the sitter opens the door. She is just a kid from across the street. I cannot lose control yet. I do not want to upset her. I pay her quickly, thank her and watch her cross the street.

Writing
from
Within:
The Next
Generation

294

My house is quiet. I check on the kids. They are asleep and Jack may not be back from his "dealer trade" tonight, if in fact he really had one. I sink onto the couch, but my body won't relax I am so tight. All my muscles hurt. I ache everywhere and realize the tension I have been under. My neck and jaw are rigid. I push myself off the couch and, using the hall wall for support, slowly head for the bedroom. I struggle to remove my clothes. "I am going to burn that dress," I tell myself. I am so cold and shaking so much that I can hardly walk to the bathroom. I want to take a hot shower. I want to cleanse myself and warm myself. I run the water real hot and step inside. It feels good but I cannot stop the shakes. After a few minutes of standing under the hot water, I know I will not get warm, so I get out. I reach for the towel and rub myself. The shaking is worse so I head into the bedroom to sit down on the bed. My head drops into my lap and I begin to rock myself back and forth.

"What's wrong with you?" I hear a voice say.

I look up and Jack is standing in the doorway. I try to say "nothing," but my teeth are chattering and no words will come.

He walks over to me. "What has happened?" he asks.

A million things flash through my mind. Should I tell him? He is my husband; he should comfort me. If I tell him, he will know I was trying to get information about his affair. He has the affairs and I go for one dinner and I get raped!! I don't understand this. He touches my shoulder and I recoil. The tears are stinging my throat. My stomach is so tight it is jerking. I feel like I am going to throw up.

"Jack . . . Jack," I sputter but nothing else comes out. He sits next to me on the bed. I am rocking faster. "Jack . . . Gene raped me." I spit out the words.

"What?!!!? What were you doing with him??" he demands, leaping up from the bed.

I am numb and feel pain all at the same time. This is not the comfort I was hoping for, but knowing Jack how could I expect anything else. My teeth are chattering and I cannot explain any further. My head feels like it will snap off at my neck. I do not want to talk anymore. I know that, somehow, Jack will blame me for the whole episode.

He begins removing his clothes, getting ready for bed. I must get out of this wet towel, I think. Then try my best to stand up.

"I can't believe you were with Gene," says Jack. "You probably deserve what you got."

That shocks me, even coming from insensitive Jack. I go numb again, then the calmness returns. I really hate this man. I cannot live with him any longer. I can't get far enough away from him. A divorce would be an improvement.

I slide under the blankets and am so tense my body doesn't seem to touch the bed. Jack climbs in next to me. He lies still and is silent.

I do not think that I can be this close to him. He is so hateful. He is even worse than Gene. I hate him. I start to turn to leave the bed. His arm wraps over me.

"Jack, please. Just leave me alone." I try to twist away from him, but he holds me down. I cannot stand being held down. Not now. Not after what happened.

"Did he hurt you?" he asks. I hear no concern in his voice.

"I don't know. I'm too cold and tense to feel anything," I say in a dull, even tone of voice. "Please let me go. I can't sleep. I'm going to make myself some tea." But his arm stays tight around me. I freeze. I know what he wants. I panic. "No. No, not again, not tonight. No!! No!!" I say as we struggle. He pushes himself on me.

I do not struggle anymore. I have been through this once tonight and this is no different. It is all the same. Jack or Gene. Gene raped me tonight but Jack has been raping me for years. I hate him. This is the last time.

"I want you to know that it doesn't matter to me," Jack whispers in my ear.

'Well, it matters to me,' I think but say nothing. He never cares or waits to see how I feel about anything. I have nothing to say to him. He pushes himself into me. It hurts. I flinch.

"I thought you said he didn't hurt you," says Jack. I say nothing. It doesn't hurt now, not anymore. I feel nothing. I don't want to feel anything. I wait. Again it doesn't take long.

'Thank you God. Why did this happen to me?' I ask God, but get no answer. I release my grip on the bottom sheet. My hands and fingers ache from holding the sheet so tight. My whole body feels like it is two inches above the bed.

Jack turns over and falls into sleep. I lie in the dark and try to think. Jack knows I will not tolerate him any longer. I know that he will try to make life difficult for me even when we divorce, but I don't care. I just have to get away from him. I will not allow him to dump any more emotional or mental abuse on me or my kids. I will divorce him and make a new life. It will be just me and the kids, but that is how it always has been anyway. I take a deep breath and begin to relax. I cannot tolerate my life with Jack anymore. If anything good came out of this evening it is the final realization that I must divorce. I cannot sleep. I must plan my escape. I must get away.

P.S. I did get away. A few days later, Jack moved out. Soon afterward I filed for divorce claiming "mental cruelty." Jack began to tell everyone that I had committed adultery. He contested the divorce, saying he wanted the kids and the house. It took two years to get into court. On our court day Jack brought Gene to testify against me. This was totally unexpected and unnerving. So I settled out of court by waiving the two years of child support that Jack had not paid and I got the kids and the house.

Three years later, while driving home from work (I now could drive and had a car), I noticed a man walking along the sidewalk. I knew him from somewhere

Writing
from
Within:
The Next
Generation

296

but couldn't place him. He looked at me. Before I realized it, my car was trying to run him down. In a flash, I knew it was Gene. When he saw me, he dashed into a store to hide. I never saw him again.

———— • • • ————

Tamara J. Randall   *Tamara's mother, a 1960s hippie, took her very young children to Mexico, where they lived hand-to-mouth for fifteen years. Tamara's stories are filled with the mystery of native religion and folkways of Mexico. She is the mother of two children.*

The Beach   *by Tamara J. Randall*

In the darkness of our *palapa* (beach hut), I awaken to the sound of the ocean waves crashing upon the beach. The air is rustling the palm leaves of our beach hut. I roll out of my hammock, landing upon my hands and knees in the soft sand floor.

Our hammocks are strung out from the center pole of the palapa like a Ferris wheel. I hear the brothers beginning to stir now. I have two brothers and three sisters. I am ten years old, the oldest in my family, and living in Mexico with my mother.

"Eric," I say, "help me open up one of the walls." Eric and I each grab one of the long forked poles that are used to hold the walls of the palapa open during the day. We spear the bottom corner of one wall with a pole and push it out and plant the poles in the sand. The ocean breeze rushes in and I can taste the salt in the ocean spray. The sea is blue green, edged in a clean white foam. The waves thunder down on the moon-shaped beach and I feel the earth shake with each wave.

We are living on a sandbar called Barra de Navidad (Bar of Christmas) that separates the ocean from a peaceful, island-filled lagoon. In the background, I hear a jungle buzzing just inland. I see the rock cliff and hillside rising up on the other side of the tip of the sandbar, making a canal which the lagoon fills and empties with the tides. At midday when the tide pulls the water out of the lagoon and back into the sea, we kids go down and jump in and are rushed by the current out to the sea waves crashing at the mouth of the canal. Then we pull ourselves out and run back to the lagoon side for another bubbly ride. I love living in a palapa, sleeping in a hammock, opening the four walls to the warm ocean breeze, and I am crazy about the outdoor shower, an old oil drum that sits on stilts.

As I stand under it and pull the rope, fresh water falls on me. I love it so much that I take several showers a day. I love never being cold, day or night. I run free, swimming and playing all day long. This is a peaceful, beautiful paradise and I feel so natural here, without a worry in the world.

Our palapa is the last one at the very end of the sandbar. We have been here for a few months now. I don't know when we are going to go back home to Ajijic, and right now I don't care. Yesterday, the old grey-bearded gringo with the hole-filled straw hat, who lives in a palapa just down from ours, shared his breakfast of oatmeal with all seven of us. This morning, though, is different from yesterday. I can't remember whether or not I had any lunch or dinner yesterday and I am starting to wonder if we are going to get any breakfast this morning. Mama is not doing anything. She just sits on the sandy floor of our palapa with my baby sister in her lap. Her light-colored curly hair falls in ringlets down around her beautiful, sad, worried face. Her blue eyes seem calm. The other kids are looking around at one another, but no one wants to be the first to ask.

"Mama, I'm hungry," my little six-year-old brother Chris says at last.

Mama looks around and takes her time answering. "I don't have any food to feed you today," she answers sadly. After a moment, as the words of "no food today" set in, she says, "All I have is this LSD. I guess we could eat it. It is all I've got to give you." We all agree we should eat the LSD. This is not the first time I have eaten LSD. "Turning on" has been a monthly event in my life for a couple of years now. Mama pulls a little container out of her purse, takes out a little white capsule and opens it up. She sprinkles a bit of the white powder from the capsule onto her baby finger and as I lick it off of her finger, I get a little shiver. It tastes salty and tickles my nose as I swallow it.

Each of us gets our share, including Mama and my month-old baby sister Sara. My sister Jill and I are playing at the edge of the lagoon. My brothers Eric and Chris and my sister Rachael are playing together nearby as Mama watches. In and out of the lagoon we move, the sun blazing down on us. As the hunger pains melt away and I forget about food, Jill and I play, laughing and giggling, rolling in and out of the lagoon. We make castles and mud pies and splash in the water. Endlessly, we play and play and play.

In the afternoon the water in the lagoon empties with the tides and so we all go down to the tip of the sandbar for our ritual of jumping in on the lagoon side and letting ourselves be rushed out by the sea waves. As fast as I can, I jump into the water, bobbing up and down in the bubbly water. I giggle and giggle and laugh loud, screaming, my body tickled all over by the rushing water as I am pulled and tossed out to meet the crashing sea waves at the great mouth of the sea.

The world is shiny, glistening, a million colors and patterns...the water and sky blend. I cannot tell where one thing begins and the other ends. I melt into a sea of everything.

After what seems like forever, I begin to feel tired of all this running, jumping, splashing, swimming and laughing.

Writing
from
Within:
The Next
Generation

298

I stop and sit. One by one, my brothers and sisters pull themselves out of the current too. We all sit at the tip of the sandbar with Mama and watch the world move, everything is breathing life.

At last we walk back over to our palapa. I stand under the old oil drum, pull the rope and am refreshed by the warm, clear, sweet water pouring down on my head. It washes through my long golden brown hair, over my body. I feel as clear and sweet as the water pouring over me; I have become sweet water.

It is late afternoon now, and everything has become very quiet and still. We are sitting next to the lagoon again. My family is all silence and peace. I lay in the sand next to Mama, looking up at her as she holds sweet little Sara, her golden hair in ringlets softly surrounding her beautiful, strong, tender face. "Mama," I say, the first words I have spoken to her all day, "you are so beautiful."

I see in my mother such beauty and tenderness, and I hold in my heart such love for her! She looks at me, and shiny blue eyes smile the most wonderful smile I have ever seen! She doesn't say a word. She doesn't have to. I am filled with her and love. I look around at my world. I see Eric standing knee deep in the calm smooth lagoon. He is watching the water.

Suddenly he yells out, "Look!" He is pointing at the water in front of him. All of us kids scurry to the water's edge to see what he is pointing at. "A big old fish!!" he exclaims. "Right there!"

I can see it now. It is just swimming in circles right in front of Eric. Eric suddenly leaps out to the water and runs as fast as he can down the beach to the palapa of a fisherman.

He comes running back, with the fisherman running right behind him, and his big round net hanging over his dark arm. *"¡Andale! ¡Corrale! ¡Mira aca! ¡Un pescado grandismo!"* ("Hurry! Run! Look here! A really big fish!")

The fisherman steps up to the water and the fish is still swimming around and around right where Eric first spotted him.

The fisherman looks very serious in his big straw hat tilted to the side and his pants rolled up past his thighs. I can see his blue blood running right through his dark brown skin, his muscles and veins tense as he prepares to cast his net.

Everyone is hushed as he steps into the still lagoon. His dark eyes follow to where Eric is pointing. *"¡Alli!"* ("There!") Eric whispers to him.

The fisherman waits for the right moment, then throws the net up and over the spot where the fish is. The circular net flies, twirling through the air, splashing down upon the flat smooth surface of the water, the fisherman pulls the net slowly and soon lands the biggest fish I have ever seen! We all gather around to get a better look. This fish is huge. It is flipping and flapping back and forth. My brother Chris gets a little too close and gets a good fishtail whack across the ankles, knocking him right off his feet.

"Wow!" he yells as he speedily gets back onto his feet.

This causes everyone to laugh great big belly laughs. The fisherman smiles and laughs too and is missing a lot of teeth.

The fish lies on the wet glistening sand, his silver scales shining out rainbow colors. He is dying slowly and isn't moving much, only his gills move as though he struggles for a breath.

"¿Que tip de pescado es?" ("What kind of fish is this?") Mama asks the fisherman.

"¡Es una Lis Grande!" ("It is a Big Lisa!") he answers.

"¿Y como se cocina un pescado tan grande?" ("How do you cook such a big fish?") asks Mama.

"En hojas de platano, en la arena," ("In banana leaves, in the sand") he replies.

Soon after that we all begin to help dig a big hole in the sand. The old gringo who has come to help is making a big bonfire in the sandpit with wood that the fisherman has brought. We kids run down to the back edge of the lagoon where there is a grove of banana trees in somebody's back yard and we are allowed to pick some leaves from them. We take them back and wrap the fish well in the leaves and secure them with some string. Soon the coals are ready and the old gringo spreads the coals out flat and he and Mama lay the fish over the coals and cover it with sand. The sun is setting and we all begin to wait for dinner. Hours pass, the night has come, and the old gringo has come to help us pull the fish from the sandpit. Mama and the old gringo carry the fish up into our palapa and we begin to wake the other children as they have fallen asleep waiting for the fish to cook. "Hey, everybody, the fish is done!" says Mama. "Come and eat. Come on." Slowly, rubbing the sleep from his eyes each child eats fish. The old gringo is very impressed by the flavor of the fish. It is the best fish I have ever tasted, especially since I don't even like fish! I feast on fish and then happy as can be fall into my hammock and sleep, thinking, "What a great ending to a great day."

P.S. I can never forget that great day on the sandbar, the innocence and the fish that came to us when we needed it. It was pure magic! From that day on, whenever I found myself in a difficulty of some kind, I always carried within me a strength and an undying faith in a power beyond what I could comprehend, and it was always there for me when I needed it.

— • • • —

Joanne Baumgart   Born in Poland, Joanne survived years of internment in the Warsaw ghetto and, later, a number of the concentration camps set up by the Nazis. Fluent in German, she stayed alive, and helped many others stay alive, by outthinking the Nazis. She is one of the true heroes of the Polish Resistance. She came to the United States shortly after the war ended.

Christmas 1944   *by Joanne Baumgart*

I have no idea what the Germans have in mind when, in mid-November, 1944, in Auschwitz, we, a group of women, are detained after the morning roll call. They encircle our group with SS men, machine guns, as usual, and tell us not to move but remain in rows of fives. After counting and counting, they command us to march, this time out of the gate, out of Auschwitz. We are forced to walk for seven days, and seven nights, through small towns, over mountains and mountains, with short rests in between to receive our small portions of bread, to an undisclosed location.

Many, many of the women perish on this walk.

We bury the bodies in shallow graves with our bare hands. Sisters and friends of the deceased try to hang on to them, but we, the rest of the prisoners, do not let them. We beg them; we tell them, "Do not cry, do not admit that they are yours."

By now we know the mentality and the methods of the SS too well. They do not like to separate families they say, and it would not surprise us if they kill their next of kin.

Exhausted and more dead than alive, we arrive at a brand new camp, a different concentration camp than anything else I have seen in all the years. There are no watchtowers, no electric wires, just miles and miles of sandy grounds, and a primitive little house.

There, we receive, for the first time after this exhausting journey, our first hot soup, which is almost inedible.

Soon male prisoners arrive. They seem to be in a hurry; they do not look at us. They carry bundles and bundles of straw into these houses while we are still standing outside in the cold. As silently as they arrive, so they leave. Suddenly cars with bright lights and SS men appear. I do not see the usual entourage, no machine guns, no dogs.

"You are here to work, you will be led by your overseers to and from your workplaces. You may not see fences or wires, but do not try to escape. You won't go far, we assure you," says one SS officer. "You may go to your rooms now."

About sixty women are assigned to a room bare except for straw on both sides of these long cement floors. Two small windows are at the end of the room. The smell of the damp cement walls and floors is awful—grey, cold, musty.

We do not have a chance to orient ourselves when SS women with their rifles and their whips enter the room.

"Attention, attention. These are your quarters, the straw by the walls has to be kept in perfect order. The walkway in the middle has to be at all times kept clean. Never let us see a strand of straw. The consequences are deadly. You soon will learn to keep the room neat and clean and the straw in perfect line."

By this time each of us has to step forward and each of us is handed a broom, and a paper bag neatly folded with a white cord to pull together on top. "There are no blankets." *As if we had blankets before,* I think without saying a word. "But here are your bags."

The SS woman opens one bag and demonstrates the bag to us, and how to use it. "You sit down and pull it over your body to your neck, keeping your arms inside so you will use less room. If one of you does not wake up in the morning, it is the duty of the person next to the deceased to pull the bag over the head of the deceased and tie it together. The body has to be brought out to the roll call and put down on the ground."

Until that moment I do not realize that these are bags for the dead, in which dead soldiers are taken away from where they have been killed or wherever their bodies have to be shipped to. I take my bag into my hands and move on. I swear to myself, *I will not put this bag on.* I can't stand to be covered up and tied to or into something. No, I won't put this on. I don't know what I am going to do, but I am definitely not crawling into that bag.

Otherwise, I find this camp livable. There are washrooms, toilets where one can flush. I hope I have not forgotten how to do that. I encourage myself. It does not bother me that we have cold water only and it is cold. Icy cold in this place. I wonder if we are still in Poland? We will soon find out, I console myself.

It is evening. I don't know what time it is. We lie next to one another on damp straw. I see the women slipping into their bags. I unfold mine but I do not slip into it. I put it on top of me. "What are you doing Joanne?" someone next to me asks. I turn my back. "Why do you do that?"

"Never mind," I say. The dim lights go out. To keep warm we move closer to each other. I hear some bags tearing. I remember an old Jewish saying, "When one puts a garment on, one is supposed to wear it in good health." I want to laugh.

I am proud to be Jewish, I say to myself, we are a smart people. Even these bags prove it. Better to wear them in good health than to be put into them dead....

I have to survive, I vow to myself. I have to prove them wrong. I must, yes, I must survive.

The next day after roll call we are marched off to work.

We walk and walk. We do not see a living soul. The air is so clean, so crisp. Where are we? I can't believe that something so beautiful still exists. Beautiful forest everywhere I look, nothing but pine trees, everywhere pine trees. What a sight. I am elated. This must be paradise. We can walk here and breathe. The Jews must have a prayer for this too. I am sure but I can't think of one. Instead, I think of a German song: "One asks who has created you, you beautiful forest it can only be a grant from above, only you, master of the universe can be praised, only you." I am afraid to move my lips but my heart sings.

Writing
from
Within:
The Next
Generation

302

We walk and walk for a long time. I don't mind. I cherish every moment until we hear the harsh sounds.

"Halt. Stop." Again we are counted and are told, one by one, to walk into an underground building. Who would think that under this beautiful forest, in this far-away place I never saw before, the Germans would build an ammunitions factory.

No one would ever suspect or think that under these pine trees is a factory in which hundreds of men and women are worked and starved to death.

The noise is unbearable. Machines, motors, men, women, grotesque-looking people with pale, sweaty faces, moving quietly back and forth.

"Oh my God. What is awaiting us here?" Above us, life. In this factory...

By now, we are a few weeks in Gebhardsdorf, Sudetenland. This long, twice-daily walk through this forest to and from work keeps us alive.

Sometimes when we walk so very early in the morning, the moon is pale but still visible and the majestic trees, their branches heavy with snow, and the silence all around us, make me truly believe in peace on earth.

I pretend that this is my world—no war, no one disturbs me. I can look as far as I want and see nothing but trees. And for such moments during these awful times I am grateful.

One afternoon, on our way back from work, it is a windy day. I see broken branches all around us. I can't resist. I bend down and pick up a branch. What a feeling! The long, soft green needles, I caress with my fingers. I suddenly realize that since fall or winter, 1939, I have never touched a flower, a leaf, or a branch.

I will bring it to our room, my mind wanders, I will let the girls touch the needles.

Too soon, I rejoice. One of the SS women who walks us (and I am sure never noticed what I did) stops me. "What do you have there?" as if she does not see it.

"A Christmas tree branch," I answer, knowing quite well that this is not really a Christmas tree branch. She pulls it out of my hand and throws it on the ground. I bend down and pick it up. She lifts her arm with the whip and she strikes out, but the whip does not touch me. I am too low or the whip is too high.

How badly do I want this branch? I know what she is going to do to me and yet I have it in my hand again. I look at her and I say, "I want this because it is Christmastime, Frau Auperchim."

"What did you say? You want this for Christmas?"

"Because it *is* Christmas," I correct her. She is surprised. "You are a...?" She does not end her sentence. By now I have the situation well in my hand. My mother is German. I, too, do not finish the sentence. I could tell her my stepmother was a German Jewish woman but I don't say that. Let's see how this works, I think to myself.

"Do the other women know that?" she asks, as she now walks beside me.

"I don't think I am the only one."

We do not talk about it. She is silent and holds the branch. I can sense that she is too long by my side. She moves away from me. The girls look at me. I do feel what they are thinking, *You stupid fool. This is not the end of it and for what? For a green branch.*

I, too, feel that this is not the end of it, but I am not afraid. My mind is already far ahead of me.... Among our inmates is a young, very pretty woman. She has the most beautiful voice I ever heard. That voice has a special quality. Sometimes when we are able to persuade her to sing, we always say, "Aguisha, sing please, we promise not to die during the night." We also know that many of us pray. On rare occasions, she does sing. I really believe that everyone wants to live.

As soon as we are in our room, I look for Aguisha. We sit down on the straw and I tell her what happened on the way home. "Joanne, you are crazy, crazy, crazy. Why do you get yourself in trouble?"

"I don't know," I say. "I just felt like it. Aguisha, will you let me teach you to sing the German words to *Silent Night, Holy Night*?"

"You know them?" she asks. I know I have her approval.

"Yes, of course, I know them." I don't know if I wished for anything more at that moment than a pen and piece of paper. This is impossible, but I can teach her and she will sing—that is important.

For a Polish-speaking person it is not easy to say these beautiful, old German words but after a few times she can say them. When she comes to *"shdat in himmlisher Ruh'"* ("sing in heavenly peace") tears are running down her face and mine as well.

The next day, on the way to work, I see the same SS woman. Does she remember me? I wonder. This time I purposely do not walk with my sister in the same row just in case. I say to myself, *let her be out of it.*

On the way back, the German SS woman is looking for me. "You may take as many branches as you can carry. Let the girls help you. After roll call, I will come to your room," she says.

Oh, my God. What did I start? I only hope that I did not go too far, but I do pick up some long branches and some of the girls do too.

After roll call that very night, the SS woman arrives at our door with a tin container to put the branches in, and orders me to tell the girls to help me to form a Christmas tree. She promises to bring white tissue paper to make some curtains for the windows. One of our women, a real artist, calls me aside and tells me, "Joanne, ask her to bring a pair of scissors and some tape, I can make something very beautiful."

"I don't believe so," I answer. "You know we are not allowed to have anything, they consider scissors weapons."

"Ask her anyway. Go ahead, ask her, Joanne."

Writing
from
Within:
The Next
Generation

304

"Alright, I will," I promise, "I will." The SS woman does not object. The very same evening she brings the scissors and tape. Martha starts knitting and creates a masterpiece. The girls are so enthusiastic to help, I think for a moment many of us forget what hell we are in.

While all this is going on, Aguisha tries to rehearse the lovely chorus. What thoughts come to my mind: Do I endanger everyone here with my crazy adventures? How do I bring a Christmas atmosphere into this Jewish concentration camp, to my people who are suffering? Will they doubt my true intentions? I, whom they trust so much; I, who has developed a reputation—"talk to Joanne" or "ask Joanne, maybe Joanne knows." What am I trying to do here, trying to convince this pale, uneducated rough SS woman, that I am half German? I am sorry that I picked up that branch, sorry that I have made this German woman bring all that stuff in the room. May God help me. At this moment, I am very unhappy.

The next day we work only half a day. It is December 24, 1944. It is Christmas Eve. As I walk through the woods I think of my homeland, of the gifts we handed out to our employees, of the hustle and bustle that goes with this holiday. How I loved it when at midnight all the church bells started to ring. When I was still a child, I tried not to fall asleep, so our maid could take me to the midnight mass at the church. I enjoyed watching people so fashionable-looking. I enjoyed listening to our maid, when every year she told me the same story—not to talk to the animals because after midnight they can talk with human voices. You should really not talk to them.

Could this world (of hate) really disappear? Will it ever end? Will I live to see that? Has religion brought such hate? I can't, I won't accept this.

We get this horrible smelling and even more horrible tasting soup. After the usual roll call, we are, so to say, on our own. The SS woman comes one more time to the room. She brings some foil paper and hands it to me. "Trim the tree," she tells me.

I walk over to Malka, the artist, and show her the silver foil.

Will I ever stop being a fool? My worries are already forgotten. "Malka, I say, do you think we have enough foil paper to make a star?"

"A star?" she looks at me. "A star?"

"Don't you know, the star of Bethlehem."

"Joanne, are you alright? You want me to make a star? A star of Bethlehem?"

"Yes, Malka," I say, "Make a star of David, our star, our Jewish star, the star of David. Please Malka, do that for me," I beg her.

She embraces me half crying, half laughing, "You are something, you are really something, Yes, I will make a Star of David."

It is evening. Girls from other rooms come in and admire our room. It really looks different. The tinfoil with the rest of the white tissue paper, Malka draped it softly around the can and the star.... Everyone says, "Our star, our Star of David, who did that?" We are laughing.

"It's our secret, do you like it?" Malka says.

At nine o'clock, no one can be in the halls anymore. Each of us has to be in her assigned room. It happens quite often that SS men or women come to check, with flashlights in their hands, that no one moves, that everyone is where they belong.

"Aguisha, please sing us to sleep," the girls beg her. She sings a lovely Jewish lullaby and I can't see, but I know that many tears are shed. We listen. We hear heavy steps in the hallway.

Aguisha changes her tune, she sings "Stille Nacht, heilige Nacht." One must hear angels' voices to listen to her.

The door opens. Our SS woman steps into our room and turns the lights on. She does not say a word. She stays next to the door. She looks for me. I get up and walk closer. She calls me out. "Come with me," she says. I must admit, I am scared, but, of course, I follow her. "That is beautiful," she says. "Just beautiful." I would like to say something myself but at the moment I do not know what to say.

"Is the girl who sang, also a *mischling*?" (A *mischling* is the offspring of parents of different religions.)

"I don't know, Frau Auperchim."

She walks again into our room and admires the beautiful cutouts on the windows. She likes what we did with the branches and sees the star. "It looks odd," she says. "It is empty in the middle."

"Yes, of course," I say. "That is the Star of Bethlehem, that is as the shepherd who saw the star."

"I never saw it that way," she says.

"Well, Frau Auperchim, that's all the foil we had."

"I see, I see."

"I am sorry that is all the foil I had."

"Don't be," she answers.

"We are satisfied and we thank you."

She does not ask who the girl is who sang so beautifully. Is she afraid to meet another German?

She calls me out again. "I am so sorry for you," she says. "You know what is going to happen to all of you, once the work is finished here?

"No, I don't. What is going to happen to us?" I ask.

With a very calm voice she says, "Oh, I can't tell you, but it is not good."

"You mean they are going to kill us?"

"Yes, they will, you see." I think she wants to excuse the Germans for what they are doing.

"Impossible," I say to her. "Frau Auperchim, they can never kill all the Jews. Impossible. They will always live, they will."

Writing
from
Within:
The Next
Generation

306

"Why do you say that?" she asks, with not such a certain voice any more.

"Because Jesus is a Jew, Frau Auperchim."

"Jesus, a Jew? How can you say that?"

"Because I know." It amuses me how calm I am. "Jesus is a Jew. The history was written three hundred years after he died and not by him."

"Really?" she asks.

"Really," I answer.

"Oh, my God, I never knew it," she says. "But you had a nice Christmas, didn't you?" she asks.

"Yes, very nice," I answer. "And I thank you for it."

"I have to go now," she says.

"Thank you Frau Auperchim, have a Merry Christmas." She leaves me standing before the door and walks off into the night.

I return to the room. "What did she say?" the girls ask.

"Not much. I think she believes I am not Jewish and I wished her a Merry Christmas."

"What???"

"See," I say to the girls, "when I lie, they believe me; when I say the truth, no one does." I really wished her a Merry Christmas. I repeat, "Good night, girls."

This was December 1944. Gebhardsdorf, Sudetenland.

The bells did not chime and the animals did not talk, but it was a memorable Christmas.

P.S. The movie *Schindler's List* has made its impact on me. Almost every newspaper I pick up has something to say about it. The film tells more in three and a half hours than the world has realized in fifty years about the destruction of the Jews during the Holocaust. "We are dealing with the unthinkable, the unimaginable, the incomprehensible, we do not have a vocabulary to communicate the scale of the hate and horror unleashed by the Holocaust," says Ben Kingsley, as he describes the events he has tried to portray in the movie. Not for me, is it unthinkable. To me it was just yesterday, when I, as I always do around Christmas, let my thoughts take me back to Christmas 1944.

— • • —

CJ Schepers *CJ Schepers is a professional ghostwriter and book editor living in Los Angeles. A former news journalist and ad copywriter, she has been writing since age twelve. After surviving a childhood that nearly crushed her, CJ found creative writing to be profoundly freeing and healing. This chapter is from her novel-in-progress* Blackcat-Whitecat: The Interdimensional Tails, *about two immortal cat beings that exist on a plane of existence far beyond what most humans know. They are on a mission to retrieve a human soul, stolen and frozen in time by a demon angel. As the story builds, the interdimensional cats move in and out of Earth's timeline, and are pulled deeper and deeper into the complex, intertwining lives of humans.*

Blackcat–Whitecat   *by C J Schepers*

Chapter 2

Bent on one knee, she is perched atop a small ice-frosted ridge, in another dimension hidden far from the world she'd once known. A cloak falls across her like liquid silver, and solid wisps of golden hair frame her narrow face. Godforsaken mountain peaks, cragged and sharpened with more age than any creature can imagine, stretch out in infinite agony beneath a starless canopy of thick gray sky.

A Scepter of Wonder as tall as the Sword of All Time balances itself between her cold childlike hands. But the most unusual part are the wings—solid as stone and three times the length of her body. Jutting out from her marblesque shoulders, their innermost curves arc toward her like the crescent Moon of Earth. Her irises, as vivid as sapphires, are locked behind pale, colorless eyelids. If only she could open them. But she is frozen in time. Or, at least, her Astral Soul is, in a place where not even the wind knows how to howl..."

Arcelia's fair fur shivered as she privately recounted the great Purisima's telling of the abduction and merciless captivity of the human female named Ruby. It was something she and Magico had secretly shared ever since the great ones, Purisima and Sirius, had enlightened them as to their purpose back on Earth. It had been the crime of eternity, one that was quickening with every second, reaching out in infinite tendrils of darkness and destruction. Even for evolved catkins as themselves, it seemed a preposterous, doomed mission. Arcelia imagined what it would be like to lose her own Astral Soul, to be permanently severed like that. Her heart began to quake as though she were fending off some mortally vicious attack.

Sunrise was coming. Even though her eyes were closed, Arcelia could sense it shifting between the edges of the dark and the light. Her lithe form sat upright in the Lotus position, and the breathing was purposeful, measured. It was a vain attempt to push away the story of Ruby, and the thoughts of what had led to the seizing of the human's soul. As far as anyone knew it was something that had *never* happened in all the levels of all the worlds and infinite time. But such thoughts only clamored about in Arcelia's consciousness, and the more she pushed them away, the more they demanded to be heard.

"Our concern, of course, is the rip in the spectrum of our interconnected cosmos and the shared Divine Will of all living kind," Sirius had told them with the gravest of voice. Arcelia reflected on the memory of the great blackcat's saffron eyes pulsating fiercely in the twilight of their astral garden amid the Gingkos. She sucked in the deepest breath and held it for a long, long moment. Nonetheless, the words of the great ones continued haunting her. "We can no more be neutral in this matter." Purisima's chest had risen and fell like crashing waves, the gold that encircled her throat with the eye of The Whole One heaving with it. "It is already beginning to affect the galaxy's chaotic order."

At this point, Arcelia realized that she might as well allow the story in her mind to retell itself as it had since they first learned of it, dozens of times. Perhaps there was a clue, a sign, a solution that they had all failed to see.

"I want to be an angel," Ruby, the human, had thinly whispered into the air one grey winter night. And, someone had heard her. It had been the first misstep across the ripples of all the universes. It had the potential to unravel into the ultimate tragedy for life kind, *all* of it. It had nothing to do with Ruby declaring that she wished for such a thing. It had everything to do with the one who had heard it. It had been *him*, Lahash, one of many fallen angels, true enough. "But this one," Arcelia recalled the words of Purisima, as she finished telling she and Magico what they needed to know. "This one, Lahash, he has a particular panache for stealing one's prayers and silent hopes, not to mention stirring awake the darkest spots in the darkest of hearts...." Arcelia couldn't help but notice that Purisima's front claws had instantly protracted at that moment, gleaming in the inky night air like freshly polished daggers. Even the great one seemed oblivious she had done so.

"...He is the one who has dared interfere with *all* our Divine Wills." Arcelia finished this last thought out loud to herself, for Magico was already away on a hunt with the first Earth cat that had crossed their paths since arriving to Earth only moments ago.

Yes, Lahash had once been a great angel; in fact, Guardian Master over thousands of other angel beings. Unfortunately, the centuries of power and authority had made him only ravenous for more. No one had seen his face in more than three thousand years, not since The One Goodness of all the galaxies had him expelled for his unforgivable crime: assembling an army of angels to steal the prayers of a human. The details of those prayers never did reach The One Goodness. They were lost forever, in turn, throwing the course of all life significantly off-kilter from that of Divine Will's.

It could have been worse, far worse for *everyone*. Despite the fact that no living creature or spirit had spoke firsthand of what this demon angel looked like, word of his presence managed to replicate itself. Generations upon generations of catkins had passed down the specifics, millennium after millennium: Lahash and his smooth, elegant words. Lahash and his dark, handsome hair that draped across the milk-white shoulders of his naked torso; the cloven feet that dangled beneath his long, black skirt. Lahash and those wings—such magnificent wings of layered feathers that soared above his chiseled head like a proud, ferocious bird. Then there was the symbol of Inca seared into his massive chest and the two slender glistening swords that he carried across his back.

"Beware," Sirius had warned them. "His weapons are not of the physical world." The tail of the great blackcat bristled forth like a thousand quills and his red-blue-gold wings began to billow wildly. "But make no mistake," Sirius's voice boomed louder, as the flapping of his wings grew fiercer, and hundreds upon thousands of Gingko leaves fell from their mother tree's delicate limbs, "they can slice through any steel, flesh, or bone as easily as a swift seizer's talons through cream." And, just as quickly as it had begun, those massive wings of his stilled themselves.

It was the last hard wind, Arcelia thought, *the eerie stillness just before a terrible storm.* The four age-versed catkins stood silently staring at the mounds of leaves that had buried their feet. Arcelia's snowy coat shivered, and she closed her eyes trying to remember everything she knew....

On that particular Earth night in that particular sliver of time and space, La-hash had stumbled upon Ruby's request for barely a moment before speaking to her in her dreams. His words, Lahash's words, had found their way in and stuck to her like barnacles on a ship, "When you hear 6...8...9, my dearest Ruby, you shall have it."

The moment that Ruby realized someone had heard and meant to grant her this wish, no more than a strong thought, she immediately spoke up to cancel the request. "Wait! I don't think I really want that, I just realized. I would like it not to happen for a very, very long time, not until I'm old and wrinkled and gray, and Eddy is gone and my children are in love and well cared for, please, but thank you. I prefer to wait a long, long—yes, a very long time."

Ruby woke from that dream to a family of sparrows chirping in the orange bougainvilleas that crawled their way up the wall of the neighbor's garage. The squirrel was clacking its mouth off as it scurried across the hot brown roof. She fumbled for her glasses on the nightstand, the memory of Lahash's face melting as fast as ice in warm-blooded hands.

It was Saturday, and Ruby and Eddy had decided to spend it lazily in the strangest of places: a giant shopping mall, filled with the buzz of ordinary humans doing ordinary things to pass the time of their ordinary lives. Ruby was taking her sweet time trying on gloves at a small vintage boutique. Even for a patient man like Eddy it was taking longer than he cared for. He told Ruby that he'd wait outside for her but by the time she'd finished, he was gone. She kept checking her phone. No one seemed to notice her mounting panic as she nervously pushed her way through the crowd. An old, familiar sense of abandonment slithered its way ever so quickly, enveloping her like a hungry python. She closed her eyes and tried to say a prayer, but it seemed so trite and pointless. Instead she began weaving more frantically through the mob of shoppers, on

Writing
from
Within:
The Next
Generation

310

the hunt for Eddy. The glimpse of something red caught her heart: There he was, his dingy red baseball cap bopping in and out of the sea of life. She released all of her breath, which had been stuck in her throat like a child's toy in a narrow drainpipe, and sprinted off. She was a quarterback near the end zone with only ten seconds left on the clock when she finally reached him, leaping so hard into his arms, that she nearly knocked them both to the ground.

Eddy's eyes glistened like chocolate jewels and she purred into his good ear, the right one. "Let's go home," Eddy said, his mouth breaking into mischief. He squeezed her hand off and on, as they made their way outside. Out of nowhere a gust caught the brim of Ruby's pink hat, the one Eddy had bought her on the boardwalk their very first summer together. His arm thrust out to catch it like a viper striking, and they both laughed in surprise. "Whew, that was a close one!" she laughed.

Across the street a tall Italian looking man with dark curly hair was dragging the arm of a little girl, who couldn't be more than four years old. "Look at that," Ruby said, turning to Eddy. A circular saw started spinning in her gut. The traffic light had changed and shoppers were crossing the street, but the little girl wasn't moving. Without warning, her father swung his right foot wrapped in a brown leather boot, and kicked her from behind. "Whadda I say?!" The girl tipped violently forward, and as a toy weighted at the bottom, she bounced right back.

Ruby's hand dropped Eddy's. Her vision narrowed as she charged toward the man who was half a mountain taller than most. He was yanking his daughter in the opposite direction now, away from the crowd, and a sick chill pop-fired across the membranes of Ruby's mind. She didn't even see the silver car coming at forty miles per hour. Normally, she was as cautious as a girl scout when it came to crossing city streets. Her body flew up and did a shocking vertical somersault, landing with a sickening crunch on the hood as the driver hammered the brakes. Somewhere in the million conversations happening at once; through the *bong-bong clump, bong-bong clump* of the drummer down the street; the pigeons cooing; and the homeless man dressed in all black rags and shaking his cup of coins, Ruby heard Eddy scream. Next thing she knew he was clutching her in his arms, and the siren one hears without much regard drew closer.

Eddy was trembling. "Don't let me die," Ruby begged him. In the loud, frenetic chorus of the living, she heard something else in the distant...6...8...9. Suddenly, to her horror, Eddy's mouth began to shrink. "Eddy..." Her voice seemed so strange to her, raspy and faint and faraway. "Don't worry, baby. I–I– can fix this." Eddy's mouth was nothing but a pinhole now, and his face fading fast, except for those warm-brown eyes.

Ruby felt herself being yanked from her body by an invisible hand. It was the opposite of gravity. Instead of falling to Earth she was rising. There was a force of something outside, yet inside her, too. It was the strangest feeling in the world.

Sounds of heavy wet sheets flapping in the wind forced her to turn her head apprehensively over her shoulder. And there, she saw it: wings jutting out of her back. Wings!

Suddenly Ruby felt strong as a god, and realized she was floating. Below her, Ruby saw Eddy holding onto her broken body. Her body's eyes were open but without light. Ambulance workers and firemen were trying to pry him away from her. Ruby continued soaring higher and higher and higher, taking in the surreal scene of her own life and death. Was this a dream? She remembered the nightmare from this morning, and a primal scream rang out of her mouth. But it was too late. From somewhere behind the fast-approaching clouds she heard a deep voice singing, and it wasn't Ol' Blue Eyes.

"I've gotttt youuuu...under my skinnn..."

Writing
from
Within:
The Next
Generation

312

Creating a Supportive, Noncritical, yet Insightful Writing Group

At this point, I want to step back from our work on technique to talk about the process of giving and getting criticism. A key aspect of succeeding as a writer is knowing when and where to get guidance, support, and assistance. Most writers need feedback from members of a writers' group, an editor, or some other trusted source. I want to suggest ways of getting positive support and feedback and tell you how to get the most out of it in order to continue to grow in your work.

Everyone has encountered criticism from different people during their lives. You probably remember how stung you felt when teachers, parents, and even friends criticized you when you were doing the best you could. Such criticism felt particularly harsh when you were doing something artistic—writing, painting, drawing, or playing a musical instrument. Often, you simply stopped doing these artistic things. Gradually, you internalized this criticism and developed your own inner critic.

Now that you are going to do some writing, you need to retrain this inner critic. Otherwise, you may not go on writing after the first bit of harsh criticism you receive when you share your work with others—and you do need feedback.

Retraining your inner critic is no small or easy task. It can be accomplished, however, by patience, discipline, and a positive outlook. The same process can also be used to retrain the critic within members of your support structure. First, consider the kind of feedback you as a writer would like to experience. Then I will outline a process by which the wild, undisciplined, even destructive critic within you can be converted to a purposeful, disciplined, insightful one.

What Is Supportive Feedback?

A group, or even one like-minded person, can help you get the kind of feedback you need. This person or group to whom you are going to turn for support needs to develop a disciplined response to your writing to protect you and make you feel safe while guiding you in the direction of better work.

That discipline involves adhering strictly to the following agreement, which each participant will make with other participants: Feedback to each writer after they share a story will be Nonjudgmental, Noninvasive, Corrective, and Affirming (NJNICA, for short). Each person giving feedback agrees to avoid any statement that sounds judgmental or invasive, no matter how innocently they intend it. During the early sessions of any group, one person may be appointed to be on the lookout for such judgmental and invasive statements.

A. Typical judgmental statements are:

You should have…. You could have…. You ought to have….

If I were you, I would….

That (story, thought, paragraph, etc.) was too (sentimental, clever, abrupt, silly, slow, confusing, boring, etc.).

B. Typical invasive questions and statements are:

Why did (or didn't) you…?

Why were you…?

You sound like you were trying….

You often…or always….

Any one of these statements can discourage a writer. Instead, ask members of your group to try

A. Nonjudgmental corrective statements, such as:

I would like to (see, feel, know, be able to follow, etc.)….

I had trouble seeing the picture.

I had difficulty following the action.

I needed to feel the character's feelings.

I found my attention wandering.

I needed to hear the characters talk to each other more.

I had difficulty finding (or following) the spine.

I didn't know what the central question of the story was.

The key question was answered before I had a chance to get involved or get excited about it.

Writing
from
Within:
The Next
Generation

314

B. Nonjudgmental affirming statements, such as:

I saw the picture clearly.

I was right there with you the whole time.

I knew what each character (or the narrator) was feeling from one moment to the next.

The dialogue drew me in and helped me know each character.

The balance of narrative, dialogue, and inner thoughts and feelings held my interest.

These are important considerations. A potential writer can listen all day to nonjudgmental, noninvasive, corrective, and affirming (NJNICA) comments. This writer can listen for only a few moments to invasive or judgmental statements. After receiving invasive or judgmental statements, writers will begin to defend themself, their creativity will turn off, and they will stop writing.

You may find that your support system is only one person, or perhaps you and a friend decide to write your life stories and share them. One person is enough if the feedback is nonjudgmental, noninvasive, corrective, and affirming.

The great advantage of working in a group or with a friend is that the writer can stop being the critic and simply create. Each person can then be a responsible critic for the other writers when they read their stories. So keep looking for one or two people with whom you can share this special journey of self-exploration.

However, if the person you select to review your work simply says, "I like it," or "I don't like it" and shows no inclination to go beyond this level of criticism, get a new partner. Likewise, if they make judgmental or invasive comments, find someone who is willing to provide NJNICA feedback. If you find yourself alone and unable to develop a writer–reviewer relationship with anyone, then try to develop these NJNICA qualities in yourself.

If you are a teacher and you wish to encourage your students to write their life stories, it is important to develop habits of NJNICA feedback in them.

The exercises below will help you develop NJNICA feedback and may be tried alone or in a group.

1. Review "Willem," starting on page 34.

2. Give yourself and your friend or group at least one session per story. Appoint one person to roleplay the "writer" of the story. If you are that writer, you may defend what has been written any time you feel the feedback is hostile, judgmental, invasive, or superficial. When the critique of "your" work is over, tell the others what it felt like. Also, point out who was providing NJNICA feedback and who was not.

3. If you are giving feedback, describe your responses to the story aloud. If you are doing this alone, talk into a tape recorder, speak aloud, or, as a last resort, write it down.

   Focus your attention on how you responded to the story rather than on how the story is written (that is, "I needed more detail," "I found my attention wandering," and so forth, rather than "It's too long, too confusing," and so forth).

   If the person roleplaying the writer begins to defend himself, it is a clue that you or others in the group are being judgmental, invasive, or superficial. Find a NJNICA comment that will make the point.

   Remember, by giving NJNICA feedback that focuses on your reactions to the story, you leave the writer room to make choices about what to change and what not to change.

   Have each person in the group defend or absorb feedback for five minutes. Continue until each person in the group has had a chance to roleplay the writer. The comments may be repetitive, but the purpose of the task is to experience (1) being a writer under the gun and (2) changing your mode of giving feedback from judgmental or superficial to NJNICA.

4. Address the following issues:
   • Is the point of view a child's or an adult's?
   • Is the story written in the present or as a recollection?
   • Is the level of language a child's or an adult's?
   • Is the situation believable?
   • Are the writer's feelings clearly expressed?

5. When the initial critique of each story is complete, read the final version of the story aloud, again appointing a writer to defend or explain the work. Remember, there are no right answers to the issues. You are attending to the task of creating feedback and promoting lively discussions.

6. After the third session, you will be ready for feedback on your own stories. If you have not written your earliest memories yet, read the first two main sections of this book and then follow the steps below if you have one or more persons giving feedback.

   A. Tell your earliest memory aloud into a tape recorder or to your friend or group. Get a few NJNICA comments and then retell the story in the present tense: "I am five years old and I am…" rather than "I was…."

   B. Write your story just as you have told it aloud. If the group is large or time is running short, do the writing at home, but try to do the writing immediately.

Writing
from
Within:
The Next
Generation

316

C. Repeat NJNICA feedback for each story.

D. Each writer in the group should repeat the storytelling/writing process until they are comfortable writing and receiving feedback. At this point, the writing can be done at home.

Remember that each new person added to the group or class needs to be taken through this storytelling/writing process. New group members need to be encouraged to listen for NJNICA feedback and given a little time to develop NJNICA feedback. With practice and time, the whole group's feedback—and unity—will be all the better for it.

*Appendix:
Creating a
Supportive,
Noncritical,
yet Insightful
Writing Group*

317

Selected Readings

Writing Models

Aiken, Conrad. "Silent Snow, Secret Snow." In *Collected Short Stories.* New York: Schocken Books, 1982.
This story allows us to glimpse a young boy's fascinating and very private world from his point of view.

Bierce, Ambrose. *The Stories and Fables of Ambrose Bierce.* Owings Mills, MD: Stemmer House Publishers, 1977.
The stories "Occurrence at Owl Creek Bridge," "The Boarded Window," and "One of the Missing" have superbly shocking, unpredictable, mind-teasing endings.

Campbell, Joseph. *Hero with a Thousand Faces.* Princeton, NJ: Princeton University Press, 1973. *The Masks of God* (4 volumes). New York: Penguin, 1970, 1976.
The path of the hero in everyone is traced through quests and temptations, weaving its way through virtually all of the world's mythologies and religions.

Doctorow, E.L. *World's Fair.* New York: Fawcett Crest, 1986.
Doctorow's novel, which displays a number of techniques of life-story writing, chronicles the events and experiences of his fictional hero's life.

Dostoevsky, Fyodor. *Crime and Punishment.* New York: Bantam Books, 1984.
The author interweaves first-person narrative, dialogue, and inner monologue in this classic story of risk-taking, crime, and conscience.

Dreiser, Theodore. *The Best Short Stories of Theodore Dreiser.* Chicago: Ivan R. Dee, Inc., 1989.
The narrator's voice in a Dreiser story is often clumsy and intrusive, a legacy of the nineteenth century, yet the stories are well worked out and often gripping and ironic.

Hemingway, Ernest. *Collected Short Stories.* New York: Charles Scribners Sons, 1938.

Hemingway's narrator remains as discreet and inconspicuous as Dreiser's is heavy-handed. The author makes his points dramatically through dialogue and occasional inner monologue.

Ibsen, Henrik. *Complete Major Prose.* New York: New American Library, 1978.
The plot structure and problems Ibsen sets for his characters and the qualities he gives them make his plays forever interesting.

Lang, Fritz. *M.* (Classic Film Scripts, a series). London: Lorrimer Publishing, 1973.
In M, we experience the forcefulness of pursuers, including the protagonist's own conscience, from the point of view of the criminal pursued.

Miller, Arthur. *Death of a Salesman.* New York: Penguin, 1977.
The struggle of a character to achieve a goal and the way he pursues it when he cannot have what he really wants gives Miller's play dignity and meaning.

O'Connor, Flannery. *The Complete Stories.* New York: Farrar, Straus and Giroux, 1971.
O'Connor offers some of the most bizarre and interesting characters in modern short stories.

Orwell, George. *Collected Essays* (4 volumes). San Diego, CA: Harcourt Brace Jovanovich, 1968.
"Shooting an Elephant" is classic autobiographical writing: crisp narrative storytelling, a clear view of the objective world facing the writer, physical action, and reflection on the meaning of the actions one takes.

Pirandello, Luigi. *Plays.* Middlesex, England: Penguin Books, 1962.
Pirandello's plays bring us into a series of delightfully separate worlds in which each character is convinced his view of the real world is correct and each character manages to convince us he is right.

Writing Process

Capacchione, Lucia. *The Creative Journal.* Athens, OH: Ohio University Press, 1979.
Clurman, Harold. *On Directing.* New York: Macmillan, 1983.
Goldberg, Natalie. *Writing Down the Bones.* Boston: Shambhala Publications, 1986.
Rico, Gabriele. *Writing the Natural Way.* Los Angeles, CA: J. P. Tarcher, 1983.
Stanislavski, Constantin. *An Actor Prepares.* New York: Routledge Theater Arts, 1989.
Ueland, Brenda. *If You Want to Write.* Saint Paul, MN: Graywolf Press, 1987.

Autobiographical Writing

St. Augustine. *The Confessions of St. Augustine.* New York: Mentor Books, 1963.

Dillard, Annie. *An American Childhood.* New York: Harper and Row, 1987.

Scott-Maxwell, Florida. *The Measure of My Days.* New York: Penguin Books, 1979.

Simon, Kate. *Bronx Primitive.* New York: Harper and Row, 1983.

Simon, Kate. *A Wider World: Portraits in an Adolescence.* New York: Harper and Row, 1986.

Wiesel, Elie. *Night.* New York: Bantam Books, 1982.

Wilde, Oscar. "Confessions." In *Complete Writings of Oscar Wilde* (10 volumes). New York: Nottingham Society, 1907.

Guides to Autobiographical Writing

Hateley, B.J. *Telling Your Story, Exploring Your Faith.* St. Louis, MO: CBP Press, 1985.

Kanin, Ruth. *Write the Story of Your Life.* New York: Hawthorne Dutton, 1981.

Keen, Sam, and Anne Valley Fox. *Telling Your Story: A Guide to Who You Are and Who You Can Be.* New York: Signet Books, 1973.

Moffat, Mary Jane. *The Times of Our Lives.* Santa Barbara, CA: John Daniel and Co., 1989.

Collections

Walker, Scott, ed. *The Graywolf Annual Three: Essays, Memoirs, and Reflections.* Saint Paul, MN: Graywolf Press, 1986.

Zinsser, William, ed. *Inventing the Truth: The Art and Craft of Memoir.* Boston: Houghton Mifflin, 1987.

Writing
from
Within:
The Next
Generation

320

Other Books by Bernard Selling

Character Consciousness: From Self-Awareness to Creativity. This book moves the experience of personal writing from the technical arena of "how to write well" into "how can we see ourselves in our writing" in a way that not only produces self-awareness but opens the door to greater creativity.

The Art of Seeing: Appreciating Motion Pictures as an Art Form and as a Business. Hollywood has created a mass audience that appreciates film in a certain way- appealing to emotions. But contemporary audiences wonder whether there might be other, more interesting ways to appreciate films. This book outlines that other way of experiencing films—by *seeing* into what's on screen in the same way that painters of the past nurtured their viewers' ability to "see" what was around them.

The Duke's Musician: A Spy at a Renaissance Court. The first in a series of docu- novels that take place during the Italian Renaissance. Told through the eyes of an ambitious, young English musician and featuring the beautiful Cecilia Gallerani (whose portrait was painted by Leonardo da Vinci), the novel follows the rise to power of the visionary Ludovico Sforza, who schemes to displace his hated brother, Galeazzo Sforza, duke of Milan, and his brother's powerful allies.

Predators: The Enemies of Milan. The second in the series of novels about the rise of Ludovico Sforza, visionary duke of Milan, and those who would cause him to fail: the pope in Rome; his sinister, rapacious nephews; and the doge in Venice.

The da Vinci Intrusion. Leonardo da Vinci's arrival in Milan causes intense dis- comfort for William Castle who must rethink his importance to the court of Milan, even as he continues his efforts to bring peace to Milan in the wake of a military victory over the Venetians.

The Hidden Treasures of Renaissance Milan: The Castles of Ludovico Sforza and Those of his Friends and Enemies. This coffee-table book (including 350 color/ b&w photos) is the product of four decades of research on Sforza's life and of the trips I have taken to Italy.

Life-Story Writing Workbooks:

First Steps to Creative and Academic Writing—Workbook I. This workbook provides the step-by-step instruction in the beginning steps as highlighted in *Writing from Within* while providing more advanced ideas and content for academic writing in grades 6 through 12.

Self-Awareness/Relationship—Workbook II. This workbook focuses on helping each of us discover the best character qualities that exist within us, as described in my book *Character Consciousness,* through additional exercises in expanding the concept of the P.S. mentioned in *Writing from Deeper Within* into a full-blown Self-Assessment as described and amplified in *Character Consciousness.*

Please go to BernardSelling.com for more information about these books.

— • • • —

The Writing from Within Series:

Writing from Within: The Next Generation. A semi-bestseller, with over 65,000 copies sold, *Writing from Within* has provided an abundance of techniques and solutions to the problems of writing life stories. Leapfrog Press called it "A seminal work in the field of autobiographical writing." This 25th Anniversary Edition integrates the best material from *Writing from Within* and the more-advanced material from *Writing from Deeper Within* into a fully rewritten book, the latest and best edition of *Writing from Within.*

Writing from Deeper Within goes deeper into the writing process, examining the components of great storytelling and expanding on the "writing from within" method. Selling describes how writers can reach and resolve a story's climax, get to the heart of their characters, and incorporate backstory and history using advanced writing strategies. He also discusses how life stories can be turned into creative stories, novels, and even screenplays.

The **Writing from Within Workbook** contains step-by-step exercises for successful life-story writing. Includes lessons on how to start, how to access and write early memories, and how to revise. Later units explain how to add narrative, inner thoughts and dialogue, character sketches, and climaxes. Sample rewrites show how your stories can grow and develop into longer forms. Available in paperback and spiral-bound editions.

For more information and to order these books visit hunterhouse.com.

Writing
from
Within:
The Next
Generation

322

Romantic
WEDDING CAKES

Romantic WEDDING CAKES

KERRY VINCENT

MEREHURST

Contents

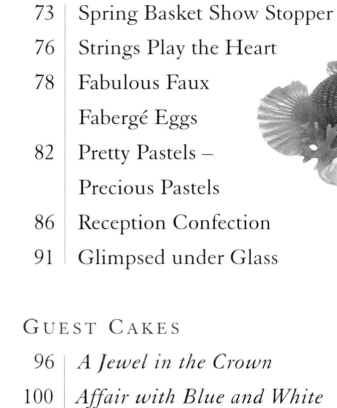

Guest Cakes

Dedication

Born in the wheat-belt region of Western Australia, I spent most of my youth in rural Mt Many Peaks before moving on to Perth. Inspired by the daily theatre of jewel-like skies, fiery sunsets and pastoral life, I took my first tentative steps in the direction of creative art. Always curious and very single minded, little did I know that I would one day leave it all behind and embark on my own odyssey around the world. My life has been an amazing tapestry, moving from one magnificent country to the next, delighting in the strands of colourful cultural experiences that each has offered and weaving them into part of me. In the course of my journey through London I met my husband-to-be, American Douglas Lee Vincent, subsequently married him there and together we embraced a transitory lifestyle that continues to this day. Currently we reside in Tulsa, Oklahoma. My husband has supported me in the time-consuming endeavour of compiling this book, and I dedicate it to him. He has my heartfelt thanks for dealing so calmly with this interruption in our lives. This book is also a homage to the memory of my parents, Roy Henry Flynn and Dorothy Frances Flynn (née Farmer), neither of whom lived long enough to see how sugarcraft impacted my life, and to my parents-in-law, Swinford Jack Vincent aged 94 and Mabel Hulin Vincent (dec).

*Wedgwood has had
the privilege of supporting the
Oklahoma State Sugar Art Show with the
Wedding Cake Competition. This is the
result of the talent and expertise
of Kerry Vincent.
Any book on the subject of Sugarcraft would
be greatly enhanced by the involvement
of Kerry Vincent.*

The Lord Wedgwood

Acknowledgements

There have been many friends who have encouraged me along the path to sugarcraft – key personalities include Patricia Simmons (Australia); Pat Ashby, Jillian Cole, Gary Chapman and Sheila Lampkin (UK); and Maxine Boyington and Eileen Walker (USA).

None of this would have been possible without the incredible support of Gene Johnson (photographer extraordinaire) and his staff – Danny Le Grange. Lynnet Leigh and Scott Johnson at Hawks Photography.

Special thanks to Barbara Croxford for finding me, then choosing to work with me at such a disparate geographical distance. Together we proved it can be done.

Do You Take This Cake?

After my initial delight at being commissioned to produce a book on romantic cakes, I then thought long and hard about the approach I would take. It seemed to me that most existing books focused primarily on flower making. Although I love to make flowers – and they are an integral part of cake design – I decided that little attention had been seriously given to modern cake design. Since many sugarcrafters are expert at making beautiful flowers, I drifted into exploring display options.

At present the cutting edge for flamboyant style appears to be in the United States. There aren't any rules or regulations about what can or can't be done, so design has no limiting restrictions. Cake styling, though slow to change, always goes round in cycles, and each country has its turn at the top. Right now I believe there is a gentle upheaval in cake design. Every aspect of our lives is affected by fashionable trends: why not the cake? It has happened before, although slowly over the past centuries. The current love affair with cakes displaying drapes and lace is evident in all the major bridal magazines. Some purists are aghast at the amount of moulding being done at the expense of extension work and other more formidable techniques of the past. However, most of us are in the business of creating cakes for real brides for serious money, and the bottom line is that we must produce what they like and what they are willing to pay for. My cakes are very expensive and custom designed. There are no repeats under any circumstances. Not everyone wants to work this way: many like to work to a formula, providing a photograph album, catalogue style, so that the client can choose the basic design before making minor changes and colour variations. This keeps pricing simple, whereas I may be obliged to prepare a quotation after reviewing the bridal requirements.

Since I am the first person in the United States whom Merehurst has commissioned to write a cake decorating book, there has been a heavy sense of responsibility alongside this challenge. If I had failed to meet the criteria demanded, it would have closed doors for others, and my wish is to see talented United States cake designers given the opportunity to showcase their skills and ideas as I have done.

To my International Cake Exploration Societé friends both here in the United States and abroad, thank you for sharing and for challenging me. This book is for you to enjoy, turn the pages, be motivated, widen your decorative horizons, make magic and create something lovely. If that goal is realized, then I will have fulfilled my responsibility.

Finally, a portion of the proceeds from this book will be set aside to subsidize a scholarship to enable a financially strapped student to attend sugarcraft classes.

Kerry Vincent

Stylish Satin Sugar Roses

CAKE AND DECORATION

- 15 cm/6 inch, 20 cm/8 inch, 25 cm/10 inch, 30 cm/12 inch and 35 cm/14 inch round cakes
- 1 kg/2 lb ivory flower paste/gum paste
- Antique silk lustre dust (VB/CK)
- 15 ml/3 tsp Tylose powder/CMC (J)
- 7 kg/14 lb ivory sugarpaste/rolled fondant
- Cornflour/cornstarch
- Moulded sugar vase (see pages 74–5)

EQUIPMENT

- 18-gauge wire
- Ivory floral tape
- Berling acanthus leaf mould (ADM – MPL 100)
- Kingston cutter formers (TOB)
- 8 cm/3 inch polystyrene/styrofoam ball
- 15 cm/6 inch, 20 cm/8 inch, 25 cm/10 inch and 30 cm/12 inch thin round cake boards
- 45 cm/18 inch round cake board
- Double scalloped crimper (PME)
- 100 mm/4 inch plaque cutter (J)
- Veining or Dresden tool (J or OP)
- 16 x 1 cm/^{1}/$_2$ inch dowel rods
- 17 x 5 mm/^{1}/$_4$ inch dowel rods
- Long sharpened dowel rod
- Matching fabric ribbon, to trim the 45 cm/18 inch cake board
- Varipin/Rosa's Roller (OP)

A BRIDE CAN TRULY PERSONALIZE HER WEDDING WITH THESE LOVELY CLASSIC TIERS. GOWNS FEATURING WRAPPED RIBBON ROSES ARE VERY FASHIONABLE, SO IT IS A SIMPLE MATTER TO CUSTOMIZE THE CAKE TO MATCH. HER DREAMS ARE REALIZED WITH THIS IVORY CONFECTION — SO VERY MUCH IN TUNE WITH FASHIONABLE TRENDS, AND DELICIOUSLY BLENDING CLASSIC DESIGN WITH CONTEMPORARY OVERTONES.

SATIN FABRIC SUGAR ROSES

1 Roll out very thin pieces of ivory flower paste/gum paste to 5 cm/2 inches wide and in varying lengths, from 8 cm/3 inches to 10 cm/4 inches long. Brush a central strip, 2.5 cm/1 inch wide, with antique silk lustre dust. Fold each strip in half lengthways, and roll up loosely. Pinch it into a base, removing the excess paste.

2 Insert a dampened, hooked 18-gauge wire into the base of the rolled-up flower head. Tightly wrap the wire with ivory floral tape (pic 1), then dry for 2–3 days. This bouquet has 250 flowers. For fewer flowers or a smaller cake, shorten each flower stem. Rolled roses for the side design are not wired and should be made when required, because soft paste pushes into position more readily than pre-dried paste. Repeat step 1 for the unwired roses.

1 Wrapping the satin fabric sugar roses

> **HOW MOIST?**
> When attaching flower paste/gum paste and sugarpaste/rolled fondant to each other, remember that wet paste to dry paste is easy, as is wet to wet. The same, however, cannot be said for dry paste to dry paste, which can on occasion be quite resistant to gluing.

ACANTHUS LEAVES

3 To make the acanthus leaves, first add the Tylose powder to 500 g/1 lb ivory sugarpaste/rolled fondant. Knead well, then double wrap in plastic wrap and leave to rest overnight.

4 Lightly dust the acanthus leaf mould with cornflour/cornstarch. Roll out the paste thickly, then push into the mould. Run over the surface with a rolling pin. Cut across the mould surface, leaving the open-work effect exposed. Tease out the leaf with a knife (or freeze it briefly and it will pop right out – although this method is much more time-consuming). Brush with antique silk lustre dust, then lay the leaf on the Kingston former and dry overnight (pic 2). You will need 150 of these acanthus leaves.

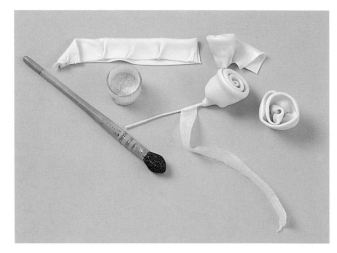

2 Making and drying acanthus leaves over the former

> **MAKING ACANTHUS LEAVES IN ADVANCE**
> Acanthus leaves are a useful side design for any cake and can be made well ahead in basic white paste. They nest easily, can be airbrushed any colour, occupy little storage space and are fabulous to have on hand to prepare an outstanding cake at short notice.

THE CENTREPIECE

5 Several days ahead, prepare the moulded sugar vase (see pages 74–5), making sure the centre is hollowed out sufficiently to accommodate the polystyrene/styrofoam ball. Decorate the sides with the stylized acanthus leaves. Brush the leaves with antique silk lustre dust while still damp. Cut the ball in half. Attach the half ball to the hollowed-out moulded sugar vase, using royal icing, and cover with a thin layer of sugarpaste/rolled fondant. Alternatively, dry a ball of sugarpaste/rolled fondant for two days, then insert in the same way. Arrange the flowers, spiralling down in even rows from the top to the bottom (pic 3).

PREPARING THE CAKES

6 Centre the cakes on the thin boards, then cover them and the 45 cm/ 18 inch board with ivory sugarpaste/rolled fondant. Crimp a row of double scallops at the upper edge of each cake. Emboss the upper surface of the top tier with the plaque cutter and veining tool (pic 4). Paint the embossed pattern with antique gold lustre dust mixed with clear alcohol.

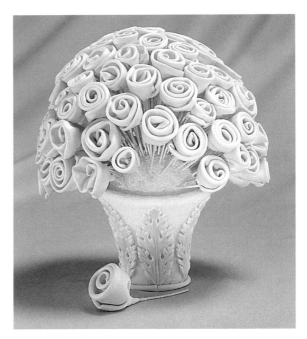

3 Arranging the roses in the centrepiece

4 Quilted decoration and plaque

7 Stack the cakes one on top of the other, dowelling each tier before proceeding on to the next (see page 142). Hammer the long sharpened dowel through all five cakes, to stop shifting. Pipe a small royal iced border, to seal the cakes. Attach the acanthus leaf side design with royal icing, then the freshly made, rolled satin effect fabric sugar roses. Arrange for two people to carry the completed cake to the event, then add the centrepiece on-site.

ASSEMBLING THE CAKE ON-SITE

8 Alternatively, it can be stacked and decorated on-site. Leave a space free on either side for the offset spatulas. After centring, fill in the empty spaces with stylized acanthus leaves, then the roses. Pack the wrapped roses in plastic containers to keep them soft. Carry the centrepiece separately to the reception site. Pipe a ball of royal icing beneath the vase, and centre it on the cake.

This cake does not have as many steps as some of the other cakes and is well within the reach of an advanced beginner. It does take some time to prepare, however, because there are so many pieces. Tiers can be added or subtracted, according to event requirements. This cake will serve 230 people when made as a madeira or sponge/pound or white cake, comfortably reserving the top for the bride to keep for her first anniversary.

Sea Shades Shimmer

CAKE AND DECORATION

- 40 cm/16 inch oval cake
- 30 ml/6 tsp Tylose powder/CMC (J)
- 5 kg/10 lb sugarpaste/rolled fondant
- Green-gold, pale green, ruby, teal, avocado-green, coral, brown, yellow, antique silk, purple, super gold and bronze lustre dusts (VB/CK)
- 2.5 kg/5 lb caster/superfine sugar or granulated/regular sugar
- 310 ml/10 fl oz/1¼ cups water
- Pale blue, brown and yellow food colourings (VB/CK)
- 1 egg white

EQUIPMENT

- 40 cm/16 inch thin oval cake board
- Mylar, cardboard or paper template for the tropical fish (see page 152)
- Veining tool (OP or J)
- Various-sized drinking straws
- Round piping tubes/tips
- Paintbrush
- Varipin/Rosa's Roller (OP)
- 5 mm/¼ inch dowel rod
- Combination cutter veiner (RVO)
- Dusty miller cutter (RL)
- Rose leaf veiner
- Coral reef and shell samples
- Large glass or metal bowl
- Aluminium foil
- Sponge foam
- 45 x 5 cm/18 x 2 inch cake dummy
- Dressmaker's tracing wheel
- 65 cm/26 inch oval cake board

HERE, JEWEL-TONED TROPICAL FISH SWARM ABOUT A WHITE CHOCOLATE GROOM'S CAKE. THIS SOPHISTICATED SPIN ON THE TRADITIONAL VERSION IS CERTAIN TO PLEASE THE MOST DISCERNING OF TASTES. SEA THEMES AND SAND DUNES EVOKE THOUGHTS OF THE IDYLLIC PLEASURES OF A HONEYMOON TO COME.

PREPARING THE DECORATION MIXTURE

1 Knead the Tylose powder into 1 kg/2 lb sugarpaste/rolled fondant. Use this strengthened mixture for all the decorations on this cake. Set aside for an hour for the gum to dissolve, then knead once more.

MAKING THE TROPICAL FISH

2 Cut out a Mylar, cardboard or paper template for the fish (pic 1). Roll out the strengthened sugarpaste/rolled fondant and cut thirteen fish. Press the veining tool into the tails and the fins, to make sharp-pleated markings, and draw the paste out so it looks wavy. Using the various-sized drinking straws, the veining tool and the round piping tubes/tips, mark the scales, eyes and gills of the fish. Dust with green-gold, pale green, ruby and teal lustre dusts.

1 Preparing the tropical fish

3 Prepare a little paste mound with the veining tool, indenting the centre where the fish will be positioned. Cut three small slits where the coral and sea grass will be inserted. Set aside for a couple of days to firm up.

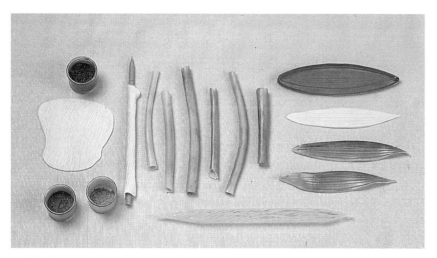

2 Making the coral tubes and sea grass

CORAL AND SEA GRASS

4 Make the hollow underwater coral tubes from various-sized strips of strengthened sugar paste/rolled fondant embossed with the Varipin/Rosa's Roller and wrapped around the thin dowel rod. Press down hard to seal the join, then colour with avocado-green, coral and pale green lustre dusts (pic 2). Set aside to dry.

5 Meanwhile, cut out the long sea grass from the strengthened sugarpaste/rolled fondant, using the combination cutter veiner. Immediately brush with pale green, teal and brown lustre dusts. Curl the tops over, then dry flat.

CORAL REEF AND SHELLS

6 The dusty miller cutter is an excellent cutter to substitute for coral. These pieces are also cut from the strengthened sugarpaste/rolled fondant, veined with a rose leaf veiner or a rose leaf from the garden, then shaded with coral, yellow, antique silk and purple lustre dusts. For the reef moulds, simply collect two or three samples from the seashore or buy them from hobby craft shops. Press them into the strengthened paste. Freeze briefly to set the shape, then dry hard for a week or two. The original reef pieces, the mould and the moulded piece are quite hard to tell apart (pic 3). They can be white, marbled or dusted.

7 For the shells, roll out the strengthened paste and press on to the back of a natural shell. Peel away, trim with a craft knife or scalpel, and brush with antique silk, super gold and bronze lustre dusts.

3 Coral reef and shell collection

TROPICAL BACKGROUND ASSEMBLY

8 Streak some royal icing with pale blue food colouring. Using a palette knife and the blue-streaked icing, ice/frost the little mound so that it resembles sea waves. Position the fish into the centre of the mound while the icing is wet. Add some foam support until dry. Meanwhile, push in the coral and sea grass. Prop everything until the icing is set hard.

BEACH SAND

9 Colour the remaining sugarpaste/rolled fondant so it resembles beach sand, using yellow and brown food colourings.

ROCK SUGAR

Rock sugar is fun to make and very realistic. Preheat the oven to 120°C/250°F/GM1/2. Line a large glass or metal bowl with the foil. Combine 1 kg/2 lb caster/superfine sugar or granulated/regular sugar with 250 ml/8 fl oz/1 cup water in a large saucepan – the sugar eventually doubling in size. Stir over low heat, taking normal precautions when boiling sugar, such as removing any scum accumulating on the top and brushing any sugar granules down from the sides of the pan. When dissolved and beginning to boil, partially cover the saucepan and bring the sugar to 124°C/255°F. If colouring is required, add it now. Continue boiling until the temperature reaches 140°C/275°F. Remove from the heat source and immediately stir in 30 ml/2 tbsp royal icing. Beat lightly; do not overbeat. The mixture will puff up like a meringue, fall a little, then rise again. For more porous rock sugar, add extra royal icing.

Immediately pour into the prepared bowl and put in the oven for 10 minutes, to set the sugar. Remove from the oven and leave for 10 hours. Chop or break it into pieces for your project – a serrated knife works best. Rock sugar lasts for ages and can be lightly airbrushed once the pieces are set in place.

MOULDED SUGAR

10 Mix together the remaining caster/superfine sugar or granulated/regular sugar, remaining water and the egg white. Substitute albumin powder, if you wish.

CAKE ASSEMBLY

11 Attach the cake with royal icing to the thin cake board. Centre the cake on the cake dummy and cover both with the beach sand sugarpaste/rolled fondant. Draw some vertical accent lines around the cake with the tracing wheel and brush with super gold lustre dust. Pile the moulded sugar on to the 65 cm/26 inch cake board using a palette knife like a trowel to pack it down and smooth the surface. Centre the cake on this board. Pipe a walnut-sized ball of royal icing in the centre of the cake, then stand the sea grass and hollow pipes upright within it. Crumble a little rock sugar over the icing so it can't be seen. Prop with sponge foam until dry.

12 Arrange three fish in a tight triangle around the grass, attaching them to the top of the cake with royal icing and surrounding them with shells. Circle the cake with individual ornamental fish and dot the moulded sugar with coral, shells and rock sugar.

Pintucks and Pansies

Cake and Decoration

- 20 cm/8 inch, 25 cm/10 inch and
  30 cm/12 inch scalloped oval cakes
- Yellow, moss-green and purple petal dusts
  (VB/CK)
- 85 g/3 oz pale lemon flower paste/gum paste
- Purple food colouring
- Purple lustre dust (VB/CK)
- 7 g/¼ oz moss-green flower
  paste/gum paste
- Sugar crystals, from Chinese food stores
- Hi-lite orange lustre dust (OP)
- 6 kg/12 lb pale lemon sugarpaste/rolled
  fondant
- Moulded sugar vase (see pages 74–5)

Equipment

- 20- and 28-gauge wires
- Paper templates for pansy petals (see page
  152) or large rose petal cutter (OP – R1)
- Ball tool • Dried cornhusk
- Medium five-petal blossom cutter (such as
  OP – F2L, or PME)
- Mid-green floral tape
- Leaf cutters (OP – OL2, OL3, OL4)
- Veining or Dresden tool
- Natural leaf veiner • Dimpled foam mat
- Polystyrene/styrofoam ball
- 20 cm/8 inch, 25 cm/10 inch and
  30 cm/12 inch thin oval cake boards
- 38 cm/15 inch scalloped cake board
- Open scalloped crimper
- 13 x 5 mm/¼ inch dowel rods
- Long sharpened dowel rod
- Fluorescent light cover pattern
- Lace mould cutters (RVO – F13 and F11)
- No.000 piping tube/tip
- Daisy centre moulds (J)
- Dressmaker's tracing wheel
- Sponge foam

SOUTACHE ACCENTS WITH PINTUCKS AND PANSIES EPITOMIZE THE VERY ESSENCE OF A SPRINGTIME WEDDING. SIGNATURE EFFECT IS CREATED WITH HUGE PURPLE AND PARCHMENT PANSIES. FEMININE SUGAR STREAMERS POOL GRACEFULLY ON THE CAKE BOARD. ADDED HINTS OF PURPLE AND GREEN IN A DRIFT OF LEMON SOUFFLÉ WOULD MAKE THIS CAKE A SUPERB HIGHLIGHT AT ANY WEDDING DAY!

THE PANSIES

1 For the central stamen, make a tiny ball of white flower paste/gum paste just large enough to support the very large pansy petals. Tinge with yellow and moss-green petal dusts and attach to the 20-gauge wire.

2 Roll out the pale lemon flower paste/gum paste and cut the petals using the template or rose petal cutter. Ruffle the edges with the side of the ball tool (pic 1). Vein the petals with the dried cornhusk. Place them on a petal pad, starting at the top of the flower and descending – right/left top petals, then right/left side petals, centre and finally the bottom petal. Touch each overlapping corner with edible gum glue and press together,

1 Creating pretty pansy faces

making sure each makes contact. Press the stamen through the centre of the flower as well as a piece of supporting aluminium foil, then set aside to dry over a glass. Paint in the dark markings with purple food colouring mixed with clear alcohol/vodka or Everclear. When dry, brush lightly with purple lustre dust.

3 Make a Mexican hat with six points from moss-green flower paste/gum paste, for the calyx. Hollow out the base, thin the edges and insert the pansy wire. Tip with a little edible gum glue. Make a blossom cutter frill and attach with edible gum glue. Wrap the stem with mid-green floral tape.

2 Sets of leaves in progress

3 Preparing sugar crystals

THE LEAVES

4 Cut out sets of leaves in moss-green flower paste/gum paste, using all the leaf cutters. Thin the edges and increase the width of the leaves by stretching with the veining or Dresden tool. Brush with moss-green petal dust and vein the surface with the leaf veiner. Insert 28-gauge wires, then wrap with floral tape (pic 2). Lay the leaves on the dimpled foam mat to dry.

SUGAR CRYSTALS

5 Brush each crystal with hi-lite orange and purple lustre dusts (pic 3). Use the crystals to support the flowers and foliage and to conceal the polystyrene/styrofoam ball.

PREPARING THE CAKES

6 Centre the cakes on matching sized thin cake boards, which have been scalloped to shape and covered with contact paper. Cover each cake and the banded, 38 cm/15 inch, scalloped cake board in pale lemon sugarpaste/rolled fondant, so it matches the pansy colour. (A small amount of yellow kneaded into

PANSY CUTTER OPTIONS

The pansies on this cake are particularly large, measuring 10 x 8 cm/4 x 3 inches. For these, use the pansy petal templates (see page 152) or a large rose petal cutter such as OP R1, although the rose petal cutter will not produce the same size. You might therefore need to adjust the decoration by making an extra flower, should this latter option be adopted. It is, however, faster to work with the cutter.

white paste is close to the colour of the natural flower and looks like lemon soufflé.) Before the surface crusts, crimp the scalloped pattern vertically into the four recessed areas of each cake, using the open scalloped crimper, and circle the cake board with the same pattern. Paint the centre of the crimped scallops with hi-lite orange lustre dust mixed with clear alcohol/vodka or Everclear. The next day, centre the bottom cake on the covered cake board, securing with royal icing.

7 Insert seven dowels 8 cm/3 inches in from the edge and follow the contour of the bottom cake (see page 142). Stack the middle tier on top and insert six dowels 8 cm/3 inches from the edge. Add the top tier after placing a blob of edible gum glue between it and the previous tier. Hammer the long central dowel through all the cakes, to stop shifting during transportation. Add double-row swags, starting and ending at the centre of each recess.

SIDE DESIGN

8 Now comes the fun part. Emboss the rolled out sugarpaste/rolled fondant with the fluorescent cover pattern. Using the small set of lace mould cutters for the top and middle tiers, and the larger set for the bottom tier, lay the embossed paste over one of the lace moulds and shallow cut. (Please note: I did not push the paste right down into the cutter moulds, because a different personalized pattern was the goal.) Lay on the tabletop and coax the pieces into the shapes shown (pic 4), one piece being cut in half vertically. Outline each piece with running dots, using the piping tube/tip, and brush immediately with hi-lite orange lustre dust.

9 Form the pattern by building out from the centre lace points (pic 5). (It doesn't have to match this one exactly – allow your imagination to take flight and create an

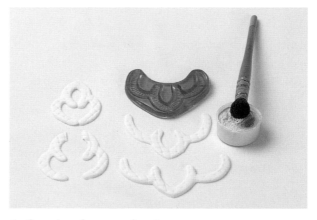

4 Creating the soutache pieces

individual masterpiece.) Attach each piece to the cake sides with edible gum glue. Cut up additional pieces to fill empty spots and make sure whatever happens on the right-hand side is repeated on the left. The back of the cake is a replica of the front. Make a range of different sized buttons in sugarpaste/rolled fondant, using the daisy centre moulds. Add these buttons in graduating

5 Stages of the lace mould process

sizes at join points, to pull the effect together – it is the key to the design work. Also cover the joins in the double-row swags with the largest buttons. Brush the buttons with hi-lite orange lustre dust.

BOW LOOPS AND STREAMERS

10 Press thinly rolled sugarpaste/rolled fondant on to the sheet of fluorescent light cover pattern, embossing the surface. Cut into a curved pointed shape (pic 6), following the template on page 152. (This template can be sized up or down to suit any cake dimension.) Turn the paste sides under, then 'stitch' along the edges with the tracing wheel. Pleat at the top and run the tracing wheel down the top end of the pleat, to form pintucks. Brush with hi-lite orange lustre dust and attach to the side of the cake with edible gum glue. There are two overlapping panels on each side and these are also repeated at the back. Add four pleated open loops, once again 'stitching' the pintucks into position with the tracing wheel before layering and attaching with edible gum glue. Finally add a fifth loop, placing it vertically (pic 7); support in position with sponge foam until dry. Cover the join with a small pleated knot.

FINISHING OFF

11 Cut four stylized leaves, long oak or something similar to the cutter shown (pic 8), in the embossed sugarpaste/rolled fondant. Following the contour of the leaf, press in

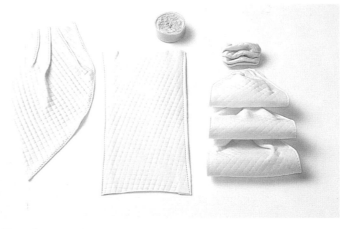

6 Bow loops and streamers

8 Satin leaves and cutters

edging dots using the piping tube/tip. Brush with hi-lite orange lustre dust and tuck the leaves under the knot, securing with edible gum glue.

12 Cover the moulded sugar vase in sugarpaste/rolled fondant and decorate with lace soutache. Circle the vase base and the rim with a thin rope, and insert styrofoam, securing it with edible gum glue. Leave for at least a day, until the glue has dried, before adding and arranging the flowers and foliage; otherwise the arrangement could topple.

7 Attaching the fifth loop

Pêche Belle La Russe

CAKE AND DECORATION

- 15 cm/6 inch, 20 cm/8 inch and 30 cm/12 inch round cakes
- 2.75 kg/5 lb 10 oz pale peach sugarpaste/rolled fondant
- 30 g/1 oz balls of green, dark peach, purple and pale blue sugarpaste/rolled fondant
- Pale green, mauve, silk-white and super gold lustre dusts (VB/CK)
- 30 g/1 oz pale green flower paste/gum paste
- 125 g/4 oz/¹/₂ cup peach caster/superfine sugar
- 15 ml/1 tbsp alcohol-flavoured, simple syrup for each bonbonière/favour

EQUIPMENT

- 100 mm/4 inch plaque cutter (J)
- Medium and large maple leaf cutters (RL)
- Natural insecticide-free rose leaf
- Selection of four different blossom cutters
- Veining tool
- Small and medium-sized half-ball sugar moulds (PME)
- Carnation cutters (OP – C1 and C2)
- Ball tool
- Berling acanthus leaf mould (ADM – MPL 100)
- Kingston cutter former (TOB)
- Plunger cutters (PME or OP – F2M and F2L)
- Broderie anglais cutter (PME)
- 15 cm/6 inch and 20 cm/8 inch thin round cake boards
- 38 cm/15 inch round cake board
- Large single scalloped crimper (PME)
- Brocade lace mould (ELI)
- Satay stick/bamboo skewer
- Parsley cutter or sharp knife
- 8 x 5 mm/¹/₄ inch dowel rods
- Bun tins/gem cake pans

TODAY'S CAKE STYLISTS ARE THROWING TRADITION TO THE WIND AS BRIDES OPT FOR MORE TRENDY, CUTTING-EDGE DESIGNS. WHITE HAS ALWAYS BEEN THE OBVIOUS CHOICE BUT MODERN BRIDES ARE NOW ABANDONING TRADITION AND CHOOSING WEDDING CAKES IN EVERY COLOUR OF THE RAINBOW. THIS COUTURE-INSPIRED CAKE DESIGN IS MEANT FOR THE ROMANTIC AT HEART.

1 Plaque cutter and maple leaves

VINCENT MARQUETRY TOP PLAQUE

1 Cut out a plaque from 60 g/2 oz of the pale peach sugarpaste/rolled fondant, using the plaque cutter. Immediately cut out three maple leaves in two sizes, and replace them with the same leaf, in green paste. Vein the leaves with a natural insecticide-free leaf. Then overcut two more leaves, one of each size (pic 1). Brush with pale green dust.

2 Using the selection of blossom cutters and 30 g/1 oz each of the dark peach, purple and pale blue sugarpaste/rolled fondant, cut into the leaves, replacing the discarded scraps with solid-coloured flowers – the more overcutting, the prettier the design. Press in a throat with the veining tool (pic 2). Brush the purple flowers with mauve lustre dust, and the others with silk-white lustre dust. Paint the plaque edge with super gold lustre dust mixed with alcohol. Paint flourishes, extending out from the spray. Make four feet from moulded sugar, using the small half-ball mould. Position under the plaque.

VINCENT MARQUETRY

Generic Vincent Marquetry plaques can be made months ahead and stored. They are extremely useful to have on hand for short-notice occasions, and are a great way to recycle coloured remnant sugarpaste/rolled fondant and flower paste/gum pastc.

2 Inlaid plaque with flowers and cutters

3 Carnation petals and cutters

CARNATIONS

3 Cut four rounds using the medium carnation cutter. Frill the edges and place the first three on top of each other, to make the flower. Press the centre with the ball tool, forcing the petal sides upwards. Fold the fourth piece into an S-shape and insert at the centre of the flower (pic 3). Repeat this method, using the small carnation cutter. You will need thirty-two carnations of each size.

MAPLE LEAVES

4 Prepare pale green, rose-veined, flower paste/gum paste maple leaves, with the maple leaf cutters and natural rose leaf veiner. Brush with pale green lustre dust (pic 4). Fold each leaf in half, to attach to the cake border beneath the carnations on the top and middle tiers. The remainder should have the sides lifted slightly before slipping beneath the flowers on the top and bottom tiers. While still damp, attach the leaves to the cake with edible gum glue or royal icing.

4 Making the maple leaves

ACANTHUS LEAVES

5 Press firm pale peach sugarpaste/rolled fondant into the mould. Cut away the excess with a very sharp knife, then shave the top away carefully, leaving the cutwork exposed (pic 5). Immediately remove the leaf from the mould, or freeze it briefly. (Freezing stops the medium from stretching and makes it easier to remove.) Brush the leaves with silk-white lustre dust, then dry over the shaped former. Twenty-four of these acanthus leaves will be required, but make a couple of extras in case of breakages.

FILLER FLOWERS

6 Make the filler flowers from the purple and dark peach sugarpaste/rolled fondant, using the large plunger cutter (pic 6). Cut out peach blossoms with the medium-sized plunger cutter and the Broderie anglais cutter. After attaching, pipe in a single stamen in white royal icing.

PREPARING THE CAKES

7 Dampen and sprinkle the 38 cm/15 inch cake board with the peach caster/superfine sugar. Place the top and middle tier cakes on matching-sized thin cake boards. Cover the three cakes with sugarpaste/rolled fondant. Centre the bottom cake on the sugar-covered cake board. Working from the bottom cake upwards, embellish the upper edge of each tier with the scalloped crimper. At the junction of each space, push in a single, medium-sized peach blossom, and finish with a piped white stamen.

BOTTOM TIER

8 Mark the edge of the lace mould 10 cm/4 inches from the base. Using this as a guide to ensure uniformity of depth, roll out the sugarpaste/rolled fondant. Press into the lace mould with a foam

5 Stylized acanthus leaf side design

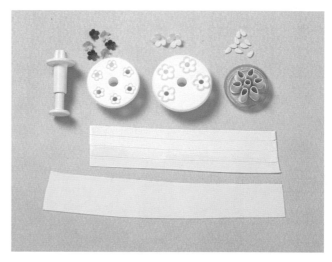

6 Filler flowers and matching cutters

sponge. Brush the raised design with silk-white lustre dust. Form into pleats with a satay stick/bamboo skewer (pic 7), and glue to the cake side, tucking the last pleat under the first, so there is no visible join.

MIDDLE TIER AND TOP TIER

9 Using royal icing, attach the acanthus leaves and carnations to the middle tier, followed by the leaves and filler flowers. Measure the circumference of the top tier and divide the cake in six. Using the parsley cutter or sharp knife, cut strips of thinly rolled sugarpaste/rolled fondant the depth of the top tier cake, then brush with silk-white lustre dust.

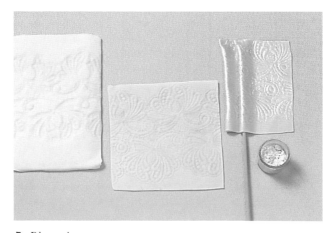

7 Pleats in progress

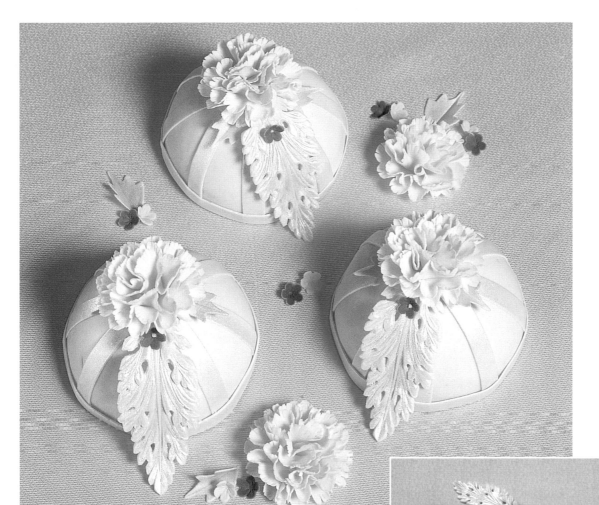

*Matching
bonbonières/favours
look spectacular
whether displayed
with the cake or
served individually*

*8 Decorating
bonbonières/favours*

Attach these strips with the minutest amount of water. Cover
each of the rough edges at the top with a single blossom. Attach
the carnations and leaves at the lower edge, using royal icing.

STACKING THE TIERS

10 Put four dowels each into the bottom and middle cakes (see
page 142), extending the dowels 2.5 cm/1 inch above each cake.
Prepare eight moulded sugar half-balls, with holes in the centre,
using the medium-sized, half-ball mould. Slip one over each
dowel to disguise the wood, and glue them to the cake surface,
using royal icing.

11 For transportation, sit each tier on a larger cake board with
non-skid rubber matting. Stack the tiers at the reception. Touch
each dowel top with a blob of royal icing and, using an offset
spatula, lift each cake into position. Add the cake top plaque,
and line the carnations up with the paste ribbon strips.

BONBONIÈRES/FAVOURS

Make the cakes in bun tins/gem pans. When
completely cool, drizzle with the alcohol-flavoured,
simple syrup, then cover with sugarpaste/rolled
fondant. Divide each cake evenly. Cut eight 5 mm/
1/4 inch strips of paste and brush with silk-white lustre
dust, then attach to the cake (pic 8). Attach the maple
leaves, acanthus leaf, medium carnation and filler
flowers with royal icing, in the order given.

Mosaic Magic

CAKE AND DECORATION

- 15 cm/6 inch, 20 cm/8 inch, 25 cm/10 inch, 30 cm/12 inch and 35 cm/14 inch round cakes
- 250 g/8 oz white flower paste/gum paste
- Purple and green powdered food colourings (VB/CK)
- Sifted white polenta/cornmeal
- Green, super gold, silk-white and brown lustre dusts (VB/CK)
- Larkspur, pale blue, white and yellow petal dusts (VB/CK)
- 7.5 kg/15 lb pale cream sugarpaste/rolled fondant (75:25 white and ivory mixed)
- Moulded sugar vase (see pages 74–5)

EQUIPMENT

- Paper templates (see pages 152–3)
- Ball tool
- Large needle
- Shallow celformer, pierced through the base
- Long thin calyx cutter from a hibiscus or rose cutter set
- 20- and 26-gauge wires
- Tiny five-petal flower cutter
- 18 x 0 line brush
- Leaf veiner
- Rose leaf cutter
- Piece of rippled foam
- Floral tape
- 15 cm/6 inch, 20 cm/8 inch, 25 cm/10 inch, 30 cm/12 inch and 35 cm/14 inch thin round cake boards
- 45 cm/18 inch round cake board
- Grosgrain ribbon, 1.5 mm/⅝ inch wide, to trim 45 cm/18 inch cake board
- Adding machine tape
- Dowel rods (see page 142)
- Textured rolling pin (EC)
- No.10 piping tube/tip (W)

MOSAIC ART HAS BEEN AROUND FOR CENTURIES. ARTISTICALLY PLEASING TO THE EYE, IT IS A TIMELESS TECHNIQUE TO CELEBRATE A COLOURFUL WEDDING. GOLDEN CONFETTI SHARDS AND LUSTROUS PEARL TILES ARE PLACED IN INTRICATE PATTERNS CREATING EXOTIC SIDE DESIGNS, WHILE HYDRANGEAS PEEP OUT BENEATH AMETHYST BALLOON FLOWERS CLUSTERED IN A STUNNING CAKE ORNAMENT.

WIRED BALLOON FLOWERS

1 Mould a marble-sized ball of flower paste/gum paste. Roll out the edges, leaving it very thick in the centre. Using the template (see page 153), cut out the star-shaped, balloon flowers. Brush heavily with purple powdered food colouring. Remove excess. Press firmly with the ball tool and hollow out the centre, so the sides of the stars begin to cup. Thin the edges of the petals and pierce the centre with a large needle, then rest in the celformer.

2 Prepare a small, inner, tube-shaped circle. Cut even little nicks into the surface and dust with purple and green powdered food colourings. Position over the needle hole in the centre of the flower.

3 With the long thin calyx cutter from the hibiscus or rose cutter set, trim the stamens to a very thin star shape (pic 1). Roll each of the five points between the thumb and forefinger. Run a thin paint line of edible gum glue along each point and sift white polenta/cornmeal over the top. Make the

1 Balloon flowers coming to life

stigma thin, dark purple and bottle shaped. Attach a hooked 26-gauge wire to it, then push through the flower centre. Dampen the join with edible gum glue. Add a tiny five-petal flower on top of the stigma. Paint dark vein lines on the petals with the line brush, using purple food colouring mixed with clear alcohol/vodka or Everclear.

2 Balloon flower: stages of calyx and buds

BACK OF THE FLOWER AND BUDS

4 The calyx is a simple five-point star with a small, elongated hip beneath. Make the buds in the same way, eliminating the flower centre (replace with a hooked wire and a pea-sized ball of paste) and close the petals (hence the balloon shape) so the centre cannot be seen (pic 2). Colour them lighter than the flowers, using purple food colouring brushed with green lustre dust. Close the petals to meet evenly in the front and to a point. The pattern is exactly the same, although smaller for the bud.

HYDRANGEA FLOWERS

5 These have anywhere between three- and five-petal combinations. Attach tiny balls of flower paste/gum paste to the 20-gauge wire, cut in 15 cm/6 inch lengths. Twelve hours later, cut out the petals in paste, using the hydrangea flower template. Thin the edges with the ball tool. Press with the leaf veiner. Arrange in the celformer, overlapping each petal. Carefully push the wired centre through and attach with edible gum glue. Dry for 24 hours before touching. Brush with larkspur, pale blue

3 Hydrangea petals and flowers

and white petal dusts with a spot of yellow at the centre (pic 3). For the side design, use the same pattern, method and colouring – no wire, of course.

FOLIAGE

6 Prepare the leaves with the rose leaf cutter. Then offset the cutter again, slicing a bit off each side. Wire the leaf. Vein the surface and lay on a piece of

4 Rose leaves trimmed to size

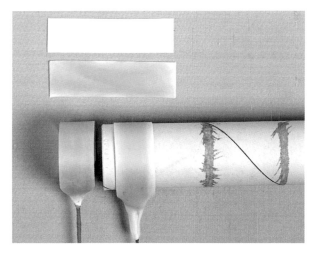

5 Shaping gold ribbon loops

rippled foam to dry. Floral tape the wires. Attach the leaves on one side of the stem only, then position immediately beneath each other, graduating from small to large (pic 4). For the side design, use the same method, pattern and colouring but omit the wire and remove the oblong piece to insert the stem.

GOLD RIBBON LOOPS

7 Dry 20-gauge wired, 2 cm/³⁄₄ inch strips of super gold-brushed flower paste/gum paste formed in a circle over a kitchen paper towel roll (pic 5). Tape all wires when the flowers and ribbons are absolutely dry.

7 Balloon flowers in the side design

6 Placing the mosaic tile pattern

MOSAIC DESIGN

The same mosaic design is repeated on the top, third and bottom tier cakes. For added interest, the second and fourth tier cakes feature complementary patterns.

MOSAIC TILES

8 Roll out strips of flower paste/gum paste and cut in 5 mm/¹⁄₄ inch squares with a craft knife or scalpel (pic 6). While still soft, brush with silk-white lustre dust. Do not separate until required – it will be easier to match the pieces. For the brown strips, prepare some thin oblong pieces by cutting each tile in quarters. Brush with brown lustre dust.

Dry thoroughly, then snap apart. Keep the colours separated. For the gold pieces, prepare long strips of thin paste. Dust with super gold lustre dust while the paste is wet. When dry, break into small pieces. (If required the pieces can be made larger than those used here – the decorating will then go much faster.)

TOP, THIRD AND BOTTOM TIER SIDE DECORATION

9 Cover each cake with the pale cream sugarpaste/rolled fondant. Divide the cakes into eight even sections and arrange the white tile outline. Roll out some flower paste/gum paste and cut out more balloon flowers. Dust with purple food colouring. Paint darker purple vein lines with the line brush, using purple food colouring mixed with clear alcohol/vodka or Everclear (pic 7). Add a thin calyx stamen topped with the mini star-shaped blossom at the centre. Dust with sifted white polenta/cornmeal. Attach the flower to the cake sides with

8 Hydrangea flowers in the side design

polenta/cornmeal. Attach the flower to the cake sides with edible gum glue. Add the hydrangea petals and green leaves. Fill the remaining space with gold pieces (pic 8).

SECOND AND FOURTH TIER SIDE DECORATION

10 Divide the cake measurement into repeat sections by folding the adding machine tape. Cut a wavy line duplicating the pattern provided on page 153. Mark the design on the cake. Glue the tiles around the top border. Glue the blossoms and foliage into position. Add more tiles and brown strips. Fill with the gold pieces.

ASSEMBLY

11 Stack the cakes, dowelling each tier (see page 142). For the hollow tubes, emboss some paste with the textured rolling pin. Wrap around the long scrap dowels. Press down to seal (pic 9). Slide off into position on the cake and cover each join with a single tile.

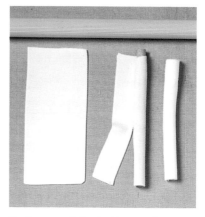

9 Stages of the hollow tubes

FLORAL CENTREPIECE

12 Prepare the moulded sugar vase (see pages 74–5). Remove an ice-cream scoop-sized ball from the centre. Once dry, fill with a round ball of sugarpaste/rolled fondant and set aside for several days. Decorate the exterior with a simple mosaic pattern. Arrange in the following order: gold ribbon loops, wired balloon flowers, hydrangea flowers and rose leaves.

A TOUCH OF ELEGANCE

Why not make tiny gift tags to match the wedding cake and place them on the serviettes at the table of honour? (It would not be advisable to suggest making these for all the guests, as they are a bit fiddly and time consuming.) Duplicate parts of the main design on to small flower paste/gum paste rectangular plaques. Punch out a round hole with the piping tube/tip. Using the other end as a cutter, cut out two round disks. Remove the centres with the same tube/tip so all the holes match. Line up on the plaque and join with edible gum glue. Fill in the mosaic pattern, then thread a strip of paste ribbon through the hole.

How Sweet it is – Cake for Two

Cake and Decoration

- 8 cm/3 inch and 10 cm/4 inch round cakes
- 750 g/1¹/₂ lb white sugarpaste/ rolled fondant
- 60 g/2 oz pale pink sugarpaste/rolled fondant
- 15 g/¹/₂ oz pale pink flower paste/ gum paste
- Orchid-pink, super pearl and cornflower-blue lustre dusts (VB/CK)
- Larkspur, lime-green and moss-green petal dusts (VB/CK)

Equipment

- 8 cm/3 inch and 15 cm/6 inch thin round cake boards
- Small double scalloped crimper (PME)
- China cake or dessert plate
- 4 x 5 mm/¹/₄ inch dowel rods
- Medium flower cutter (PME – plunger or medium blossom)
- Mini leaf cutter
- Grosgrain textured rolling pin (EC)
- Dressmaker's tracing wheel
- Sponge foam
- Petal pad (OP)
- Dresden tool
- Veining tool
- 8 cm/3 inch diameter carnation cutter (J)
- Celformer (CC)
- Soft medium paintbrush
- Aspic bird cutter
- 18 x 0 line brush

A PRETTY PINK PORCELAIN-LIKE CAKE AS FRESH AS A SUMMER BREEZE AND READY TO ACCOMPANY THE BRIDE AND GROOM ON THEIR HONEYMOON. OFTEN OVERWHELMED BY THE EXCITEMENT OF THE DAY, THE BRIDAL COUPLE HAVE LITTLE TIME TO REALLY ENJOY THEIR RECEPTION CAKE, SO SUGGEST MINIATURE TIERS FROM THE MAIN CAKE DESIGN, BEAUTIFULLY BOXED, FOR LATER.

31

CAKE PREPARATION

1 Place the top tier cake on the 8 cm/3 inch cake board. Trim the board with a craft knife or scalpel, if necessary, so the diameter is slightly less than the cake. Cover the cake with sugarpaste/rolled fondant right down over the edges of the board. Also cover the bottom tier cake with paste, while it is on a temporary board.

2 Cover the 15 cm/6 inch thin cake board with sugarpaste/rolled fondant. Embellish the edges with the double scalloped crimper. Attach sugar grosgrain ribbon to the edge of the board (see step 3). Centre the cake board on the china cake plate, and glue with royal icing. One day later, gradually ease a palette knife under the bottom cake and lift into position at the centre of the cake board. Custom measure, then cut and insert the dowels (see page 142). Add the top tier.

CAKE BASE DECORATION

3 Measure the base of each cake, then add an extra 1 cm/ $^1/_2$ inch. Cut two 3 cm/1$^1/_4$ inch wide strips of sugarpaste/ rolled fondant by the expanded circumference measurement, and emboss with the flower and leaf cutters. Brush the flowers with orchid-pink lustre dust and larkspur dust. Using lime-green dust, tint the flower centres and leaves (pic 1), and attach to each cake base. Remove overlapping paste. Emboss pink sugarpaste with the textured rolling pin. Cut 5 mm/$^1/_4$ inch strips and attach a strip above and below the floral side panels with gum glue, then brush with super pearl.

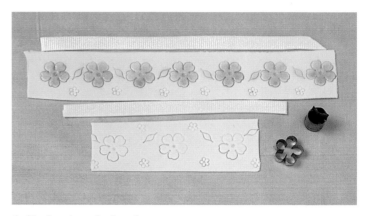

1 Embossing the band

THE BOW

4 Prepare the offset bow with pale pink sugarpaste/rolled fondant, using the same embossing technique as for the cake base. Cut two ribbon tails, each 13 x 15 cm/5 x 6 inches. Run the tracing wheel along the longer, base edge, to simulate stitching. Fold the sides under and gather the top edge. Cut 13 x 8 cm/5 x 3 inch strips from the remaining embossed paste, for the ribbon bow loops. Fold under the sides and pinch in the raw edges (pic 2). Attach the tails and bow loops to the cake, with the royal icing or edible gum glue. Support the bow pieces with sponge foam. To give a sense of movement, add some strips of sugar grosgrain ribbon, guiding them to follow the drape of the bow, then prop them up. Position the bow centre, and accent the edge with grosgrain ribbon.

2 Making an embossed bow

DECORATING THE CAKE BOARD

5 Using the flower cutter, cut out the blossoms from sugarpaste/rolled fondant. Place on a petal pad. Thin the edges with the Dresden tool, and press in the centre throat, using the veining tool. Turn the flowers upside down to dry in shape, or use a commercial drying rack. When dry, pipe a tiny dot of white royal icing into the flower centre and tint with orchid-pink lustre dust (pic 3). Attach to the cake board, with royal icing. Cut out the leaves with the leaf cutter. Brush with moss-green petal dust and attach in position with a water-dampened paintbrush.

3 Sets of flowers and leaves for cake board embellishment

CARNATION PREPARATION

6 Cut ten layers of petals from pale pink flower paste/gum paste, using the carnation cutter, and place under plastic wrap, to prevent drying out. Using a craft knife or scalpel, cut nicks into the petal edges, and ruffle them with the Dresden tool. Brush them with a combination of orchid-pink and cornflower-blue lustre dusts, adding tints of lime-green petal dust (pic 4). Partially dry the petals in a shallow celformer. Stack each layer on top of the other, propping with foam to separate. When the space at the top becomes very small, fold the final round in half, then in quarters/fourths, forming an S-shape. Fit into the space and tease the ruffled edges evenly with a soft paintbrush. It may be necessary to clip a little off the base, for uniform height. Attach to the top of the cake with royal icing or gum glue, and allow to dry.

4 Making the large carnation

THE BIRD

Create a small bird in the flower paste/gum paste, using the bird cutter. Brush with orchid-pink lustre dust. Mix a little of the orchid-pink lustre dust with clear alcohol/vodka or Everclear, and paint tiny dots on the body with the fine paintbrush (pic 5). Attach to the cake with a tiny dot of royal icing. Paint an orchid-pink lustre dust flourish beneath the bird, and another trailing away behind it.

5 Birds take flight

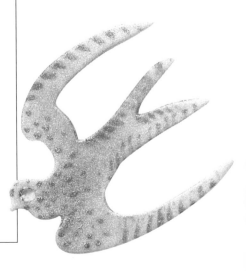

Picture Perfect Couture Cake

CAKE AND DECORATION

- 15 cm/6 inch, 25 cm/10 inch, 35 cm/ 14 inch and 40 cm/16 inch round cakes
- Small, round, moulded sugar vase (see pages 74–5)
- 750 g/1½ lb flower paste/gum paste and sugarpaste/rolled fondant in a 50:50 mixture
- 7 kg/14 lb champagne-ivory sugarpaste/ rolled fondant
- Super gold and antique silk lustre dusts (VB/CK)

EQUIPMENT

- Small jar
- Daisy button mould (J)
- Rose garland stencil – with small and large graduated pattern (CSD)
- Scallop-edged broderie anglais cutter (PME)
- 20-gauge wire
- White floral tape
- Sponge foam
- 15 cm/6 inch, 25 cm/10 inch and 35 cm/14 inch thin round cake boards
- 50 cm/20 inch round cake board
- Double open-scalloped crimper (PME)
- Veining tool
- Paintbrush
- Electric pasta machine (optional)
- Satay sticks/bamboo skewers
- 14 x 1 cm/½ inch dowel rods
- 5 x 5 mm/¼ inch dowel rods
- Double-sided lace mould (ELI)
- Varipin/Rosa's Roller (OP)
- Rose leaf cutters (OP – R6 and R6A)
- Cardboard former
- Long sharpened dowel rod

GLEAMING WITH GOLDEN HIGHLIGHTS, THIS GRACEFUL CAKE DUPLICATES THE LUSTRE OF FINE SILK. A DISTINCTIVE LAYERED OVER-SKIRT CASCADES FROM TIER TO TIER IN PERFECT SYMMETRY. GILDED, COILED ROSETTES ARRANGED IN A FRAGILE FLOUNCED VASE ADD ROMANTIC FLAIR TO THIS SPLENDID DECORATIVE DESIGN. MAGICAL SUGAR WITH A MIDAS TOUCH.

VASE PREPARATION

1 Prepare a moulded sugar vase (see pages 74–5), hollow out the centre and allow to dry. Turn the vase upside down on a small jar and attach two gathered panels of stencilled 50:50 flower paste/gum paste and sugarpaste/rolled fondant mixture, hiding the joins in overlapping folds and gluing the seams. Make bisque daisy buttons, and attach at the base. After drying overnight, carefully return to the upright position. Press a golf ball-sized piece of sugarpaste/rolled fondant into the hollowed-out, moulded sugar vase. Dry overnight.

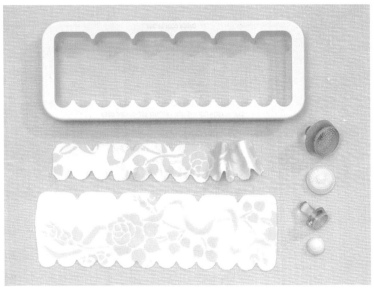

FANTASY FLOWER ROSETTES

2 Prepare the large flower rosettes for the centrepiece from the 50:50 mixture by stencilling the paste with the small stencil pattern. Cut two lengths, full width, with the broderie anglais cutter, pleat and circle each length into a rosette. Join the ends with edible gum glue, and insert the wire. When dry, wrap the wire with white floral tape.

3 To form the smaller rosettes, use just half the width of the broderie anglais cutter (pic 1). Proceed as above, without the wire. Make daisy button centres, dust with super gold, then add to all the flower rosettes (pic 2). Dip the flower stems in royal icing/buttercream; arrange and support them in the vase.

1 Paste cut to full and half widths by the broderie anglais cutter

PREPARING THE CAKES

4 Place all the cakes except the bottom tier on matching-sized, thin cake boards. Centre the bottom tier on greaseproof/waxed paper and place on a temporary cake board. Cover the 50 cm/20 inch round cake board with sugarpaste/rolled fondant, allow to crust overnight, and centre the bottom tier on it. This is easy to do by sliding the cake across from one board to the other, while pulling the greaseproof/waxed paper. Cover the cakes with paste, bringing it over the board edges. Form a pretty edge with the double scalloped crimper. Also crimp within the circle on the top tier. Add extra interest with the side of the veining tool. Paint the raised centre of the crimped edge with super gold lustre dust mixed with clear alcohol/vodka or Everclear.

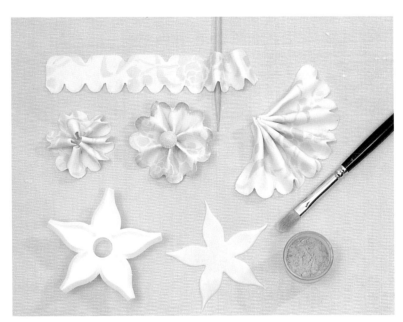

2 Fantasy flowers coming together

MAKING THE GATHERS

5 Measure the circumference of each cake and divide by five, marking the places to ensure accuracy when placing the swags later. Working on the bottom tier first, roll out the mixture of flower paste/gum paste and sugarpaste/rolled fondant. Cut out 9 x 30 cm/3¹/2 x 12 inch

sheets – using an electric pasta machine will save time (see page 143). If long pieces seem daunting, shorten the lengths.

6 Measure the depth of each tier and mark the rose garland stencil accordingly, to help keep the pattern repeat level. Press the paste sheet into the large rose garland stencil pattern, using a sponge. Turn over and brush with super gold lustre dust. Carefully remove the panel, then lay flat. Gather evenly, using satay sticks/bamboo skewers, then press down firmly at the top and glue to the cakes. Continue overlapping the panels until the last, which should be slipped under the first, forming a continuous skirt. Repeat for the second and third tiers, using the smaller rose garland stencil (pic 3).

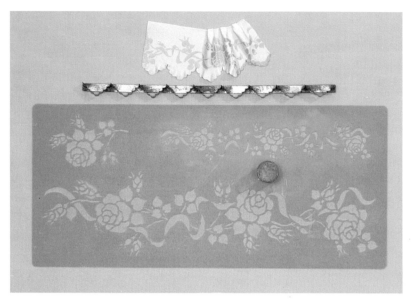

3 *Rose garland stencils and short gathers*

SUGGESTIONS FOR THE BRIDE

This cake was designed to be built in individual tiers, depending on the number of servings required. The top tier alone would serve about seventy-five guests with fruitcake but only sixteen if prepared with madeira or sponge/pound or white cake. As the guest list grows, add extra tiers. The visual effect will not be compromised.

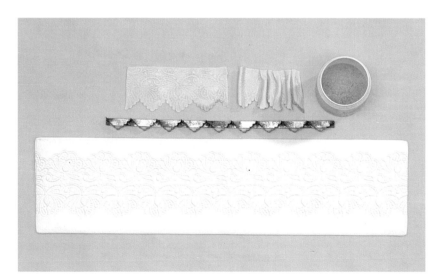

4 *Embossed lace, mould and lustre dust*

5 *Stencilled swag ready to attach*

STACKING THE CAKES

7 Using seven 1 cm/^{1}/$_2$ inch dowel rods each for the bottom and third tier and five 5 mm/^{1}/$_4$ inch ones for the second tier, push in a circle of dowel rods, to support the cakes when stacked (see page 142). Stack each ascending tier after inserting the dowels. Completely decorate each tier before adding the next.

LACE FLOUNCES

8 The top tier has two gathered rows of embossed lace. Roll out sheets of champagne-ivory sugarpaste/rolled fondant. Press into the lace mould with a dry sponge. Remove carefully. Cut into 30 x 8 cm/12 x 3 inch strips and brush with antique silk lustre dust (pic 4). Gather panels using a satay stick/bamboo skewer and attach to the side of the cake, with edible gum glue. Attach the first level of flounce at the centre of the cake and the second to the top, so they overlap. Add a dollop of buttercream or royal icing between each tier, to stop sliding. Paint the edges with super gold lustre dust and clear alcohol/ vodka or Everclear.

THE SWAGS

9 Stencil the swags, using the small pattern on the rose garland stencil. Graduate the lengths, according to the measurements taken on each cake, and fold the sides under (pic 5). Add the swags, taking care to line them up evenly. Paint the edges of the skirt with super gold lustre dust mixed with clear alcohol/vodka or Everclear. Experiment with the mixture to be sure it is thick enough to be visible – if there is too much alcohol, the edging will have no impact.

FABRIC-EFFECT LEAVES

10 Texture some sugarpaste/rolled fondant with the Varipin/Rosa's Roller. Cut the leaves in two sizes, with the rose leaf cutters. Brush with super gold lustre dust and attach immediately, using a slightly water-dampened paintbrush. Leave a few textured leaves to dry over the cardboard former (pic 6), to add extra

6 Textured leaves curled over the former

interest to the shape. Using royal icing, attach the dried leaves on the top tier, so the leaves curl back towards the centre of the cake. Centre a fantasy flower and leaves on each join where the swags meet.

FINISHING

11 Measure and hammer the long sharpened dowel through the three assembled tiers. Nip the top so the dowel does not protrude above the paste, using pruning shears kept specifically for this job. Keep the top tier separate and slip it on at the reception site, adding a little blob of royal icing under the board for security. Finally add the centrepiece.

SERVING SUGGESTIONS

If the completed cake is three tiers or more, pack the top tier and centrepiece separately and attach it at the reception site. Arrange for two people to carry the dowelled cake. When the cake is to be cut, break away the side decorations with a chef's knife before cutting to serve. Remember that the long lace mould is double sided, and the reverse was used for the side design on Pêche Belle La Russe (page 21). This is indeed excellent mileage from one product.

Valentine's Heart Sublime

Cake and Decoration

- 30 cm/12 inch heart-shaped cake
- 175 g/6 oz white flower paste/gum paste
- 30 g/1 oz moss-green sugarpaste/rolled fondant
- 3.5 kg/7 lb white sugarpaste/rolled fondant
- Super pearl lustre dust (VB/CK)
- 125 g/4 oz white flower paste/gum paste and sugarpaste/rolled fondant in a 50:50 mixture

Equipment

- Medium blossom cutter (OP – R2)
- Gardenia cutter set (NL)
- Veining or Dresden tool
- Sponge, for support
- Paper templates for gardenia leaf (see page 153)
- Leaf veiner
- 38 cm/15 inch cake board
- Varipin/Rosa's Roller (OP)
- Greaseproof/waxed paper
- Medium daisy button mould (J)
- Lace mould (SB – 8N395)
- Shallow, slightly curved dish
- Brocade cutter mould (RVO)
- Make-up sponge
- Dressmaker's tracing wheel

THERE IS NO MISTAKING THE MESSAGE THIS SUGAR-CLAD HEART EVOKES — AFFECTION, FLIRTATION AND LOVE'S PROMISE. THIS SWEET TREAT IS ENHANCED WITH A SINGLE GARDENIA TRIMMED WITH SATIN BIAS AND LOVELY TOUCHES OF LACE. SHINING WITH HIGH GLOSS PEARL, A SIMPLY CUT BOW WITH STREAMERS WRAPS AROUND THE SIDES OF THE HEART. PURE BLISS FROM CUPID'S CAKE STYLIST DEAR VALENTINE!

THE GARDENIA

1 Cut two sets of small white flower paste/gum paste blossoms with the medium blossom cutter, for the flower centre. Thin the edges and curl one side only inwards on each petal (pic 1). Furl into a rosette, then wrap the second set around the first.

2 Cut the small set of gardenia petals, and thin the edges. Run the veining or Dresden tool around the outer edge, forcing the petals upwards. Turn the petals back to the right side. Make two more petal sets, but with the larger gardenia cutter. Layer the petals by offsetting them and attaching with edible gum glue. Twist to add some movement and shape, then prop into position with the sponge. Finally add the rosette centre.

1 Gardenia whorls and leaves

FOLIAGE PLATE

3 Using the gardenia leaf template (see page 153), cut the four-point leaf 'plate' from moss-green sugarpaste/rolled fondant. Emboss each segment with the leaf veiner, pinch the tips together and set aside to dry flat. Glue the completed gardenia flower into the centre of the leaf.

PREPARING THE CAKE

4 Cover the cake board with white sugarpaste/rolled fondant and texture the surface edge with the Varipin/Rosa's Roller, then set aside to dry. Meanwhile position the cake on greaseproof/waxed paper. Paint a little edible gum glue into the centre of the prepared cake board. Cover the cake with white sugarpaste/rolled fondant and slide on to the cake board. Carefully trim the greaseproof/waxed paper.

BANDS AND SCALLOPS

5 For the continuous 'bias' bands at the base of the cake, cut three 90 x 10 cm/36 x 4 inch strips of white sugarpaste/rolled fondant. Attach with edible gum glue, beginning and ending at the centre back of the cake. Trim neatly, and brush with super pearl lustre dust. Cover the join with medium rounded buttons, made from paste using the daisy button mould.

6 Divide and mark each cake side in three even scallops, using a scalloped arc. Angle each one slightly down to the front. Cut 15 x 2.5 cm/6 x 1 inch strips of white sugarpaste/ rolled fondant and brush with super pearl lustre dust. Fold in half and coax into a gentle curve, then glue to the cake, following the scalloped arc.

LACE DECORATION

7 To make the side decoration, brush the inside of the lace mould with super pearl lustre dust. Roll out a thick piece of the white flower paste/gum paste and sugarpaste/rolled

fondant paste mixture. Press into the mould,
cover and press firmly with a rolling pin.
Remove the excess paste, tidy the edges, then
freeze. Remove from the mould, and cut out
the accent eyelets. Attach to the cake side,
slightly overlapping the scallop decorations.
Fill any spaces between joins with little lace
pieces. Done carefully and with thought, the
lace decoration will appear seamless.

8 For the top, prepare three more lace pieces,
keeping one flat for the top of the cake, at the
front. Place the other two in the shallow,
slightly curved dish, to dry (pic 2). Attach
securely at the back of the cake, with the
gardenia centrepiece placed between.

2 Curved lace decoration with bands and scallops

BROCADE

9 Roll out fairly thin, very firm flower paste/gum paste.
Brush the brocade cutter mould with super pearl lustre dust,
then press the paste into the mould with a make-up sponge.
Roll across the cutting edge with the rolling pin, then remove
the piece from the mould. Lay flat to dry. Fit these brocade
pieces end to end around the edge of the board and cake top,
attaching with edible gum glue.

THE BOW

10 Cut three 20 x 10 cm/8 x 4 inch strips of white
sugarpaste/rolled fondant. Diagonally trim the tails of two
strips, then turn the side edges under all of them. Brush with
super pearl lustre dust, and run the
dressmaker's tracing wheel along the
edge of each, to simulate stitching
(pic 3). Position the bow tails on the
back of the cake and drape across
the board slightly, curving around
the edge of the cake and attaching
with edible gum glue. Split the
remaining strip evenly, then fold in
half and cut in the centre. Pinch the
ends together and attach with edible
gum glue at the back of the cake.
Cover the join with a gathered and
glued knot of super pearl-dusted,
white flower paste/gum paste.

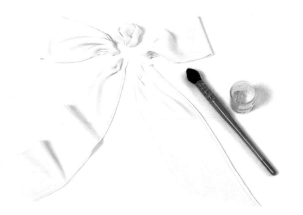

3 Putting the bow together

Romancing the Dome

CAKE AND DECORATION

- 15 cm/6 inch, 20 cm/8 inch, 30 cm/12 inch and 40cm/16 inch round cakes
- 7 kg/14 lb pale ivory sugarpaste/rolled fondant (50:50 white and ivory mixed)
- 125 g/4 oz white flower paste/gum paste
- 30 g/1 oz moss-green flower paste/ gum paste
- Super pearl and avocado lustre dusts (VB/CK)
- 10 ivory roses (see pages 94 and 119)
- 10 blue hydrangeas (see page 28)
- Buttercup petal dust (VB/CK)

EQUIPMENT

- 15 cm/6 inch polystyrene/styrofoam ball
- 15 cm/6 inch, 20 cm/8 inch and 30 cm/12 inch thin round cake boards
- Two 40 cm/16 inch round cake boards
- 45 cm/18 inch round cake board
- Ivory ribbon, to trim cake board
- Pale blue dupioni silk
- Parsley cutter
- Lace rose mould (SB – 8F955)
- Medium paintbrush
- Rose leaf cutter (OP – R5)
- Natural or commercial rose leaf veiner
- Sliver leaf cutter (RVO)
- Plunger cutters (PME or OP – F2M and F2L)
- Pointed-tipped large blossom cutter (RL)
- Ball tool
- Large tea rose cutter (PC)
- Checked stencil (CSD)
- Satay stick/bamboo skewer
- Dowelling (see page 142)
- Daisy button centre (J)
- Long sharpened dowel

IMPERIAL DOMES CROWN MOST OF THE GREAT CITIES OF THE WORLD. THEY HAVE ALWAYS REMINDED ME OF THE ULTIMATE WEDDING CAKE. OUT OF A SOFT SUMMER SKY COMES THIS ROMANTIC INTERPRETATION. IMPOSING CAKE LAYERS ARE TRIMMED WITH RICH RIBBON TAPES AND CHECKED SATIN PLEATS. CREAMY WHITE TEA ROSES AT THE SIDE ARE ACCENTED BY DAINTY BLUE HYDRANGEAS.

PREPARING THE CAKES

1 Cut the polystyrene/styrofoam ball in half and attach with royal icing to the 15 cm/6 inch thin round cake board. Cover each cake with pale ivory sugarpaste/rolled fondant and centre the top three tiers on identically sized thin round cake boards. Glue two 40 cm/16 inch cake boards together and attach the pale blue dupioni silk to the 45 cm/18 inch cake board, using spray adhesive. Make sure each board is very secure before adding the cake. Centre the bottom cake on the board, using royal icing as the gluing agent.

THE DOME AND TOP TIER

2 Centre the dome on top of the upper tier and glue together with a generous spoonful of royal icing or buttercream. Measure the depth of the ball and the depth of the top tier cake, then divide the circumference into eighths.

3 Prepare 5 mm/1/4 inch strips of sugarpaste/rolled fondant with the parsley cutter, and attach eight pairs to the surface of the dome and the cake sides. Cover the joins at the dome top with the moulded lace rose, brushed with super pearl lustre dust (pic 1). Using the double strips of ribbon as the centre guide, decorate an inverted 'V' of tiny, small and medium blossoms and foliage.

1 Moulded rose dome accent

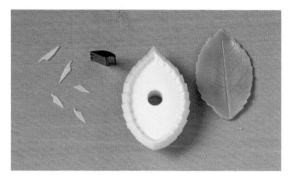

2 Stages of rose and miniature leaves

FOLIAGE

Make large rose leaves from moss-green flower paste/gum paste, using the rose leaf cutter, then vein them with a natural or commercial rose leaf and brush with avocado lustre dust (pic 2). Dry fairly flat before attaching between the second and third tiers. Attach one leaf on each side of where a rose will sit, using royal icing. Make tiny pale ivory leaves with the leaf sliver cutter or cut them freehand; brush with super pearl dust and attach with royal icing.

FLOWERS

The template and instructions for hydrangea flowers are given on pages 28 and 152, and for the rose on page 94. Attach the hydrangeas between the rose leaves, then sit the roses on top. Make the flowers for the dome and decorative accents elsewhere with the plunger cutters and the pointed-tipped large blossom cutter (pic 3). Having cut them out, soften the edges and press in the centre throat with the ball tool. Attach to the cake with royal icing or push directly into the cake.

3 Making hydrangea and filler flowers

THE SECOND TIER

4 Measure the depth of the second tier plus 8 cm/3 inches, and cut 5 mm/1/4 inch strips with the parsley cutter, then brush with super pearl lustre dust. Extend the ribbons 8 cm/3 inches over the top and down over the cake sides, and attach. This cake needs seventy strips.

THE THIRD TIER

5 Very thinly roll out the white flower paste/gum paste and drape over the cutting edge of the large tea rose cutter. Press in gently with a sponge (pic 4) and leave to stand for a minute to set, then turn right side up and cut down. Let the paste remain in the cutter for another minute, then turn out on to the work surface.

6 When fairly firm, brush with super

4 Pressing paste into the cutter

5 Dusting the appliqué roses

pearl lustre dust (pic 5) and highlight the rose with buttercup petal dust. Without disturbing the puffed effect, attach immediately to the side of the third tier. At the top and base of the rose appliqué, add three medium blossoms.

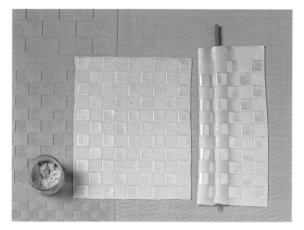

6 Adding lustre before forming the pleats

THE BOTTOM TIER

7 Cover the dupioni silk on the 45 cm/18 inch cake board with plastic wrap before making the pleats. Roll out the sugarpaste/rolled fondant and press on to the checked stencil. Brush with super pearl lustre dust. With a light touch, cut 15 x 15 cm/6 x 6 inch square panels while still on the stencil. Peel away and form into uniform pleats with the satay stick/bamboo skewer (pic 6). Attach the panels to the bottom cake with gum glue (see page 143).

HOLLOW TUBE DECORATION

8 Measure the spaces between the paired paste ribbons in the top tiers. Stencil thin strips of paste, using the checked stencil (pic 7). Form around the dowel, pressing down to close the join. Cut and attach a tube between the ribbons. Make daisy button centres to cover the joins on all the tiers.

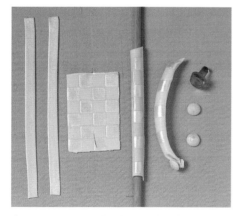

7 Stages of the hollow tube decoration

ASSEMBLY

9 Dowel (see page 142) and stack the three lower cakes for transportation. Add the top tier at the reception. This cake will be very heavy, so, if the cake stylist is delivering alone, box the tiers separately. Pack the roses and prepare the hollow tubes and daisy centres at the last minute, cover with plastic wrap and seal in a plastic container. Attach the hollow tubes, leaves, hydrangeas and roses with royal icing when the cakes are finally assembled on the table of honour. Alternatively, instead of the hollow tubes, simply pipe borders around the cakes.

Tiers in a Teacup

CAKE AND DECORATION

- 8 cm/3 inch round cake, 5 cm/2 inches deep
- 5 cm/2 inch round cake, 4.5 cm/1³/4 inches deep
- 2.5 cm/1 inch round cake, 3 cm/1¹/4 inches deep
- 500 g/1 lb sugarpaste/rolled fondant
- Super gold lustre dust (VB/CK)
- Gold highlight powder (VB/CK)
- Pale blue, lavender, yellow and pale green food colourings
- Rubine and cerise petal dusts (OP)
- 55 g/2 oz flower paste/gum paste
- Moss-green and pale lemon petal dusts (VB/CK)

EQUIPMENT

- Plastic drink coaster or lace doily
- 10 cm/4 inch cake board
- Shell tool (J)
- 2 x tiny foil-covered thin round cake boards
- Three-piece tea set
- Satay stick/bamboo skewer
- Posy mould (SB – 4662)
- 18 x 0 line brush
- Miniature rose leaf cutter (OP – R16)
- Tiny flower cutters (RVO)
- Small centre from the Garrett frill set (OP – GF3) or round paper template (see page 153)
- Oval paper template (see page 153)
- Ovate, pointed leaf cutter (RVO)
- Medium blossom cutter (OP – F2L)
- Veining tool
- Quilting pin
- Electric pasta machine (optional)

TINY TIERS PERCHED ON TEA-SET PLACE SETTINGS MAKE AN ALTERNATIVE CHOICE TO THE RECEPTION WEDDING CAKE. WEAVING NEW TRENDS INTO AGE-OLD TRADITION, SOME COUPLES ARE NOW OPTING FOR THESE DRAMATIC INDIVIDUAL DESSERTS. CREATE YOUR OWN TINY TEACUP CAKES, MATCHING DIFFERENT PATTERNS TO SEASONAL OCCASIONS, AND LET YOUR DESIGNER SPIRIT FLY.

PREPARING THE CAKES

1 Emboss some sugarpaste/rolled fondant with a lace pattern, using the plastic coaster or doily (pic 1). Cover the cake board with lace-embossed paste. Paint with super gold lustre dust and gold highlight powder mixed with clear alcohol/vodka or Everclear. Bind the edge with a strip of sugarpaste/rolled fondant and emboss with the shell tool. Centre the paste-covered bottom cake on the board.

2 Make a foil-covered, thin round cake board for the middle tier a smidgen smaller than the cake's diameter, and another for the top tier. Position each cake on the appropriate board. Colour some sugarpaste/ rolled fondant to match the tea set, although this may prove difficult because the colour of white china and porcelain varies tremendously – some having a really creamy cast while other varieties look quite blue. Kneading in the tiniest touch of blue was a good choice for the colour match here. Cover the cakes, bringing the paste right down over the edge of the foil-covered boards. Stack the cakes, putting a little dab of royal icing or buttercream between each tier. Push a satay stick/bamboo skewer through the centre of all three. Clip off flush with the top.

1 Lace-embossed paste covering for the cake board

2 Moulding the miniature floral centrepiece

DECORATIVE VARIATION

Miniature cakes such as this two-sided one are especially popular with the New York élite. If there is plenty of preparation time and only a few are required, make the cake in its entirety. If not and the order is for up to 200 cakes, put the back design on the front and leave the back undecorated – a simple, effective and time-saving solution. Make sure the cake is facing out from the table when serving. Each cake will serve two people and can be shared. Place on the table between each couple if this is the case.

FLORAL CENTREPIECE

3 Prepare the miniature flower centrepiece, using the posy mould (pic 2). Paint the predominant flowers with rubine and cerise petal dusts mixed with clear alcohol/vodka or Everclear. Using the line brush, decorate the remaining flowers with lavender, yellow and pale blue food colourings mixed with clear alcohol (pic 3).

4 Prepare miniature pointed leaves with flower paste/gum paste, using the rose leaf cutter. When dry, hand paint the leaves with

3 Paint palette indicating centrepiece colours

4 Creating the side floral design

moss-green. Attach the leaves to the cake top in two overlapping rings, using edible gum glue. Add the posy mould and fill in the space at the side with tiny lavender, yellow and blue flowers to match the china.

SIDE FLORAL DESIGN

5 Check the centre of the middle tier and mark a circle, using the small centre from the Garrett frill set or the round paper template (see page 153). Beneath this circular decoration, centre and mark the oval floral decoration on the bottom tier (see template on page 153). Prepare pale mint-coloured, ovate leaves in flower paste/gum paste, with the ovate, pointed leaf cutter. Use these to create an outer rim of leaves on the circular and oval marks. For the middle rim, make leaves of the same shape but darker moss-green in colour, and pinch the tips together (pic 4). For the inner rim, attach tiny leaves, made with the miniature rose leaf cutter, coloured with moss-green dust and highlighted with pale lemon dust.

6 Fill the remaining space with miniature roses. For the rose centre, roll up a small strip of flower paste/gum paste, rubbing 2.5 mm/^{1}/$_8$ inch from the strip top, till the short end falls off. Cut four paste flowers with the medium blossom cutter. Thin the edges and stack three on top of each other, offsetting the petals each time. Press together in the centre with the veining tool. Cut the last blossom in two, so there are three petals in one unit and two in the other. Wrap the rose centre with two petals, then use edible gum glue to attach the remaining three, offsetting them, into the flower base. Moisten the rose centre base and push into the flower, using the quilting pin. Brush liberally with rubine and cerise dusts (pic 5).

5 Making miniature roses

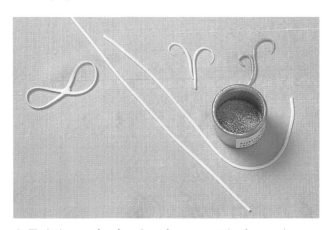

6 Twisting and colouring the paste strip decoration

FINISHING OFF

7 Cut and run a thin strip of sugarpaste/rolled fondant around the base of each cake. Also prepare two bow loops and tails. Attach these at the base of the top tier, curling the tails on to the cake board. Cover the join with a single rose, miniature blossoms and foliage. The lower tiers look prettier and more delicate with just a single blossom and two miniature rose leaves covering the join. Accent the centre designs with thin rolled scrolls of sugarpaste/rolled fondant or flower paste/gum paste painted with gold highlight powder and clear alcohol/vodka or Everclear.

8 To prevent the cake from slipping on the china, form a thin paste rope and attach with edible gum glue to the inner mouth of the cup. Dry overnight. Place the cake on top of the tea place setting at the reception.

All that Glitters

CAKE AND DECORATION

- 15 cm/6 inch, 20 cm/8 inch and 30 cm/12 inch round cakes
- 6 kg/12 lb white sugarpaste/rolled fondant
- Super gold and super pearl lustre dusts (VB/CK)
- 30 g/1 oz white flower paste/gum paste

EQUIPMENT

- 15 cm/6 inch, 20 cm/8 inch and 30 cm/12 inch thin round cake boards
- Square-patterned embossing tool or similar (see step 1)
- Paper templates for side design (see page 153)
- Fine and medium paintbrushes
- 4 mm and 6 mm beadmaker (CK)
- Medium blossom cutter (RL)
- Dressmaker's tracing wheel
- Quilting pin
- Veining tool
- Lace cutter
- Miniature blossom cutter
- 38 cm/15 inch round cake board
- White ribbon, to trim 38 cm/15 inch round cake board
- 6 x 1 cm/¹/₂ inch dowel rods
- 5 x 5mm/¹/₄ inch dowel rods
- Long sharpened dowel rod

FOR A LANDMARK WEDDING, WHEN ONLY THE GRANDEST CAKE WILL DO. DRESSED WITH DRAMATIC GOLD SCROLLS, PRECIOUS SUGARED PEARLS AND DAINTY CORONET, THIS IS SURELY A CAKE FIT FOR A QUEEN! WATCH HER FACE GLOW WITH PLEASURE WHEN SHE SEES THIS RICH SCULPTED FANTASY WITH ORNATE BAROQUE DETAIL. DELICIOUS EDIBLE MEMORIES CERTAIN TO PROVOKE COMMENT!

PREPARING THE CAKES

1 Freeze the cakes overnight. Sculpt the top and bottom tiers identically, with a very sharp knife, by paring 1 cm/1/2 inch from the base of each cake graduating up to the top – cut nothing from the top edge. Check to see all sides are even by spinning on a turntable. For the middle tier, carve from the base upwards and the top downwards, creating a gradual curve and forming a waist 1 cm/1/2 inch deep. Do not remove excessive amounts of cake, because it doesn't take much to alter the silhouette (see page 140). Centre each tier on a matching-sized thin cake board, then cover each cake with sugarpaste/rolled fondant. Immediately emboss a circle of repeat square patterns into the upper edge surface of the top and bottom tiers, using any decorative embossing tool such as a decorative cutlery/flatware handle, button or commercial embossing tool (pic 1).

2 Divide the middle tier into six panels and the bottom tier into twelve. Measure the circumference of the top and bottom cakes with adding machine tape if preferred. Mark the divisions on the tape. Prick each division point with a pin, to act as a guide.

1 Embossed paste and tool

TOP AND BOTTOM TIER SIDE DESIGN

3 Knead, hand roll and mould sugarpaste/rolled fondant scrolls, C-shapes and teardrops. Using the side design templates (see page 153), draw the scroll and C-shapes on a sheet of paper, making sure they fit into the appropriate panels. Use this as a guide to mould each piece so they are a uniform shape. Prepare the teardrops freehand.

4 Paint the moulded pieces using super gold lustre dust mixed with clear alcohol (pic 2). Be careful not to over-paint on to the cake surface or leave fingerprints; over-paint mistakes can be rectified by repainting with pure Everclear and a clean brush. (Everclear does not leave a hole in the paste, nor will there be shiny marks.) Glue the shapes in a repeat pattern on the sides of both cakes (see page 145).

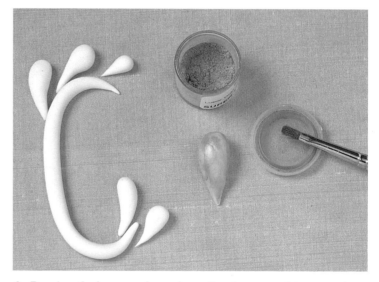

2 Dusting C-shapes and teardrops for the top and bottom tiers

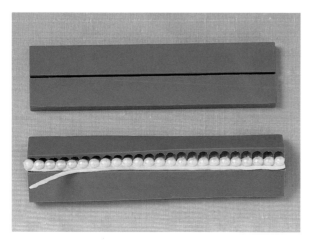

3 Pearl beads in the beadmaker

PEARLS

5 First brush the inside of the beadmaker with super pearl lustre dust. Insert a thick rope of white flower paste/gum paste. Push in firmly and press down over the closure with a rolling pin. Open the mould (pic 3) and tease out the pearls with a palette knife. Cut the bead strips to size. Trim the excess strip with fine scissors.

6 Outline the moulded scrolls and C-shapes on the top tier with 4 mm pearls and on the bottom tier with 6 mm pearls (pic 4), and attach with edible gum glue. Cut out and impress medium blossom flowers into the flower paste/gum paste within the pattern border. Finish off with 16 mm/⅝ inch hand-moulded pearls on the bottom tier.

MIDDLE TIER

7 Measure the depth of the cake. Cut strips of white sugarpaste/rolled fondant 3 cm/1¼ inches wide by the cake depth. Following the line of a ruler, run the dressmaker's tracing wheel down the centre of each. Glue the panels lightly to the cake. (This cake was not measured because it is unimportant how wide the final strip is for the front. The last one is always narrow. If by miscalculation a wider slot appears, split it with an extra row of pearls and add two rows of buttons.) Cover each join with a vertical strip of pearls.

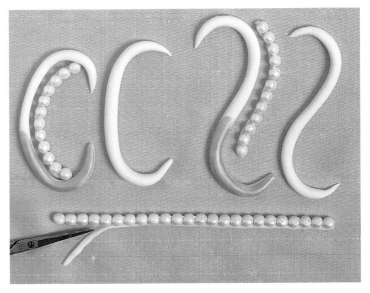

4 Further decorative stages of the scrolls, C-shapes and pearls

5 Painting floral jewellery

FLORAL JEWELLERY

8 For the moment, forget that flower paste/gum paste is always prepared paper thin, and cut out thick paste flowers with the medium blossom cutter. Prick the entire surface with the quilting pin and press in a throat with the veining tool. Paint with super gold lustre dust mixed with clear alcohol/vodka or Everclear (pic 5). Make another strip of pearls and cut them apart with scissors. Attach single pearls to the centre of each 'flower' with gum glue.

CORONET

9 Cut a 18 x 5 cm/7 x 2 inch strip of flower paste/gum paste, then run the lace cutter along one side (pic 6). Allow to firm up for a few minutes. Guide the paste into a small circle using a small tin/can (anything round with a straight edge). Seal the join with a dab of edible gum glue. Attach a thin strip of paste to the base. Paint the edges of the lace with super gold lustre dust mixed with clear alcohol/vodka or Everclear. Carefully attach handmade 2 mm/1/16 inch baby pearls to each of the coronet points, using royal icing. On top of these, add tiny super gold and clear alcohol painted miniature blossoms, each cupping freehand teardrop pearls (pic 7).

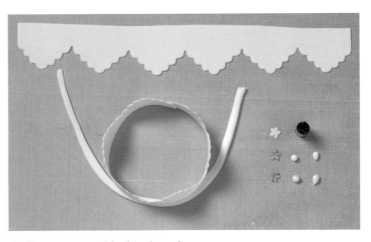

6 Coronet assembly for the cake top

7 Coronet: bird's eye view

EMBELLISHMENT

10 On the centre tier, fit a tiny puffed swag of sugarpaste/rolled fondant between each row of vertical pearls at the top, and cover the join with gold floral jewellery (pic 8).

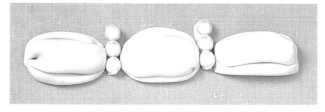

8 Puffed swags with pearl stations

ASSEMBLY

11 Cover the 38 cm/15 inch round cake board with sugarpaste/rolled fondant and band with white ribbon. Edge with 6 mm pearls. Centre the bottom tier on the board.

12 Dowel each tier and stack (see page 142). Sharpen the long dowel and measure alongside the lower two cakes, cut and hammer in centrally. (Normally the dowel would be hammered through all tiers; however, since the top of the cake can be seen through the coronet it would not be visually practical.) Attach the top tier with royal icing. Seal the top and bottom tiers with 6 mm pearl rope borders.

13 Add puffed swags and floral jewellery to the base of the middle tier. Attach gold floral jewellery between the embossed squares on the top cake surface. Glue the coronet on to the top tier, or carry separately to the reception site and then place in position. (Ask the caterers to pack it for the bride once the cake is served.)

SERVING SUGGESTIONS

Before serving, instruct the caterers to remove the heavy scrollwork and beads with a sharp chef's knife. Photocopy the cake cutting chart provided on page 138 and hand to the caterers for a suggested serving procedure.

Marquise de Pompadour

CAKE AND DECORATION

- 15 cm/6 inch, 20 cm/8 inch, 25 cm/10 inch and 30 cm/12 inch oval cakes
- 5 kg/10 lb ivory sugarpaste/rolled fondant
- Aztec-gold, super pearl, oyster and antique silk lustre dusts (VB/CK)
- 15 ml/3 tsp gelatine
- 15 ml/3 tsp Karo syrup or liquid glucose
- 500 g/1 lb ivory flower paste/gum paste

EQUIPMENT

- Piece of costume jewellery or commercial mould if available
- Model magic, latex or silicone
- Kingston cutter former (TOB)
- Medium-sized paintbrush
- Kingston cutters (TOB – medium set)
- 38 cm/15 inch oval cake board
- Ivory ribbon, 1 cm/¹⁄₂ inch wide, to trim 38 cm/15 inch cake board
- 15 cm/6 inch, 20 cm/8 inch, 25 cm/10 inch and 30 cm/12 inch thin oval cake boards
- Brocade-textured rolling pin (RVO)
- Lace cutter (FMM – M8)
- Dressmaker's tracing wheel
- Satay stick/bamboo skewer
- 19 x 5 mm/¹⁄₄ inch dowel rods
- Grosgrain-textured rolling pin (EC)
- Sponge foam (optional)
- 3 mm beadmaker (CK)
- Long sharpened dowel rod
- Veining or Dresden tool
- Moulded floral centre cutter (SB – 4662)
- Oval biscuit cutter/cookie cutter (W)

INSPIRED BY THE LAVISH EIGHTEENTH-CENTURY LIFESTYLE OF THE MARQUISE DE POMPADOUR, THIS WEDDING CAKE PAYS TRIBUTE TO SOME OF THE SPECIAL THINGS SHE LOVED: JEWELLERY, BOWS AND ROSETTES. ELEGANT BEYOND BELIEF, THE MARQUISE MADE THE BOW AND ARTIFICIAL FLOWERS HER TRADEMARK; BOTH ARE AS COMPLEMENTARY TO CAKE DESIGN AS THEY ARE TO FASHION.

COSTUME JEWELLERY

1 Create a mould of the chosen piece of costume jewellery, using the model magic, latex or silicone – the last was used in this project (pic 1). Press the sugarpaste/rolled fondant firmly into the mould, then freeze. Remove from the freezer and pop out, right side up, on to a non-stick surface. The paste will sweat a little, but don't touch the surface; just allow it to dry naturally. Trim any excess paste from the edges with a craft knife, scalpel or scissors. Lay on the upper edge of the Kingston former so each piece has a slightly convex shape that conforms to the rose leaf side designs. Dry, then paint with lustre dusts mixed with clear alcohol/vodka or Everclear, using aztec-gold lustre dust for the central 'golden topaz', super pearl lustre dust on the bezel stone surround and oyster lustre dust on the outer 'stones'. Dissolve the gelatine in 30 ml/6 tsp cold water,

1 Handmade sugar costume jewellery

then leave it to sit for 10 minutes until it is spongy, then microwave for a few seconds to liquefy. Add the Karo syrup or liquid glucose, and sit the container in a hot water bath (au bain-marie). Do not cook the mixture, just melt it. Paint the paste jewellery quickly, with the medium-sized brush. Reheat if the mixture begins to thicken and gel.

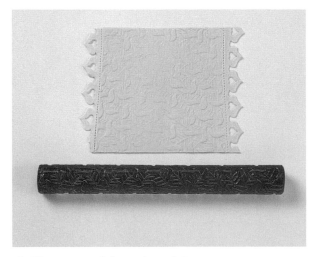

2 Stylized rose leaves, former and cutters

3 First stage of the embossed drapes

2 Roll out the flower paste/gum paste quite thinly and cut the side designs using the Kingston cutters (pic 2). Lay on the Kingston former and dry overnight. For uniformity of curve, make one rose leaf, dry it and rotate it as the first on each former as a guide. Paint with antique silk lustre dust mixed with clear alcohol/vodka or Everclear. Glue the jewelled piece on to the rounded upper end of the rose leaf side design, with royal icing. Set aside until ready to attach to the cake sides.

PREPARING THE CAKES

3 Cover the 38 cm/15 inch cake board with sugarpaste/rolled fondant and set aside to dry overnight. Cover the edge with matching ivory ribbon. Centre and glue each cake on the matching-sized, thin oval cake boards, then cover with paste, bringing it right down over the edge of each board. Centre the bottom tier on the 38 cm/15 inch cake board, securing with a blob of royal icing or a flattened sticky piece of sugarpaste/rolled fondant.

THE DRAPES

4 Prepare four 23 x 23 cm/9 x 9 inch squares of sugarpaste/rolled fondant, using a brocade-textured rolling pin. Thin the edges with a smooth rolling pin. Brush the entire piece with antique silk lustre dust. Embellish the edges with the lace cutter, and run a stitching line with the tracing wheel (pic 3). Brush over the edges with oyster lustre dust. Gather into folds using the satay stick/bamboo skewer (pic 4) and lay carefully on the bottom tier cake. Be alert: the lace pieces can distort

very quickly if you are not paying attention. Pull the corners into a central point at the sides and rest them on the cake board. Flatten the folds where the next tier will sit. Coax the edges into a gentle folded curve with a fluffy paintbrush. Cover the corners with fan-shaped, lace-edged, matching drapes, then highlight with pieces of the paste costume jewellery.

STACKING THE CAKES

5 Insert seven 5 mm/^{1}/4 inch dowels into the bottom tier cake (see page 142), following its oval shape. Add the next tier as quickly as possible, because the drapes will crack under the weight of the cake if the sugarpaste/rolled fondant dries too hard. Add a 5 mm/^{1}/4 inch band of grosgrain-textured ribbon paste around this third tier cake, using the grosgrain-textured rolling pin. Seal with a small piped bead of ivory royal icing.

4 Second stage of the embossed drape

(Note that the piping on this tier will not be straight because of the flow of the sugar drape.) Attach the jewellery pieces to the rose leaf side designs, with royal icing. As they are top heavy and inclined to slide a little, make sure they aren't slipping before moving on to the next jewellery piece – or support with pieces of foam.

6 Add five 5 mm/^{1}/4 inch dowels to the third tier cake, once again following its oval shape. Position the second tier and add the grosgrain-textured ribbons, beads and side designs, as in step 5. Then dowel the second tier cake, centre the top cake on it and decorate the sides, as for the other tiers. Hammer the long sharpened dowel through the centre of the cakes, to stop them slipping (see page 142).

ADVICE TO BEGINNERS

After adding the four top drapes, lightly cover the upper surface of the bottom tier cake with plastic wrap to slow the drying rate. This will give you time to arrange the sides, add the second tier cake, then the fanned corner drape and jewellery.

RUFFLED ROSETTE

7 Cut a 38 x 2.5 cm/15 x 1 inch strip of sugarpaste/rolled fondant or flower paste/gum paste. Trim one side with the lace cutter and frill the edge with the veining or Dresden tool. Gather the edges gently on the unfrilled side, gradually curving into a circle and drawing into the centre (pic 5). Cover the centre with a moulded floral posy. Attach to the ruffled rosette, then brush the whole piece with antique silk lustre dust, and highlight the edges with oyster lustre dust.

BOWS

8 Prepare the grosgrain-textured bows on the front and rear of the bottom tier by texturing some sugarpaste/rolled fondant, using the grosgrain-textured rolling pin. Cut four pieces 4.5 x 13 cm/1³/₄ x 5 inches, pinch each in at the centre, and attach with royal icing, for the loops. To make the tails, cut eight pieces 4.5 x 18 cm/1³/₄ x 7 inches, pinch each in at one end, and attach. Make sure the royal icing holding the ribbon loops and tails in place is dry before adding the paste jewellery on the bow centre at the front and the ruffled rosette at the back – there is a lot of weight accumulating here.

5 Ruffled rosettes and equipment

DOMED JEWELLERY BOX

9 Cut out an ivory flower paste/gum paste base, using the biscuit cutter/cookie cutter. Roll out another piece of paste with the brocade-textured rolling pin. Brush the surface with antique silk lustre dust, then drape over the sharp side of the cutter and leave it for 10–15 minutes (pic 6). Turn it over and cut down hard. Do not touch the dome for an hour or so, until it is set. Measure the circumference of the oval; this will be the length. Cut a 2 cm/³/₄ inch strip by the length measurement, and use it to edge the oval base, cutting neatly at the back and joining all seams with minute dabs of water. When completely dry, add an edging of 3 mm sugar pearls around the domed top and to the box top and base. Brush the beads with antique silk lustre dust.

TRANSPORTING THE CAKE

10 If this cake is too heavy to be carried completely assembled, stack the bottom two tiers and box them. Position the dowels in the next tier and box this and the top tier separately. Temporarily leave off the side designs at both ends of each cake, so there is room for the offset spatulas to be inserted while manoeuvring the cake into position. At the reception, centre the cake into position, pipe the upper borders and add the missing side designs. Wait a few minutes before leaving to be sure the side designs are firmly attached.

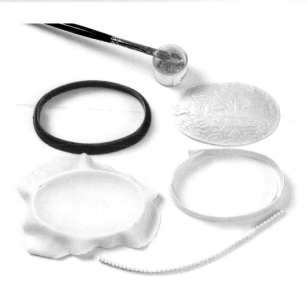

6 Sugar pieces for the domed jewellery box

Tussie Mussie – Vintage Glamour

BOUQUET HOLDER AND DECORATION
- Cream horn former or ice-cream cone
- Cornflour/cornstarch
- 55 g/2 oz white flower paste/gum paste
- Super pearl lustre dust (VB/CK)

EQUIPMENT
- Parchment paper
- Paper template for bouquet holder (see page 154)
- Eyelet cutter (RVO)
- Linen-like fabric, textured rolling pin or lace plastic doily
- Lacy decoration (see step 2)
- Veining tool
- Sponge or cotton wool/cotton balls
- Lace mould (RVO)
- 24-gauge wire
- Rippled foam pieces

The word 'tussie' refers to the bouquet, and 'mussie' to the moss that kept the flowers moist. Tussie mussie holders were mostly made of silver plate and sterling silver, although some were of mother-of-pearl. With the current nostalgia for times past, it seemed appropriate to include this romantic symbol of a bygone era. Indeed, mothers of the bride already commonly carry tussie mussies at prestigious weddings in the United States. This reproduction vintage bouquet holder will hold a petite bouquet that will also make a perfect and unusual cake top.

TUSSIE MUSSIES ARE SMALL POSY HOLDERS AND WERE ORIGINALLY CARRIED BY FORMAL LADIES OF FASHION IN THE VICTORIAN ERA. THESE TINY CONE-SHAPED VASES, FILLED WITH FRAGRANT BOUQUETS, WERE HELD IN THE HAND, MAKING A STROLL IN THE STREET MORE AROMATICALLY PLEASANT.

BASIC TUSSIE MUSSIE CONE

1 Wrap a cream horn former or ice-cream cone with parchment paper and dust with cornflour/cornstarch. Roll out the flower paste/gum paste and cut out the bouquet holder template with a craft knife or scalpel. Decorate the edge of the paste with the

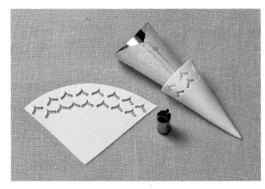

1 Basic paste cone preparation

eyelet cutter, then wrap around the former, overlapping slightly at the back (pic 1). Barely dampen the join with edible gum glue and press firmly together. Brush with super pearl lustre dust, then turn upside down on the former to dry.

2 When the cone is firm enough to handle without collapsing, emboss a strip of flower paste/gum paste with any linen-like fabric or even with a textured rolling pin or lace plastic doily. Fold the embossed paste in half and attach to the inside wall of the cone (pic 2), checking that it is all the same width. Emboss a 5 mm/ ¼ inch strip of flower paste/gum paste on some lacy decoration such as the brass metal strip used here. Cover the rough edge of the join on the paste cone with the embossed paste strip. Brush completely with super pearl lustre dust.

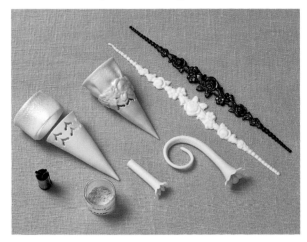

2 Assembly of the decorative stages required

THE HANDLE

3 Prepare a 5 mm/¹/4 inch log of flower paste/gum paste. Hollow out one end, using the veining tool, then flatten the hollowed-out end and cut eight pointed petals with scissors. Thin them between the thumb and forefinger. Taper the other end to a point and curl round. (If preferred, leave the handle straight, and shorter.) Using the sponge or cotton wool/cotton balls, support the handle until dry. Insert the paste cone into the handle and attach with royal icing; support until dry.

3 Creating the wired lace pieces

LACE PIECES

4 Brush the lace mould with super pearl lustre dust. Press thinly rolled flower paste/gum paste into the mould, then roll across the cutting surface with a non-stick pin. Remove the lace piece carefully and cut eyelet holes in it with a craft knife or scalpel. Attach to the 24-gauge wire. Dry on the rippled foam, to create unusual shapes (pic 3).

FINISHING OFF

5 Fill the tussie mussie with a flower posy of your choice, such as a pair of tea roses, buds and foliage, as used here, in addition to the wired lace pieces.

Well Dressed in Tulle

PURSE AND DECORATION

- 185 g/6 oz/³/₄ cup sugar
- 30 g/1 oz white flower paste/gum paste (double this if the handle ribbon is also made of paste)
- Red pearl lustre dust (VB/CK)

EQUIPMENT

- 68 cm/27 inches cotton tulle, 23 cm/¼ yard wide (this is more than is needed but the width is necessary)
- Kitchen paper towel
- Large embroidery hoop
- Paper templates for purse (see page 156)
- Piece of stiff plastic or mylar
- Pink ribbon, 2 mm/¹/₁₆ inch wide, to trim the handle (optional)
- Lace mould or embossed material such as lace (see step 5)
- Broderie anglais cutter (PME)
- Plain Lucite stand (optional)

UGAR SYRUP FOR COTTON TULLE

1 For the sugar syrup, mix the sugar and 125 ml/ 4 fl oz/¹/₂ cup water until it dissolves. Bring to a gentle boil in a small saucepan before reducing to simmer for 10 minutes. Brush down the sides of the pan to incorporate any stray sugar crystals and check that the sugar stays quite clear in colour, with no hint of caramelization. Cool and store in a sealed container in the refrigerator until needed.

CLASSIC CHIC: THIS PETITE EVENING PURSE MAKES A STUNNING ORNAMENTAL STATEMENT. GLEAMING WITH PEARLIZED VINTAGE FRAMEWORK AND CUSTOMIZED INITIAL, IT OFFERS A NEW TWIST FOR THE UP-TOWN GIRL LOOKING FOR SOMETHING FRESH AND DISTINCTIVE.

PREPARING THE COTTON TULLE

2 Dip and saturate the cotton tulle in the sugar syrup. Drain off the excess and blot lightly. Stretch the tulle in the embroidery hoop (pic 1) and dry completely. Remove the syrup-soaked tulle from the hoop and cut out the purse, using the template.

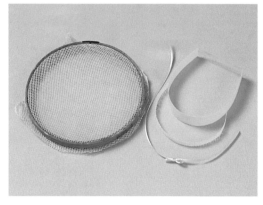

1 Tulle in the hoop, and the handle former

THE HANDLE

3 Cut out a 20 x 1 cm/8 x ¹/₂ inch syrup-soaked tulle strip for the handle. Bend the piece of stiff plastic or mylar into a horseshoe shape and tape in position. Lay the syrup-soaked tulle handle over it, and tape in place, to form an arch. Leave overnight to dry. Cut the material ribbon to size, or make one with flower paste/gum paste, and attach to the handle with edible gum glue. Add a tiny bow of ribbon or paste at the top, before removing the handle from the former.

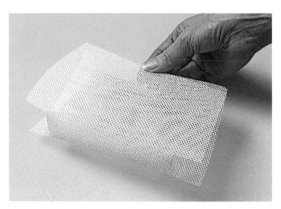

2 Folding and shaping the tulle

MAKING THE PURSE

4 On the purse tulle piece, cut two 1 cm/ ¹/₂ inch slits at the centre of each end and running parallel to the sides (pic 2). Set aside. Mark the folds with very faint lines so they won't be seen, then bend the purse piece

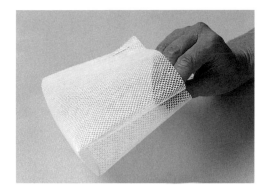

3 Setting the side seams

in half. Press the sides in and push up the triangular tab at the base (pic 3), so it stays in place without stitching. Make one knotted stitch each at the top right and top left, to hold the purse together. Pin the four darts and stitch a single over-sew knot at the top of each dart. Gently encourage the darts to taper off half-way down the front of the purse.

SIDE DECORATION

5 Using the templates (see page 156), prepare an identical pair of moulded top frames and eight triangular edging pieces from the flower paste/gum paste. Brush with red pearl lustre dust. Emboss these paste pieces with the lace mould or any embossed material – mine came from a company specializing in brass furniture mouldings (pic 4). Dry the frames flat. Attach the embossed triangular pieces while damp so that they follow the contour of the tulle, using minute amounts of royal icing. Less is best! Put on the embossed paste frames when dry.

6 Since the 'K' initial is in fact mine, it might be nice to personalize the purse with your own. Draw a pattern of the initial required. Form very thin rolls of flower paste/gum paste, occasionally breaking the lines of the letter by adding broderie anglais paste pieces arranged into flowers. Form the larger, melon-shaped pieces freehand. Brush everything with red pearl lustre dust, then attach with royal icing. Add the handle, slipping the purse top between the vertical slits; secure with royal icing.

4 Decorative lace frame and corners

OPTIONAL TOUCH
Prepare a simple filler flower bouquet resting on a single leaf, and hook over the edge of the purse framework.

Romantic Foot First

SHOE AND DECORATION

- 75 g/2¹/₂ oz flower paste/gum paste
- Peach, antique silk, lime, super gold, copper, super pearl, pink and teal lustre dusts (VB/CK)
- Yellow, lemon, black and buttercup petal dusts (VB/CK)

EQUIPMENT

- Clean aluminium drink can
- Adhesive tape
- Sturdy cardboard
- Paper templates for the shoe (see page 154)
- Plastic wrap
- Textured fabric or embossed rolling pin
- Tiny cutters for eyelet (RVO)
- Curved cardboard
- Tiny rose petal cutter (OP – R4)
- Natural non-toxic leaf
- Tiny filler blossom cutters
- Rose leaf cutter (OP – R5)
- Chrysanthemum cutter (OP – N4)
- Celformers (CC)
- Oak leaf cutters (OP – OL1, OL2, OL3)
- Cotton wool/cotton balls or sponge foam
- Base plaque (OP – P5)

COMPOSING THIS FLORAL GALLERY OF FANTASY FOOTWEAR WAS A DESIGNER INDULGENCE. A MODERN BRIDE LOVES SPECIAL VIGNETTES, SO CREATE A PERSONAL SLIPPER ECHOING THE PATTERN OF HER DRESS, BOUQUET OR TROUSSEAU. THIS WOULD BE A FLATTERING DESIGN CONCEPT!

MAKING THE SHOE

1 Prepare a shoe 'last' from a clean aluminium drink can and tape it vertically on a piece of sturdy cardboard (pic 1). Using the shoe templates (see page 154), cut out the sole and the vamp of the shoe from flower paste/gum paste. Cover the vamp with plastic wrap, then shape the sole over the shoe 'last'.

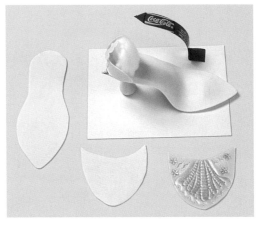

1 Stages of shoe construction

2 Make a freehand paste heel, referring to the templates on page 154. Insert the heel in position and attach with edible gum glue. Imprint the vamp with the textured fabric or embossed rolling pin, then cut eyelet holes (pic 2), using the tiniest cutters available to retain the scale. Attach the vamp to the front of the shoe with edible gum glue

2 Winter White Rose Delight shoe assembly

and push in a piece of curved cardboard to maintain the open shape. Cut out the back of the heel in paste, using the template on page 154, and fix it in position with edible gum glue.

SHOE ASSEMBLY

3 Cover the basic shoe with a selection of paste leaves and flowers. Floral shoes are more entrancing if the leaves are twisted and curved; flowers are generally left alone with little or no distortion. Use the celformers to create different heels by building up leaf combinations, as shown with the oak leaf. Colouring can be matt or pearlized. Normally I work with white or ivory paste and build the colour up as required; however, that does not mean the flower paste/gum paste can't be coloured.

4 Since each shoe is custom designed, cut the leaves in batches of four or five, then colour and add after twisting and curling. It is hard to estimate how many are needed, because each shoe varies. Sometimes the layers can be quite tight, and at other times loose and airy. Be sure to have a sufficient supply of cotton wool/cotton balls or sponge foam, to support the different stages of assembly. Cut out the base plaque, decorate if preferred, then attach the shoe (see also page 69).

SOFT SHADES OF SPRING

Spring finds romance afoot with monochromatic dogwood blossoms and accent foliage. For the dogwood flower, cut out tiny rose petals in flower paste/gum paste, using the rose petal cutter, then brush with a combination of peach and antique silk lustre dusts and attach to a freehand moulded button centre. To vein and shape the dogwood petals, see page 130. Cut leaf slips freehand with a craft knife or scalpel and vein with the natural non-toxic leaf. Brush with peach and antique silk lustre dusts, then twist and curl the paste leaves, before attaching to the back and side of the shoe. Add tiny filler blossoms for extra detail. Form the paste heel, coloured in the same manner as the rest of the shoe, by placing three large rose leaves upside down and drying in the celformer.

SUMMER BLISS SWEET ART'S KISS

Trip into summer with an inlaid embossed vamp, featuring purple and yellow filler blossoms. Take care that the cutters selected are in scale with the shoe. For Vincent Marquetry inlay technique, see page 22. Decorate the vamp with eyelets formed by any combination of very small cutters, making sure the outside edge of the base paste pattern is not distorted. Outline the heel with twisted leafy spears brushed with lime lustre dust and highlighted with super gold lustre dust, then secure with edible gum glue.

Make the tiny button paste chrysanthemums using the chrysanthemum cutter, brush with yellow and lemon petal dusts, and tip the centre with black petal dust. Prepare the leaves for the heel in the same way as for the spring shoe, except they are coloured with lime and super gold lustre dusts.

AUTUMN ESSENTIALS UNCOVERED

Discover nature's ornaments, tiny acorns nestled in satiny copper oak leaves, then pulled together with tiny filler blossoms. Make the acorns freehand, with flower paste/gum paste. Using the graduated set of oak leaf cutters, cut and vein paste leaves and brush on copper lustre dust. Build up the leaves on the shoe back, supporting them with cotton wool/cotton balls. Prepare the heel as for the spring shoe, then dry in the celformer. The only other colours used here were super pearl lustre dust and buttercup petal dust for the accent blossoms.

WINTER WHITE ROSE DELIGHT

Put your best foot forward clad in pretty pink roses and soft teal leaves, made in flower paste/gum paste. The special accents featured on this shoe include a full-blown pink rose heel; winter-white, embossed vamp, and rose foliage forming the outer silhouette. For the pink rose, the petals must be damp when centring the heel. Build up the back of the heel, then add a miniature rose bud for accent. Brush this shoe with super pearl, teal and pink lustre dusts. (To make the roses, see page 94.)

FLORAL SHOES

Making floral shoes can be tricky and requires patience. The method outlined on pages 66–7 is for a basic shoe, which can be decorated in any manner required. Each shoe is about 13 cm/ 5 inches from toe to heel and, for display purposes, is on a base plaque. It can, however, be attached directly to the cake top. Most brides prefer to keep their shoe as a permanent souvenir, and a plaque does help to inhibit breakage as the shoe is not handled.

Petite Gilded Cottage

COTTAGE AND DECORATION

- 500 g/1 lb white flower paste/gum paste
- Super gold and super pearl lustre dusts (VB/CK)
- 30 g/1 oz/2 tbsp caster/superfine sugar

EQUIPMENT

- Thin cardboard templates for the gilded cottage (see pages 154–5)
- Square broderie anglais cutter (PME)
- Veining tool
- Sponge foam
- Ball tool
- Paintbrush
- Small plastic bridal umbrella, with handle removed

THE STAR OF ITS OWN SHOW, THIS TINY TREASURE COULD STEAL YOUR HEART AWAY. THE FAÇADE SHIMMERS UNDER A GENTLE MANTLE OF POWDERED SUGAR SNOW. A SPECIAL CONFECTION DEDICATED TO LORD WEDGWOOD, WHO HAS ENCOURAGED MY SUGARCRAFT ENDEAVOURS FOR MANY YEARS.

THE WALLS

1 Prepare a paper template of the cottage (see pages 154–5), marking the fold lines of the walls and cutting out slightly enlarged window and door positions. Roll the flower paste/gum paste into an oblong. Lay the paper template on top of the paste and cut around the

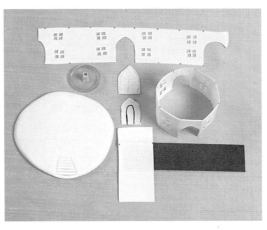

1 Basic walls and cottage base

perimeter of the walls, with a sharp craft knife or scalpel, being careful not to drag the paste; continually wipe the knife with a damp cloth if the paste seems to resist. Cut out the windows with the square broderie anglais cutter, then the front door and rear arch with the knife. Discard the window pieces but retain the door shape. Mark in the door mouldings and the knob; brush with super gold lustre dust, and paste on to a slightly larger piece of paste similar in shape (pic 1). Using the veining tool, press into the paste to form the frame around the front doorway, taking care not to distort the shape. Lightly brush the door frame and door with super gold lustre dust.

2 Bend the straight-edged piece of cardboard at the fold lines for the walls. Lay the paste walls on top of this cardboard template, to ensure the lines are straight, and gently adjust it to follow the bends in the cardboard. Stand the paste walls upright against the base of the cardboard template. Join the walls at the back arch using edible gum glue. Remove the cardboard, add the front door from the inside, and fill the interior with sponge foam, for support. Leave the wall structure until absolutely dry.

THE BASE

3 Mould a slightly elevated flower paste/gum paste mound and shape it to fit into the base template (see page 155). Make the central area, where the structure will sit, perfectly flat. Press in the steps with the veining tool, and roll the ball tool along the edge, to form a little bank. Set aside to dry. Move the wall structure into position and attach with royal icing. Using a paintbrush, lightly dampen the base with water and sprinkle with caster/superfine sugar to create a snow blanket effect.

THE ROOF

4 Using the template (see page 155), cut the ceiling support from flower paste/gum paste and dry thoroughly. Using the plastic bridal umbrella as a base former, prepare paste spokes and arrange them in eight even separations (pic 2). Allow to dry. Cut an extremely thin sheet of paste for the overhanging roof (see template on page 154) with its diameter 1 cm/^{1}/$_2$ inch larger than that of the ceiling support, and dry.

5 Make a central post of flower paste/gum paste to support the spokes and centre on the ceiling support piece. Assembling the roof will be a fragile exercise, so do take care. Very gently remove the spokes from the former and centre on the ceiling support (pic 3). Gingerly drape the extremely thin overhanging roof paste over the spokes, bringing it right over the edges of the ceiling support. Smooth between the spokes, running the finger tips up and down and forming soft channels. Using a slightly dampened, very sharp craft knife or scalpel, cut the excess away, following the base shape. Insert minute edible gum glue spots under the edge, to hold the roof in place. When thoroughly dry, attach the cottage roof to the walls with royal icing. Paint a 5 mm/^{1}/$_1$ inch stripe with a water-dampened brush around the edge of the roof and dust with caster/superfine sugar, to suggest snow.

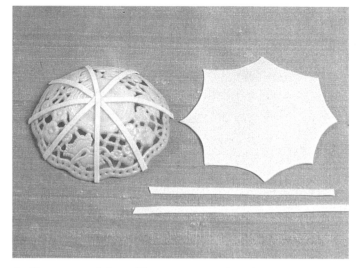

2 First stage of the ceiling support and spokes

3 Second stage of the ceiling support and spokes

THE CHIMNEY

6 Using the chimney template (see page 155), mould the chimney with flower paste/gum paste, and attach to the cottage roof with royal icing. Paint thin horizontal rings around it, using a soupy mixture of super gold lustre dust and clear alcohol/vodka or Everclear.

FINISHING OFF

7 Decorate the walls with miniature white flowers and foliage brushed with super pearl lustre dust. Add accent brush stroke flourishes with super gold lustre dust mixed with clear alcohol/vodka or Everclear before outlining the window treatments and archway.

Spring Basket Show Stopper

BE-RIBBONNED MOULDED SUGAR BASKET CONTAINS A SPRING CONCOCTION OF IVORY TEA ROSES FLECKED WITH TOUCHES OF MAUVE, PAPER WHITE JONQUILS AND WOODLAND VIOLETS. HONOURS THE FRENCH HOUSE OF LESAGE, MAKERS OF EXQUISITE LACES AND EMBROIDERY.

BASKET AND DECORATION

- 30 g/1 oz mauve flower paste/gum paste
- 15 g/¹/₂ oz white flower paste/gum paste
- Mustard-yellow food colouring (VB/CK)
- Buttercup petal dust (VB/CK)
- 250 g/8 oz/1 cup caster/superfine sugar
- 55 g/2 oz ivory flower paste/gum paste
- Antique silk lustre dust (VB/CK)
- 15 woodland violets (see page 118)
- 4 white tea roses (see page 94)

EQUIPMENT

- Veining or Dresden tool
- Purple stamens
- Green floral tape
- 26-gauge wire
- Set of mini jonquil cutters (Angela Priddy) or a mini chrysanthemum cutter and a small blossom cutter
- Throat tool
- Original vase or oval-shaped container to be duplicated
- Melon baller or spoon
- Fine-grain sandpaper or emery board
- Parsley cutter or sharp knife
- Dressmaker's tracing wheel
- Petal pad
- Sturdy, plastic handle former
- Daisy centre mould (J)
- Small polystyrene/styrofoam block, to fit inside basket

LILAC BLOSSOMS

1 Form a small cone of mauve flower paste/gum paste, then cut into four equal sections using a pair of fine scissors. Holding the paste flower between the thumb and forefinger, roll each of the stubby petals back and forth with the veining or Dresden tool until quite thin. Trim the petals into a point, then soften them with the finger tips before scoring the top surface with the tip of the scissors (pic 1). Hollow the centre with the thin point of the veining or Dresden tool. Thread a purple stamen through the centre. Attach with floral tape to short lengths of 26-gauge wire and tape into small bunches.

1 Lilac blossom assembly and equipment

2 Paper white jonquil in progress

PAPER WHITE JONQUILS

2 Prepare a small cone of white flower paste/gum paste, then flatten into a Mexican hat. Press the larger jonquil cutter down over the cone and pull away the excess paste. Then cut out the smaller jonquil blossom (pic 2). Thin the petals and centre the smaller trumpet over the larger.

Bond them together at the centre with the throat tool. Paint the calyx on with a little mustard-yellow food colouring mixed with clear alcohol/vodka or Everclear. Brush a tiny spot of buttercup petal dust in the centre. Floral tape the stems.

MAKING THE MOULDED SUGAR BASKET

3 Mix the caster/superfine sugar with 10 ml/2 tsp water – the texture should be like damp sea sand. Firmly pack the dampened sugar into the vase or oval-shaped container to be duplicated (pic 3), then up-end on to a flat dry surface such as dry cardboard, just like making a sandcastle. Transfer to an oven set at 95°C/200°F/GM¼, and dry for about 15 minutes.

This will create a 5 mm/¼ inch hard shell on the outside. Hollow out the centre by gently removing the soft sugar with the melon baller or spoon (pic 4), taking care to follow the contour of the mould. Use a fine-grain sandpaper or emery board to neaten any rough edges. If the moulded piece breaks, just crush the sugar back into its original damp sea-sand state, and remould. Turn off the oven and put the moulded piece back in it, to dry thoroughly.

BASKET SIDE DESIGN

4 Brush thinly rolled ivory flower paste/gum paste with antique silk lustre dust and run the parsley cutter or sharp

3 Packing down the dampened sugar

knife across it, forming ribbons. Decorate the ribbon edges
with the tracing wheel, and glue to the moulded basket (pic 5).   *4 Hollowing out the sugar mould*

BASKET HANDLE

5 Using the petal pad, roll one or two thin ropes of ivory flower paste/gum paste to uniform thickness, depending if a
plain or twisted handle is required. For the latter, twist the ropes together as tightly as possible, without stretching or
breaking them. Brush with antique silk lustre dust. Insert a sturdy plastic handle former inside the moulded basket.
Drape the twisted ropes over the plastic former and allow to dry thoroughly. Cover the joins at the sides with decorative
paste buttons made with the daisy centre mould.

5 Side design and handle attachment

SUGAR MOULDING

This simple method of sugar moulding is taken
to new heights by adding elegant finishing
touches. It is an interesting way to create shapes
suitable for applying all types of decorative side
design. Lots of basic shapes can be made using
all sorts of readily available household items
from yoghurt cups to crystal vases. Pieces can
be combined to create unique containers: for
example, a saucer shape atop a candleholder
base makes a very nice pedestal compote.

FINISHING

6 Make a large soft embossed bow from ivory flower paste/gum paste. Brush
with antique silk lustre dust and attach to the side of the moulded basket.
Insert the polystyrene/styrofoam block in the moulded basket and secure with
edible gum glue. Fill with flowers of your choice. Prepare the lilac and paper
white jonquils as described here. For the woodland violets and tea roses, see
pages 118 and 94. Touches of violet in any flower arrangement add striking
contrast, which in turn accents the dominant flower.

Strings Play the Heart

VIOLIN AND DECORATION
- 55 g/2 oz white flower paste/gum paste
- Super pearl lustre dust (VB/CK)
- 10 paper white jonquils (see page 73)

EQUIPMENT
- Paper templates for the violin (see page 155)
- Palette knife
- Cocktail stick/toothpick
- Cotton wool/cotton ball
- Tiny five-petal flower cutters
- Tiny rose leaf cutter
- Paper white cutter

Before beginning this project, take a look at a picture of a real violin

FOR CENTURIES THE VIOLIN HAS CAPTURED THE ESSENCE OF ROMANCE. PERHAPS THIS DAINTY FLORAL INTERPRETATION IS AN APPEALING ALTERNATIVE TO THE TRADITIONAL SPRAY. TO CONVEY A ROMANTIC THEME, SURROUND IT WITH A COLLAGE OF SUGAR FLOWERS, RIBBONS AND MUSICAL NOTES.

THE BODY

1 Roll out the flower paste/gum paste fairly thinly and, following the template, cut out the top and the bottom of the instrument body. Using a very sharp craft knife, scalpel or other suitable cutter, incise a pair of thin scrolls on the upper surface of the violin body. This will be the top of the instrument. Allow both sides to dry, then brush with super pearl lustre dust.

2 Measure the exterior perimeter of the instrument casing, then cut a 1 cm/½ inch wide strip of flower paste/gum paste of the same length plus a little surplus, to be on the safe side. Let the paste set for a few minutes. Paint a very thin strip of edible gum glue just a fraction inside the perimeter of the instrument bottom. Following the contour of the body, stand the strip up on the glue line, like a little dam (pic 1). Don't fight the paste – it will respond to gentle guidance. Trim to fit, then allow to dry before adding the instrument top and attaching with edible gum glue. Fill any discrepancy where the joins meet with royal icing, adding it from the inside. Carefully trowel away any residue with the palette knife.

THE NECK

3 Form the neck of the violin freehand, checking against the template that it is the correct size. Puncture two holes on either side with a cocktail stick/toothpick and push in string pins made from paste. Roll and curl the neck end to form a graceful scroll. While soft and malleable, attach the neck to the casing with edible gum glue, then prop to dry for twenty-four hours. Glue the fret in place.

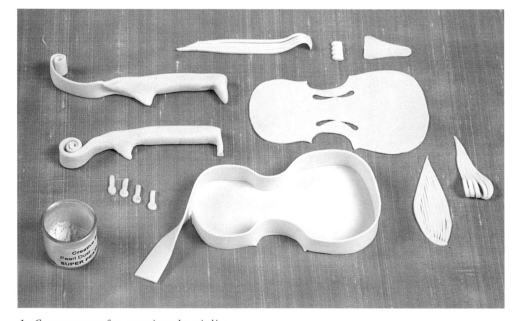

1 Components for creating the violin

76

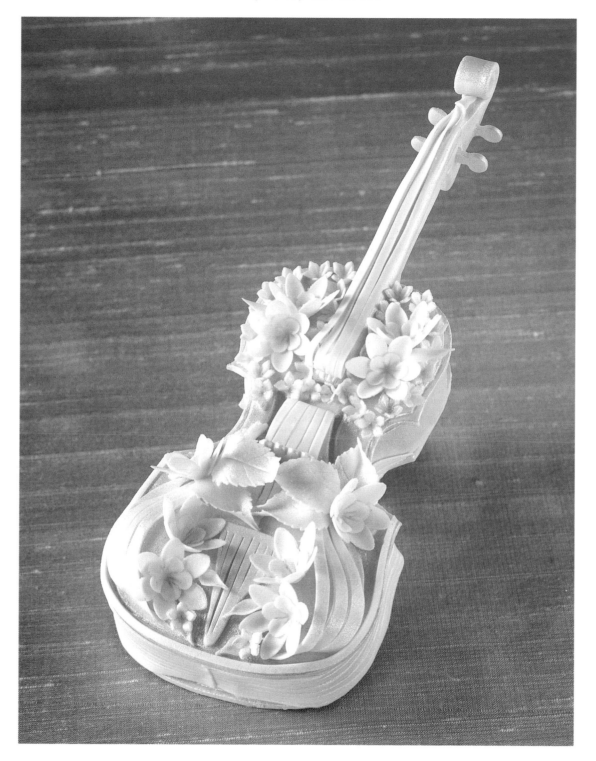

STRINGS AND DECORATION

4 For the strings and other ornamentation, cut strips of flower paste/gum paste and incise without separating them. Allow them to dry slightly before twisting under and guiding into an easy scroll. Don't be in a hurry. Prop them with a puff of cotton wool/cotton ball, if necessary.

5 To decorate the violin, cut out any miniature filler flowers – they can be any basic five-petalled flower – and rose leaf foliage. Use the paper white cutter to make the ten large paper white jonquils in flower paste/gum paste (see page 73).

Fabulous Faux Fabergé Eggs

EGG AND DECORATION

- 1 kg/2 lb white chocolate (summer coat)
- Classic ivory, seafoam and peach-coloured white chocolate (summer coat) pastilles (or substitute with oil-based colours specifically for chocolate)
- 55 g/2 oz white flower paste/gum paste
- 55 g/2 oz seafoam flower paste/gum paste
- 55 g/2 oz peach flower paste/gum paste
- Super pearl and avocado-green lustre dusts (VB/CK)
- Cornflour/cornstarch

EQUIPMENT

- VIP Whistler or double boiler
- 18 cm/7 inch egg mould (CK)
- Paintbrush
- Fine cotton gloves (optional)
- Egg stand mould (CK)
- Cocktail stick/toothpick
- Rose leaf cutters (OP – R6 and R6a)
- Rose petal cutter (OP – R3)
- Lace-embossed moulds (SB)
- Small filler blossom cutters (PME – plunger small and medium; or OP – F2M and F2L)
- 4 mm beadmaker (CK)
- Berling reproduction mould (ADM – SLL 100)
- Thin kitchen rolling pin
- 5 cm/2 inch egg mould (CK)
- Carnation cutter (OP – C2)
- Ball tool
- Maple leaf cutters (RL)

EXCLUSIVE CONFECTIONS, IMPOSSIBLY DELICIOUS, IMPERIAL HIGH STYLE. CUSTOM-DESIGNED, ELEGANT EGGS MAKE ULTIMATE WEDDING FAVOURS. THOSE WHO SHARE THE LOVE OF FINE TASTE AND THE CONFECTIONER'S ART WILL UNDOUBTEDLY TREASURE THESE BEAUTIFUL EGGS.

MAKING THE EGG

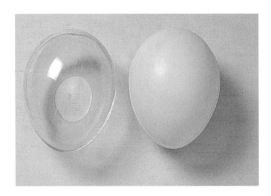

1 Pour water into the spout of the VIP Whistler and replace the whistle. Heat until warm to the hand. The temperature will be maintained for 20 minutes. Gently re-warm as necessary. If using a double boiler, heat the water until hand hot, then proceed. Add the white chocolate and allow to melt (see page 134). Transfer 250 g/8 oz at a time to a clean mixing bowl and add a coloured white chocolate pastille, to create the required colour. Make one 18 cm/7 inch egg in each colour: classic ivory, seafoam and peach.

1 Basic ivory egg and mould

2 Pour the coating into the egg mould and swish up the sides with a paintbrush. Refrigerate for a few minutes and paint the sides again from the pooled chocolate in the base. This will strengthen the sides. Return to the refrigerator for 10 minutes, until the chocolate begins to separate from the mould. Remove from the mould; if the chocolate egg is a little stubborn, just tap the mould open side down on the work surface/countertop and it will pop right out when it is ready. If you force the egg out, ugly dull patches will appear. Wearing fine cotton gloves to protect the egg surface, touch the edges of each matching pair of egg halves to the surface of a warm, non-stick frying pan and self-glue together. Very quickly, check from all sides to be sure they are even (pic 1).

EGG DECORATION

3 Cover each basic egg with a selection of decorative pieces, attaching them with tiny dabs of melted chocolate.

Classic czarina (left); Empress Catherine (back); Princess peach (right)

CLASSIC CZARINA

1 Prepare the classic ivory-coloured white chocolate egg. For the stand, pour some ivory-coloured, white chocolate into the egg stand mould (pic 2). Allow to set, then remove and attach to the base of the egg.

2 Prepare the seven stephanotis flowers by forming some white flower paste/gum paste into a Mexican hat (pic 3). Hollow out the centre with the cocktail stick/toothpick and divide equally into five petals. Snip, shape to a point with scissors, and pinch the petals. Dust with super pearl lustre dust.

2 Classic ivory egg stand and mould

3 Stages of the stephanotis flowers

3 For the five rose leaves, cut some white flower paste/gum paste with the rose leaf cutter (R6). Vein, shape and allow to dry. Dust with super pearl lustre dust. Make the three roses by cutting white paste petals with the rose petal cutter. Prepare the centre cone and allow to dry. Add two petals, then three, and then sets of five, offsetting each row from the last. Twist the petals so they look life-like (pic 4). Prepare three rose buds. Set aside to dry. Brush over all with super pearl lustre dust.

4 Prepare the two lace-embossed pieces. Press thinly rolled, white flower paste/gum paste into the lace moulds, remove and trim the edges if necessary. Brush with super pearl lustre dust. Cut two slits at the centre and open out (pic 5). Lay on the top of the egg immediately, attaching with melted chocolate.

4 Rose, leaves and cutter

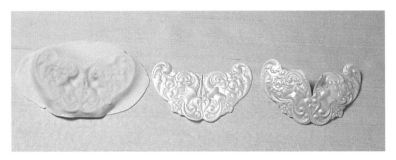

5 Lace-embossed pieces in three stages

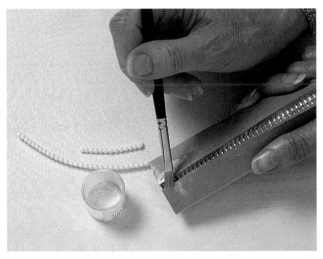

6 Brushing the pearl beads with lustre dust

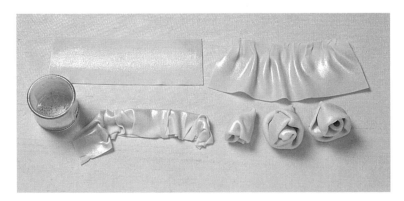

7 Making fabric-effect roses

5 Make the filler flowers, using the small blossom cutters, and follow in a gentle arc at the front of the egg, outlining the lace-embossed pieces. Prepare the pearls in the beadmaker, then brush with super pearl lustre dust (pic 6). Attach a strip of pearls within the arc, at the centre and base. Make the filigree paste shape. Build up the pattern with the roses, buds and stephanotis, then the filigree shape and rose leaves.

EMPRESS CATHERINE

1 Prepare the seafoam-coloured white chocolate egg. For the twelve fabric-effect roses, roll out 15 x 4 cm/6 x 1¹/₂ inch strips of seafoam flower paste/gum paste. Brush only the centre with super pearl lustre dust. Gather one side, then fold in half lengthways. Turn one corner down, then loosely roll up (pic 7). To make the six fabric-effect leaves, cut another paste strip of the same size and brush only the centre strip with super pearl lustre dust. Fold in half, then fold both tails down, to create a triangular point. Pinch the ends together and trim (pic 8).

2 For the twelve latticework leaves, roll out some seafoam flower paste/gum paste. Dust the Berling reproduction mould lightly with cornflour/cornstarch, then press in the paste. Trim the paste, then razor across the top of the mould with a sharp knife.

Remove carefully. Immediately attach six of these latticework leaves in a flower pattern on top of the seafoam egg. Leave the remaining six leaves draped over a thin kitchen rolling pin, to allow them to dry in shape (pic 9). Then attach the latticework leaves and fabric-effect roses and leaves.

PRINCESS PEACH

1 Prepare the peach-coloured white chocolate egg. Make the solid 5 cm/ 2 inch egg in peach-coloured white chocolate. To make each of the eight carnations (pic 10), you should cut four peach-coloured flower paste/gum paste pieces, using the carnation cutter. Frill the edges of all four of them and place three pieces on top of each other. Press the centre gently with the ball tool, forcing the sides upward. Fold the fourth piece into an S-shape and insert it in the centre.

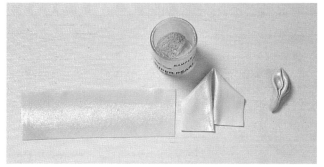

8 Preparing the fabric-effect leaves

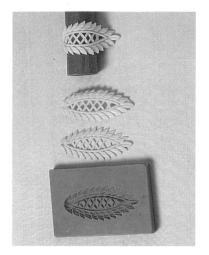

9 Latticework leaves and mould

2 Measure and divide the large egg into eight equal parts. Prepare and attach eight peach flower paste/gum paste swags with melted chocolate. Prepare and attach eight tightly controlled drapes, to cover the joins.

3 Cut seventeen maple leaves from white flower paste/gum paste with the maple leaf cutter. Vein, shape and colour them with avocado-green lustre dust. Also in white paste, make a pair of thin bow loops and three twisted tails, and brush with super pearl lustre dust. Glue the 5 cm/2 inch egg on top of the large egg with melted chocolate, add the maple leaves, then the carnations, bow loops and twist tails.

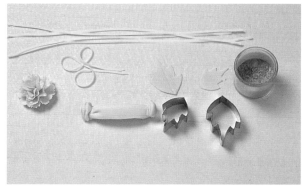

10 Stages of the carnations and maple leaves

Pretty Petals — Precious Pastels

CAKE AND DECORATION

- 2 x 18 cm/7 inch firm-textured, round cakes, 8 cm/3 inches deep, such as chocolate mud or madeira/pound cakes
- 15 cm/6 inch round cake, 2.5 cm/1 inch deep
- 175 g/6 oz ivory flower paste/gum paste
- Ruby and antique silk lustre dusts (VB/CK)
- 1.5 kg/3 lb champagne-coloured sugarpaste/rolled fondant
- Salmon-pink and white liquid or powdered food colourings

EQUIPMENT

- 18-gauge wire
- Medium and large rose petal cutters (OP – R2 and R1)
- Stripes and spots stencils (CSD)
- Plastic lace doily
- Small make-up sponge
- Celformer (CC)
- Drying rack
- Medium blossom plunger cutter (PME)
- Cream floral tape
- Medium and large rose leaf cutters
- 25 cm/10 inch round cake board
- Spray bottle
- Corrugated cardboard (recycle the white liner from biscuit or cookie packets)
- 2 x 18 cm/7 inch thin round cake boards
- 5 x 5 mm/1/4 inch dowel rods
- Small fan brush
- 3 mm beadmaker (CK)
- Tassel stencils (CSD or Delta)
- Dressmaker's tracing wheel
- Veining or Dresden tool
- Celpick (CC)

A NEW TAKE ON THE CAMELLIA. THIS IS AN UPDATED CONTEMPORARY CAKE APPEALING TO THOSE WITH A MORE WHIMSICAL SENSE OF STYLE. FANTASY TAKES FLIGHT AS EACH WHORL OF PETALS IS EITHER STRIPED OR SPOTTED, THEN FABRIC EMBOSSED. NOTE THE EXUBERANT PAINTED SIDE DESIGN, ALL HAND APPLIED IN WARM SHADES OF ROSE AND GOLD WITH GENTLE WAVES OF SMUDGED IVORY PEEPING THROUGH.

CAMELLIA FLOWERS

1 Form the flower centre freehand with ivory flower paste/gum paste and attach to a hooked 18-gauge wire; then dry overnight. For the innermost layer of petals, cut five medium rose petals in paste and thin the edges. Stencil the striped pattern with ruby lustre dust. Lay the petals face down on the plastic lace doily; do not move them about or they will smudge. Emboss the petals on the doily by pressing on the back of each petal with a small make-up sponge; take great care not to distort the coloured stripes. Attach them around the flower centre, overlapping each petal, before slipping the final petal beneath the first, so the effect is continuous.

2 Clean the board surface and stencils (both front and back) with a piece of foam sponge each time they are used, to avoid ghost images and smudging. It is too time-consuming to wash the stencil each time, so roll the flower paste/gum paste on a separate board to the one on which colour is used.

3 Prepare five petals for the second layer, again using the medium rose petal cutter, stencilling with stripes and embossing. Shape each petal in the celformer, curling the top of the petal back over

1 Building up layers of petals

2 Fantasy foliage

the top. As soon as the petals begin to hold their shape, attach with edible gum glue to the flower and hang upside down on a drying rack.

4 Prepare the third and fourth layers as in step 3, except that the large rose petal cutter is used and the third layer is stencilled with spots (pic 1). Hang upside down to dry completely. Make the paste 'calyx', using the medium blossom plunger cutter, and attach beneath the flower. Steam lightly about 30 cm/12 inches from the boiling water source. Dry without touching. Floral tape the wires in cream.

ROSE LEAVES

5 Cut the leaves from flower paste/gum paste, using the medium and large rose leaf cutters. Stencil the spots and stripes and emboss on the lace doily (pic 2). Allow to dry on a slightly uneven surface, to suggest movement.

PREPARING THE CAKE

6 Cover the 25 cm/10 inch round cake board with sugarpaste/rolled fondant, and dry overnight. Mist with water from the spray bottle, and sponge with a combination of salmon-pink and white food colouring. While the surface is still wet, use the piece of corrugated cardboard to create fanciful patterns (pic 3). After the design has dried, brush with antique silk lustre dust.

7 Centre each 18 cm/7 inch cake on a similarly sized, trimmed thin cake board. Stack them both and provide dowel support (see page 142). Cover with sugarpaste/rolled fondant and allow to firm overnight, then add a 15 cm/6 inch, paste-covered cake on top. Centre on the cake board and attach with royal icing. Masking the cake board with greaseproof/wax paper, mist with water and sponge with a combination of salmon-pink and white food colouring. When dry, highlight the surface with broad, fan-brush strokes of ruby lustre dust mixed with clear alcohol/vodka or Everclear, then soften with antique silk lustre dust.

3 Cake colouring and painting steps

RIBBONS AND PEARLS

8 Add a strip of stencilled sugarpaste/rolled fondant around the base of the cake, then another strip folded in half around the top cake. Band the folded strip with a row of 3 mm pearls, made with the beadmaker and coloured with ruby lustre dust. Prepare a wide strip of stencilled paste, then fold the edges under and drape around the board, adding stencilled knots at even intervals.

THE TASSELS

9 Make two paste tassels with the appropriate stencils, pushing them well into the stencil so they are thick and have good definition. Colour with ruby lustre dust before removing from the stencil (pic 4), then 'stitch' along the edge with the tracing wheel before shredding the ends of the tassels with a craft knife or scalpel. Finally thin the edges with the veining or Dresden tool and attach offset to the left side of the cake. Dry and glue into position on the cake board. Add a camellia corsage at the centre. Press the celpick deep into the centre of the cake, then arrange the camellias. Slip the foliage beneath the flower arrangement and secure with edible gum glue.

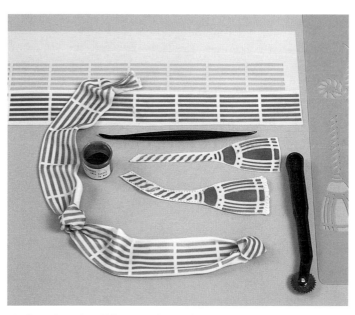

4 Creating the ribbons and tassels

Reception Confection

CAKE AND DECORATION

- 15 cm/6 inch and 20 cm/8 inch round cakes
- 2 kg/4 lb soft lavender-blue sugarpaste/ rolled fondant
- Super gold, antique silk, golden bronze and avocado-green lustre dusts (VB/CK)
- 125 g/4 oz milk chocolate-coloured flower paste/gum paste
- 15 g/½ oz mid-green flower paste/ gum paste
- 85 g/3 oz soft lavender-blue flower paste/ gum paste
- Two-toned roses and buds (see page 106)
- Cake separator mould (see step 7)

EQUIPMENT

- 15 cm/6 inch and 20 cm/8 inch thin round cake boards
- Small double-edged scalloped crimper (PME)
- Large and small stylized leaf cutters (RVO) or paper templates (see page 157)
- Fine quilting pin
- Dressmaker's tracing wheel
- Ribbon insertion tool (J)
- Plastic lace cake stand (W)
- 14 cm/5½ inch cake plate
- 38 cm/15 inch round cake board
- Soft lavender-blue ribbon, 1.5 cm/⅝ in wide
- Grosgrain-textured rolling pin (EC)
- Double-sided lace mould (ELI – 305)
- Arch cutter (FMM – 1)
- Tiny leaf cutter (RVO)
- Primrose cutters (OP – F3S and F3M)
- Throat tool
- Round piping tube/tip (W – 2)
- Tiny five-petal blossom cutter (RVO)
- Drying rack

A GENTLE WASH OF SOFT LAVENDER-BLUE SUGAR BISQUE ACCENTED WITH SHIMMERING, SOFT, MILK CHOCOLATE-COLOURED GROSGRAIN RIBBONS. FANTASY PRIMROSES AND NEW-LOOK CLASSIC ROSES DECORATE A SUMMER WEDDING CAKE TO TOUCH YOUR HEART. THE SIMPLE CAKE STAND MASQUERADES AS A TIERED CAKE, ADDING EXTRA HEIGHT AND THE ILLUSION OF SIZE.

SCULPTING THE CAKES

1 Freeze the cakes overnight. Starting at the top, pare away thin uniform layers until the cakes appear evenly graduated (see page 140). Be sure to take the height of the cake separator into consideration. Remove a 2.5 cm/1 inch diameter centre from the matching-sized, thin round cake boards, then centre the cakes on them.

PREPARING THE CAKES

2 Cover each cake with soft lavender-blue sugarpaste/rolled fondant, bringing the paste over the edge of the thin round cake boards. Decorate the upper surface of the top tier with the scalloped crimper. Remove a 2.5 cm/1 inch core from the centre of the bottom cake. Hollow out a small amount from the base of the top tier to accommodate the capping bolt on the post.

3 Divide the cake into four. Using the paper templates (see page 157) and quilting pin, prick the flower placement design on the sides of the cakes. Imprint a sunray pattern of branch lines with the tracing wheel. Paint along these lines with super gold lustre dust mixed with clear alcohol/vodka or Everclear. Cut slits into the upper surface and into the cake sides between the repeat floral design, using the insertion tool and following the curve of the ribbon template (see page 157).

1 Stages of the stylized leaves

STYLIZED LEAVES

4 Roll out milk chocolate-coloured flower paste/gum paste and cut out the leaves using the stylized leaf cutters or paper templates (see page 157) – the small cutter is for the top tier and the larger one for the bottom. Brush with antique silk lustre dust and highlight with golden bronze and avocado-green lustre dusts (pic 1).

CAKE STAND

5 Remove the centre column from the plastic lace cake stand. Cover the stand top and base with soft lavender-blue sugarpaste/rolled fondant. Layer the column with paste stylized leaves, securing them in position with edible gum glue. Reassemble the stand and dry overnight.

CAKE BOARD

6 Cover the 38 cm/15 inch round cake board with soft lavender-blue sugarpaste/rolled fondant. Glue the decorated cake stand in the centre with royal icing. Dress the base edge of the cake stand with additional paste leaves. Trim the board with ribbon.

MOULDED SUGAR VASE

7 Prepare a moulded sugar vase (see pages 74–5), using a simple container matching the visible height

of the centre post – this one was recycled from a takeaway meal. Hollow out the centre to match the 2.5 cm/1 inch diameter of the centre post.

RIBBON STRIPS

8 Roll out and emboss milk chocolate-coloured flower paste/gum paste with the grosgrain-textured rolling pin. Cut in strips, using a parsley cutter, craft knife or scalpel. Run along both edges with the tracing wheel. Brush with antique silk lustre dust. Set the ribbon strips aside until needed, by covering with plastic wrap, then placing a damp towel on top. They will be usable for a day kept in this manner.

3 Miniature leaves and blossoms

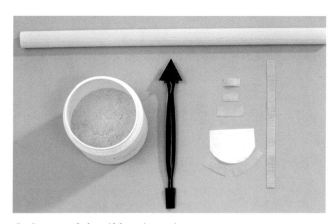

4 Making primroses for the side details

5 Stages of the ribbon insertion

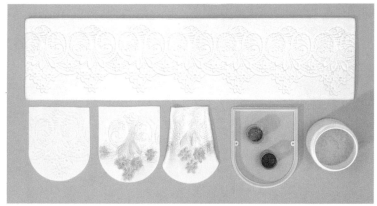

2 Decorative panels for the cake stand

DECORATIVE PANELS

9 Roll out soft lavender-blue sugarpaste/rolled fondant into a strip, then press into the lace mould. Cut out eleven lace-embossed panels using the arch cutter. Brush with antique silk lustre dust, then colour the lace-embossed flowers and leaves with golden bronze and avocado-green lustre dusts (pic 2). Fold the sides under and attach each panel over the edge of the cake board, yet far enough into the centre so that when the cakes are positioned they will cover each panel top.

DECORATING THE CAKES

10 Gum glue the stylized leaves to the cake sides. Emboss mid-green flower paste/gum paste, using the grosgrain-textured rolling pin. Form tiny leaves with the leaf cutter (pic 3) and attach to the cake sides along the golden branch lines.

PRIMROSES

11 Cut out soft lavender-blue flower paste/gum paste primroses, using the primrose cutters (pic 4). Thin the edges and press straight into the side of the cake with the throat tool. Using the round piping tube/tip, add a tiny bead of royal icing to each flower centre. Add extra definition along the branch lines by cutting out and pressing in tiny, blue, five-lobed blossoms.

RIBBON INSERTION

12 Using the ribbon strips that have already been prepared, cut and shape small curved pieces (pic 5) for the ribbon insertion. Using the insertion tool, press curved ribbon strips into slits on the upper surface and cake sides, between the repeat floral design.

RIBBON LOOPS

13 Cut more embossed-paste strips into pieces 9 cm/3½ inches long, then double them over to form ribbon loops. Pinch the ends together, then hang on a drying rack to retain shape (pic 6).

CAKE TOP CENTREPIECE

14 Pipe a little royal icing in the centre of the top tier. Arrange the ribbon loops in a circle with the ends in the piped royal icing. Begin to layer them and in between tuck two-toned roses and buds (pic 7; although the unusual colour combination and the alternate petal placement are just for this project). Support in position with sponge foam until quite dry.

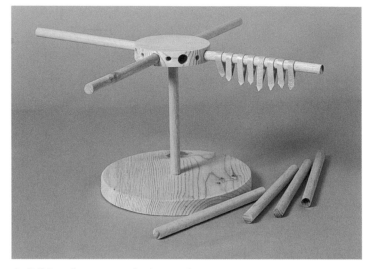

6 Ribbon loops on a drying rack

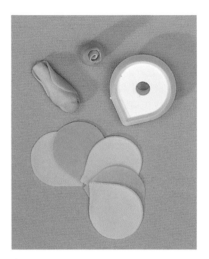

7 Rose blossom assembly

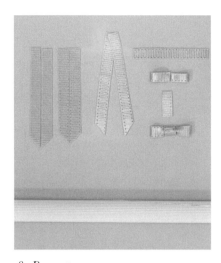

8 Bow stages

BOWS

15 Make the bows in the same way as for the ribbon strips (step 8). Fold two loops into the centre. Cover the join with a small strip and pinch in at the back (pic 8). If the paste is drying too quickly, moisten with a very little water. Cut the tails in pairs, making sure they are long enough to drape over the panels, and attach with edible gum glue. Secure the prepared bow loops at the top of the tails with gum glue.

FINISHING

16 Centre the bottom cake on the cake stand. Insert the centre post through the cake and attach it to the cake stand, then slip the moulded sugar vase over the top of it. Cover the join at the base with two little circles of soft lavender-blue flower paste/gum paste rope, and allow to dry. Fold a 5 x 65 cm/2 x 26 inch strip of soft lavender-blue sugarpaste/rolled fondant in half. Trim evenly using a ruler as a guide. Encircle the bottom cake and neatly join at the back. Pipe a small bead of royal icing to seal the join, and attach the bows to the edge of the cake board. Add the ribbon border to the top tier. Connect a custom-made 14 cm/5½ inch cake plate to the centre post above the separator. Carefully position the top tier after the cake is delivered to the reception site.

Glimpsed under Glass

Cake and Decoration

- 15 cm/6 inch round cake
- Flower paste/gum paste (optional, for glass dome decoration)
- 850 g/1³/4 lb sugarpaste/rolled fondant
- 2.5 ml/¹/2 tsp Tylose powder/CMC (J)
- Pink, green and pale teal food colourings (VB/CK)
- Pale pink and buttercup petal dusts (VB/CK)
- Small moulded sugar vase (see pages 74–5)

Equipment

- 50 cm/20 inch reproduction glass dome
- Ribbon (optional, for glass dome decoration)
- Plastic lace, lace fabric or a lace press
- Rose cutter box base (OP) or paper template for cake plaque (see page 154)
- Rose leaf cutter (OP – R7) or any other small rose leaf cutter
- Small soft pointed paintbrush
- Veining tool
- Small and medium five-petal blossom cutters
- Miniature daisy cutter
- Throat tool
- Tiny leaf cutter (RVO)
- 15 cm/6 inch thin round cake board
- 25 cm/10 inch round cake board
- Celformer (CC)
- Rose petal cutter (OP – R2)
- Ball tool
- Plastic spoons
- 20-gauge wire
- Calyx cutter
- Floral tape
- Satay stick/bamboo skewer
- Lace edge cutter (FMM – M5)
- Small circular Lucite disk

THE ESSENCE OF ELEGANCE AND A CELEBRATION OF STYLE. CRISP PASTEL HIGHLIGHTS AND A SPLASH OF ROSES COMBINE WITH ROMANTIC VINCENT MARQUETRY. THIS TECHNIQUE CAN BE COMPARED WITH FRENCH FURNITURE INLAY – PATTERNS ARE FORMED BY THE INSERTION OF CUTTER LEAVES AND FLOWERS IN A SUGARPASTE VENEER. NEW MAGIC AT WORK WITH THE DOME PRESENTATION.

THE CAKE PLAQUE

1 Knead the Tylose powder into 250 g/8 oz sugarpaste/rolled fondant, then set aside for an hour to rest. Prepare separate walnut-sized balls of pink, green and white from the Tylose-strengthened paste. Colour the remaining strengthened paste with pale teal food colouring.

2 Roll out the pale teal sugarpaste/rolled fondant and emboss with plastic lace, lace fabric or a lace press. For this 15 cm/6 inch petal-shaped plaque, use the rose box base as a cutter or the paper template (see page 154) and cut the outline with a craft knife or

1 Creating the Vincent Marquetry cake plaque

scalpel. Gently pull the excess paste away. Immediately cut out the rose leaves, using the rose leaf cutter. Remove each leaf with the point of the craft knife or scalpel and replace it with a pale green, strengthened-paste replica. There is no need to add any moisture as the paste is self sticking. A small soft pointed paintbrush is useful to manoeuvre stubborn pieces into position. Vein the leaf with the veining tool. Repeat the process, cutting into the corners of the original leaf and being sure to overlap them, since this is part of the charm of this technique.

3 Make and add the flowers in the same way and in the following order. Cut and insert pale pink flowers into an empty spot of the same size, using the medium five-petal blossom cutter; then repeat this process with the white flowers, using

the small five-petal blossom cutter. Finish with the miniature white daisies, using the daisy cutter. Mark each flower with the throat tool and press the veining tool into its petals, to suggest movement (pic 1) – remembering the paste markings are difficult to correct later. It is a good idea for beginners to cover the parts not being worked on with plastic wrap, and lay a barely damp tea towel over the wrap, to avoid dry and brittle edges.

4 Complete the design with miniature leaf accents, cutting these with the tiny leaf cutter. Edge the plaque with strips of strengthened paste folded in half and attached with water to the underside of the plaque. Dry the decorated plaque thoroughly.

CAKE BOARD DECORATION

5 Cover the 25 cm/10 inch cake board with pale teal strengthened sugarpaste/rolled fondant. For the cake board decoration, repeat the same basic Vincent Marquetry method as used for the cake plaque, but varying the pattern (pic 2).

THE ROSE

6 Using an ice pick or knitting needle, pierce a hole through the base of the celformer, then line with greaseproof/wax paper. Prepare the centre cone and allow to dry. Cut out the first five rose petals with the rose petal cutter. Wrap the first pair beneath the cone. Add the next layer using the remaining three, then set aside. Cut four more sets of five rose petals. Thin the petal edges with the ball tool and brush them with pale pink petal dust, then highlight the base with buttercup petal dust. Press each petal into the palm of the hand, to vein it, then shape over the back

2 Close up of the Vincent Marquetry cake board

of a plastic spoon. Place the shaped petals in the celformer, working from the outside to the centre. Support each petal with a foam sponge, if necessary. Using royal icing, glue the petals in position, offsetting each petal from the one above it. Gently push the prepared centre through the rose and the celformer, and place over a cup to dry. Next day, make the calyx with the calyx cutter, nick and trim it (pic 3) and then attach around the base of the rose petals. Wire and floral tape the stem. For the leaves, see page 119.

3 Components for creating the roses

SIDE DECORATION

7 Centre the cake on the thin round cake board and then cover it with pale teal sugarpaste/rolled fondant, bringing the paste right down over the board edges. Centre on the inlaid cake board and attach with a little royal icing. Divide the cake in 3 cm/1¼ inch sections. Cut 10 x 3 cm/4 x 1¼ inch panels. Gather with the satay stick/bamboo skewer, then press down hard on to the non-stick board, to keep the ruched pleats together. Trim and neaten the edges with a craft knife

WHY THE DOME PRESENTATION?

After the cake has been cut, the top tier is usually boxed and set aside for the family to take home. Always the prettiest tier, it never made sense just putting it away. Solving this dilemma became a personal priority. One day, browsing in Kansas City, Missouri, I visited an antique shop and discovered some reproduction blown-glass domes and wondered whether the top cake tier and ornament would fit beneath one – which it did. For many years since then, these blown-glass domes have been my personal trademark. Normally I add a bow of flower paste/gum paste or ribbon around the glass knob, but for clarity of photography it has been omitted here. My brides just love the idea of displaying their cake under a glass dome.

or scalpel. Attach the ruched pleated panels to the side and cover the joins with zig-zag strips of 5 mm/¼ inch pale teal paste made using the lace edge cutter (see page 144). Roll some pale teal paste into a long sausage and circle around the base of the cake. Make flowers with the small five-petal blossom cutter. Brush with pale pink petal dust and attach between the ruched pleated panels with royal icing.

FINISHING TOUCHES

8 Centre the plaque on the cake, supporting it with the Lucite disk so it just clears the tops of the panels. Fill a small moulded sugar vase with the sugar moulded roses and place on top. Measure the height of the cake and the flowers, and check to see there is room to fit everything under the dome. (The first time I did this, I misjudged the height and came very close to smashing every flower in the arrangement.) The illusion can be deceiving, the glass appears to be taller than it really is and one can be fooled into thinking there is plenty of room. It is also worth noting that the inside dimension is smaller than the outside. Carefully cover the cake and flowers with the glass dome.

A Jewel in the Crown

GUEST CAKE BY SCOTT FERGUSON

CAKE AND DECORATION

- 13 cm/5 inch round cake, 8 cm/3 inches deep; 20 cm/8 inch round cake, 10 cm/4 inches deep; and 30 cm/12 inch square cake, 13 cm/5 inches deep
- 1 kg/2 lb white chocolate (summer coat)
- 125 g/4 oz each white, ivory and dark peach flower paste/gum paste
- Silk-white and super pearl lustre dusts (VB/CK)
- 500 g/1 lb pale peach flower paste/ gum paste
- Cosmos, orange, magenta and yellow petal dusts (VB/CK)
- 3.5 kg/7 lb ivory sugarpaste/rolled fondant
- 125 g/4 oz royal icing

EQUIPMENT

- Original elephant to be duplicated
- 1 kg/2 lb thixotropic silicone or kneadable silicone clay
- 2.5 mm/$\frac{1}{8}$ inch dowel rods
- Pointed tweezers
- Cold porcelain • Five-point throat tool
- Oval mould, domed in the centre
- Kingston cutter former (TOB)
- Lace leaf mould (ADM – LD300)
- Mexican hat pad (OP)
- Small circle cutter • White 30-gauge wire
- Templates (see page 158) • Sugarcraft gun
- Plunger cutters (FMM – LV1 and B1)
- Quick rose cutter (OP – F6)
- 13 cm/5 inch and 25 cm/10 inch round cake boards
- Peach ribbon, 5 mm/$\frac{1}{4}$ inch wide, to trim
- 5 mm/$\frac{1}{4}$ inch dowel rods
- Endless lace cutter (OP – LA1)
- 30 cm/12 inch square cake board

DELICATELY CARVED IVORY WITH THE ALLURING PERFUME OF JASMINE AND ROSES ARE SYMBOLIC OF THE ROMANTIC FAR EAST. UNDER AN EXQUISITE CANOPY, NOBLE CHOCOLATE ELEPHANTS OFFER FLOWER GARLANDS (MALAI) TO THE HONOURED BRIDAL COUPLE. WHO COULD RESIST THIS EXOTIC WEDDING CAKE?

DUPLICATING THE ELEPHANT

1 Mix the thixotropic silicone or kneadable silicone clay, as per the manufacturer's directions, and apply a smooth shell at least 5 mm/^{1}/4 in thick over the elephant to be duplicated. Using a craft knife or scalpel, cut the cured mould away, into three or more pieces (pic 1). Wash; dry then reassemble the mould, securing with rubber bands.

2 Melt the white chocolate (summer coat) as per the manufacturer's directions. Prop the mould upside down and pour the coating into each of the legs (pic 2), gently tapping to release any air. Insert 2.5 mm/^{1}/8 inch dowels into each leg while the coating is liquid. When cool, carefully remove the mould. Remove any seam marks with a knife, then polish with nylon ladies' stocking/hose.

1 Elephant and prepared silicone mould

CROWN FLOWERS

3 Modify the tweezers by moulding a small amount of cold porcelain around the tweezer points and forming two tiny, opposing, bean-shaped pads. Allow to harden thoroughly. Form a sausage shape from some white flower paste/gum paste, and insert the throat tool into one end. Clip indentations with scissors and pull each section into a rounded point (pic 3). Insert a cocktail stick/toothpick

right through the sausage. Slightly dampen the back of each point and tightly roll under, into a volute. Roll the sausage between your fingers to form a ball and pinch off the excess paste. Using a

2 Pouring the white chocolate into the mould

palette knife, make vertical indentations between each volute. With the modified tweezers, pull out each section and form a dimple. When dry, remove from the cocktail stick/toothpick, and dust with silk-white lustre dust. Make one hundred crown flowers.

3 Stages of making the crown flowers

LACE LEAVES

4 Wash the oval domed mould thoroughly and fill with remnant flower paste/gum paste. Level back, then remove the 'pad' from the mould, place it on the Kingston former, and allow to dry. Make eight such temporary support pads.

5 Using some stiff ivory flower paste/gum paste, work in more shortening and cornflour/cornstarch until the mixture slices easily. Dust the leaf lace mould with cornflour/cornstarch and press the paste into the mould. Slice off the excess paste with a palette knife (pic 4). Patch any holes, trimming a second time if needed. Remove the paste lace from the mould and place on the Kingston former, centring over a support pad. When dry, brush with super pearl lustre dust. Make twenty-eight lace leaves.

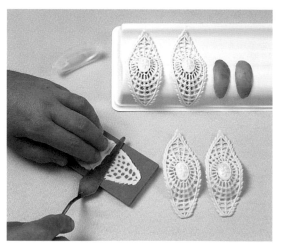

4 Removing the excess paste from a lace leaf

MINI BELLS

6 Press some white flower paste/gum paste into a hole on the Mexican hat pad and roll until the top is even and thin. Remove the paste from the pad, invert, neaten up, and cut with the circle cutter (pic 5). Insert dampened wire into the top of each 'bell' and allow to dry. Brush with silk-white lustre dust. Make twenty mini bells.

FRAMED FILIGREE PANELS

7 Tape greaseproof paper/wax paper over the filigree paper template (see page 158). With the ridged ribbon disk in the sugarcraft gun, form the frame with ivory flower paste/gum paste, mitring the edges and securing with water on an artist's brush (pic 6). Make four of these frames and allow to dry.

8 Cut out the filigree paper template. Prick each hole centre with a pin so you can feel it on the underside (like Braille). Roll a sheet of dark peach flower paste/gum paste with a pasta machine. Place the template over it and press lightly to transfer the dot grid on to the paste. Cut the perimeter of the template with a craft knife or scalpel, but do not remove the excess paste. Lift off the template. Centre the LV1 plunger cutter over each dot, cut and remove each flower, then remove the excess paste. Make four filigree panels. Using edible gum glue, attach the ivory frames to filigree panels. For the four teardrop shapes, repeat steps 7–8 but using the teardrop template (see page 158).

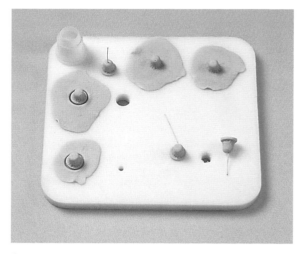

5 Creating the mini bells

OTHER FLORAL DECORATIONS

9 Make 150 roses (see page 94) with pale peach flower paste/gum paste and the rose cutter, then paint them with cosmos, orange, magenta or yellow petal dusts mixed with clear alcohol. Make 100 jasmine finger flowers with white flower paste/gum paste, painting the centres with yellow petal dust. Insert 10 cm/4 inches of dampened wire into only twelve jasmine flowers.

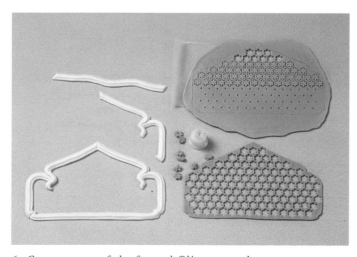

6 Components of the framed filigree panels

ASSEMBLING THE TOP TIERS

10 Cover the two round cakes and matching boards with ivory sugarpaste/rolled fondant. Glue the peach ribbon to the larger cake board. Dowel and stack the top two tiers (see page 142). With royal icing, glue eleven lace leaves around the top tier and seventeen around the middle tier. Alternate jasmine and rose blossoms between the two tiers, and on the top dome. With the endless lace cutter, cut a lace strip in ivory paste and gum glue it over the ribbon. Insert bell wires under the lace. Trim each lace leaf with a small leaf and B1 plunger cutter.

THE BOTTOM TIER

11 Mitre the corners of the square cake, then place on its matching board and cover with ivory sugarpaste/rolled fondant. Insert 5 mm/¼ inch dowels into the cake at each elephant leg location. Gum glue the filigree panels to the cake sides.

12 String crown flowers on to wire and form loops and drops (see pic 3). Attach three drops to each loop. Support a floral garland on each elephant's trunk. Arrange the remaining roses around the base of the bottom cake and around the elephants.

Affair with Blue and White

GUEST CAKE BY LOYDENE BARRETT

CAKE AND DECORATION

- 30 cm/12 inch and 25 cm/10 inch scalloped oval cakes
- 20 cm/8 inch oval cake
- 5 kg/10 lb white sugarpaste/rolled fondant
- Delphinium-blue and moss-green paste colourings (W)
- 750 g/1½ lb white flower paste/gum paste
- Buttercup-yellow, brown, moss-green, sage-green, forest-green and cinnamon petal dusts (VB/CK)
- Super pearl lustre dust

EQUIPMENT

- 45 x 40 cm/18 x 16 inch scalloped oval plywood cake board, 7.5 mm/³/8 inch deep
- 32 cm/13 inch oval cake board
- Starburst and small curved leaf cutwork cutters (EC)
- White 26- and 30-gauge wires
- Veining tool
- White stamens
- Celboard (CC)
- White ginger cutters (R)
- Orchid veiner (R)
- Ball tool
- Green floral tape
- Green 26-gauge wire
- Celstick (CC)
- 12 x 5 mm/¼ inch dowel rods
- Long sharpened dowel rod
- Round piping tube/tip (W – 2)
- Varipin/Rosa's Roller (OP)
- Freesia cutter
- Airpen syringe (SPC) or small piping bag
- 18 x 0 line brush
- 3 x 35 cm/14 inch lengths of plastic tubing, 5 mm/¼ inch wide

REFLECTING SUMMER SKIES AT THE HEIGHT OF THE WEDDING SEASON, THESE TIERS OF PRISTINE WHITE WITH DELPHINIUM-BLUE HIGHLIGHTS BLEND LACY CLASSIC DESIGN WITH CONTEMPORARY CHARM. ON THE CAKE, A STRIKING CONTRAST OF BLUE CUTWORK AND FRENCH KNOT DRAPES IS ACCENTED WITH SPRAYS OF WHITE GINGER AND ORCHIDS.

COVERING THE CAKE BOARD

1 Cut out the scalloped oval cake board from the plywood. Tint 1 kg/2 lb of sugarpaste/rolled fondant with delphinium-blue paste colouring. Roll it out and use to cover the scalloped board. Allow the board to dry for several days. Place the 32 cm/13 inch oval cake board on the scalloped board. Roll out 370 g/12 oz of white sugarpaste/rolled fondant and cut it to a scalloped shape before placing it over both cake boards. Working quickly, trim the white covering 5 mm/¼ inch from the edge of the blue board. Using the starburst and curved leaf cutters, cut out the design on the edge of the white sugarpaste/rolled fondant (pic 1).

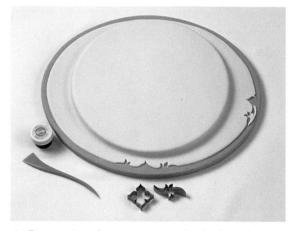

1 Decorating the paste-covered cake board

WHITE GINGER FLOWERS

2 Make the pistil by bending a small hook in a piece of white 30-gauge wire. Form a very small piece of white flower paste/gum paste similar in shape to a grain of rice. Insert the hook end of the wire into the 'grain of rice', positioning it close to one end. With the pointed end of the blade tool, make an indentation across the top. Insert a white stamen in the end away from the wire. When dry, brush with buttercup-yellow petal dust, then tint with brown petal dust on the top. Dust moss-green petal dust on the stamen.

3 Roll out a small ball of flower paste/gum paste on the celboard. Cut out one petal, using the round white ginger cutter. Moisten the white 26-gauge wire and insert into the ridge. Pinch the base close to the wire and lightly vein with the orchid veiner. Place the petal on the petal pad and soften its edges with the ball tool. Dry on ridged packing foam. Make and wire the remaining petals but vein only the oval ones. Using the oval white ginger cutter, cut one petal, then flip the cutter over and cut a second one, so there is a right and left oval petal. Finally cut three petals, using the narrow white ginger cutter, and fold in half lengthways. Colour the base, front and back of each petal with buttercup-yellow petal dust, and tint with moss-green petal dust (pic 2).

4 Bend the wire of the pistil in an S-shape. With one-third width of floral tape, bind the pistil to the round petal and then the three narrow petals. Position the oval petals between the narrow ones. Prepare seven more of these white ginger flowers, repeating steps 2–4.

2 Creating the white ginger flowers

3 Making the white ginger leaves

LEAVES

5 Tint a small amount of flower paste/gum paste with moss-green paste colouring and roll out on the celboard. Cut out the leaves using the round white ginger cutter. Moisten the green 26-gauge wire and insert into the ridge. Place on the petal pad and soften its edges. Lightly vein with the orchid veiner. Pinch the leaf together up the centre, and dry on ridged packing foam. When dry, colour the leaf with sage-green and forest-green petal dusts. Brush stripes on the leaf surface with cinnamon petal dust, as well as the edges (pic 3). Prepare six more leaves.

FILLER ORCHIDS

6 Roll a pea-sized ball of white flowerpaste/gumpaste into a cone and hollow out with the celstick. Using small scissors, cut the cone into four equal petals. Cut two opposite petals in half, so there are two wide petals and four narrow ones. Thin all but one wide petal between your thumb and finger. Fold the outside edge of the thick petal into the centre and create a channel. Insert a stamen at an angle through the centre, and secure. Colour the centre buttercup-yellow and the base with moss-green petal dust. Make buds by inserting a moistened white 26-gauge wire into a pea-sized ball of paste, and dust each base with moss-green (pic 4).

4 Stages of making the filler orchids

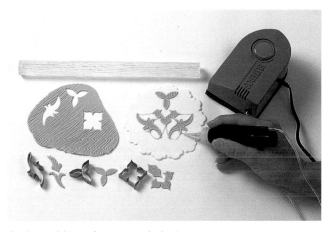

5 Assembling the cutwork design

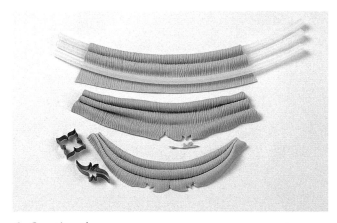

6 Creating the swags

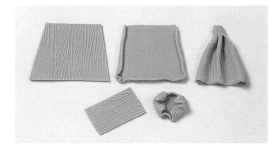

7 Making the French knot drapes

STACKING THE CAKES

7 Cover the cakes with white sugarpaste/rolled fondant. Dowel and stack each one (see page 142). Pipe a snail trail around the base of each cake.

CUTWORK

8 Roll out some delphinium-blue sugarpaste/rolled fondant and texture with the Varipin/Rosa's Roller. Using the cutwork and freesia cutters, cut the paste (pic 5), moisten and position on the top and middle tiers. Fill the airpen syringe or small piping bag with royal icing and outline the cutwork pieces. Pipe royal icing from one piece to another until you have created the look of Belgian lace. After attaching each string, use the moistened line brush to neaten the joins.

SWAGS AND FRENCH KNOT DRAPES

9 Roll out some delphinium-blue sugarpaste/rolled fondant and texture with the Varipin/Rosa's Roller. Using a craft knife or scalpel, cut the swag. Space three lengths of plastic tubing 5 mm/¼ inch apart and lay the textured paste over them. Squeeze the tubing together to gather up the paste swag. Using the starburst and small curved leaf cutters, cut out the swag edge. Remove the tubing, pinch the ends together (pic 6), moisten and position on the cakes.

10 For the drop, roll out the remaining blue paste and texture with the Varipin/Rosa's Roller. Cut out a flared piece 6 cm/2½ inches long. Gather at the narrow edge, moisten and attach at the end of each swag. For the knot, cut out a 5 x 2.5 cm/2 x 1 inch rectangle (pic 7). Shape and gather into a knot; position over the drop. Brush the entire cake with super pearl lustre dust.

Invitation to a Summer Wedding

GUEST CAKE BY CAROLYN WANKE

CAKE AND DECORATION

- 18 cm/7 inch, 28 cm/11 inch and 38 cm/15 inch round cakes
- 90 g/3 oz each pink and egg-yellow flower paste/gum paste
- 5.5 kg/11 lb white sugarpaste/ rolled fondant
- 55 g/2 oz white flower paste/gum paste
- 270 g/9 oz green sugarpaste/rolled fondant

EQUIPMENT

- Teardrop rose cutters (2.3 cm/^{7}/8 inch and 2.8 cm/1^1/8 inch)
- Ball tool
- Petal pad
- 2 baroque moulds
- Paper templates for the baroque pieces (see page 158)
- 5 cm/2 inch square cutter
- Aluminium flashing
- Basketweave rolling pin (PME)
- 5 mm/^{1}/4 inch wooden skewer
- Wooden cushion nail
- Reusable adhesive
- Piping tubes/tips (W – 4, 349)
- 45 cm/18 inch round plywood cake board
- 140 cm/56 inches braid or ribbon, 1.5 cm/^{5}/8 inches wide, to trim board
- Glue gun
- 18 cm/7 inch, 28 cm/11 inch and 38 cm/15 inch thin round cake boards
- 10 x 5 mm/^{1}/4 inch dowel rods
- Long sharpened dowel

SEARCHING FOR A SPECIAL CAKE, THE BRIDE-TO-BE WOULD NOT BE DISAPPOINTED WITH THIS PRETTY DESIGN, ESPECIALLY SUITED TO A SUMMER WEDDING. WHIMSICAL BASKETS FILLED WITH MINIATURE ROSES REFLECTING RAINBOW HUES ARE PULLED TOGETHER WITH TWISTED SUGAR RIBBONS. ROMANTIC BLISS INDEED!

THE ROSES

1 For each closed bud, roll out coloured flower paste/gum paste and cut with the appropriately sized teardrop cutter. Thin the petal edges using the ball tool and petal pad. Roll the petal into a tight bud, lengthening the bottom portion to form a solid pointed stem (pic 1). Make 140 small buds and thirty large buds of each colour. Dry completely. Set aside sixty small buds of each colour.

2 For each open bud, lighten the coloured flower paste/gum paste with same amount of white flower paste/gum paste. Repeat step 1 for rolling, cutting and thinning petals. Wrap two or three petals around each of the remaining buds to make an open bud.

3 For the open rose, use six small open buds and thirty large open buds of each colour. Repeat step 2 for colouring the flower paste/gum paste, rolling, cutting and thinning petals. Add five petals to each open bud to form the rose.

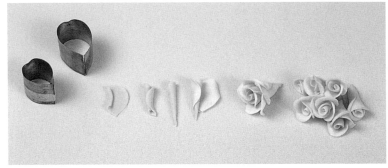

1 Stages of the rose blossoms

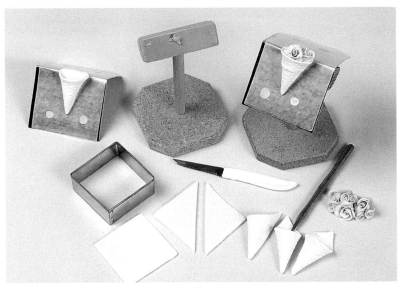

2 Making the basketweave cones

TOP BAROQUE PIECES

4 Press white sugarpaste/rolled fondant into the two baroque moulds, unmould and trim to fit the paper templates (see page 158). Glue the two sides back to back with white royal icing, and trim the edges to match. Make three double pieces and allow to dry.

BASKETWEAVE CONES AND BOWS

5 Cut six 9 x 15 cm/3³/₈ x 6 inch pieces of aluminium flashing and fold the 15 cm/6 inch side in half to a 90 degree angle. Cut six 8 x 15 cm/3 x 6 inch pieces of greaseproof/wax paper and fold in half. Roll out 55 g/ 2 oz white sugarpaste/rolled fondant to 2 mm/¹/₁₆ inch thick, with the basketweave rolling pin. Cut three squares, positioning the cutter so that the weave goes from corner to corner; then cut each square in half on the horizontal weave line. Form a cone with each triangle and flatten the seam by rolling with the wooden skewer. Trim top points, leaving just enough paste to fold over the corner of the flashing. Thin and flare the top edge of each cone by gently pinching. Dry overnight on the flashing (pic 2).

6 When dry, attach a 4.5 mm/³/₁₆ inch, white flower paste/gum paste ribbon, 5.5 cm/2¹/₄ inches long, around each cone 1 cm/¹/₂ inch from top.

7 Secure the flashing to the cushion nail with a small amount of reusable adhesive. Use royal icing to attach greaseproof/wax paper to the flashing, the cone on to the greaseproof/wax paper, and the roses in the cone.

Cut rose stems as required. Hold the cushion nail and turn or twist the nail to get the proper angles for piping leaves, with green royal icing and the No.349 piping tube/tip. Release the flashing from the cushion nail by holding it on either side of the bend and gently moving from side to side. Set aside for the icing to dry. Repeat step 7 for each of the remaining five cones.

8 Make six small bows, 2 cm/³/4 inches wide, in white flower paste/gum paste, and allow to dry.

PREPARING THE CAKES

9 Cover the 45 cm/18 inch cake board with white sugarpaste/rolled fondant and attach ribbon or trim around the edge of the board with the glue gun. Place cooled cakes on matching-sized thin cake boards and cover with paste. Cut dowels to the cake heights and insert into the two bottom tiers (see page 142). Stack the cakes on the covered cake board, securing with royal icing and the long sharpened dowel.

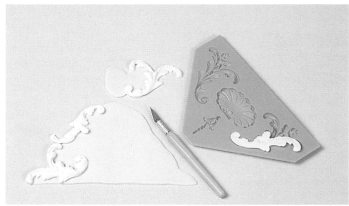

3 Creating the baroque pieces

BAROQUE TRIM

10 Customize paper templates for the baroque trim (see page 158) by measuring one-sixth the circumference of your cake by its height. Line up and mark the base of each tier in sixths. For the bottom tier, press four white sugarpaste/rolled fondant pieces in the baroque mould, and trim to match (pic 3). Place greaseproof/wax paper over the paper template panel and form paste pieces to fit in the space. Arrange five more sets of baroque pieces on greaseproof/wax paper and freeze all until needed. Use the same technique for the top tier.

UNDERLAY PIECES

11 Draw paper templates for the underlays (see page 158). Roll out green sugarpaste/rolled fondant, transfer to greaseproof/wax paper, place the template on top, and cut to shape with a sharp craft knife or scalpel. Mark the centre bottom of each underlay for the bottom tier. Freeze until needed. Cut six underlays for the bottom tier and six for the top tier.

FINISHING

12 As each underlay is removed from the freezer, match the underlay centre mark with the cake mark on the bottom tier, and attach. For the top tier, place the centre of the piece 2.5 cm/1 inch above the cake mark. With the No.4 piping tube/tip, pipe royal icing at the base of each tier. Using royal icing, attach each set of baroque pieces over the edges of the underlays, fasten the three baroque pieces to the top tier, and secure the basketweave cones to the middle tier. Place large roses on the top cake and at the base of the bottom tier. Use the small roses to fill in and complete the arrangements. Pipe green royal icing leaves with the No.349 piping tube/tip. Join the cones with 4.5 mm/³/16 inch strips of twisted, white flower paste/gum paste. To finish, attach streamers, 10 cm/4 inches and 13 cm/5 inches long, and paste bows to each cone.

Here Comes the Groom

CAKE AND DECORATION

- 40 x 31 cm/16 x 12½ inch oval cake
- 125 g/4 oz each very pale green and mid-brown flower paste/gum paste
- Moss-green, golden-yellow, brown and dark green petal dusts (VB/CK)
- 500 g/1 lb white flower paste/gum paste
- Green, brown, black and yellow airbrush colours
- Black, brown and moss-green paste food colourings (VB/CK)
- 1 kg/2 lb brown pastillage (see page 134)
- 250 g/8 oz Chinese rice noodles/ cellophane noodles/rice sticks
- Green, brown, black and white powdered candy colours (VB/CK)
- 2.5 kg/5 lb chocolate-brown sugarpaste/ rolled fondant
- 250 g/8 oz ivory sugarpaste/rolled fondant

EQUIPMENT

- White 18- and 20-gauge wires
- Brown floral tape • Angled tweezers
- Pale gold embroidery floss
- Heavy cardboard, 4 cm/1½ inches wide
- Paper templates (see page 152)
- Leaf board
- Applecrate/apple box divider
- Veining tool
- Bubble foam or eggcrate foam
- Airbrush • Wire coat hanger
- Heavy aluminium foil • Wire brush
- 55 x 45 cm/22 x 18 inch polystyrene/ styrofoam board, 5 cm/2 inch thick
- 40 x 31 cm/16 x 12½ inch oval sturdy board
- 55 x 45 cm/22 x 18 inch oval heavy board
- Fabric covering for cake board (EM)
- Biscuit/cookie press • Sugarcraft gun

WHILE THE GROOM'S CAKE IS CONSIDERED TO BE A SOUTHERN AMERICAN TRADITION, IT IS FAST GAINING POPULARITY IN OTHER AREAS. IT HAS GONE THROUGH MANY INCARNATIONS, FROM A SMALL PIECE OF CAKE PACKED IN A BOX GIVEN TO THE GUEST TO TAKE HOME, TO ITS MOST POPULAR FORM TODAY – A RICH CHOCOLATE CAKE WITH CHOCOLATE ICING.

MAGNOLIA CENTRES

1 Roll a ball of the very pale green flower paste/gum paste, then taper it into a slightly rounded cone (pic 1). Cut three pieces of 18-gauge wire, one being slightly longer than the other two. Bend a hook in the longer piece and bind all three wires together with the floral tape. Dip the wire in edible gum glue and insert securely into the base of the cone. Using fine scissors and beginning about two-thirds of the way down the cone, make fine cuts moving towards the point of the cone. After every few cuts, carefully curl the ends down. Then, using angled tweezers, pinch vertical lines on the lower third of the cone. With fine scissors, clip the top half of each of these lines, so they flare out slightly from the cone but should not curl back. Allow the cone to dry thoroughly.

1 Making the magnolia flower centres

2 Wind the embroidery floss 8–10 times around heavy cardboard. Carefully slip the floss off the cardboard, wire the centre and cut all loops. Moisten with gum glue, and spread the 'stamens' apart. Two of these will be needed for each flower. Place on each side of the central cone and bind with floral tape. Trim to just slightly larger than the cone base. Dust between the curled points with moss-green petal dust. Dust the curled points and the extensions at the cone base with golden-yellow petal dust. Add a touch of brown to the tips of the curls. The more open the flower, the darker these curls.

MAGNOLIA PETALS

3 Magnolias normally have nine petals, in three sizes. For the inner petal, put a slight curve into the end of a piece of white 20-gauge wire. Roll the white flower paste/gum paste on the leaf board and cut three petals with the craft knife or scalpel, using the inner petal template (see page 152). With a large ball tool, thin the petal edges, being careful not to ruffle them more than necessary. Using the ball tool or the rounded end of a rolling pin, work the inside of the petal to begin cupping it. Pinch a small pleat at the tip of the petal. Insert the prepared wire into the ridge made by the leaf board. Taper the end of the petal around the wire and lay the petal in the former, to obtain the desired shape, forcing the centre down and being sure that the curved part of the wire follows the curve of the petal. (A divider used in apple-crates/apple boxes makes a good former.) Make three middle and three outer petals in the same way.

4 Attach the petals to the flower centre with the floral tape, placing the inner ones equidistant around the cone, the middle petals between the inner ones, and the outer petals behind the inner petals (pic 2). Thicken the magnolia stems with extra wire or several layers of floral tape, until they are the desired width.

2 Stages of the magnolia petals

MAGNOLIA LEAVES

5 Magnolia leaves are large and fairly straight, with a definite curve at the centre vein and slight curves under at the edge. They are glossy dark green on top and soft brown underneath. Darken the green flower paste/gum paste, then roll it and mid-brown paste together on the largest slot on the leaf board, with the brown side facing down. Cut the leaf with a craft knife, using either leaf template (see page 152). Place the brown side up on a soft pad and thin the edges with the ball tool – this will also create a gentle curve under the leaf edge. Since most commercial leaf veiners are not large enough for these leaves, use the veining tool to mark the veins in the leaves. Make a sharp crease down the centre and insert a piece of 20-gauge wire. Place the leaf on bubble foam or eggcrate foam, positioning it so that the centre is between the bubbles and the outside edges curve over them. When completely dry, dust the leaf underside with brown petal dust, using a wide soft brush, and then lightly with cornflour/cornstarch, to give the velvety look of a natural leaf. Dust or airbrush the green side with dark green petal dust or green airbrush colour (pic 3), then make the green side glossy by holding the completely dried leaf over a steaming kettle.

3 Preparing the magnolia leaves

MAKING THE LOG

6 Build the log on a wire armature such as a wire coat hanger, bending it to the desired shape and building up the design with heavy aluminium foil. Cover with the brown pastillage. As long as the foil doesn't show through, don't worry about any cracks in the pastillage – they will lend more authenticity to the look of the log. Use the wire brush to add extra graining to the log. Also add knots and smaller stems, as desired. Dry thoroughly, and then airbrush with very dark brown, possibly with some black added. Spray this on, then wipe with a kitchen paper towel. This will leave the dark colour in the cracks and give more dimension to the log. Airbrush the log with a paler brown airbrush colour, and possibly some green and yellow airbrush colour, to create the desired look (pic 4).

4 Airbrushing colour into the log

SPANISH MOSS

7 Boil water in a saucepan, then add some black, brown and moss-green food colourings. Place the rice noodles/cellophane noodles/rice sticks in the boiling water for just a minute or two, until they are soft. Remove and spread out on kitchen paper towels to dry – this can take up to a day, at room temperature.

8 Mix the desired 'moss' colour using green, brown and black powdered candy colours. When the noodles are almost dry, sprinkle the powder mix over and through them, until they look like natural Spanish moss (pic 5). White powdered candy colour may need to be added to get the desired colour. Remove as much excess powder colour as possible. If the 'moss' is to be placed on a

5 Making Spanish moss

surface other than sugarpaste/rolled fondant, move it at this point, while not quite dry. Any moss that is going to touch sugarpaste/rolled fondant must be completely dry or it will mark the paste. For a specific shape, such as moss draping over the edge of the cake, use a cake tin/cake pan as a former.

6 A rope border made using a sugarcraft gun

ASSEMBLING THE CAKE

9 Bevel the polystyrene/styrofoam at the top, then set on the 55 cm/ 22 inch heavy board. Gather the fabric cover, at the top and bottom, with elastic, and pull over the prepared base board. (To order instructions for this base, see page 159, Earlene Moore.) Place the oval cake on the matching-sized, sturdy board. Cover with chocolate sugarpaste/rolled fondant, and centre on the fabric-covered base.

10 For the rope border, push ivory sugarpaste/rolled fondant through a biscuit/cookie press, or roll freehand. Twist two 'rope' pieces together, and cut the ends on a diagonal (pic 6). For the tassels, press ivory paste through the sugarcraft gun using the die with many small holes. To cover the seam where the tassels join the rope, make a small string with the single-holed die on the gun, then wrap it over the join.

Fantasia Roseta Romántica

GUEST CAKE BY ROSA VIACAVA DE ORTEGA

CAKE AND DECORATION

- 15 cm/6 inch, 20 cm/8 inch, 25 cm/10 inch and 30 cm/12 inch round cakes
- 500 g/1 lb white flower paste/gum paste
- White sparkle dust (VB/CK)
- Pink and lime petal dusts (VB/CK)
- Rose buds and leaves (see pages 94 and 119)
- Filler flowers
- 3.5 kg/7 lb white sugarpaste/rolled fondant
- 1.5 kg/3 lb white flower paste/gum paste and white sugarpaste/rolled fondant in a 50:50 mixture

EQUIPMENT

- 26-gauge wire
- Jasmine cutter and veiner mould (RVO – F108)
- Sponge foam
- Petal pad
- Ball tool
- Former
- Cake boards (see step 3)
- 3 mm beadmaker (CK)
- Dotted Swiss rolling pin (RVO – F33)
- Lace cutter (RVO – F06)
- 5 x foam twisty hair rollers or 1 cm/½ inch plastic tubing
- Large and medium fantasy leaf cuttters (RVO) or paper templates (see page 157)
- Round piping tube/tip (W – 3)
- Lace rolling pin (RVO – F32)
- Kitchen paper towel tube former
- Separated cake stand (HD – Nancy)

TOUCHED WITH A SENSE OF PURE FANTASY, THIS EXQUISITELY CRAFTED WEDDING PRESENTATION IS TRULY A BRIDE'S DELIGHT. A DREAMY WHITE CLOUD GLISTENS WITH SPARKLING ACCENTS, WHITE BOWS AND UNIQUE LEAF OVERLAYS. TULLE BILLOWS AND SWIRLS BENEATH EACH CAKE, CREATING THE ILLUSION THAT THEY ARE SUSPENDED IN AIR.

FANTASY FLOWERS

1 For the flower centre, hook the 26-gauge wire and dip in edible gum glue. Attach a flat-topped teardrop of flower paste/gum paste to the wire. Brush with white sparkle dust and leave to dry. Prepare a Mexican hat in paste. Brush the jasmine cutter and veiner mould with white sparkle dust and press the Mexican hat into the mould. Trim the petal edges with the sponge, then remove the flower from the mould. Place on the petal pad and soften the edge with the ball tool. Push the flower centre through the flower, attaching with edible gum glue. Brush the flower with pink and lime petal dusts (pic 1), then place in the former to dry.

2 Make up four top posies, using a variety of small pink rose buds, fantasy flowers, filler flowers and rose leaves.

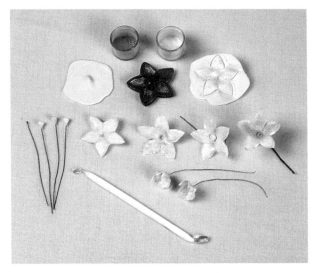

1 Follow these steps for the fantasy flowers

CAKE SIZE	BOARDS
15 cm/6 inch	18 cm/7 inch and 20 cm/8 inch
20 cm/8 inch	23 cm/9 inch and 25 cm/10 inch
25 cm/10 inch	28 cm/11 inch and 30 cm/12 inch
30 cm/12 inch	32.5 cm/13 inch and 35 cm/14 inch

PREPARING THE CAKES

3 Cover each cake with white sugarpaste/rolled fondant. Glue two boards together for each cake (see box, left). Cover the combined boards with paste, taking it over the edges. Centre the cakes on the boards and attach. Brush the inside of the beadmaker with white sparkle dust. Press flower paste/gum paste into the mould, then firmly push a rolling pin over the beadmaker. Open the mould and carefully remove the pearls (see page 54). Attach pearls to the base of each cake and to the second tier of each board.

RUCHED DRAPES

4 Roll out a 25 x 13 cm/10 x 5 inch strip of 50:50 mixture of flower paste/gum paste and sugarpaste/rolled fondant

2 Preparing the ruched drapes

using the dotted Swiss rolling pin. Create a decorative edge with the lace cutter, then remove the centre of each scallop. Lay each piece over the foam hair rollers or plastic tubing, forming folds by gathering at the top (pic 2). Leave to firm up. Attach to the top of the cake, using edible gum glue, drape over the sides and plump the drapes to create a ruched effect.

FANTASY LEAVES

5 Roll out more 50:50 mixture of flower paste/gum paste and sugarpaste/rolled fondant using the dotted Swiss rolling pin. With the fantasy leaf cutters, cut out large and medium leaves from the embossed paste, then brush with white sparkle dust. Using the piping tube/tip, create an open-work edge around each leaf (pic 3). Gather the top of each leaf into two folds. Overlap the drapes with the leaves, supporting with the sponge foam until dry.

3 Fantasy leaves with matching cutters

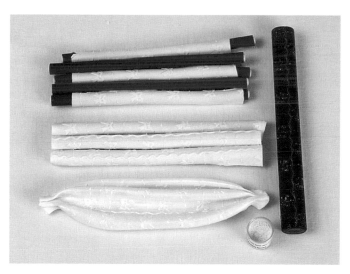

4 First stages of making the bow loops

BOWS AND RIBBON TAILS

6 Prepare a 23 x 13 cm/9 x 5 inch strip of 50:50 mixture of flower paste/gum paste and sugarpaste/rolled fondant, with the lace rolling pin. Using the foam hair rollers or plastic tubing, make three folds. Remove the rollers and pinch the paste at each end (pic 4). Bend each folded paste piece over a tube former and pinch together, to make the bow loops. Leave until dry (pic 5). Decorate each cake as illustrated and arrange on the cake stand.

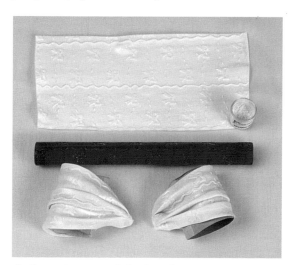

5 Second stages of the bow loops

Simply Pretty in Pink

CAKE AND DECORATION

- 15 cm/6 inch, 20 cm/8 inch and 25 cm/10 inch round cakes
- 10 g/¹/₃ oz white flower paste/gum paste
- Purple and lime petal dusts (VB/CK)
- Purple and pale leaf-green powdered food colourings (VB/CK)
- Fine polenta/cornmeal
- 3.5 kg/7 lb pale pink sugarpaste/rolled fondant
- 500 g/1 lb white sugarpaste/rolled fondant
- Super pearl, avocado and silk-white lustre dusts (VB/CK)
- 55 g/2 oz pale pink flower paste/gum paste
- 10 g/¹/₃ oz green flower paste/gum paste
- One large rose, 10 cm/4 inches across (see page 106)

EQUIPMENT

- Ball tool
- Trumpet modelling tool (J)
- 18 x 0 line brush
- 28-gauge wire
- Floral tape
- 15 cm/6 inch, 20 cm/8 inch and 25 cm/10 inch thin round cake boards
- 30 cm/12 inch round cake board
- Dowelling (see page 142)
- Sharp knife
- Round piping tube/tip (W – 1)
- Daisy centre mould (J)
- Rose leaf cutter (OP – R5)
- Veining tool
- Small and medium blossom cutters (OP – F2S and F2M; RVO or PME)

SIMPLE IN DESIGN, THIS CAKE HAS VISUAL IMPACT. PERFECT FOR A SMALL WEDDING, OR SUMMER BRIDAL TEA, IT IS DECORATED WITH AMERICAN VIOLETS, NOT THE TRADITIONAL ENGLISH VARIETY. TOPPED WITH A SUPERB FULL-BLOWN, OLD-FASHIONED ROSE, THE DRAPE TWISTS DOWN THE SIDE OF THE CAKE, ACCENTING THE OFFSET PLEATED JABOT BEFORE CURLING ON TO THE SERVING BOARD.

THE VIOLETS

1 Prepare a Mexican hat with white flower paste/gum paste and cut into five points using the scissors (pic 1). Thin the petals with a ball tool. The upper pair will be wider and longer than the rest; the lower outside set curled forward, then backward; and the central base petal, which is more square, is cupped forward.

2 Deepen the throat of the flower with the trumpet modelling tool. Brush the entire flower, except the throat, with purple petal dust. Tint the throat with lime petal dust. With the line brush, paint some fine dark purple lines at the base of the throat, using clear alcohol/vodka or Everclear mixed with purple food colouring.

3 Insert two tiny white ball-shaped flower paste/gum paste stamens at the front and dust with a little sifted polenta/cornmeal. Add a hooked 28-gauge wire, and bind with floral tape. Paint the calyx with alcohol-diluted, leaf-green food colouring. Dry.

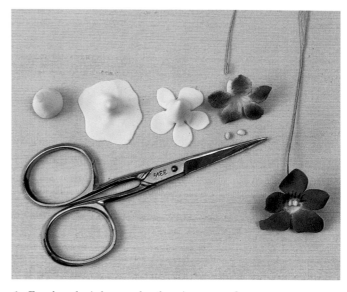

1 Freehand violets and colouring procedure

PREPARING THE CAKES

4 Freeze the cakes before sculpting. Gradually and evenly sculpt 2.5 cm/ 1 inch away from the base of each cake, using a wide-bladed knife (see page 140). (The tops will still be at the original measurement but the bases will have decreased by 2.5 cm/1 inch.) Centre the cakes on the matching-sized thin cake boards. Cover with pale pink sugarpaste/ rolled fondant.

ROLLED STRIPS

5 Cut out continuous rolled strips, alternating pale pink and white sugarpaste/rolled fondant. Starting at the top edge of each cake and working towards the base, attach with a little edible gum glue (pic 2). Do not panic if each roll is not exactly even; they are meant to be slightly varied.

ROLLED STRIP GUIDE

Approximate circumference measurements for each cake:

15 cm/6 inch = 50 cm/20 inch strips
20 cm/8 inch = 65 cm/26 inch strips
25 cm/10 inch = 80 cm/32 inch strips

Make each strip approximately 6 cm/2½ inch wide, then fold in half.

6 Cover the 30 cm/12 inch cake board with a thin layer of pale pink sugarpaste/rolled fondant. Beginning at the edge of the board and working towards the centre, add continuous paste strips, making the first strip 100 cm/40 inches long, then reducing the strip length by 5–8 cm/2–3 inches each time as you progress towards the centre. Continue until about 10 cm/ 4 inches in depth from the edge has been covered. Brush all the rolled strips with super pearl lustre dust.

CAKE ASSEMBLY

7 Centre the bottom tier cake on the 30 cm/ 12 inch cake board. Add the other tiers, centring and dowelling each time (see page 142). Using the piping tube/tip, pipe a snail trail of royal icing or buttercream, to seal the cake edges, then add another continuous strip to cover the join, which should be offset to the left front.

2 Applying the rolled strips to the cake side

PLEATED RUFFLES

8 Cut 2.5 cm/1 inch strips of pale pink paste. Prepare a double pleated ruffle (pic 3) and attach over the rolled strip joins. Add a plain paste strip; make buttons in the daisy centre mould and brush with super pearl.

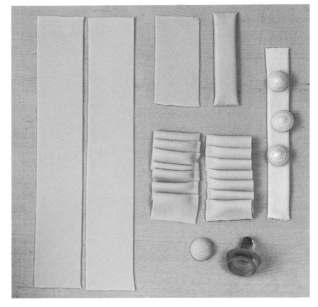

4 Rose leaves and cutter

CAKE DRAPE

9 Roll out two 45 cm/18 inch strips of pale pink flower paste/gum paste, pinch in two pockets, then drape and twist down the side of the cake. Attach only at the centre of the top cake.

---

3 Stages of making the pleated ruffles

ROSE LEAVES

10 Cut out ten rose leaves from the green flower paste/gum paste, using the rose leaf cutter. Vein each leaf and brush with avocado lustre dust (pic 4). Dry two of them within the pockets of the drape so they will fit.

5 Stages of the filler flowers

6 Attaching the full-length drape

FILLER FLOWERS

11 Right at the last moment, just before they are needed, make the filler flowers in pale pink flower paste/gum paste, using the small and medium blossom cutters (pic 5). Cut out as many as required, cup with the veining tool, and brush with silk-white lustre dust.

FINISHING OFF

12 Slip the violets and rose leaves in the pockets created in the folds, and glue scattered filler blossoms down the drape (pic 6). Attach the large rose on top, then tuck rose leaves beneath it, securing with royal icing. Decorate the serving table with a circle of ruched silk fabric. Position the cake, then scatter paste violets and leaves on the fabric.

Love is in the Air

CAKE DECORATION

- 10 cm/4 inch, 15 cm/6 inch and 20 cm/8 inch round cakes
- 5 ml/1 tsp Tylose powder/CMC (J)
- 2 kg/4 lb pale teal sugarpaste/rolled fondant
- Antique silk lustre dust (VB/CK)
- Cornflour/cornstarch

EQUIPMENT

- 10 cm/4 inch, 15 cm/6 inch and 20 cm/8 inch thin round cake boards
- 25 cm/10 inch cake board
- Pale teal ribbon, 1.5 cm/⅝ in wide, to trim cake board
- Open scalloped crimper (PME)
- Double-sided, saw-edged open scalloped crimper (PME)
- Adding machine tape
- Dotted Swiss rolling pin (RVO – F33)
- Lace cutter (FMM – M7)
- Broderie anglais cutter (PME)
- Floral rose posy mould (SB – 7865)
- 10 x 5 mm/¼ inch dowel rods
- Long sharpened dowel rod
- Paintbrush
- Garrett frill cutter (OP – GF1) or any round, scallop-edged, 9 cm/3½ inch cutter such as scone or biscuit/cookie cutter
- Plastic parasol bridal ornament

BRODERIE ANGLAIS – THE MOST FEMININE OF LACES – IS SEEN HERE IN A NEW LIGHT. UPDATED IN SOFTEST TEAL, WITH SOPHISTICATED, HAND-PAINTED, ANTIQUE SILK EYELETS, IT IS THE STUFF OF DAYDREAMS. BRIDES WILL BE ENCHANTED WITH THE SIMPLICITY OF THIS DRESDEN EFFECT. AN EPICUREAN MOMENT OF UNABASHED GLAMOUR FOR THE PERFECT FINISHING TOUCH.

PREPARING THE DECORATION

1 Add the Tylose powder to 250 g/8 oz sugarpaste/rolled fondant and knead thoroughly. Cover well with plastic wrap and set aside for a couple of hours. Knead again before using this strengthened paste.

2 Centre each cake on its matching sized board. Trim the 25 cm/10 inch cake board with the ribbon and cover with unstrengthened paste. Then cover all the cakes with more of this paste. Embellish the paste edges, alternating the two crimpers (pic 1). Paint every second crimped space with antique silk lustre mixed with clear alcohol/vodka or Everclear. Once the bottom tier paste has firmed up, centre it on the cake board.

1 Sample of the scalloped design

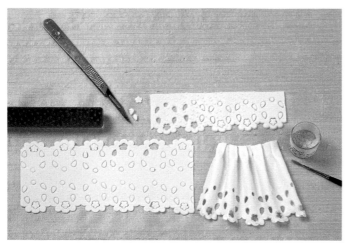

2 Creating the eyelet flounce

BOTTOM TIER

3 For the base flounce, run a strip of the adding machine tape around the bottom tier cake, marking a line of pinpricks at the top. Roll fairly thin strips of the strengthened sugarpaste/rolled fondant – these were 6 x 30 cm/2½ x 12 inches. Emboss with the dotted Swiss rolling pin (pic 2). Enhance the edge using the lace cutter, then add extra decorative touches with the broderie anglais cutter. Check that the paste flounce is the same depth as the adding machine tape. Remove all the little eyelet pieces, using the point of a craft knife or scalpel. (These can be saved and recycled later for other projects requiring a raised embroidery pattern.) Circle the holes with antique silk lustre dust mixed with clear alcohol/vodka or Everclear. Once the alcohol has evaporated – after a minute or two – gather and attach the flounce to the cake, hanging it from the line of pinpricks. Make the second row much shorter, measuring the depth from the edge of the cake and overlapping the base flounce but not covering the eyelets. Proceed in the same manner as the base flounce but using the shorter depth – the depth was only 4 cm/ 1½ inches on this cake.

4 Trim the top edge with a double folded swag and tidy up with a dainty textured bow (pic 3), both made with the strengthened paste. Cover the join with a rose posy, also made with this paste and the floral posy mould. Dowel and stack the cakes (see page 142), using five dowels per cake, finishing with the long sharpened dowel.

SECOND TIER AND TOP TIER

5 Note the depth and circumference of both the second and top tiers. Add a 2.5 cm/1 inch overlap to the circumference measurement, for a clean cut. For the second tier, roll out the strengthened sugarpaste/rolled fondant. Emboss with the dotted Swiss rolling pin. Cut a lace edge on both sides using the lace cutter, plus a double row with the broderie anglais cutter. Make

3 Swag, bow and rose posy

> ### OPTION FOR A LARGER CAKE
> Add two flounced tiers at the base of a five-tier cake, with three wrapped tiers above.

---

sure the measurement corresponds to the depth at the greatest point. Paint the eyelets with the antique silk medium. Once the paint is dry, attach the strip to the cake so it is slightly off-centre at the back, using the barest amount of boiled water on a paintbrush and taking care not to distort the eyelets. For the top tier, repeat step 5.

6 Cover the joins with grosgrain ribbon (made from sugarpaste/rolled fondant), 5 mm/¼ inch wide (pic 4), draping it all the way from the top centre of the top tier to the top edge of the bottom tier cake. Attach another ribbon of similar length, offsetting it the same distance to the

left. Gently push the ribbons into the waist of the cake with the fingertips. Make a large posy from the strengthened paste, using the floral rose posy mould, and attach with edible gum glue so it keeps the ribbons correctly positioned. Add smaller, single moulded roses to the base of the tails.

4 Grosgrain ribbons and rose posy

> ### HELP FOR BEGINNERS
> The side design can be added before the stacking process, just in case some might feel nervous handling large pieces at a height.

DOME CENTREPIECE

7 Cut out a circle from sugarpaste/rolled fondant, with the Garrett frill cutter or other scalloped-edged cutter. Divide the circle evenly and cut eyelets with the broderie anglais cutter (pic 5). Lightly dust a plastic parasol bridal ornament with cornflour/cornstarch and place the paste over it. When completely dry, paint the eyelets with antique silk lustre dust mixed with clear alcohol/vodka or Everclear. Centre the dome centrepiece on the top tier, attaching with edible gum glue or, for a perfect match, dissolve a pea-sized ball of strengthened sugarpaste/rolled fondant in a few drops of hot water for two seconds in the microwave and use this to attach the centrepiece. Add a moulded rose posy on top. The cake also looks good from the side and can be displayed that way if preferred.

5 Stages of the dome centrepiece

Breathtaking in Bride's Lace

CAKE AND DECORATION

- 15 cm/6 inch, 20 cm/8 inch, 25 cm/10 inch
  and 35 cm/14 inch oval cakes
- 55 g/2 oz white flower paste/gum paste
- Moss-green, brown and lime-green petal
  dusts (VB/CK)
- 5 ml/1 tsp fine polenta/cornmeal
- 15 g/½ oz green flower paste/gum paste
- Super pearl lustre dust (VB/CK)
- 7 kg/14 lb white sugarpaste/rolled fondant

EQUIPMENT

- 18- and 28-gauge wires
- Green floral tape
- Large rose petal cutter or paper template
  for lisianthus (see page 155)
- Ball tool
- Celformer (CC)
- Sponge foam
- Calyx cutter
- Lace medallion cutter (ELI – 501)
- Rounded former
- 3 mm, 4 mm and 8 mm beadmakers (CK)
- 15 cm/6 inch, 20 cm/8 inch and
  25 cm/10 inch thin oval cake boards
- 43 cm/17 inch oval cake board
- Wood-graining tool
- 21 x 5 mm/¼ inch dowel rods
- Long sharpened dowel rod
- Lace wrap mould (ELI – 201)
- Lace cutter (FMM – M7)
- Lace rose mould (SB – 8F955)
- Scalloped-edged cutter (FMM – M7)
- Satay stick/bamboo skewer
- Textured fabric or ribbon, at least
  2.5 cm/1 in wide
- Dressmaker's tracing wheel

INSPIRED BY A LOVE OF VICTORIAN ACCENTS, FLUID VINTAGE RIBBON ARRANGEMENTS DRAPE OVER GRACEFUL LACE. WHITE ON WHITE WITH ITS EXTENDED PALETTE OF NEUTRALS ARE NATURALS FOR A ROMANTIC FORMAL WEDDING. THIS CAKE DESIGN PAYS TRIBUTE TO PARISIAN FASHION DESIGNER CHRISTIAN LACROIX WHOSE MAGNIFICENT WORK INSPIRED ONE OF MY FAVOURITE WEDDING CAKES.

LISIANTHUS CENTRE

1 Using white flower paste/gum paste, make three small flat seed pods. Glue each to 28-gauge wire. Bind together with the floral tape. Brush with moss-green petal dust and colour the point with brown petal dust. For the stamens, mould five tiny rounded ovals with white paste. Glue each stamen to 28-gauge wire, then dampen slightly and dip into sifted fine polenta/cornmeal. Form a small fat sausage with green flower paste/gum paste. Push the taped seed pod wires into the top and through the sausage. Arrange the five stamens at equal distances around the sausage and position the pollen heads beneath the seed pods. Tape to the wires at the sausage base. Tape the whole lisianthus centre to an 18-gauge wire and continue taping to the stem base (pic 1).

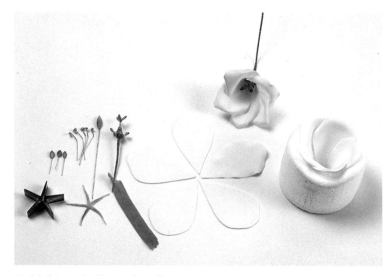

1 Making the lisianthus flowers

LISIANTHUS FLOWERS

2 Roll white flower paste/gum paste very thinly before cutting five petals, using the rose petal cutter or the lisianthus template (see page 155). If the rose petal cutter is used, slice the sides off the petals, as a lisianthus petal is much narrower than the rose. Although each petal can be wired, those shown here are not. Thin the petal edges with the ball tool and press into the palm of the hand to create veining. Glue the right side of each petal at the base for about one-third of its depth. Stack the petals into a fan, each overlapping by half. Furl the petals into a cone, checking that their bases are connected into a dull point.

Roll up and place into a celformer that has been pierced through the base and dusted with cornflour/cornstarch. Separate the petals and prop with foam. Dust the merest hint of lime-green petal dust in the throat and at the flower tips. Push the wired stamens through the centre of the glued petals and secure with royal icing at the base. Check that the flower has not stuck to the former.

3 Cut the calyx from green paste, using the calyx cutter. Thin the sides with the ball tool, and pinch along the centre with tweezers. Glue in place beneath the petals.

THE TIARA

4 With the lace medallion cutter, prepare a lace-embossed, white flower paste/gum paste medallion. Brush with super pearl and then remove the eyelet holes. Cut the medallion base straight, using a craft knife (pic 2). Cover the rounded former with plain paper and lay the medallion on it until dry. Stand the piece up and

2 Tiara method from mould to former

embellish with three rows of stacked, graduated, 8 mm, 4 mm and 3 mm, white sugarpaste/rolled fondant beads (see beadmaking page 54). Brush with super pearl. Add two very thin single ribbons to tie at the back. For the finishing touch, attach two tiny four-looped bows at either side, covering the ribbon tapes. Add a single 4 mm bead at the centre of each bow.

STACKING THE CAKES

5 Centre the top three cake tiers on their matching-sized, thin cake boards, then cover each cake, including the bottom tier cake, with white sugarpaste/rolled fondant. Cover the 43 cm/17 inch oval cake board with white paste and emboss it with the wood-graining tool (pic 3). Brush the embossed board with super pearl lustre dust, then centre the bottom cake on it. Dowel and stack the cakes (see page 142).

3 Wood-grained cake board covering

LACE WRAPS

6 Run the sugarpaste/rolled fondant through a pasta machine on setting three, or hand roll. Press into the lace wrap mould and rub with the palm of the hand. Turn the mould over; allow the paste to drop out by itself, then trim the scalloped edge with a craft knife or scalpel, and brush liberally with super pearl lustre dust (pic 4). Dampen the sides of the cake with a little boiled water. Once the lace embossed paste has firmed, lay it face downwards on the lace wrap mould. Using the mould as support, attach one or two lengths of the lace-embossed paste to the side of each tier. Each wrap is 55 cm/22 inches long and goes right around the top tier, with a single join at the back. The second, third and bottom tiers each need two lace wraps. Seal the cakes with 8 mm sugarpaste/rolled fondant beads brushed with super pearl lustre dust.

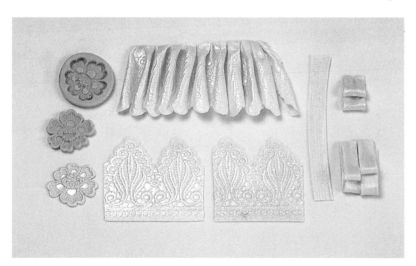

4 Stages of the lace wrap, appliquéd flowers, bustle and vintage ribbons

This cake design would take centre stage at a typical American wedding. Made to be viewed from the front, back or side, it doesn't matter where it is placed at the event. Lisianthus or prairie gentians (*Eustoma grandiflorum*) are native to Texas, although the Japanese first popularized these long-lasting cut flowers. The pretty arc of each flower as it bends forward creates a soft and elegant silhouette.

DRAPES AND SWAGS

7 Measure and divide the bottom tier into four, finding the centre front and back, then the sides. Using these measurements, cut four panels of embossed lace in sugarpaste/rolled fondant, using a craft knife or scalpel. Embellish the edges with the lace cutter, then brush with super pearl lustre dust. Fold the top over and add an extra fold in the centre (pic 5). Attach each piece to the side of the bottom tier, draping from the centre front to the side, then side to back, back to side and finally side to front.

8 For the swags, measure the bottom tier cake on both front and back at mid-point between the centre front and centre back and the sides. Using these measurements, prepare the swags in the same way as the drapes. Make the appliquéd flowers by pressing sugarpaste/rolled fondant into the lace rose mould. Freeze the paste until the flower readily pops out of the mould. Leave to dry, brush with super pearl and attach each flower over a join on the cake board.

BUSTLE AND VINTAGE RIBBONS

9 Prepare a 50 x 9 cm/20 x 3¹/₂ inch panel of lace-embossed sugarpaste/rolled fondant, for the bustle. Trim the edge into scallops with the scalloped cutter and gather using a satay stick/bamboo skewer. Leave to firm, then attach to the cake back with a little boiled water.

10 To make the vintage ribbons, emboss thinly rolled sugarpaste/rolled fondant with textured fabric or ribbon. Cut 2.5 cm/1 inch strips, fold the edges under, then fold in half. Vary the lengths so they balance the bustle. Layer these textured ribbons both front and back and on the sides. Prop with sponge foam, if the bustle begins to flatten.

5 Lace-edged drape and mould

FINISHING

11 For the back, make another sugarpaste/rolled fondant flounce of embossed lace, measuring 50 x 6 cm/20 x 2¹/₂ inches, and gather so it fits the space over the top of the ribbons. Pleat a neat little lace-edged paste fan, dry it and then attach at the base of the third tier in the empty space behind the bustle and between the cake. Cover the join on the side ribbons with two more appliquéd lace flowers. Using the same texturing medium, cut four 50 cm/20 inch paste ribbons and attach with a tiny amount of water to the cake side. Trim diagonally, then zip down the edge with the tracing wheel. Gently guide the ribbons to the centre front and attach with very little water. Add a 6 cm/2¹/₂ inch ball of white flower paste/gum

paste at the centre of the long ribbons. Hide the front and sides by extending the ribbon loops up and almost over, just leaving spaces for the lisianthus. Dry overnight. Attach the flowers, dipping each stem in royal icing and pushing it into the ball of flower paste/gum paste. Brush away any unattractive residue. Prop with sponge foam. (Back view of cake on page 149.)

(Back view of cake on page 149.)

AT THE RECEPTION

Add the top tier at the event site, then prepare and attach the pearl bead border. If only one person is available to carry this extremely heavy cake, it might also be worth adding the long ribbon loops on-site; then it would be necessary to carry only two tiers stacked. The tiara can be permanently attached into position with royal icing or be boxed and carried separately, to be retained as a souvenir.

And the Bride Chose Dogwood

CAKE AND DECORATION

- 15 cm/6 inch, 20 cm/8 inch, 25 cm/10 inch and 30 cm/12 inch round cakes
- 15 g/¹/₂ oz mid-green flower paste/ gum paste
- 250 g/8 oz ivory flower paste/gum paste
- Moss-green, pale yellow, lime and mushroom petal dusts (VB/CK)
- Silk-white lustre dust (VB/CK)
- Brown food colouring (VB/CK)
- 6 kg/12 lb ivory sugarpaste/rolled fondant
- Teacup mould for centrepiece base (see step 9)
- Champagne sugar crystals

EQUIPMENT

- Greased tulle netting
- 24-gauge wire
- Medium rose cutter (OP – R2, or similar)
- Paper templates of elongated petal and dogwood leaf (see page 157)
- Small blossom cutter
- Veining tool
- Aluminium foil
- Round piping tube/tip (W – 110)
- Fine tweezers
- 15 cm/6 inch, 20 cm/8 inch, 25 cm/10 inch thin round cake boards
- 35 cm/14 inch round cake board
- Ivory ribbon, 1.5 cm/⁵/₈ inches wide, to trim the 35 cm/14 inch cake board
- Grosgrain-textured rolling pin (EC)
- Turntable (optional)
- Sponge foam
- 7 x 1 cm/¹/₂ inch dowel rods
- 12 x 5 mm/¹/₄ inch dowel rods

SAVING THE BEST FOR LAST! GLOWING WITH SUBTLE MOTHER-OF-PEARL SHEEN, DELICATE TRACERIES OF DOGWOODS ENCIRCLE THIS ELEGANT WEDDING CAKE, ILLUSTRATING SKILFULLY BLENDED, CLASSIC DESIGN AND CONTEMPORARY OVERTONES. ANOTHER SPECIAL SUGAR-ART TOUCH: THE FOOTED VASE WITH ITS SIMPLE CLUSTER OF MATCHING FLOWERS.

DOGWOOD FLOWERS

1 For the centre, press a pea-sized ball of mid-green flower paste/gum paste into the piece of greased tulle netting. Remove and check the shape is round. Gum glue miniscule ivory flower paste/gum paste cones on top of the centre, to suggest buds and florets. Make and wire seven such flower centres, and set aside to dry. Paint with clear alcohol/vodka or Everclear mixed with moss-green and pale yellow petal dusts.

2 Cut a pair of ivory flower paste/gum paste petals using the medium rose cutter or similar (two options are shown in pic 1), then cut another pair using the elongated petal template. Remove a small U-shape from the tops of both pairs, using the side of the small blossom cutter.

3 Thin the petal edges, then deeply vein with long strokes from top to base of each petal. Push the veining tool point into each cutout, so creating a slight hump across the petal tip. Lay the first pair of petals on a piece of shaped aluminium foil and gum glue together, then attach the elongated pair, forming a crucifix. Glue the flower centre over the join. Set aside to dry. Highlight the petals with lime petal dust, then silk-white lustre dust. Paint the cutouts with brown food colouring diluted with clear alcohol/vodka or Everclear. When thoroughly dry, dust the cutouts with mushroom petal dust. Make forty unwired flowers.

TO DRY WIRED FLOWERS

Push the wire on each flower through a hole in some shaped aluminium foil positioned over a tall drinking glass, resting the flower head on the foil. Leave until thoroughly dry.

DOGWOOD STEMS

4 Form a slim roll of ivory flower paste/gum paste and thread on to each wire. Bend in the desired stem shape, before drying. Brush with moss-green and lime petal dusts. Make small paste leaves freehand, and attach to the stems.

DOGWOOD FOLIAGE

5 For the side design, real dogwood leaves were used (see page 157 for the paper templates). Using the template or a commercial leaf cutter, cut out ivory flower paste/gum paste leaves, vein, brush with silk-white lustre dust and highlight with lime petal dust. Prepare about ninety leaves.

DOGWOOD SEED PODS

6 Prepare small cones freehand from ivory flower paste/gum paste. Impress the top with the piping tube/tip, and form ridges with fine tweezers. Brush with silk-white lustre dust, then lime and mushroom petal dusts. Dry.

GROSGRAIN RIBBON

7 Cover the cakes and boards with ivory sugarpaste/rolled fondant. Attach the ribbon to the board edge.

8 Emboss ivory sugarpaste/rolled fondant with the grosgrain-textured rolling pin. Measure the base of each cake, cut the embossed paste in appropriate, single lengths, and allow to firm up for a few minutes. Attach a strip to each cake, using a turntable if available, or placing the cake

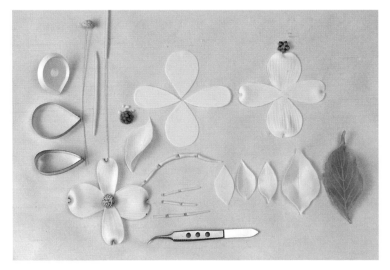

1 Stages of the dogwood flowers and leaves

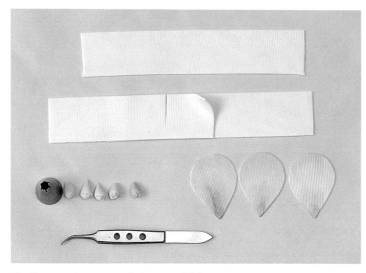

2 Grosgrain-textured dogwood blossoms

FINISHING

11 Stack the cakes using dowel support (see page 142). Attach the dogwood flowers, foliage and seed pods to the cake sides, with royal icing; particularly check each flower before moving on to the next. If nervous, prop the flowers with pieces of sponge foam until the royal icing is dry. The foliage and seed pods are much lighter and not likely to fall off while the royal icing is still wet.

12 Scatter and attach several leaves and seed pods on the paste-covered cake board. The day before moving the cake to the reception site, position the floral centrepiece centrally on the top cake, and secure with royal icing. (If the centrepiece is required as a family memento, pack separately and position on the cake on-site.)

board on a slippery surface and turning it by hand; start at the back and allow the paste ribbon to wrap itself round the cake. Cut overlapping ribbons for a perfect join and seal with royal icing. Remove the excess pieces of paste.

CENTREPIECE BASE

9 Create an ivory moulded sugar vase (see pages 74–5), using a prettily shaped teacup. Gouge out the centre with a teaspoon and dry thoroughly. Fill the centre with a ball of stiff sugarpaste/rolled fondant, flattened on the surface. Sprinkle with the sugar crystals and dry for a day. Emboss ivory flower paste/gum paste with the grosgrain-textured rolling pin and cut out single dogwood petals (pic 2). Attach to the outer surface of the moulded sugar vase. Cover the join of the sugar base with a thin strip of embossed, ivory flower paste/gum paste; then add miniature rolls of paste dusted pale lime.

10 Dip the stems of the wired flowers in thinned royal icing and push into the paste ball. Support in position with sponge foam until completely dry.

PRESENTATION

This cake can be set up on a table of honour, around which the guests can walk at the reception site. The design is continuous and since there is little difference from the front, back and sides there is no necessity for a special background.

PACKAGING

At the reception site, be sure to leave a strong cardboard box, written instructions for the staff, and the material for the cake top centrepiece to be repacked after the cake has been cut.

International Notes and Recipes

INGREDIENT VARIATIONS

• American butter is sold in pound packs. These are separated into 4 oz blocks known as sticks, each of which is marked on the side of the wrapper in 1 tbsp increments. One stick equals 4 oz, which is 115g; 1 tbsp equals ½ oz, which is 15g.

• Large eggs are used in all recipes in this book.

• American mills prepare plain flour/all-purpose flour from a combination of hard and soft wheat varieties, while UK mills use primarily soft wheat. British and Australian bakers preparing these recipes should therefore combine 50 per cent plain flour sifted together with 50 per cent strong bread flour.

• American 'Bakers' Special' (used professionally) or superfine sugar very closely resembles British and Australian caster sugar. Use any of these sugars in the recipes.

MEASURING INGREDIENTS

• American home bakers very rarely weigh ingredients, preferring to 'dip and sweep' with a measuring cup. When using a cup to measure flour, either spoon the flour into the cup or if the bin is wide and deep enough, dip the cup, then remove the excess by sweeping across the top of the cup with a flat spatula. Do not pack the flour down. There may be discrepancies with this method, because it is possible to repeat-weigh these dip-and-sweep ingredients six times and have six entirely differing results, some varying by as much as 55 g/2 oz. This is a major problem if you are expecting the perfect cake. By not using a set of scales, it is much easier to make a mistake in formulating the correct ratio of ingredients. Also cup and spoon measuring sets themselves can vary in capacity.

• The recipes in this book can be followed by using either metric or avoirdupois (imperial) measuring sets. Use only one set of measures.

• Finally, metric sets are slightly larger than imperial sets, so it follows that metric cake tins/pans should be used when using metric measurements and imperial cake tins/pans for imperial measuring sets.

ADJUSTMENTS FOR ALTITUDE

The recipes in this book were developed at sea level, so make alterations if you are baking at high altitude. Every 300 m/1,000 feet of altitude requires an additional adjustment. The most common changes to consider are:

• a reduction in bicarbonate of soda/baking soda or baking powder;

• a reduction in sugar;

• an increase in liquid weight. This can be accomplished with the addition of an egg white/yolk/or both;

• an increase in flour;

• an increase in oven temperature.

HEATING CONES

Prior to baking, fill the cake tin/pan to a smidgen over half full. To ensure even baking results in 8 cm/3 inch deep madeira/pound cakes, especially those of 30 cm/12 inch diameter or more, insert a heating cone. Grease the cone and lightly dust with flour both inside and out, position in the centre of the cake tin/pan, then half fill with the cake mixture/batter. After the cake has cooked and cooled, remove the heating cone. Turn out the cone-shaped cake, then return it to the space in the centre of the cake. Place the entire cake on a wire rack and allow to cool.

CAKE DECORATION ASSEMBLY TIMING

Directions for the assembly order in this book apply to Genoise, madeira/pound and sponge/white cakes, as these are perishable cakes and have to be made and decorated in a short time frame. Fruitcakes allow much more preparation time and can be made and decorated at whim.

CHOCOLATE
MELTING CHOCOLATE

There are many ways to melt dark or white chocolate and summer coat, from the inexpensive, familiar double boiler to the top-of-the-line Chocolate Sinsation. Something in between – the VIP Whistler – is a specialized pot that keeps chocolate or like products at an even temperature for dipping or pouring. Because the temperature of the Whistler is automatically controlled by the hydrothermic action of steam heat within the jacket lining, there is no burning or boiling over. It does not hold temper. At an average cost of £16/US$25, it is within the reach of most semi-professional and amateur sweet/candy makers.

WHITE CHOCOLATE

White chocolate as such really doesn't exist, as it does not contain any cocoa solids. However, you can buy two types of white colored chocolate: one contains cocoa butter as the only fat, and the other vegetable oil. Opt for a good brand such as Callebaut, Lindt, Nestlé, Tobler or Valrhona, all of which contain cocoa butter. Beware of inexpensive white chocolate – it will invariably be the inferior, vegetable oil variety. The shelf life of white chocolate is fairly limited, so be sure to use a retail source that sells it briskly. Use and eat immediately. Do not store for extended periods of time or, before you know it, it will have become quite rancid. Freezing is an option.

THE DOUBLE BOILER

Chocolate melts at 29°C/84°F. If using a double boiler, melt – don't cook – the chocolate over hot, not boiling, water. Take care: chocolate burns easily, so do not heat dark chocolate above 49°C/120°F or white above 43°C/110°F. Chocolate is often spoiled not only by overheating but also by steam contaminating the mixture, which makes the chocolate seize and so become almost useless, although it can still be piped. This will not happen with the VIP Whistler, as the steam is contained and the heat controlled.

THE MICROWAVE

The microwave can also be used to melt chocolate. Break the chocolate into small pieces and pile into a glass bowl. Melt uncovered with frequent bursts of low power (30 per cent), stirring frequently. The pieces will hold their shape and can trick one into overheating and burning the product.

RECIPES
SUGARPASTE/ROLLED FONDANT

Many sugarpaste/rolled fondant recipes are heavy to mix; this recipe shared by pastry chef Maria Velasquez of Texas is usable immediately and is not a strain to make.

INGREDIENTS
- 30 g/1 oz powdered gelatine
- 125 ml/4 fl oz/¹/₂ cup water
- 1 kg/2 lb sifted icing/confectioner's sugar
- 30 ml/1 oz/¹/₄ cup/2 tbsp glycerine
- 125 ml/4 oz/¹/₂ cup karo or light white corn syrup

Soften or bloom the gelatine in the water, then heat, but not to boiling point. Meanwhile warm the icing/confectioner's sugar in the oven at the lowest setting, then switch off (the sugar should only be body temperature). Add the glycerine and karo syrup to the warmed sugar. Combine both mixtures together. A heavy-duty machine on low speed using the dough hook can initially mix this. If the motor begins to strain, tip out on to the work surface, grease the hands with white vegetable shortening and finish manually. The mixture might look and feel a little lumpy but will smooth out during the kneading process.

COLOURING SUGARPASTE/ROLLED FONDANT

Always a laborious process, I find the easiest way to incorporate the colour with sugarpaste/rolled fondant is to dip a cocktail stick/toothpick into the chosen colour medium, which can be paste, liquid or powder – the last never seems to be as strong – and incorporate it into a small ball of paste. Knead a sufficiemt amount of colour into the ball until it reaches a shade several times deeper than required. Cut the ball in half and incorporate it into the paste. If the resultant mixture is too pale, add more from the remaining half ball until the desired shade is reached. Acting conservatively with colour is preferred, since once it is incorporated into the sugarpaste/rolled fondant, there is no way it can be reversed. Always wear food-approved gloves when using colouring paste, liquid or powder, to avoid colouring your hands and staining them semi-permanently.

ROYAL ICING
INGREDIENTS
- 1 egg white at room temperature (substitute with pasteurized/albumin powder, if necessary)
- 185–250 g/6–8 oz/1¹/₂–2 cups sifted icing/confectioner's sugar

Remove any embryonic tail from the egg white. Put the egg white in a glass bowl and break it up with a wooden spoon. Add the sugar 5 ml/1 tsp at a time, incorporating it thoroughly each time. Only once the egg white readily accepts the sugar can the amount of sugar added be increased. Hand mixing generally takes about 20 minutes.

ROYAL ICING TIPS

• The quantity of sugar required depends on whether soft, medium or firm peak royal icing is preferred; use the lower amount for soft peak, more for firmer icing.

• When only small amounts of royal icing are required, make up a single recipe of royal icing, then divide it into generous 5 ml/1 tsp increments. Double wrap in plastic wrap, double bag, and place in the freezer until it is required.

FLOWER PASTE/GUM PASTE

INGREDIENTS

• 1 egg white at room temperature (or pasteurized/albumin powder)
• 185–250 g/6–8 oz/1½–2 cups sifted icing/confectioner's sugar
• 15 ml/3 tsp Tylose powder/CMC (J)
• 5–10 ml/1–2 tsp firm white vegetable shortening

Proceed as for royal icing until the sugar reaches soft peak stage, then add the Tylose powder. Even though the mixture will immediately seize, continue adding sugar until the mixture is no longer sticky. Warm the shortening in the palms of the hands, then knead it into the mixture. Double wrap the paste tightly in plastic wrap and store in the refrigerator or freezer.

PASTILLAGE

INGREDIENTS

• 500 g/1 lb/4 cups icing/confectioner's sugar
• 15 ml/1 tbsp gum tragacanth
• 60 ml/2 fl oz/¼ cup water

Grease the bowl, paddle/beater and hands. On a slow setting, mix all the ingredients together, except for about ⅔ cup sugar. Grease the work surface/countertop, pour on the rest of the sugar and knead into the mixture.

The pastillage can be used immediately. However, it will dry out a faster than flower paste/gum paste so don't use it for anything that takes a long time to make.

DECORATOR'S BUTTERCREAM

This recipe makes sufficient to ice/frost and decorate a 25 cm/10 inch round cake or 23 x 33 cm/9 x 13 inch rectangular/sheet cake.

INGREDIENTS

• 25 ml/5 tsp meringue powder (substitute with 15 ml/3 tsp albumin powder, if necessary)
• 1.5 kg /3 lb icing/confectioner's sugar
• 2.5 ml/½ tsp cream of tartar
• 250 g/8 oz/1 cup unsalted/sweet butter and firm white vegetable shortening in a 50:50 mix (or 25:75 in hot temperatures)
• 185 ml/6 fl oz/¾ cup water
• 15 ml/1 tbsp pure vanilla (substitute with white imitation, if necessary)

1 Sift the dry ingredients in a large mixing bowl. Add the rest, blending well at low speed in an electric stand mixer, then beat at high speed for 5 minutes.
2 For icing/frosting the cake, mix in more fluid. For piped decorations, add a little more sugar.

ITALIAN MERINGUE BUTTERCREAM

This is sufficient to ice/frost a 20 cm/8 inch, double-layered cake.

INGREDIENTS

• 6 large egg whites
• 440 g/14 oz/1¾ cups caster/superfine sugar
• 1.25 ml/¼ tsp cream of tartar
• 500 g/1 lb/4 sticks unsalted butter/sweet butter at room temperature
• 15 ml/1 tbsp vanilla essence/extract

1 Using an electric hand mixer, beat the egg whites over hot water in the top of a double boiler until soft peaks appear. Add the sugar and cream of tartar in small increments, beating continuously until a ribbon begins to form, when the mixture reaches 40°C/105°F.
2 Remove from the heat source and continue beating until the mixture cools to room temperature. This may take 20 minutes or so.
3 Chop the butter in small pieces and introduce gradually. Increase the size of the pieces once half of the butter is incorporated into the mixture. Add the vanilla gradually.

CITRON VODKA CAKE

This cake is extremely rich, very delicious and not for anyone watching their calories.

Makes a 25 cm/10 inch round cake, 8 cm/ 3 inches deep.

CAKE INGREDIENTS

• 250 g/8 oz/2 sticks butter, softened
• 440 g/14 oz/1¾ cups caster/superfine sugar
• 5 ml/1 tsp vanilla essence/extract
• 4 large eggs
• 600 g/1¼ lb/5 cups plain flour/all-purpose flour
• 5 ml/1 tsp salt
• 5 ml/1 tsp baking powder

- 2.5 ml/$^{1}/_{2}$ tsp bicarbonate of soda/baking soda
- 250 ml/8 fl oz/1 cup buttermilk
- 10 ml/2 tsp lemon essence/extract
- 60 ml/2 fl oz/$^{1}/_{4}$ cup lemon juice
- Zest of two large lemons

SAUCE INGREDIENTS
- 250 g/8 oz/1 cup caster/superfine sugar
- 125 g/4 oz/1 stick butter
- 10 ml/2 tsp lemon essence/extract
- Juice of one lemon, made up to 125 ml/4 fl oz/$^{1}/_{2}$ cup with Stolichnaya Citron (Lemon) Vodka. Do not substitute.

1 Grease a 25 cm/10 inch round cake tin/pan, 8 cm/ 3 inch deep. Preheat the oven to 170°C/325°F/GM3. Cream the butter and sugar until light and fluffy. Add the vanilla, then the eggs, one at a time. Sift the dry ingredients and add alternately with the buttermilk and lemon essence, starting and ending with flour. Mix for 2 minutes at medium speed. Add the lemon juice and zest.
2 Fill the cake tin/pan, put in the preheated oven and bake for 60–65 minutes. (If the mixture has been divided between two shallower, 25 cm/ 10 inch tins/pans, check earlier, after about 45 minutes.) Test with a skewer before removing from the oven.
3 Meanwhile, about 10 minutes before the cake is ready to come out of the oven, mix the ingredients for the lemon vodka sauce. Heat the ingredients together, just enough to melt the butter. Do not allow the mixture to boil. Immediately prick the cake all over with a satay stick/bamboo skewer and pour the lemon vodka sauce over the hot cake. This will not hurt the cake as the holes will fill with the sauce and the cake crumb will absorb the liquid and begin to swell. Do not remove it from the tin/pan until it is properly cold.

ITALIAN CREAM CAKE

This is an excellent alternative to a fruitcake for a wedding, and it can be made at least five days ahead.

Makes two 25 cm/10 inch round cakes, 5 cm/2 inches deep.

INGREDIENTS
- 125 ml/4 fl oz/$^{1}/_{2}$ cup vegetable oil
- 125 g/4 oz/1 stick unsalted butter/ sweet butter
- 500 g/1 lb/2 cups caster/superfine sugar
- 5 ml/1 tsp vanilla essence/extract
- 5 large eggs, separated
- 5 ml/1 tsp bicarbonate of soda/ baking soda
- 250 ml/8 fl oz/1 cup buttermilk
- 1.25 ml/$^{1}/_{4}$ tsp salt
- 250 g/8 oz/2 cups plain flour/ all-purpose flour
- 125 g/4 oz/1 cup chopped pecans
- 65 g/2$^{1}/_{4}$ oz/1 cup flake coconut (frozen is best if you can get it, otherwise use moist dried)

1 Lightly grease two 25 cm/10 inch round cake tins/pans, 5 cm/2 inches deep with margarine, then dust with flour. Alternatively, prepare the tins/pans using a commercial spray or paint them with a whipped mixture of equal parts vegetable oil, plain flour/all-purpose flour and vegetable fat. Set the oven at 180°C/350°F/GM4.
2 Mix the oil and butter, then add the sugar, and cream well. Add the vanilla, and then the egg yolks one at a time until the mixture is light and fluffy but not curdled. Combine the bicarbonate of soda/baking soda with the buttermilk. Add salt to the cake mixture/batter, then sifted flour alternately with the buttermilk. Finally stir in the pecans and coconut. Beat the egg whites until stiff, and fold into the mix in three batches.
3 Fill the cake tins/pans and bake in the preheated oven for 40–50 minutes, depending on the oven. Check with a cake tester. This cake will be very moist, providing plenty of time to decorate.

If this recipe has been baked in a 25 cm/10 inch round cake tin/pan, 8 cm/ 3 inches deep, drop the oven temperature by 10°C/50°F. To keep the surface of this heavier-textured cake from drying out, create steam by adding a small pan of water in the lower part of the oven.

ROSELLA GINGER PECAN TORTE

This cake was a national finalist in a wedding cake competition held in the United States. It can be made and assembled five days before a wedding. In fact, the maturing process improves the combination of flavours. This recipe can be made 'as is' or mix and match to suit.

Makes two 25 cm/10 inch round cakes. Reduce them by a third for two 20 cm/8 inch round cakes.

CAKE INGREDIENTS
- 125 g/4 oz fresh pineapple (or drained crushed pineapple, if necessary)
- 360 g/12 oz ripe Anjou pears (or well-drained canned pears, if necessary)
- 440 g/14 oz/1$^{3}/_{4}$ cups caster/ superfine sugar
- One lemon, sliced
- Stick lemon grass/lemon serai (optional)

- 410 g/13 oz/3½ cups plain flour/
all-purpose flour
- 5 ml/1 tsp salt
- 15 ml/1 tbsp baking powder
- 23 ml/1½ tbsp powdered ginger
- 250 g/8 oz/2 sticks butter
- 15 ml/1 tbsp Madagascar bourbon
vanilla essence/extract (NM)
- 125 g/4 oz/½ cup brown sugar
- 4 large eggs
- 80 ml/3½ oz/½ cup oil
- 30 ml/2 tbsp golden syrup/golden
cane syrup
- 250 g/8 oz/2 cups toasted pecans,
finely chopped (Wichita's and Elliott)
- 60 g/2 oz/¾ cup fresh grated coconut
(substitute with desiccated coconut, if
necessary)
- 125 g/4 oz/½ cup glacé baby ginger,
chopped small (B)

SYRUP INGREDIENTS
- 45 ml/3 tbsp sugar
- 90 ml/6 tbsp water
- 120 ml/8 tbsp ginger wine (S)

1 Steam, drain and chop the pineapple
in the food processor. Poach the pears,
adding 45 ml/3 tbsp of the sugar, lemon
slices and lemon grass/lemon serai to the
steaming water. Grate the pears, then
drain and press for one hour before
using. Grease, flour and parchment-line
two 25 cm/10 inch cake tins/pan. Preheat
the oven to 180°C/350°F/GM4.
2 Sift together the flour, salt, baking
powder and ginger, and set aside. Beat
the butter, vanilla and remaining sugar
until light and fluffy. Add eggs one at a
time, beating well between each addition.
Add the sifted ingredients, then the oil
and syrup. Mix for 2 minutes on medium
speed – this gives time to activate the
flour then fold in the nuts and ginger.

3 Pour the mixture/batter into the
prepared cake tins/pans and bake for 45
minutes, but check after 30 minutes, in
case your oven is not properly calibrated.
Cool for 20 minutes, then turn on to a
cooling rack and pour over the ginger
syrup. (I used a hypodermic to distribute
the syrup evenly.)
4 To make the ginger syrup, simmer the
sugar in the water until it dissolves
entirely. Cool completely, then add the
ginger wine.

MERINGUE DACQUOISE
- 6 large egg whites
- 250 g/8 oz/2 cups icing/
confectioner's sugar, sifted
- 250 g/8 oz/2 cups toasted pecans,
coarsely ground
- 23 ml/1½ tbsp plain flour/all-purpose
flour, sifted
- 23 ml/1½ tbsp potato flour, sifted
- 8 ml/1½ tsp sifted Madagascar
bourbon vanilla powder (NM) (or
5 ml/1 tsp vanilla essence extract)
- 8 ml/1½ tsp good-quality cocoa
(Droste or Guittard), sifted

5 For the meringue, first preheat the
oven to 180°C/350°F/GM4. Draw two
25 cm/10 inch circles on parchment, and
place on an oven tray. Whip the egg
whites until they are stiff but not dry.
Add the sugar in three stages, mixing
well between each addition. Then, add
the nuts. Sift together the two flours,
powdered vanilla and cocoa, then add to
the mixture, folding in the flours and
powders carefully with a light hand. (For
competition, sift and add separately.)
Spoon the mixture into the circles, level
and bake in the preheated oven for
20 minutes, or until they have turned a
pale golden brown.

STRAINED GINGER MARMALADE
- 300 g/10 oz jar baby ginger
marmalade (B)
- 30 ml/2 tbsp lemon juice
- 45 ml/3 tbsp water
- 30 ml/2 tbsp butter
- 45 ml/3 tbsp ginger wine (S)

6 Heat the ginger marmalade, lemon
juice, water and butter gently in a double
boiler. Purée in the food processor, strain.
When cool add the ginger wine.

GINGER AND CHOCOLATE GANACHE
- 300 g/10 oz plain bitter/bittersweet
chocolate
- 315 ml/10 fl oz/1¼ cups double
cream/heavy cream
- 55 g/2 oz baby ginger, finely chopped (B)
- 85 g/3 oz/¾ cup toasted pecans, finely
chopped
- 45 ml/3 tbsp ginger wine (S)

7 Melt the chocolate over hot, not boiling,
water. Add the cream, ginger and pecans.
After cooling, add the ginger wine. Stir
well and allow to thicken.

MY MOTHER'S WASHED CREAM
- 250 g/8 oz/1 cup unsalted/sweet butter
- 15 ml/1 tbsp Madagascar bourbon
vanilla essence/extract (NM)
- 30 ml/2 tbsp uncooked honey
- 100 g/3½ oz/½ cup caster/
superfine sugar

8 For the cream, whip all ingredients until
light and fluffy. Remove the bowl from the
mixer. Cover with chilled water, swirl and
squeeze through the fingers for a minute,
drain the water thoroughly and re-beat

until light and fluffy. Repeat six times until white and the sugar is totally dissolved. Keep covered in a cool place, without refrigeration, or stored tightly covered in the refrigerator for up to a month.

ASSEMBLY

9 Level the cakes if necessary (see page 140). Secure greaseproof/wax paper to the cake board with royal icing. Place the meringue dacquoise on the greaseproof/ wax paper. Smooth a layer of washed cream, chocolate ganache and ginger marmalade on the meringue disc. Top with one of the cakes. Repeat the layers of washed cream, ganache and ginger marmalade with the second meringue disc. Top with washed cream, ganache and marmalade, then add the second cake. Trim the meringue discs. Coat the entire cake with washed cream, then the strained marmalade. Cover with plastic wrap for twenty-four hours. Chill. Cover with white chocolate sugarpaste/ rolled fondant.

WHITE CHOCOLATE SUGAR-PASTE/ROLLED FONDANT

For every 1 kg/2 lb sugarpaste/rolled fondant (see page 134), melt 250 g/8 oz either high-ratio cocoa butter white chocolate or chocolate couverture (compound). (If using couverture, add 85 g/ 3 oz/$\frac{1}{2}$ cup sifted Dutch-processed cocoa to the melted chocolate and knead well.) Pour the chocolate into the rested paste and knead until incorporated. If flaking occurs, microwave in 5 second increments until the paste warms. Leave overnight. This results in a soft and easy to manage sugarpaste/rolled fondant. Warm in the microwave for a few seconds before kneading. Roll out on sifted icing/confectioners' sugar or cocoa.

CAKE CUTTING CHARTS

The following cake-cutting directions are intended for madeira or sponge/pound or white cake. Triple the suggested numbers for fruitcake servings. Be reminded, wedding cake servings are not as large as those for dessert, and cake servers do not always cut exactly the same-sized slice. The chart is only as a general guide.

ROUND CAKES

DIAMETER	NO. PEOPLE SERVED
15 cm/6 inch	15
20 cm/8 inch	25
25 cm/10 inch	40
30 cm/12 inch	60
35 cm/14 inch	85
40 cm/16 inch	100
45 cm/18 inch	125

OVAL CAKES

SIZE	NO. PEOPLE SERVED
20 x 15 cm/8 x 6 inches	10
28 x 20 cm/11 x 8 inches	25
32 x 25 cm/13 x 10 inches	40
40 x 32 cm/16 x 13 inches	24

HEART-SHAPED CAKES

WIDTH	NO. PEOPLE SERVED
15 cm/6 inch	10
23 cm/9 inch	25
30 cm/12 inch	40
38 cm/15 inch	80

ALTERNATE WAYS TO CUT A ROUND CAKE

Method 1

Cut a circle 5 cm/2 inches in from the edge of the cake. Cut pieces approximately 2.5 cm/1 inch wide around that circle, with the knife pointing towards the centre of the cake all the time. Move in another 5 cm/2 inches, cut a circle and continue cutting and making further circles until the tier is served.

Method 2

Make a cut across the cake approximately 5 cm/2 inches from the edge. Slice off in approximately 2.5 cm/1 inch wide slices (end pieces will be a little larger because of the curve of the cake). Continue making cuts every 5 cm/2 inches and slicing in 2.5 cm/1 inch pieces until the tier is served.

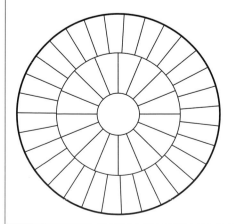
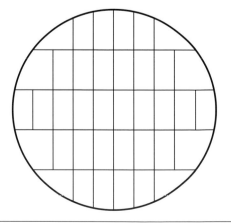

Bake it...Design it...Create it

COVERING A CAKE BOARD

Roll out the sugarpaste/rolled fondant to slightly larger than the cake board size. Slightly dampen the board and cover entirely with the paste. If liked, decorate with a textured rolling pin or crimper, depending on the pattern required (pic 2). Trim around the edge with a sharp knife, then smooth the rough edges with your hand or a set of smoothers. To disguise the raw edge to the board, attach a pretty ribbon or upholstery fabric, using fabric spray adhesive or a gum stick. For fruitcakes, an alternative method of covering a cake board is to roll out a strip of sugarpaste/rolled fondant and position it only between the cake and the board edge.

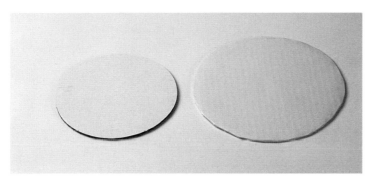

1 Thin American cake boards covered with plastic contact

Thin foil cake boards usually need to be trimmed to size – the board must not be visible beyond the edge of the cake itself. In the United States, thin boards (pic 1) are not covered with protective foil so they have to be taken care of individually. Plastic contact shelf covering is the preferred method. Cut the size required in ivory or white, then peel off the paper backing and attach to the thin card board on both sides. This is especially necessary for sugarpaste/rolled fondant cakes, because of the passage of time needed to complete the design work. If not protected, the board might absorb moisture, then warp or buckle, and the cake could collapse.

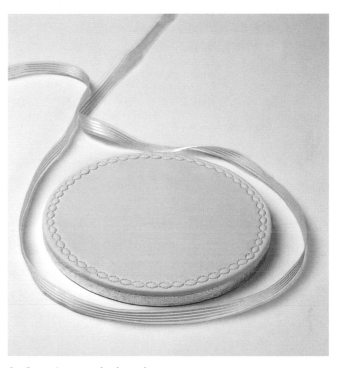

2 Covering a cake board

AN ADDITIONAL NOTE FOR CAKE STYLISTS

Dry sugarpaste/rolled fondant-covered cake boards overnight before adding cakes larger than 30 cm/12 inches in diameter. If the paste is not dry, it is very hard to centre the cake and move it on the board without marring the surface. Position each madeira or sponge/pound or white cake on a thin cake board. Bring the paste right down over the cake board edge before centring and stacking on the main cake board. These cakes are fragile so handle them gently.

LEVELLING A CAKE

Freeze or chill the cake overnight to firm the crumb, then place it on a cake board. To level the cake top, either cut right across with a long knife (pic 3) or use a professional cake leveller (pic 4) – the latter being invaluable when dealing with a cake as large as 50 cm/20 inches diameter. Turn the cake over, so the bottom of the cake is now the top, and there will be fewer noticeable imperfections.

3 Levelling a cake by hand

SCULPTING A CAKE

To sculpt a cake so its sides gradually incline inwards from the top, use a wide blade and cut down evenly, angling the knife inwards, until only a bare 1 cm/½ inch is removed at the base (pic 5). When doing this, err on the conservative side: the first time I attempted sculpting in this way, I chopped away large chunks and this was a mistake. Shaving the cake gradually is the correct way to proceed. Reception Confection cake (see page 86) has such sculpted sides.

To sculpt a 'waisted' cake, use a long, thin, very sharp knife to carve from the base up and the top down, creating a gradual inward curve and a shallow waist, 1 cm/½ inch deep. It doesn't take much cutting to achieve the 'waist' effect. (Also remember the more cake that is discarded, the fewer people it will serve, and this cost is passed on to the client.) The middle tier on All that Glitters cake (see page 52) is typical of this 'waisted' shape.

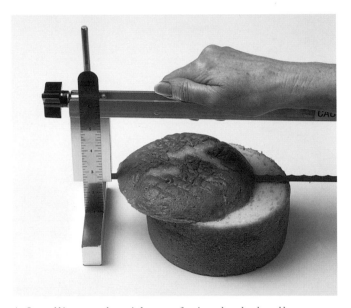

4 Levelling a cake with a professional cake leveller

5 Sculpting a cake with sloping sides

6 Sculpting a 'waisted' cake

COVERING A CAKE

First, sandwich layered cakes with chosen filling. Paint the surface of the cake with a thin coat of seedless raspberry jam/jelly. Make no mistake: if this coating is lumpy the paste will not be forgiving. Remove any visible pieces of fruit by pulsing in a food processor, then sieving before use. Cover the cake with a thin layer of buttercream or the Italian meringue version (pic 7), then with sugarpaste/rolled fondant.

To cover a cake with sugarpaste/rolled fondant using lifters, brush the surface of the paste lifters with a very thin coating of white shortening, then wipe off the excess with a paper towel, and dust the surface with sifted cornflour/cornstarch. Roll out the sugarpaste/rolled fondant on the lifter's metallic surface, and trim away the excess. Lift the rolled paste over the cake (pic 8) and drop the lifter down over the cake board. You should have a perfect result every time. Smooth the surface with your hands or a commercial smoother, and trim away excess paste. I use a very large, thin, commercial scraper to cut away the excess from the edge of the cake (pic 9), and it can double up as a smoother. Polish the cakes with a ball of scrap sugarpaste/rolled fondant. Leave them to sit overnight before decorating.

7 Cake first covered with jam, then Italian buttercream

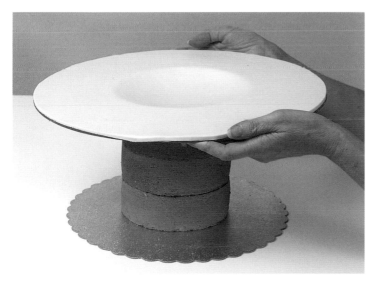

8 Sugarpaste/rolled fondant on a cake lifter

9 Trimming excess sugarpaste/rolled fondant

OTHER WAYS TO COVER A CAKE WITH SUGARPASTE/ROLLED FONDANT

Roll out the sugarpaste/rolled fondant roughly to the required size, and lift it over the cake with your hands or a rolling pin. This method becomes almost impossible as the cake size increases; when this happens, forget the rolling pin and lift the paste across both forearms, sharing the weight equally. Alternatively, roll out between two sheets of very thick plastic, peel away the top sheet, turn it over and lay over the cake before peeling away the other sheet.

DOWELLING A CAKE

Stacked cakes require the support of dowel rods to stop them collapsing. Currently I use wooden dowels to support my cakes; others prefer hollow plastic ones. However, some high-quality Stress-Free Cake Supports have recently become available (see Supplier's list, page 159), and these are so strong a person can stand on them. Each stainless-steel separator plate, in sizes ranging from 10 cm/4 inches to 40 cm/16 inches, will not warp and has four adjustable, nylon legs.

Whatever support material is used, the placement of the dowels is basically the same. Take the dowel measurement for each cake and cut to size. Evenly space in a circle and push into the cake with a finger (pic 10). Touch each dowel top with a blob of royal icing and, using an offset spatula, lift each cake into position. To avoid sliding or shifting problems when transporting or setting up the cake, especially with softly textured cake, hammer a long sharpened dowel, 5 mm/¼ inch thick, through the centre of the stacked cakes (pic 11). Mark where the dowel is even with the top of the cake, pull it out a little, clip it off with pruning shears kept especially for this purpose, and hammer it back down to its original position level with the top of the cake.

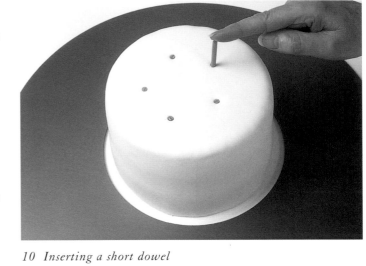

10 Inserting a short dowel

11 Inserting a long central dowel

Use 1 cm/½ inch dowel rods for the following cakes:
45 cm/18 inch cake – 11 dowels
40 cm/16 inch cake – 9 dowels
35 cm/14 inch cake – 9 dowels
30 cm/12 inch cake – 7 dowels

Use 5 mm/¼ inch dowel rods for the following cakes:
25 cm/10 inch cake – 7 dowels
20 cm/8 inch cake – 5 dowels
15 cm/6 inch cake – 5 dowels

For tiers second from top, use 2.5 mm/⅛ inch dowel rods. Dowels vary by cake. Heavier cakes require more substantial support. Each cake must be assessed on its own merit, according to the density of crumb.

AT THE RECEPTION

The dowels should be removed by the cake server. First remove the long central dowel, separate the cakes to serve, then remove the shorter ones as each cake is cut. Always indicate when a cake is dowelled.

FABRIC-LIKE FLOURISHES

Because the main emphasis of this book has been focused on romance, there have been a variety of gathers, pleats, ruching and swag methods included. The following overview shows these techniques being hand applied.

GATHERS

Measure the depth of each cake. Roll out either flower paste/gum paste and sugarpaste/rolled fondant in a 50:50 mixture or just sugarpaste/rolled fondant alone, using a pasta machine if available. Cut out panels of the required size. Shorter, more manageable lengths will not compromise the design if long panels seem

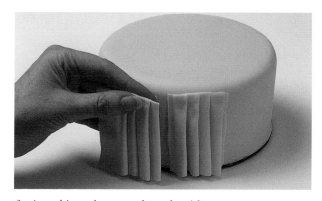

1 Attaching gathers to the cake side

a bit daunting. Gather evenly, using satay sticks/bamboo skewers. While still soft, remove the sticks/skewers, press down firmly at the top and attach to the cakes with edible gum glue (pic 1). Hiding each join under the previous panel, continue overlapping panels until the last, which will slip under the first and so form a continuous skirt. Encourage the skirt to billow by teasing the edge out with a paintbrush. See also Picture Perfect Couture cake (page 35) for reference.

2 Using a pasta machine

ELECTRIC PASTA MACHINES

The pasta machine is especially useful for creating gathers, pleats, ruches, swags and flowers. It is a marvellous time-saver, too, and a must for anyone with carpal tunnel problems. Such a machine can be set at any thickness required for flower paste/gum paste or sugarpaste/rolled fondant, and it is also possible to produce extremely long strips of sugarpaste/rolled fondant without tearing (pic 2). However, if the same piece of sugarpaste/rolled fondant is fed through the machine more than three or four times, the stainless-steel rollers can affect the paste colour, giving it a grey tinge and making it overworked. The rubbery texture problem also occurs after repeatedly using a non-stick rolling pin on the same piece of paste, but there is no colour change.

PLEATS

Roll out the sugarpaste/rolled fondant by hand or with an electric pasta machine. With a craft knife or scalpel, cut the panels to the size required. Form into uniform-sized pleats with satay sticks/bamboo skewers (see pic 6, page 47). While still soft, remove the sticks and attach the pleated panels to the side of the cake with edible gum glue (pic 3). The last pleat will tuck under the first, so there will be no visible join. See also Romancing the Dome cake (page 44) for reference.

3 Attaching pleats to the cake side

RUCHING

Divide the cake evenly into 3 cm/1¼ inch sections. Roll out some sugarpaste/rolled fondant and cut it into 10 x 3 cm/4 x 1¼ inch panels. As each cake measurement differs, some adjustment may be necessary. After gathering (see page 143), press down hard to keep the ruched pleats together. Separate with a craft knife or scalpel. Attach the ruched panels to the side of the cake (pic 4) and cover the joins with strips of 5 mm/¼ inch paste using a lace edge cutter (FMM – M5). See also Glimpsed under Glass cake (page 91) for reference.

SWAGS

These are simple pre-measured panels of sugarpaste/rolled fondant divided with two or three folds. Measure and divide the cake into as many sections as required. After cutting the panels, use

4 Applying a ruched panel to the cake side

satay sticks/bamboo skewers or slim pieces of wood dowelling to separate and hold the folds in place evenly (see pic 6, page 47). While the paste is still soft, remove the sticks, pinch both ends together, and attach to the side of the cake with edible gum glue (pic 5). Cover the joins with decorative accents. See also Love is in the Air cake (page 120) for reference.

5 Attaching a swag to the cake side

CONTINUOUS ROLLED STRIPS FOR CONTINUOUS FOLDS

Run the sugarpaste/rolled fondant through the pasta machine and cut strips about 10 cm/4 inch wide by the circumference measurement of the cake. Trim the edges, fold each strip in half and attach to the cake with edible gum glue, starting at the top edge and progressing down the cake sides (pic 6). The strips can alternate in colour or remain solid, as in Simply Pretty in Pink (see page 116).

6 Applying a rolled strip to the cake

PINPRICKING THE SIDE DESIGN

TRANSFERRING THE PATTERN

1 Draw the side design on thin kitchen parchment or greaseproof/wax paper. (For quick repeat patterns, use parchment rather than paper in a photocopier.) Attach the paper pattern to the cake base with a pin at each side. Pinprick the design on to the cake side by pushing a pin repeatedly along the pattern outline (pic 1). Repeat the design, as necessary.

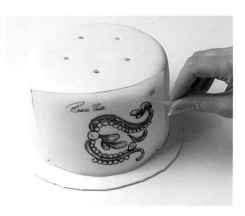

1 Pinpricking on to the cake

THE PASTE DECORATION

2 Place a copy of the pattern on the work surface/countertop and hand mould the scrolls, C-shapes and pearls. Check for the correct size and proportion by laying the prepared sugarpaste/rolled fondant pieces directly on to the pattern itself (pic 2). Paint the decorative pieces with the appropriate colours. (Here I have used super gold lustre dust mixed with clear alcohol/vodka or Everclear for the hand-moulded pieces, and super pearl lustre dust for the pearl accents).

3 Beginning with the largest pieces, attach the paste decoration to the cake side with edible gum glue. Correct any thinly painted spots with super gold lustre dust mixed with clear alcohol/vodka or Everclear (pic 3). (See All that Glitters on page 52.)

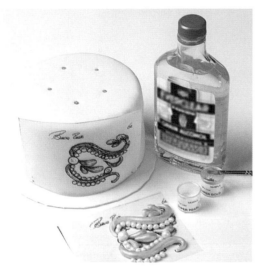

2 Checking the shape of the paste decoration

4 Hand mould the comma shapes, checking that they conform to the pattern. Paint in the same manner as in steps 2 and 3, and glue to the cake surface (pic 4). Fill in the base pattern with the pearl rope accents, pressing gently with the fingertips to ensure the gum glue makes direct contact with the cake surface (pic 5).

3 Touching up the paste decoration   *4 Building up the pattern*

EDIBLE GUM GLUE

To make edible gum glue, mix 15 g/¹/₂ oz sugarpaste/rolled fondant with enough water to dilute it into a thick syrupy mixture. Hurry it along with a couple of medium-temperature, 2 second bursts in the microwave. Store in the refrigerator in a capped container.

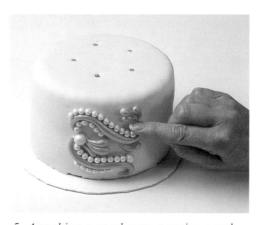

5 Attaching a pearl rope, pressing gently

A NEW SPIN ON CAKE PLATES

Scott Ferguson gave a demonstration on this technique, which I felt it was important to include here. An extremely classy cake plate or tray can be made for very little money and, if mislaid at a reception, is no one's loss.

EQUIPMENT
- Cake plate to be duplicated
- Foam core art board
- Clear craft spray
- Remnants of sugarpaste/rolled fondant or flower paste/gum paste
- Assorted moulds and textured rollers, such as smocking roller, fabric roller or a sheet of plastic cross-stitch canvas
- Edible gum glue
- Spray adhesive
- Plain florist's foil (without waterproof backing)
- Stiff brush, such as a basting or stencil brush
- Assorted sizes of ball tool
- Non-toxic artist's acrylic paint in colour of your choice
- Artist's brush

1 Embellishing the embossed board

PREPARING THE CAKE PLATE

1 Select a pattern to complement your cake, even using a cake tin/pan the same shape but a larger size than the cake itself. Allow at least a 5 cm/2 inch border around the cake. Duplicate the shape of the cake plate on the foam core board and cut out. Seal both sides with the clear craft spray, to help prevent warping.

2 Roll an even layer of flower paste/gum paste on to the board and emboss with a smocking roller, fabric roller or a sheet of plastic cross-stitch canvas. Embellish the embossed board with flower paste/gum paste, sugarpaste/rolled fondant or pastillage moulded in swags or lace wraps, secured with edible gum glue, or even royal icing piping (pic 1). Allow to dry thoroughly.

FOIL COVERING

3 Spray the entire top surface and edges with adhesive. Cut a piece of foil at least 5 cm/2 inch larger than the plate and gently lay over the embellished board, only pressing on to the adhesive when properly positioned. Starting from the centre and using a gentle, pouncing, circular motion, press the foil into the embossed paste with a stiff brush (pic 2). Gradually work your way towards the outside of the board, then over the edges and tuck under.

4 With a large ball tool, gently burnish the foil, working from the centre to the outside until every surface has been rubbed. Take a smaller ball tool and repeat the process. Use as many tools as you have and work down to a stylus-sized tool if you want a lot of detail. Cover the back with foil, if desired.

5 To dull the foil surface if it looks a bit too shiny and bright, apply an antique finishing solution of water-thinned acrylic paint

2 Stages of covering the embossed board with foil

over the entire surface; to simulate a natural patina, use a red-umber glaze on gold foil, black glaze on silver, dark brown or turquoise on copper. After application, immediately rub off the paint to reveal the moulded highlights (pic 3). This paint is non-toxic, but may be sealed if desired.

3 Completed plates with burnished finish

CAKE PLATES FOR HEAVY OR LARGE CAKES

If the cake is too large or heavy for a foam core art board, add a smaller commercial drum under the board 'plate' for support. Alternatively, cut the plate shape from hardboard or plywood.

SHIPPING CAKES

Is it possible to have a cake shipped across country? Yes. Will it arrive damage free? Maybe, but not necessarily and one definitely can't guarantee. You can't get the design of a cake you have seen by a particular cake stylist out of your head? Research then reveals their premises is 1000 miles away, so the shipping option comes immediately to mind.

Although it is possible to have a cake shipped long distance damage free, I would suggest that you first try to find someone in your own area to duplicate the design – or even improve on it. Give the local cake designer some artistic flexibility; most really don't want to reproduce exact copies.

If you reject the local option, look for a door-to-door courier that provides a pickup and delivery service. The price is likely to be hefty, starting from £200/US$300 for a three-tiered cake, and variables will depend on destination and weight.

Shipped cakes should always include detailed instructions for assembling the cake at the reception site. Even insuring a cake in transit, however, does not guarantee that you will have a cake at the reception. Each tier should be wrapped separately. Packing may or may not include dry ice, depending on the type of cake and the time of year. Fruitcake would not require ice; however, it is a must for chocolate couverture, buttercream icings, and madeira/pound cakes with tender fillings, especially when outside temperatures are above 15°C/59°F.

All decorative designs for the cake should be chosen with shipping in mind. Commercial flower paste/gum paste flowers are less likely to break than the finest handmade flower paste/gum paste flowers, as they are much thicker and more robust. Plaques, moulded flowers and close-to-the-surface, decorative work are also more likely to survive. If an accident happens, the responsibility lies with the baker unless the client signs a waiver. Having been a guest at several weddings where the cake was shipped in and damage was very noticeable, I later questioned the baker about responsibility and the airy reply was 'oh the resident chef will always fix it'. In my opinion, it is not the resident chef's business; he is not being paid to fix anything, since the cake was commissioned outside the establishment. On each occasion, no-one had put in a call to the chef to say that a cake was arriving by air and, should minimal damage occur in transit, would they consider patching it up as a professional courtesy. Even if the cake stylist arranges for a local baker to be available to assemble the cake and correct damage at the reception site, this might still not result in a top-quality cake. Respected bakers will already be involved with their own creations and deliveries, and it would be most embarrassing for their company profile to be seen dealing with another's mistakes. I feel similarly: I would not want to be anywhere near a disaster, as it would be a direct reflection on my business.

Fortunately, some companies provide transport and are willing to send a driver and the cake to distant parts. This is usually satisfactory, as the driver will assemble the cake on arrival, then repair damage if necessary. The charge is assessed on mileage and an hourly rate for the driver, and can quickly escalate to around £380/US$500.

Romantic Table Trends

GUEST DESIGNS BY DONNA DAVIS

THE UNDER-SKIRT

Under-skirting is usually a straight piece of fabric slightly shorter than the height of the display table. Polyester double-knit is a good choice, since the cut edge will not unravel; however, any fabric of the desired colour may be used. The colour may match the over-skirt or may complement the colour used on the cake.

THE OVER-SKIRT

Over-skirting may be assembled as one piece, long enough to go around the table, or in 1.2 m/4 feet lengths, depending on the type of fabric chosen. The latter may allow for easier cleaning after use – if just one panel is stained, it can be laundered independently.

AMERICAN WEDDINGS ARE STAGED PRODUCTIONS WITH A HINT OF THEATRE. FULL-SIZED, FABRIC-DRAPED CANOPIES, LATTICE GAZEBOS AND ENTIRE CEILINGS DECORATED WITH GREENERY AND TWINKLING MINIATURE LIGHTS PROVIDE THE PERFECT BACKDROP FOR THE CAKE.

Great thought is given to table linen and floral centrepieces. Backs of slip-covered chairs are matched with elaborate bows and flowers. Most often, these accessories are custom made just for the day. The table of honour is always lavishly decorated with fresh flowers and beautiful linen. It is the main focus of attention after the bride. Generally set up in the foyer or in the middle of the function room, the cake is seen from all angles.

TABLE 1

PREPARING THE OVER-SKIRT

1 To drape a table with material such as this heavily embroidered, pearl-beaded, double-edged, scalloped fabric, you will need one and one half times the circumference of the table. Measure the distance from the top of your chosen table to the floor, and add 2.5 cm/1 inch. Measure up this amount from the heavily decorated edge of the fabric. Trim the excess material from the lightest embroidery edge, then turn the trimmed edge so the right sides of both pieces are facing up. Place cut edges together. Turn under 5 mm/¹/4 inch towards the wrong side of the fabric and press. Turn under an additional 2 cm/³/4 inch and press. This will make the casing to run a drapery drawstring through. Sew two lines of stitching, one at the bottom edge of the casing, and one near the top edge, which will make a small ruffle at the top of the skirting. Insert the drawstring. This will make a full-length drape with a short ruffle accent at the top.

PREPARING THE TRIM

2 To accent this table, use a 10 cm/4 inch wide bias polyester satin trim (see Making a continuous bias strip on page 150). For a tailored look, the ends of the trim may be hidden behind the table or, for a Victorian look, they may be arranged in any manner you wish, such as bows or streamers.

DRAPING THE TABLE

3 Cover the top of the table with a cloth either in a colour that matches the over-skirt or in a contrasting one. Pin the straight under-skirt to the tablecloth with pearl-headed corsage pins or straight pins, inserting them vertically into the material. (It is helpful at this stage to put something heavy on the tabletop to keep the fabric from shifting.) Gather the over-skirt to fit around the table and pin it on with pearl-headed corsage pins (pic 1). Pin the bias trim to the edge of the

1 Attaching the over-skirt

2 Attaching the bias trim

tabletop, placing the seam edge of the bias strip next to the gathered edge of the over-skirt, with the outside of the bias strip on the tabletop (pic 2). Pin to the tablecloth, each pin very close to the next. Every 30 cm/12 inches or so, turn the

bias trim over the edge of the table to be sure the pinning is not too tight or too loose. When completed, fold the trim over the gathered edge of the over-skirt. On this table, the ends of the bias strip have been allowed to hang as streamers, off-centre to the side of the table. To create a decorative accent to the table, add a corsage of fresh roses and ivy.

MAKING A CONTINUOUS BIAS STRIP

Cut a square of fabric, using the width of your chosen material to determine the size. Fold the square diagonally (along dotted line in diagram, right); cut on this diagonal line. Sew section A to the far side of section B, making a parallelogram.

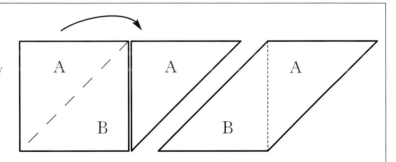

Key * = For a double bias trim, double width of finished trim plus 2.5 cm/1 inch

To make the double-sided bias trim, as used on Table 1, draw cutting lines diagonally on the fabric along the long side of the parallelogram as shown on the diagram, making them double the desired finished width plus 2.5 cm/1 inch. (My example required 23 cm/9 inch strips.) Mark the drawn strips, beginning with the letter A along the top of the fabric. Along the bottom, ignore the first strip and then mark the remaining strips, also beginning with the letter A (see diagram). Fold the marked edges, right sides together, matching A to A, B to B, etc. (It will be offset one strip; see diagram, right.) After sewing, the fabric will resemble a tube. Press seam allowances in one direction. Cut continuously along the drawn line until the whole piece is cut through. Fold the bias strip in half lengthways, right sides together. Stitch across the end, making a pointed end, and along the long side, leaving an opening in the centre of the strip, to allow for turning. Turn, press and handstitch the open portion.

TABLE 2

PREPARING THE OVER-SKIRT

1 This over-skirting is made of georgette, a very soft, flowing material with a drawstring top and a deep hem. Measure the distance from the floor to the tabletop. Turn under 2 cm/³/4 inch on the selvage edge and stitch as for Table 1, to make the casing. If a larger ruffle is desired at the top of the table, increase the amount turned under. Measure from the top stitching line down to the desired finished length of the drape. Turn up the balance of the fabric to make a wide hem, then stitch.

3 Attaching the under-skirt

PREPARING THE TRIM

2 This table has a double trim. The first is an all-over, heavily embroidered fabric with a scalloped edge on each selvage. Cut the fabric in half lengthways and seam to make one long piece. For the drawstring casing, turn under a very narrow hem plus 1 cm/¹/2 inch and stitch, leaving a long drop from the top of the table. Insert the drawstring. Make the second trim from the georgette – to measure three-quarters of the table's circumference. Cut this piece in half lengthways and seam together to make a swag one and a half times the table's circumference.

4 Attaching the first trim

DRAPING THE TABLE

3 Cover the tabletop, then add the under-skirt (pic 3) and over-skirt, as described for Table 1. Gather the first trim and attach with pearl-headed corsage pins (pic 4). Fold the swag in half lengthways to find the centre. Place this at the centre front of the table and gather at even intervals, pinning to make the swags (pic 5). Add fresh or silk flowers and ivy to each point of the swag.

5 Pinning the swag and flowers

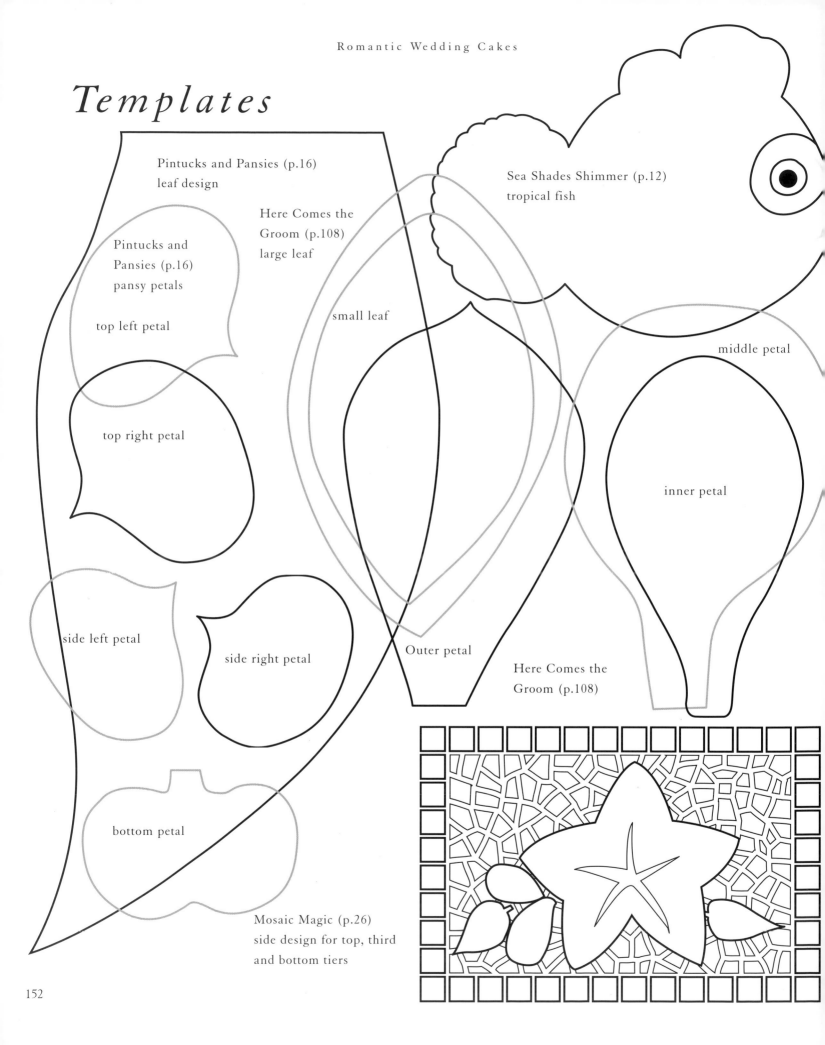

Templates

Pintucks and Pansies (p.16)
leaf design

Sea Shades Shimmer (p.12)
tropical fish

Here Comes the
Groom (p.108)
large leaf

Pintucks and
Pansies (p.16)
pansy petals

top left petal

small leaf

middle petal

top right petal

inner petal

side left petal

side right petal

Outer petal

Here Comes the
Groom (p.108)

bottom petal

Mosaic Magic (p.26)
side design for top, third
and bottom tiers

Mosaic Magic (p.26)
hydrangea flower –
medium petals

Mosaic Magic (p.26)
side design for second
and fourth tiers

side design for
bottom tier

side design for
top tier

Tiers in a Teacup (p.48)

Mosaic Magic (p.26)
star-shaped balloon
flower

Mosaic Magic (p.26)
hydrangea flower – large
and small petals

Valentine's Heart Sublime (p.40)
four-pointed gardenia leaf

All That Glitters (p.52)
side design for bottom tier

All That Glitters
(p.52)
side design for
top tier

153

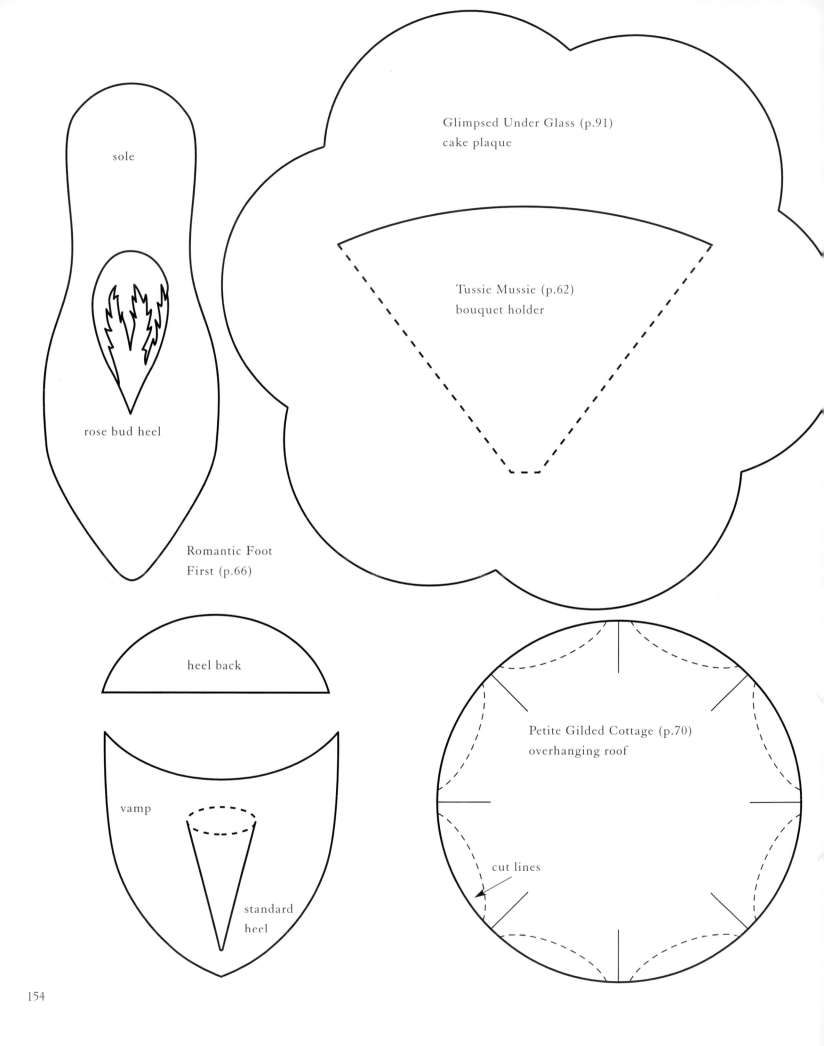

sole

rose bud heel

Romantic Foot
First (p.66)

Glimpsed Under Glass (p.91)
cake plaque

Tussie Mussie (p.62)
bouquet holder

heel back

vamp

standard
heel

Petite Gilded Cottage (p.70)
overhanging roof

cut lines

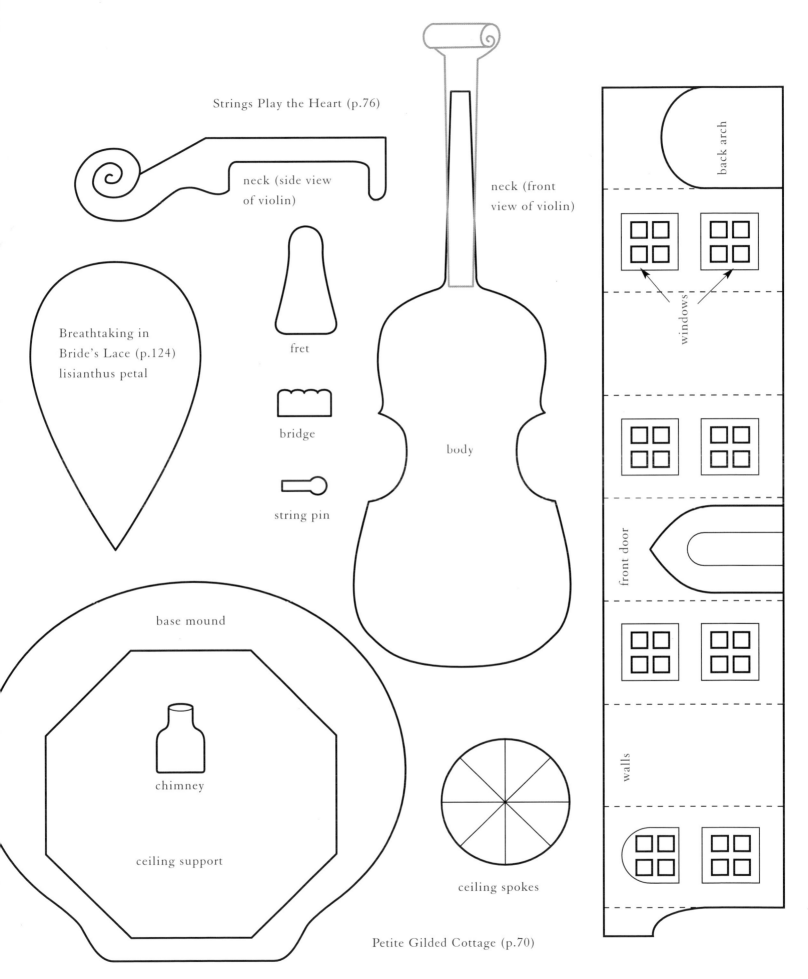

Strings Play the Heart (p.76)

neck (side view of violin)

neck (front view of violin)

Breathtaking in Bride's Lace (p.124) lisianthus petal

fret

bridge

body

string pin

back arch

windows

front door

walls

base mound

chimney

ceiling support

ceiling spokes

Petite Gilded Cottage (p.70)

155

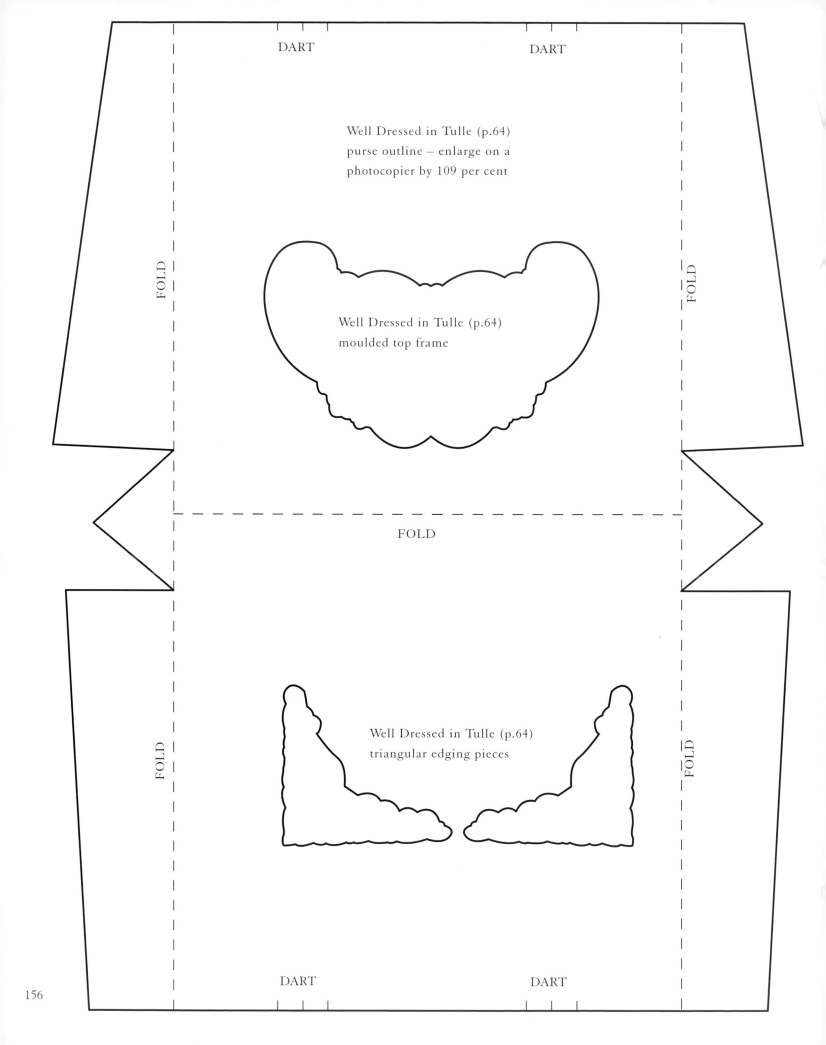

DART

DART

Well Dressed in Tulle (p.64)
purse outline – enlarge on a
photocopier by 109 per cent

FOLD

FOLD

Well Dressed in Tulle (p.64)
moulded top frame

FOLD

Well Dressed in Tulle (p.64)
triangular edging pieces

FOLD

FOLD

DART

DART

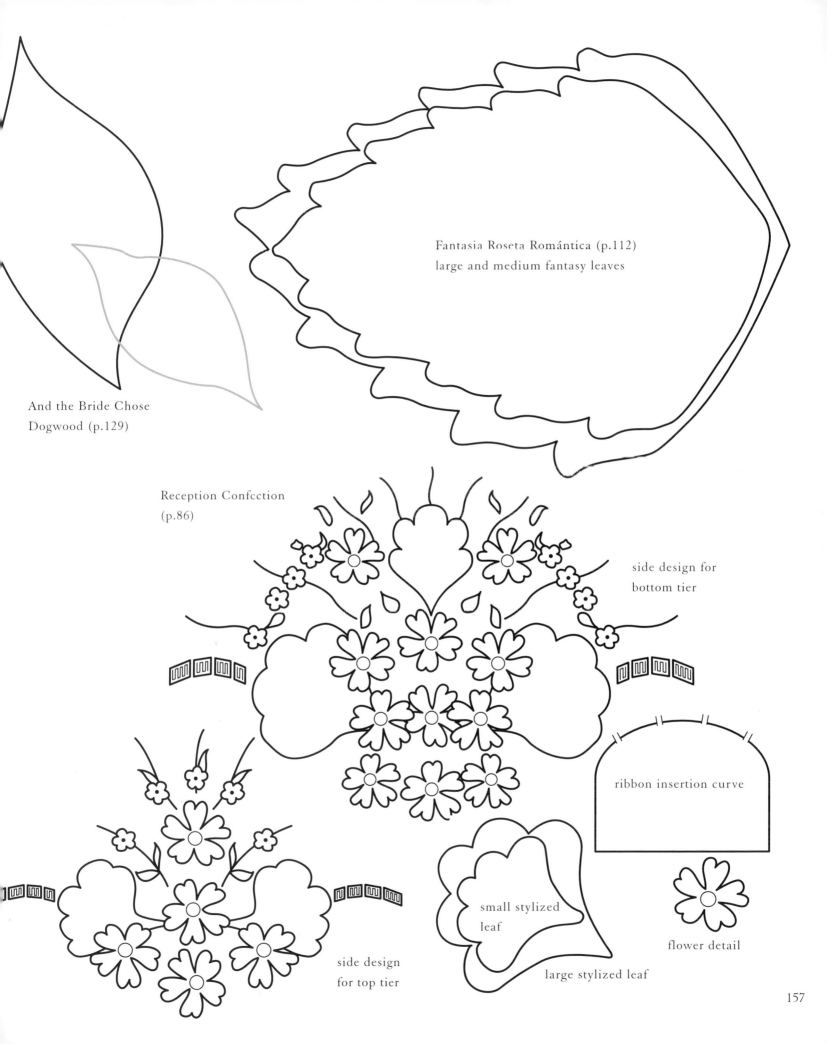

And the Bride Chose
Dogwood (p.129)

Fantasia Roseta Romántica (p.112)
large and medium fantasy leaves

Reception Confection
(p.86)

side design for
bottom tier

ribbon insertion curve

small stylized
leaf

side design
for top tier

large stylized leaf

flower detail

baroque trim for top tier
(turn pattern over for
left-hand design)

Invitation to a Summer
Wedding (p.104)

underlay for top tier

baroque trim for bottom
tier (turn pattern over
for left-hand design)

underlay for bottom tier

A Jewel in the Crown
(p.96)
filigree pattern

A Jewel in the Crown (p.96)
teardrop

Suppliers

UNITED KINGDOM
Hawthorne Hill (HH)
Milvale Studios
Milvale Street
Stoke on Trent
Staffordshire ST6 3NT
01782 811 877
(moulds)

Patchwork Cutters (PC)
3 Raines Close
Greasby, Wirral L49 2QB
0151 6785053

P.M.E. Sugarcraft (PME)
Brember Close
South Harrow
Middlesex HA2 8UN
020 8864 0888

Creative Stencil Designs
(CSD)
Flanders Moss
Station Road
Buchlyvie
Stirlingshire FK8 3NB
01360 850389

Culpitt Cake Art
Culpitt Ltd
Jubilee Industrial Estate
Ashington
Northumberland NE63 8UQ
01670 811545

Squires Kitchen (SK)
Squires House
3 Waverley Lane
Farnham, Surrey GU9 8BB
phone: 01252 711749
fax: 01252 714714

Guy, Paul & Co Ltd
Unit B4 Foundry Way
Little End Road
Eaton Socon
Cambs PE19 3JH

Vee Bee (VB)
19 Main Street (The Cross)
Kilbirnie, Ayrshire KA25 7BX
0150 568 3689
(petal and lustre dusts)

Celcakes and Celcrafts (CC)
Springfield House
Gate Helmsley, York
Yorkshire T04 1NF
01759 371447

The Old Bakery (TOB/RVO)
Kingston St Mary
Taunton, Somerset TA2 8HW
phone: 01823 451 205
email: theoldbakery@
hotmail.com

Torbay Cake Craft (TCC/EC)
5 Seaway Road
Preston, Paignton
Devon TQ3 2NX
01803 550178

FMM
Unit 5, Kings Park Ind. Estate
Primrose Hill
Kings Langley
Herts WD4 8ST
phone: 01923 268699
fax: 01923 261226
email: clements@
f-m-m.demon.co.uk

Orchard Products (OP)
51 Hallyburton Road
Hove, East Sussex BN3 7GP
phone: 01273 419418
fax: 01273 412512
email: gsfashby@aol.com

British Bakels Ltd
Granville Way,
Off Launton Road
Bicester Oxon OX6 OJT
phone: 01869 247 098
fax: 01869 242 979
email:
anyone@bakels.demon.co.uk

Wilton (W)
Knightsbridge Bakeware
Centre (UK) Ltd
Chadwell Heath Lane
Romford, Essex RM6 4NP
phone. 028 590 5959
fax: 0208 590 7373
email: kbc@where.co.uk
www.cakedecoration.co.uk

UNITED STATES
Earlene Moore (EM)
1323 E. 78th
Lubbock TX 79404
email:
Earlene@earlenescakes.com

Nicholas Lodge (NL)
The International Sugar Art
Collection
6060 Mcdonough Drive
Suite D
Norcross GA 30093 1230
freephone: 1-800 662 8925
phone: 770 453 9449
fax: 770 448 9046
email: nichlodge1@aol.com

America Cake Decorating
Supplies, Inc
3100 N.W. 72nd Ave. Unit 101
Miami FL 33122
phone: 305 592 6414
fax: 305 592 6415
email: americacake@aol.com
www.yp.bellsouth.com/
americacakedecorating

Airpen
Silkpaint Corporation (SPC)
PO Box 18
Waldron, MO 64092
www.silkpaint.com
email art@silkpaint.com
freephone: 1-800 563 0074
phone: 816 4891 7774
fax: 816 891 7775

Airpen UK agent:
Suasion
35 Riding Horse Street
London W1P 7PT
phone: 020 7636 4287
email: Suasion@aol.com

Thompson's Costume
Trim & Fabric
1232 Southwest 59th Street
Oklahoma City OK 73109
phone: 405 631 8850
fax: 405 631 3450
(fabric supplier for Romantic
Table Trends)

J. Boyer
Designer Fabrics,Ltd
8142 S Harvard
Tulsa OK 74137
phone: 918 491 4776
(fabrics in this book)

Stress Free Cake Supports
Arlene House
42551 299th Street
Scotland D57059

Beryl's Cakes Decorating
P.O. Box 1584
North Springfield
VA 22151 – 0584
freephone: 1-800 4882749
fax: 703 750 3779
email: beryls@beryls.com
www.beryls.com

*All sugarpaste/rolled fondant
used in this book was
provided by*
American Bakels Inc
8114 Scott Hamilton Drive
Little Rock AR 72209
freephone: 1800 799 2253
phone: 501 568 2253
fax: 501 568 3947
email: ambakels@swbell.net
www.bakels.com

Agbay Products, Inc.
11 Hampton Street
Auburn MA 01501
phone: 508 743 5169
email: maureen@
agbayproducts.com
www.agbayproducts.com
(cake levelling tool)

John and Judy Shelton
Decotek
2108 El Camino Ave
Sacramento CA 95821
phone: 916 564 2253
fax: 916 344 3145
email: decotek@aol.com
(fondant lifter)

Darla Avra
102 West Mike
Sapulpa OK 74066
Phone: 918 227 4623
www.cakinbake.com
email:
cakinbake@cakinbake.com

Sugar Bouquets (SB)
23 North State Drive
Morristown, New Jersey 07960
freephone (US): 1-800 203
0629
phone: 973 538 3542
fax: 973 538 4939
www.sugarbouquets.com
email:
mail@sugarbouquets.com

E.M. Berling reproduction
silicone molds
Beatrice Knapik (ADM)
3 Crestview Lane
Sutton, MA 01527
508 865 2755

CK Products (CK)
310 Racquet Dr
Fort Wayne IN 46825
phone: 219 484 2517
fax: 219 484 2510
email: mail@ckproducts.com
www.ckproducts.com
(beadmakers and colours)

Vi Whittington
Country Kitchen Sweet Art
4621 Speedway Drive
Fort Wayne, IN 46825
freephone: 1-888 497 3927
email: cntryktchn@aol.com
www.countrykitchensa.com

Jack Gerber
HIS Designs (HD)
7279 Road 87
Paulding OH 45879
phone: 419 399 3535
email: hiscake@bright.net
www.weddingcakestands.com

The Dummy Place
44 Midland Drive
Tolland CT 06084
phone: 860 875 1736
email:
SLLEE@compuserve.com
(cake dummies)

Wilton Industries (W)
2240 W 75th Street
Woodbridge IL 60517
freephone: 1-800 794 5866Ö
1800 7 WILTON
freefax: 1-888 824 9520
phone: 630 963 7100
fax: 630 810 2256
email: info@wilton.com
www.wilton.com

AUSTRALIA
Major Cake Decoration
Supplies
900 Albany Highway
East Victoria Park
Western Australia 6101.
phone/fax: 618 9362 5202
Classes and equipment.

Cake & Icing Centre
651 Samford Road
Mitchelton, Queensland 4053
617 3355 3443

The Cake Decorating Centre
32-34 King William Street,
Adelaide 5000
618 8410 1944

Cake Decorating School of
Australia
Shop 7 Port Phillip Arcade
232 Flinders Street
Melbourne, VIC 3000
03 9654 5335

Cupid's Cake Decorations
2/90 Belford Street
Broadmeadow, NSW 2292
phone: 02 4962 1884
fax: 02 4961 6594

Susie Q Cake Decorating
Centre
Shop 4, 372 Keilor Road
Niddrie VIC
Australia
613 9379 2275

NEW ZEALAND
Hitchon International
220 Abtiqua Street
Christchurch
64 33653843

IRELAND
Cakes and Co
25 Rock Hill
Blackrock Village
Co. Dublin
35312836544

PERU
Rosa Viacava de Ortega (RVO)
Av. Brasil 1141 Jesus Maria
Lima 11, Peru
phone: 511 423 4210
phone/fax: 511 423 5986
email:
ortega viacava@hotmail.

ARGENTINA
Ediciones Ballina Codai SA
Av. Cordoba 2415 1st Floor
Buenos Aires
Argentina C1120AAG
54 11 4962 5381

SOUTH AFRICA
JEM Cutters (J)
P.O. Box 115 Kloof 3640
Kwazulu Natal
South Africa
0027 31 7011431
maytham@iafrica.com

Eleanor Rielander (RL)
P.O. Box 1138 Mondeor
Johannesburg 2110
South Africa

Index

First published in 2001 by Merehurst Limited.
Merehurst is a Murdoch Books (UK) Ltd imprint.

ISBN 978-1-85391-859-9
A catalogue record of this book is available from the
British Library.

Text copyright © Kerry Vincent 2001
Photography copyright © Merehurst Limited
Kerry Vincent has asserted her right under the Copyright,
Designs and Patents Act, 1988.

Commissioning Editor: Barbara Croxford
Project Editor: Joanna Chisholm
Designer: Maggie Aldred
Photography: Hawks photography, Oklahoma, USA

CEO: Robert Oerton
Publisher: Catie Ziller
Publishing Manager: Fia Fornori
Production Manager: Lucy Bryne
Group General Manager: Mark Smith
Group CEO/Publisher: Anne Wilson

Murdoch Books (UK) Ltd
Ferry House, 51–57 Lacy Road,
Putney, London, SW15 1PR
Tel: +44 (0)20 8355 1480; Fax: +44 (0)20 8355 1499
Murdoch Books (UK) Ltd is a subsidiary of Murdoch
Magazines Pty Ltd.

Murdoch Books
GPO Box 1203,
Sydney, Australia, 1045
Tel: +61 (0)2 9692 2347; Fax: +61 (0)2 9692 2559
Murdoch Books is a trademark of Murdoch Magazines
Pty Ltd.

Distributed in North America, South America & Canada by:
Tuttle Publishing
364 Innovation Drive, North Clarendon, VT 05759-9436
Tel: 1 (802) 773 8930; Fax: 1 (802) 773 6993
Email: info@tuttlepublishing. com
www. tuttlepublishing.com

Printed in Singapore
15 14 13 12 11   10 9 8 7 6 5 4 3